# The Death of Deaths in the Death of Israel

# The Death of Deaths in the Death of Israel

*Deuteronomy's Theology of Exile*

KENNETH J. TURNER

WIPF & STOCK · Eugene, Oregon

THE DEATH OF DEATHS IN THE DEATH OF ISRAEL
Deuteronomy's Theology of Exile

Copyright © 2011 Kenneth J. Turner. All rights reserved. Except for brief quotations in critical publications or reviews, no part of this book may be reproduced in any manner without prior written permission from the publisher. Write: Permissions, Wipf and Stock Publishers, 199 W. 8th Ave., Suite 3, Eugene, OR 97401.

Wipf & Stock
An Imprint of Wipf and Stock Publishers
199 W. 8th Ave., Suite 3
Eugene, OR 97401
www.wipfandstock.com

ISBN 13: 978-1-60608-788-6

Manufactured in the U.S.A.

*To Robert Selph and Daniel Block,
my fathers in the faith, pastors, mentors, friends*

# Contents

*List of Abbreviations ix*

*List of Tables xiii*

*Preface xv*

*Acknowledgements xvii*

1 Introduction 1

2 The Vocabulary of Exile 33

3 The Texts and Contexts of Exile, Part 1 77

4 The Texts and Contexts of Exile, Part 2 179

5 The Theology of Exile 224

*Bibliography 255*

# List of Abbreviations

| | |
|---|---|
| AB | Anchor Bible |
| *AcOr* | *Acta Orientalia* |
| AnBib | Analecta Biblica |
| *ANET* | James B. Pritchard, ed., *Ancient Near Eastern Texts* |
| AOTC | Apollos Old Testament Commentary |
| ATANT | Abhandlungen zur Theologie des Alten und Neuen Testaments |
| AV | Authorized Version |
| *BA* | *The Biblical Archaeologist* |
| BBB | Bonner biblische Beiträge |
| BBC | Broadman Bible Commentary |
| BDB | Francis Brown, et al., *Hebrew and English Lexicon of the Old Testament* |
| BETL | Bibliotheca Ephemeridum Theologicarum Lovaniensium |
| *BHS* | Karl Elliger and Wilhelm Rudolph, eds., *Biblia Hebraica Stuttgartensia* |
| *Bib* | *Biblica* |
| BibOr | Biblica et Orientalia |
| *BK* | *Bibel und Kirche* |
| BKAT | Biblischer Kommentar: Altes Testament |
| *BO* | *Bibliotheca Orientalis* |
| BN | *Biblische Notizen* |
| BSac | *Bibliotheca Sacra* |
| *BTB* | *Biblical Theology Bulletin* |
| BWANT | Beiträge zur Wissenschaft vom Alten und Neuen Testament |
| *BZ* | *Biblische Zeitschrift* |

| | | |
|---|---|---|
| | BZAW | Beihefte zur Zeitschrift für die alttestamentliche Wissenschaft |
| | *CBQ* | *The Catholic Biblical Quarterly* |
| | ConBOT | Coniectanea biblica, Old Testament |
| | DSB | Daily Study Bible |
| | ETL | *Ephemerides Theologicae Lovanienses* |
| | ESV | English Standard Version |
| | *ExpTim* | *Expository Times* |
| | FRLANT | Forschungen zur Religion und Literatur des Alten und Neuen Testaments |
| | HKAT | Handkommentar zum Alten Testament |
| | HSM | Harvard Semitic Monographs |
| | *HTR* | *Harvard Theological Review* |
| | IBC | Interpretation: A Bible Commentary for Teaching and Preaching |
| | *IBS* | *Irish Biblical Studies* |
| | ICC | International Critical Commentary |
| | *Int* | *Interpretation* |
| | *JAOS* | *Journal of the American Oriental Society* |
| | *JBL* | *Journal of Biblical Literature* |
| | JETS | Journal of the Evangelical Theological Society |
| | *JNES* | *Journal of Near Eastern Studies* |
| | *JNSL* | *Journal of Northwest Semitic Languages* |
| | JPSTC | The Jewish Publication Society Torah Commentary |
| | JSJSup | Supplements to the Journal for the Study of Judaism in the Persian, Hellenistic and Roman Period |
| | *JSNT* | *Journal for the Study of the New Testament* |
| | *JSOT* | *Journal for the Study of the Old Testament* |
| | JSOTSup | Journal for the Study of the Old Testament Supplement Series |
| | *JTS* | *Journal of Theological Studies* |
| | LXX | Septuagint |
| | NAC | New American Commentary |
| | NASB | New American Standard Bible |

| NCB | New Century Bible |
| NIBC | New International Biblical Commentary |
| NICOT | New International Commentary on the Old Testament |
| *NIDNTT* | C. Brown, ed., *The New International Dictionary of New Testament Theology* |
| *NIDOTTE* | Willem A. VanGemeren, ed., *The New International Dictionary of Old Testament Theology and Exegesis* (Grand Rapids: Zondervan, 1997) |
| NIV | New International Version |
| NIVAC | NIV Application Commentary |
| NJB | H. Wansbrough, ed., *New Jerusalem Bible* |
| NKJV | New King James Version |
| NLT | New Living Translation |
| NRSV | New Revised Standard Version |
| NSBT | New Studies in Biblical Theology |
| OBO | Orbis Biblicus et Orientalis |
| OBT | Overtures to Biblical Theology |
| OL | Old Latin |
| OLA | Orientalia Lovaniensia Periodica |
| OTG | Old Testament Guides |
| OTL | Old Testament Library |
| *OTS* | *Oudtestamentische Studiën* |
| PTMS | Pittsburgh (Princeton) Theological Monograph Series |
| *RB* | *Revue biblique* |
| *RevExp* | *Review and Expositor* |
| RSV | Revised Standard Version |
| SB | Sources bibliques |
| SBLASP | Society of Biblical Literature Abstracts and Seminar Papers |
| SBLDS | Society of Biblical Literature Dissertation Series |
| SBLSCS | Society of Biblical Literature Septuagint and Cognate Studies |
| SBLSymS | Society of Biblical Literature Symposium Series |
| SBT | Studies in Biblical Theology |

| | |
|---|---|
| SBTS | Sources for Biblical and Theological Study |
| SO | Symbolae osloenses |
| SP | Samaritan Pentateuch |
| Syr | Syriac |
| Tbü | Theologische Bücherei |
| TDNT | G. Kittel and G. Friedrich, eds., *Theological Dictionary of the New Testament* |
| TDOT | G. J. Botterweck, et al., ds., *Theological Dictionary of the Old Testament*. Translated by Douglas W. Stott (Grand Rapids: Eerdmans, 1999) |
| Tg | Targum |
| Tg. Ps.-J. | *Targum Pseudo-Jonathan* |
| TJ | *Trinity Journal* |
| TLOT | E. Jenni and C. Westermann, eds., *Theological Lexicon of the Old estament* Translated by Mark E. Biddle (Peabody, MA: Hendrickson, 1997) |
| TOTC | Tyndale Old Testament Commentary |
| TRu | *Theologische Rundschau* |
| TWOT | R. L. Harris, et al., eds., *Theological Wordbook of the Old Testament* (Chicago: Moody, 1980) |
| TynBul | *Tyndale Bulletin* |
| UF | *Ugarit-Forschungen* |
| Vg | Vulgate |
| VT | *Vetus Testamentum* |
| VTSup | Vetus Testamentum Supplements |
| WBC | Word Biblical Commentary |
| WO | *Die Welt des Orients* |
| ZAW | *Zeitschrift für die alttestamentliche Wissenschaft* |

# List of Tables

Synonyms and Parallels

אבד in Deuteronomy

שמד in Deuteronomy

Division of Deuteronomy 4

Structural Options for Deuteronomy 30:1–10

Covenant Reversals in Deuteronomy 28

# Preface

THE THEOLOGY OF DEUTERONOMY is and should be recognized as complex. It was my own recognition of this that led me to write my doctoral dissertation (Southern Baptist Theological Seminary, Louisville, 2005) of which the following study is a minor revision. My interest in the topic of Deuteronomy's theology of exile developed through research in several doctoral seminars I attended while enrolled at the Southern Baptist Theological Seminary. First, in a seminar on the theology of the Prophets under Elmer Martens, I developed a theology of Zechariah based on various aspects of theological tension in the book, including the question concerning the end of the exile. I found that Zechariah takes the notion of restoration and projects it into the future for ultimate fulfillment. Conversations with Peter Gentry about the use of Zechariah in the Gospels further piqued my interest. Second, in a New Testament theology seminar under Thomas Schreiner, I was exposed to the work of N. T. Wright. One of Wright's central theses is that Jesus' preaching of the kingdom and the forgiveness of sins is tied up with the nation's expectations of the return from exile, which is fulfilled in his death and resurrection. Wright often turns to Deuteronomy for support of his position. In some ways, the present work is a beginning of a response to Wright's thesis and some of the implications he draws. Third, in a seminar on the theology of Deuteronomy under Daniel Block, I attempted to tackle the theology of exile in Deuteronomy. I was surprised in my research by how few resources were directly related to the subject.

## MAJOR CONTRIBUTIONS OF THE STUDY

The thesis of the following study consists of three major aspects: (1) the theological construct that exile constitutes the death of Israel; (2) the pervasiveness of the theme of exile in Deuteronomy; and (3) the significance of the theme of exile for understanding and developing the theology of the book. While the theological connection between exile and death is not new, this study attempts to ground this association in the vocabulary of the text (see chap. 2). This, in turn, will open up a more nuanced reading of the entire book in which the persistent presence and influence of the theme of exile on Deuteronomy's overt message, underlying theology, and structure will be recognized.

A secondary goal of this study is to show that Deuteronomy can and should be read in its present form. Whatever its history of composition and transmission, the present form of the book seems viable and intentional. Specifically, Deuteronomy 1–3 should be recognized as an essential part of the message of the book; our development and understanding of Deuteronomy's theology of exile would be significantly different if chapters 1–3 were not considered (as some views of the Deuteronomistic History would have it). Also, we will find that tensions or apparent contradictions in the text should not be immediately considered as differences among hypothetical sources or editors. This study will show how many of the tensions in Deuteronomy are part of the overall message of the book. Hence, excising or discounting texts as late or secondary (e.g., Deut 4:25–31; 30:1–10)—simply because they introduce tension—will be seen as unwarranted.

## PROPOSALS FOR FURTHER INVESTIGATION

This study naturally serves as a part of and step toward several broader areas of research. Many tensions and questions are raised in Deuteronomy that require resolution, perhaps by later revelation. Thus, an examination of the rest of the Old Testament is necessary. We would hope that this would yield three important results: first, the development of a theology of exile throughout the Old Testament that will specifically aid a fuller recognition of the theme in the Pentateuch, Deuteronomistic History, and the Prophets; second, entrance into the debate over the theme of exile in New Testament studies for which points of contact become readily visible in the following pages (e.g., the status of the individual as it pertains to covenant membership); third, a fuller treatment of the questionable absence of the major verbs for exile—גלה and שבה—in Deuteronomy. We will focus in this study on providing a rationale for the terms used regularly in the book (e.g., אבד and שמד), an angle that helps in grounding the notion that exile constitutes Israel's death in the terminology of the text itself. Further work is needed, however, concerning the absence of the more common terms.

# Acknowledgements

THIS STUDY WOULD HAVE been impossible without the loving support and assistance of many individuals. Though I cannot name them all, may Yahweh reward each one who has helped me along the way. I am especially grateful to the many professors and professional colleagues in the OT Ph.D. program who spurred me to greater scholarship and personal devotion to God.

This work is dedicated to the two most influential men in my life. Robert Selph, my first pastor, was God's instrument to bring me to faith in Jesus Christ and nurture my calling to the gospel ministry. He modeled for me a life of humility, self-denial, trust in God, and love for the church. Daniel Block has been the same type of model for me during my seminary years and beyond. Though I am extremely thankful for his supervisory role over this project, he has meant far more to me as a mentor, pastor, and brother in Christ.

I cannot express adequately my love and appreciation for my wife, Raegan, and daughters, Sydney, Piper, and Eden. Raegan has been my strength and support. Her perseverance, dedication, and encouragement through this project truly make this a joint effort.

Finally, I thank my God for his grace and faithfulness in sustaining me. May he use this study for the exaltation of his name and the expansion of his kingdom.

Kenneth J. Turner<br>
Dayton, Tennessee<br>
July 2010

# 1

# Introduction

THE BABYLONIAN EXILE OF the sixth century BC was a watershed in the life and faith of Israel. Its historical, political, and theological realities demanded a reconsideration of what it meant to be the "people of God." Scholars generally agree that the experience and aftermath of this crisis provided a context for the production of "fresh theological literature."[1] For all successive Jewish faith, exile would become a major paradigm for self-understanding, and a theological construct for interpreting life and anticipating the future. Even in a "post-exilic" setting, exile can be considered as an ongoing, unresolved experience.[2]

When read in a canonical context, the notion of exile arises long before the historical experience of the nation in the sixth century.[3] Exile underlies many other biblical accounts: Adam and Eve's banishment from the garden of Eden; Cain's wandering through the land of Nod; Abraham's journey to the land of Canaan; Jacob's flight from his homeland; Joseph's deportation to Egypt; Moses' wandering in the wilderness; David's escape from Saul; and Assyria's deportation of the Northern Kingdom. The major theological contours of the nation's exile and restoration are first developed, however, in Deuteronomy. The notion of exile arises in covenantal contexts as a threat to Israel if she persists in idolatrous worship (Deut 4:25–28), and serves as the climax of the covenant

---

1. See Brueggemann, "Shattered Transcendence," 169–82.

2. See Ezra 9:6–15; Neh 9:36–37; Dan 9. This irony of a "post-exilic exile" continues beyond the Hebrew canon. See the relevant essays in Scott, ed., *Exile*; and idem, *Restoration*. N. T. Wright has created a lively debate in NT studies with his claim that part of Jesus' mission was to bring about the end of Israel's "exile." See the discussion at the end of this chapter.

3. On exile as the theme of the "metanarrative" of the Hebrew Bible, see Hatina, "Exile," 348; Carroll, "Exile! What Exile," 63; idem, "Deportation and Diasporic Discourses," 64.

curses (28:15–68). Both of these texts are followed by the possibility of restoration (Deut 4:29–31; 30:1–10). Thus, even before the Israelites enter the land of promise, Moses predicts its loss and repossession.

The book of Deuteronomy and the notion of exile represent two important topics in biblical studies today. Current research in each area is moving beyond previous trends and consensuses. Such shifts redirect the respective theological discussions as well. The time is ripe for an exploration of their juxtaposition.

## THESIS AND OVERVIEW

The present work explores Deuteronomy's understanding of exile. While the book speaks of a potential historical experience in the nation's future, "exile" is also a dynamic theological concept. In short, exile represents the death of Israel. In losing her land, Israel apparently also loses her identity, history, and covenant relationship with Yahweh. Restoration from exile, then, is a resurrection from death to life. Since exile is a recurring theme in Deuteronomy, the theology of the book must be considered in light of its vision of exile and restoration. Following the introduction, the thesis is developed first through an examination of the vocabulary for exile and restoration in Deuteronomy (chap. 2). The next two chapters analyze the progression of our theme in Deuteronomy: chapter 3 examines the major texts and their immediate contexts; chapter 4 surveys the rest of Deuteronomy, and includes exploration of the macrostructure of the book. The study then summarizes the theological dimensions of exile and related themes (chap. 5).

To my knowledge, no one has written a full-length monograph on the theology of exile in Deuteronomy. Though Deuteronomy is often referred to in the current discussion of exile, no scholar has "settled down" in the book and approached the subject from within its own theological contours.

The limitations to the present study are driven primarily by its theological concerns. The extent of the exegetical and text-critical treatment of the passages dealing with the subject will depend on each case's relative importance to the study; not every passage can receive the same amount of detailed attention. Diachronic concerns that occupy historical-critical investigation will not be dismissed or ignored, but this study begins with Deuteronomy in its final form and canonical position. Finally, a focus on exile necessarily interacts with other topics that cannot be given full treatment, but relies on the work of others.

## HISTORY OF RESEARCH

As stated, one of the reasons for this study is that a full theology of exile in Deuteronomy has yet to be written. Apart from a few articles that deal more directly with the topic,[4] the topic is discussed briefly in various types of works: theologies of exile; biblical-theological treatments of related issues (e.g., land); theologically-sensitive commentaries and works on Deuteronomy and the Deuteronomistic History; and exegetical treatments of specific texts. Though it is important to discuss the current state of research on both Deuteronomy and exile in biblical studies, the massive amount of literature on these topics precludes a full treatment of the history of interpretation in every relevant area in this section. Therefore, we will limit this discussion of the history of research in two ways. First, we will focus on research of the Pentateuch and the Dueteronomistic History in their direct influence on understanding the book of Deuteronomy itself. Second, for the research on exile, this section is limited to a discussion of full-length works that purport to give a theology of exile in Old Testament literature. We conclude with a brief summary of the debate taking place in New Testament studies concerning the theme of exile.

The purpose of this section is not to provide critical assessment of the various positions presented. Rather, this brief sketch of the history of research serves to support our claim that the study of exile in Deuteronomy is a worthy undertaking. As we shall see, the present state of research also affects the methodology of the present study.

### *Deuteronomy in Context: Historical, Literary, and Canonical Considerations*

Deuteronomy can be examined on its own. The book, consisting largely of Moses' speeches, has a clear beginning, middle, and end. Its distinctive vocabulary and phraseology has long been recognized,[5] and its struc-

---

4. See especially McConville, "Restoration in Deuteronomy," 11–40. A less extensive, but helpful, work is Head, "Curse of Covenant Reversal," 218–26. See also McConville, "Faces of Exile," 519–34; and Hoffman, "Deuteronomist and the Exile," 659–76.

5. Driver, *Critical and Exegetical Commentary on Deuteronomy*, lxxvii-lxxxviii; cf. Weinfeld, *Deuteronomy and the Deuteronomic School*, 320–65.

tural resemblance to ancient treaty forms has occupied much scholarly energy in the last several decades. These brief observations argue for the literary independence of Deuteronomy.

But Deuteronomy's autonomy is only relative. In some sense, it is an intrusion into the larger narrative, which would naturally progress directly from the arrival in the Transjordan at the end of Numbers to the conquest of the Cisjordan in Joshua. The only new narrative elements in Deuteronomy are the installation of Joshua as Moses' successor (Deut 31:7ff.) and Moses' death (Deut 34:1ff.). The rest of the "history" in the book appears in retrospective and prospective texts; Deuteronomy reviews Israel's story of wanderings, and promulgates a body of laws by which Israel was to live when she settled in Canaan. Thus, with Deuteronomy marking a pause at a critical point in Israel's history, its reach extends both backwards and forwards.[6] Deuteronomy, therefore, holds a unique canonical position, serving as the conclusion to the Pentateuch and the introduction to the "historical" books (Joshua to Kings), thus constituting the opening of what has been called the "Deuteronomistic History." Ongoing discussions of Deuteronomy's relationship to both those books that precede it and to those that follow it in the canon insure its transitional significance.[7] As Römer states, "Deuteronomy remains the touchstone of every theory of the formation of the Torah and of the deuteronomistic movement."[8]

---

6. Cf. Brueggemann, *Deuteronomy*, 22: "Deuteronomy looks both *backward to rootage* and *forward to crisis*, and interprets at the precise place where *rootage* and *crisis* intersect." Cf. the statement in Sanders ("Exile and Canon Formation," 43): "One can read from the end of Numbers to the beginning of Joshua and not miss a beat. Deuteronomy intruded between the two to cast its light backward to Genesis and forward to the Prophets."

7. It is not surprising that some have proposed Deuteronomy as the "center" of the entire Old Testament. Cf. Hermann, "Die konstruktive Restauration," 155–70. Of course, this would be disputed by those who deny that the authors of Deuteronomy knew of and used the non-Priestly traditions of the Tetrateuch. See the discussion by Römer, "Deuteronomy in Search of Origins," 113, including the statement, "For some exegetes (Martin Rose, John Van Seters, and others), Deuteronomy, traditionally considered an interim conclusion, has become instead a 'cornerstone' on which was built first the edifice of the Deuteronomistic History and second, as an expansion of this original corpus, the texts of the Pentateuch labeled 'Yahwist.'" See the discussion of the Pentateuch below.

8. Römer, "Deuteronomy in Search of Origins," 113–14.

## Deuteronomy and the Deuteronomistic History

Martin Noth's foundational proposal of the "Deuteronomistic History"[9] is based on the conviction that the core of Deuteronomy (chaps. 12–26) provided the theological lens through which an exilic individual—the "Deuteronomist" (Dtr)—judged Israel's history, and wrote "a literary entity and unity"[10] we know as Joshua, Judges, Samuel, and Kings.[11] The fall of Judah and Jerusalem can be explained in terms of failure to keep the covenant; the history of Israel is a record of "ever-intensifying decline," and her collapse as a nation was "final and definitive" and "expressed no hope for the future."[12] Noth held that extensive texts and traditions preceded the Deuteronomistic History, and in many cases were incorporated into it; but instead of simply being inserted, these disparate materials were shaped and interpreted in light of Dtr's own creation of retrospective and anticipatory comments inserted at crucial points in the history.[13] Dtr also attached a prologue (Deut 1:1—3:29) to the existing law-code of Deuteronomy and added parts to the end of the book (parts of chaps. 31 and 34). These additions serve as the beginning of the narrative, and explain how a law-code became an introduction to the history.[14]

Because of the continued dominant scholarly opinion that Deuteronomy serves as the introduction to the "unified" historical cor-

---

9. Noth, *Überlieferungsgeschichtliche Studien.*" For the latest English edition (of the first part of this work) see Noth, *Deuteronomistic History*.

10. Noth, *Deuteronomistic History*, 13.

11. Noth based his hypothesis on four observations: (1) Seven deuteronomistic passages gave a structural organization to the literary work (Josh 1, 12, 23; Judg 2:11ff.; 1 Sam 12; 1 Kgs 8; 2 Kgs 17:7ff.); (2) because of this, the textual divisions did not coincide with the divisions into books, but were instead marked by Josh 23, 1 Sam 12, and 1 Kgs 8; (3) a chronology that gives the figure of 480 years (1 Kgs 6:1) is based on texts Noth attributes to the history; and (4) the uniformity of the deuteronomistic structural sections pointed to deuteronomistic composition, in marked contrast with the diversity of the older traditions. See Noth, *Deuteronomistic History*, 22–33. The exilic location of the history's composition was due, according to Noth, to the numerous references to the exile (ibid., 134).

12. Noth, *Deuteronomistic History*, 122, 143.

13. For Noth, Dtr puts his own analyses into the mouths of characters: Moses (Deut 1–3[4]; cf. 29–31); Joshua (Josh 1; 23); Samuel (1 Sam 12); Solomon (1 Kgs 8); and the narrator (Josh 12; Judg 2:11ff.; 2 Kgs 17:7ff.). Some add 2 Sam 7. See the discussion in Klein, *Israel in Exile*, 23–24; cf. Cross, *Canaanite Myth and Hebrew Epic*, 274–89.

14. Cf. Noth, *History of the Pentateuchal Traditions*, 12–17.

pus of Joshua-Kings,[15] it is not surprising that analyses in the study of Deuteronomy often parallel current revisions of the Deuteronomistic History. There are also historical and hermeneutical issues that can be considered "parallels" (in an extended sense) in order to organize our more-focused discussion on the current state of research on Deuteronomy itself.

The first "parallel" is the use of an extended "discovery" in order to date and interpret the material. The identification of Deuteronomy—at least its core—with the scroll found in the Temple during the reign of Josiah (2 Kgs 22:8) was the crucial historical link for both the source-critical documentary hypothesis and tradition-historical Deuteronomistic History.[16] Thus, the standard view of Deuteronomy's historical setting is largely dependent on data not found in the book itself, which "is by

---

15. For a full history of criticism, see McConville, "Old Testament Historical Books," 3–13; Knoppers, *Two Nations under God*, 17–56; and Römer and de Pury, "L'historiographie deutéronomiste," 9–120. For a collection of recent studies building on Noth's work, see McConville and Knoppers, *Reconsidering Israel and Judah*.

16. Modern critical study of Deuteronomy had always connected the book with the Old Testament historical books. In his 1805 dissertation, de Wette identified Deuteronomy with the "Book of the Law" associated with King Josiah's religious reform in 621 BC (2 Kgs 22:8). Wellhausen revised de Wette's hypothesis, reducing the contents of the scroll found in the Temple in Josiah's time to what is found in Deut 12–26, which Wellhausen considered a law-code (Wellhausen, *Prolegomena*, 279–80). But de Wette's establishment of a historical anchor became key in the later source-critical formulation of the Documentary Hypothesis, which maintains that the Pentateuchal literature originates from distinct periods of Israel's history and is composed from four source documents: J, E, D, and P (see the well documented accounts in Mayes, *Deuteronomy*, 29–55; and Tigay, *Deuteronomy*, xix–xxvi).

This position that the core of Deuteronomy—focused on the centralization of the cult as its main aim (based on the altar law of Deut 12:5)—is a seventh-century composition connected with religious reform continues to be the consensus, though scholars disagree about the exact "reform movement" with which Deuteronomy's original composition should be associated. Some continue to defend the Josianic dating (e.g., Clements, *Deuteronomy*, 70–71). Others look at the conservative movement against King Manasseh in 686–42 BC (e.g., Driver, *Deuteronomy*, xlix–lv), or the even earlier reform in the reign of Hezekiah (Weinfeld, *Deuteronomy and the Deuteronomic School*, 91).

Noth's approach signaled a shift from source criticism to transmission of history. Though earlier critics had found various strata in Deuteronomy (C. Steuernagel and W. Staerk argued for a "redactional" model based on the *Numeruswechsel* [see nn. 26 and 36]; G. von Rad spoke of late additions [*Studies in Deuteronomy*, 72]) and "D" elements in the historical books of Joshua through Kings, Noth was the first to speak of the whole corpus as a more-or-less literary unity controlled by a single writer.

its nature opaque as regards its specific period and purpose."[17] A further external discovery that has affected this aspect of scholarly research includes the parallels drawn between Deuteronomy and ancient Near Eastern treaties.[18] Though early attempts were made to locate the book in the second millennium BC,[19] others insist that these parallels substantiate the traditional seventh-century dating.[20] Either way, it is clear that Deuteronomy draws on the ancient Near Eastern treaty tradition, heightening the covenantal aspects of the book.[21] It also invites the use of comparative studies on other issues related to the book.[22]

The second "parallel" is the search for original settings and sources. Usually dismissing Noth's ideas of a single exilic editor (Dtr) and a consistently negative portrayal of the monarchy, more recent scholars have favored the idea of multiple editorial layers behind the present text. Noth's own caveats and qualifications actually began this trend. Since, for him, Dtr was a redactor as well as an author, discrepancies between passages were explained as the outcome of redacting disparate sources. But more

17. McConville, "Restoration in Deuteronomy," 11.

18. Moses' second speech (4:44—28:68) had already been considered as a covenant treaty form by von Rad, *Deuteronomy*, 26–33.

19. The argument is based on formal comparisons: Deuteronomy is more similar to early Hittite treaty forms than to later neo-Assyrian treaties. See Mendenhall, "Covenant Forms in Israelite Tradition," 50–76; Baltzer, *Covenant Formulary*; Kline, *Treaty of the Great King*; Kitchen, *On the Reliability of the Old Testament*, 283–307; idem, *Ancient Orient and Old Testament*, 90–102; Wenham, "Structure and Date of Deuteronomy," 206–12; Craigie, *Book of Deuteronomy*, 24–29.

20. Proponents of this view emphasize the lexical similarities between Deuteronomy and the Vassal Treaties of Esarhaddon (ca. 680–669 BC). The main surveys of parallels are Hillers, *Treaty-Curses and the Old Testament Prophets*; Frankena, "Vassal-Treaties of Esarhaddon," 122–54; Weinfeld, *Deuteronomy and the Deuteronomic School*, 116–29; idem, "Traces of Assyrian Treaty Formulae in Deuteronomy," 417–27; McCarthy, *Treaty and Covenant*, 172–82; cf. Nicholson, "Covenant in a Century of Study since Wellhausen," 78–93; Steymans, *Deuteronomium 28 und die adêzur Thronfolgeregelung Asarhaddons*.

21. In the final analysis, Deuteronomy is not a treaty document *per se*, for the final chapters (chaps. 30–34) do not find correspondence to the extant treaties. But the similarities drive a theological point. Cf. the statement by Whybray (*Introduction to the Pentateuch*, 88) that the similarities to ANE treaties point to the probability that "in Deuteronomy we have the earliest comprehensive theological statement about the relationship between Yahweh and Israel, and that the notion of the vassal treaty, here called a 'covenant' . . . has played some part in the development of this theology."

22. E.g., the use of Ugaritic material in Craigie, "Deuteronomy and Ugaritic Studies," 109–22.

recent schools of thought—the two main ones are associated with Frank Cross[23] and Rudolf Smend[24]—argue that the thematic heterogeneity extends beyond the sources themselves and indicates diversity in editorial comments and stages as well. Cross argues for a two-stage redaction: the main edition (Dtr¹) dates to the time of King Josiah, in which there is a stated thematic contrast between the sin of Jeroboam and the promises of David; a second, exilic edition (Dtr²) revised the earlier work, recorded the destruction of Jerusalem, and introduced a subtheme of Manasseh's apostasy as the reason for the destruction. Smend agrees with Noth of an exilic Dtr (more specifically DtrH), but argues that the work of a nomistic deuteronomistic editor (DtrN), whose dominant concern is obedience to the Torah of Moses, is also present. Walter Dietrich revises Smend's analysis and adds a prophetically-oriented redaction (DtrP), which stands between DtrH and DtrN.[25]

These revisions of Noth still assume a more-or-less unified composition in the final redaction, but they argue more strongly (and logically) for the presence of different—even competing—voices and/or theological horizons in the present text. Both the Cross school and the Smend school include adherents that concentrate on Deuteronomy itself.[26] A

---

23. Cross, *Canaanite Myth and Hebrew Epic*. Cross modifies his hypothesis of a two-stage redaction of the Deuteronomistic History in "Themes of the Book of Kings," 79–94. This double redaction theory is also expounded in Nelson, *Double Redaction of the Deuteronomistic History*; and Friedman, "From Egypt to Egypt," 167–92.

24. Smend, "Law and the Nations," 95–110.

25. Dietrich, *Prophetie und Geschichte*. For Dietrich, all three redactions date to the Babylonian exile, but Smend places DtrN in the early postexilic period. A somewhat similar view of locating multiple Dtr redactions in the exile is Wolff, "Kerygma of the Deuteronomistic Historical Work," 83–100.

The differences between these various approaches should not be overstated. Halpern, for instance, notes the essential similarity of the methodologies in that all agree that a final hand selected and shaped already extant literature; see Halpern, *First Historians*, 110–18.

26. Cross' double redaction theory is applied specifically to Deuteronomy in Mayes, "Deuteronomy 4 and the Literary Criticism of Deuteronomy," 195–224. After establishing the unity of Deut 4:1–40 and the unit's independence over against the preceding chapters (Noth was in doubt concerning chap. 4), Mayes argues that the unit is the work of Dtr². He then determines other texts that probably came from the same hand (Deut 6:10–19; 7:4–5, 7–15, 25–26; 8:1–6, 11b, 14b–16; 10:12—11:32 [omitting 10:19; 11:29–30]; 26:16–19; 27:9–10; 28:1–6, 15–19; 29:1—30:20 [31:1]; 32:45–47). According to Mayes, it was through the work of this editor that Deuteronomy "became imbued with specifically covenant or treaty thought forms and terminology" (ibid., 222).

A Smend-type approach is found in Veijola, "Principal Observations," 137–46.

similar debate concerns the possible sources for Deuteronomy; that is, can one identify the participants in the formative process of the book? The hypotheses that have been advanced include Levitical, prophetic, and (wisdom) scribal sources.[27] But many now recognize that no single hypothesis can account for everything in the book. The multi-perspective view of Brueggemann is typical: "More likely, the book of Deuteronomy emerged from the best efforts of many interpretive enterprises in Israel; it represents a hard-fought consensus in Israel about the key claims of Yahwistic faith."[28]

The third "parallel" between the ongoing study of the Deuteronomistic History and Deuteronomy itself is in fundamental challenges to certain, heretofore, scholarly consensuses and methodological assumptions.[29] Some have called into question the identification of the book of

---

Veijola favors the retention of traditional literary criticism, while explicitly rejecting "new literary approaches" to the study of Deuteronomy, particularly the "rhetorical analysis" of Robert Polzin (see below). Veijola's work also illustrates a more traditional interpretation of the so-called *Numeruswechsel*, i.e., accounting for the alternations between second-person singular and second-person plural forms by recourse to a redactional theory of the growth of the text (cf. n. 36).

27. For the view that Levitical teachers are the force behind the book, see von Rad, *Studies in Deuteronomy*, 66–67. For the view that the prophetic movement is the proper origin of the book see Nicholson, *Deuteronomy and Tradition*, 69. For the claim that Deuteronomy originated in wisdom and scribal schools see Weinfeld, *Deuteronomy and the Deuteronomic School*. Cf. the discussions in Miller, *Deuteronomy*, 5–8; Whybray, *Introduction to the Pentateuch*, 88–90.

28. Brueggemann, *Deuteronomy*, 21. See especially Römer, "Deuteronomy in Search of Origins," in which the author deals with the relationship between Deuteronomy and the rest of the Deuteronomistic History, and argues that both speak with more than one voice on the question of Israel's national origins. Others discern an overarching unity in the figure of Moses; so Blenkinsopp, *Pentateuch*, 217: "Whoever it was that actually wrote the book, it seems that it was this constituency that found a voice, the voice of Moses, in the political, social, and religious program of Deuteronomy. Cf. also the discussion in Miller, *Deuteronomy*, 5–8.

29. After reviewing scholarship on the Deuteronomistic History, Preuss ("Zum deuteronomistischen Geschichtswerk," 394) argues that theories about sources and editorial layers are *system immanent*, i.e., a scholar's results are predetermined by the perspective of his or her historical-critical school; cf. the critiques of McConville, "Faces of Exile," 519–26; idem, *Grace in the End*, 33–44, 78–90. Recently, Knoppers noted, "Within the past decade an increasing number of scholars have called into question a number of central tenets and assumptions of the Deuteronomistic History hypothesis. For these scholars, the hypothesis itself, and not just particular aspects of it, needs to be completely revised or rejected altogether" (see his editorial introduction to *Reconsidering Israel and Judah*, 3). Part 4 ("New Directions") of the same volume (ibid., 446–614) contains nine essays, all of which challenge Noth's Deuteronomistic History

Deuteronomy with the scroll found in the Temple during the reign of Josiah.[30] This corresponds to the rebuttals of scholars like Wenham, who takes issue with the time-honored conclusion that "Deuteronomy demands centralization of all worship at a single sanctuary, and therefore that its composition must be associated with Josiah's attempt to limit all worship to Jerusalem."[31] Also, whereas Cross emended Noth's redactional analysis by positing a Josianic edition and exilic edition, others are contending for multiple pre-exilic editions that precede these two.[32] Still others go a step further and contend that large blocks, even books, have their own, independent process of composition before being brought together.[33] With these and other challenges to the Deuteronomistic History hypothesis, the critical interpretation of Deuteronomy will continue to be diverse and complex.

Perhaps a more fundamental "challenge" to the traditional (albeit often modified) literary and redactional energies is a hermeneutical one. Deuteronomy and the Deuteronomistic History have not escaped the trend of explicit text-immanent approaches arising from (post)modern literary-critical theories, as well as greater sensitivity to "canonical" approaches, whether they derive primarily from literary, theological, or historical concerns.[34] The elevation of aesthetic and theological concerns

---

hypothesis in very fundamental ways and offer competing hypotheses.

30. See the discussion in Lohfink, "Recent Discussion on 2 Kings 22–23," 36–61. The historicity of the report of these chapters has been variously assessed; see Nicholson, *Deuteronomy and Tradition*, 1–17; Mayes, *Deuteronomy*, 85–103.

31. Wenham, "Deuteronomy and the Central Sanctuary," 94. Wenham refers to several others who have had difficulty with the supposition of the demand for centralization when Deut 12:5 is interpreted in its context. Cf. McConville's view—that the silence of Deuteronomy on the identity of "the place that Yahweh your God will choose" is more than a device to preserve the Mosaic fiction, but allows for a succession of "places"—in McConville and Millar, *Time and Place*, 89–139.

32. E.g., Lemaire, "Concerning the Redactional History of the Books of Kings," 446–61, where Lemaire envisions a several-hundred year period in which a basic work was continually being updated and expanded. In the introduction to this volume, Knoppers notes, "In advancing this general point of view, Lemaire is not alone" (*Reconsidering Israel and Judah*, 13).

33. Westermann, *Die Geschichtsbücher des Alten Testaments*; McConville, "Faces of Exile," 533. This approach offers a different way of accounting for the text's unity and diversity; unity of the larger entity is retained, yet discrete redactional units are identified within it.

34. The historical side of canonical approaches with respect to Deuteronomy and the Pentateuch will be given more attention in the next section. The philosophical

and foci has by no means created a monochromatic interpretive grid. At one end of the spectrum are scholars who tend to ignore rather than rebut the historical issues. A prominent example related to the present issue is Robert Polzin, who is writing a series subtitled *A Literary Study of the Deuteronomic History*.[35] Others have not dismissed altogether traditional concerns for text history, but have subjugated these concerns to literary and theological ones. These scholars tend to presuppose the integrity of the final form of the text, or at least find more unity in texts that have generally been claimed to betray disparity.[36] With respect to exile and restoration, McConville has shown great balance, demonstrating that a "canonical" study of the Deuteronomic literature can give significant attention to historical questions while also doing more justice

---

underpinnings of this so-called "trend" have been well-rehearsed in the literature. See Gunn, "New Directions," 566–77. Gunn thinks it is too simplistic to reduce the methodological difference to one between diachronic and synchronic concerns, for many recent literary studies (i.e., postmodern, reader-oriented theories) have rejected the possibility of achieving a normative reading of the text (ibid., 570). Though focusing on the Pentateuch, a standard reference for modern literary techniques is Alter, *Art of Biblical Narrative*. A complement can be found in Schökel, "Narrative Art in Joshua–Judges–Samuel–Kings," 255–78. For the most complete bibliography on modern literary analyses of biblical narrative see Ska, *"Our Fathers Have Told Us"*.

35. So far Polzin has published three of the volumes: Part One is *Moses and the Deuteronomist*; Part Two is *Samuel and the Deuteronomist*; Part Three is *David and the Deuteronomist*. Cf. also Polzin, "Reporting Speech in the Book of Deuteronomy," 355–74. Polzin is the central object of attack in a rejection of "new literary approaches" and "rhetorical analysis" in Veijola, "Principal Observations," 137–46. Veijola's study illustrates that traditional literary criticism continues despite newer approaches and concerns.

36. On the structural unity of the Deuteronomistic History, see McCarthy, "Wrath of Yahweh," 99. The literary coherence of the present form of Deuteronomy is now commonly recognized, even by those still interested in some measure with the text's literary history. This is not necessarily a rejection of disparate voices in the text, but an awareness that all these voices have been intentionally brought together in a sophisticated and overall unifying way. Christensen (*Deuteronomy 1:1—21:9*, lxviii–lxix) discerns Lohfink's "stylistic" approach to the study of Deuteronomy 5–11 as a major impulse or turning point in the study of Deuteronomy; see Lohfink, *Das Hauptgebot*. According to Christensen (*Deuteronomy 1:1—21:9*, lxix), Lohfink "tended to find unity in the text in spite of the apparent diversity in surface form, which led Steuernagel, and others after him, to posit complex theories of redactional growth." This reference to Steuernagel raises the issue of the *Numeruswechsel* (cf. n. 26). Against Steuernagel and others, Lohfink (and now many others) argues that this is a stylistic device that cannot be used to discern diverse redactional layers. For an alternative explanation that interprets the phenomenon as part of the complex set of signals for rhythmic boundaries, see Christensen, "*Numeruswechsel* in Deuteronomy 12," 394–402.

to theological considerations than Cross' double-redaction theory or Smend's multiple exilic-redaction theory.[37]

## Deuteronomy and the Pentateuch

While debates concerning Deuteronomy's relationship with the Former Prophets continue, scholars are also reconsidering the book's relationship with Genesis to Numbers.[38] We have reserved our discussion of Deuteronomy's position in the Pentateuch until now because current trends in this area flow in part from developments of and challenges to the study of the Deuteronomistic History. It is unnecessary for us to go into as much detail on the varying positions concerning the Pentateuch as we did in the previous section, but a proper grounding in the study of both Deuteronomy and the exile requires discussion of some of the main tenets of modern Pentateuchal research.[39] In some sense, refocusing on Deuteronomy's place in the Pentateuch is itself a challenge to Noth's hypothesis, which could not adequately account for the present structure of the Hebrew canon.[40]

The classical formulation of the documentary hypothesis has fallen out of favor, partly because it is dependent on a particular view of the history of Israelite religion that is now considered untenable. Because presuppositions have changed, current Pentateuchal research is intertwined with ongoing discussions and debates concerning canonical criticism and the nature of Israelite historiography.[41] Trends in these

---

37. McConville, "Restoration in Deuteronomy," 11–40. According to McConville, neither the Cross approach nor the Smend approach can adequately account for the polarities of pre-exilic hope and exilic disappointment, for each necessarily emphasizes one pole to the neglect of the other.

38. On the relationship of Deuteronomy with Genesis-Numbers see the discussion and references in Römer, "Deuteronomy in Search of Origins," 112–38; cf. Lohfink, "Deutéronome et Pentateuque," 35ff.

39. On the Pentateuch generally, see Sanders, *Torah and Canon*; Whybray, *Making of the Pentateuch*; Blenkinsopp, *Pentateuch*; Crüsemann, *Torah*. Cf. the more recent discussion of certain issues as they relate to a theology of exile in Smith-Christopher, *Biblical Theology of Exile*, 30ff.

40. Noth's book on the Pentateuch (*History of Pentateuchal Traditions*) is actually a reconstruction of the origin and development of the traditions in the Tetrateuch only. Still trying to follow the traditional documentary hypothesis, Noth found practically no traces of "D" in Genesis-Numbers. For him, the Pentateuch was formed by a simple expedient of detaching Deuteronomy from the Deuteronomistic History and attaching it to the Tetrateuch.

41. On Israelite historiography, see the relevant essays in Long, *Israel's Past in Present*

areas tend to focus on the historical and/or existential aspects of the Babylonian exile. The sixth-century crisis and its aftermath, including the concerns of the postexilic community and its competing schools, provide for many the appropriate context in which to interpret the final form of the Pentateuch and its pride of place in the canonization process. Placing the final form and achievement of canonical status in the sixth or fifth centuries is not new; this has been the consensus since Wellhausen. But the point of emphasis or significance has shifted from the *process*, whereby sources and/or traditions (whether real or fictive) have developed and been incorporated into the final form, to the *function* or *authority* these traditions have in the exilic/post-exilic context. This change in attitude is evident in the comment by Whybray: "Any attempt to discover the process by which the Pentateuch reached its present form must explain not only *how*, but also *why* its compiler or compilers acted as they did."[42]

There is no longer a consensus—except that there is no consensus—regarding the existence of, or at least availability to identify, continuous narrative sources behind the present text of the Pentateuch. However, given Noth and his successors, more attention is now given to Deuteronomistic influence throughout the Pentateuch, which calls into question the other sources. The E source has long been considered problematic as an independent source. Still, some are now eliminating the J source as well, or at least trivializing it by displacing it to a much later date.[43] Though P has fared better, it is debated whether P is a distinct narrative source or a secondary redactional stage, and some even date it earlier than D.[44] It is not uncommon, then, to find scholars who, like Rendtorff, speak of a redaction of the Pentateuch which "in its ideas and language is closely related to Deuteronomy."[45]

---

*Research*, esp. 142–206, 280–491, 552–56. At the center of the debates is the "minimalist" position, most notably associated with the writings of John Van Seters, Philip R. Davies, and Thomas L. Thompson: Van Seters, *In Search of History*; Davies, *In Search of Ancient Israel*; Thompson, *Historicity of the Patriarchal Narratives*; idem, *Mythic Past*.

42. Whybray, *Making of the Pentateuch*, 15 (emphasis added).

43. On this, see the discussion and references in Blenkinsopp, *Pentateuch*, 23–25, 29–30 n. 9.

44 On the date of P as not necessarily late, see Hurvitz, "Evidence of Language," 24–56; Haran, "Behind the Scenes of History," 321–33.

45. Rendtorff, *Problem of the Process of Transmission*, 99.

If one then broadens the enquiry, what is emerging may be a "new consensus" that the Pentateuch was composed as a corpus linked in some way, either as a theologically-motivated introduction or as a politically-driven complement, to the Deuteronomistic History.[46] The first nine books of the Hebrew Bible, then, form a connected historical continuum, with the exodus-exile nexus controlling the narrative. Either exilic or post-exilic concerns account for the canonical separation of Torah and Former Prophets, resulting in an elevation of the Torah. On the one hand, the Pentateuch provides hope for those in exile—and so outside the land of promise—for they are in a similar position as the nation prior to the conquest. On the other hand, the post-exilic community, in need of a theological and political compromise between varying schools of thought, would find in the Pentateuch the normative narrative of the Mosaic age to serve the interests of Second Temple Judaism.[47]

## Conclusion

Some of the issues raised in the preceding discussion affect the methodology adopted for the present project. First, our theological reading will be affected by the extent to which we give attention to the relationship between Deuteronomy and the rest of the Deuteronomistic History, both diachronically and synchronically. McConville is particularly helpful in this regard; he shows how both the nature of the literature (Deuteronomy and the Deuteronomistic History) and the nature of the subject matter (exile and restoration) call for theological sensitivity to multiple horizons and their interrelationship.[48] This will help establish

---

46. For the various options, see Blenkinsopp, *Pentateuch*, 229–43; Whybray, *Making of the Pentateuch*, 221–42. Even those skeptical of the Deuteronomistic History hypothesis are comfortable with a focus on Genesis–Kings as a unit; cf. McConville, "Faces of Exile," 533. The radical position that the Pentateuch was somehow authorized by the Persian court is summarized and critiqued in Watts, ed., *Persia and Torah*; cf. Smith-Christopher, *Biblical Theology of Exile*, 34–38.

47. Less attention has been paid to the fivefold division of the Pentateuch into distinct books. Blenkinsopp, *Pentateuch*, 42–47, argues that theological rather than pragmatic concerns are behind the division, and that one cannot dismiss the possibility that Genesis and Deuteronomy existed at one time as independent texts.

48. See McConville, "Restoration in Deuteronomy," 11–40. For McConville, "canonical" need not be reduced to "synchronic" or "final form" alone: "Simple 'final form' strategies will not handle all the questions that arise in this connection" (ibid., 12). Cf. McConville, "Faces of Exile," 522, where, with respect to the lack of consensus on historical and redaction issues, he regards a "text alone" approach as a pragmatic response, "which simply lays aside questions that appear to be unanswerable." While McConville

our understanding of Deuteronomy's programmatic, yet multifaceted, stance on exile and restoration.

Second, with a new scholarly focus on the *why* more than the *how* of Pentateuchal formation, the Torah is read—and *intentionally* meant to be read—as a story, with a forward-driven purpose and an overriding unity (despite possible discrepancies, multiple voices, etc.). Diachronic and synchronic concerns, therefore, find common ground in giving primary consideration to the final form of the text.[49]

Third, Deuteronomy is of central importance in understanding larger corpora, both the Pentateuch and the larger block of Genesis-Kings. Note especially the following statement by Whybray concerning Deuteronomy:

> It has a unique status not only in the Pentateuch but also in the Old Testament. In the hands of the final editors it presents a complete, more or less coherent theology—the only fully conceived theology in the Old Testament, and one which was to have a profound influence on subsequent thought, as may be seen espe-

---

operates with a more skeptical view of the Deuteronomistic History hypothesis, this attention to multiple horizons that affect a theological reading is also noted by Helga Weippert, who works within the normal limits of the hypothesis. Weippert has proposed multiple redactions and preexisting blocks of material for the Deuteronomistic History ("Das deuteronomistische Geschichtswerk," 213–49); but she also finds unity within the disparate sections in the promise-fulfillment schema first recognized by von Rad (Weippert, "'Histories' and 'History,'" 47–61). A significant contribution of her work is that the prophecy-fulfillment pattern works on both short-range and long-range levels.

49. Even those who have written on the formation of the Pentateuch concede this much. Note the following statements in Blenkinsopp, *Pentateuch*: "It is the text in its narrative integrity, and not this or that source, which in the last analysis is the object of interpretation" (p. 33); "It should ... be obvious that literary analysis must precede historical reconstruction" (p. 175). Cf. Whybray, *Making of the Pentateuch*, 9: "In so far as this new emphasis [i.e., the concentration on the final form] is likely to lead to a greater appreciation of the literary and theological qualities of the Pentateuch, it is to be welcomed."

Note the insight of Gunn, "New Directions," 566–77, that the more fundamental divide is between modern and postmodern epistemological presuppositions rather than diachronic and synchronic methodological approaches. This is highlighted in the "Afterword" of Clines' popular book, *Theme of the Pentateuch*, 127–41. After twenty years since the original publication of his work, Clines admits that his book betrays assumptions of textual unity and determinate meaning that are no longer acceptable to him.

cially in the Deuteronomistic History and in the final editions of several of the prophetic books.[50]

In other words, even on historical grounds, Deuteronomy ought to be seen as transitional and programmatic. More than a century ago, Wellhausen remarked that "the connecting link between old and new, between Israel and Judaism, is everywhere Deuteronomy."[51]

## Exile: Its History and Theology

The foregoing discussion was important to show how the scholarly study of Deuteronomy is caught up with the sixth-century exile itself. Brueggemann states baldly, "Old Testament scholarship has advanced to see that the Old Testament itself, in its canonical form, arises from and responds to the crisis of exile."[52] The focus is now on the reuse of purported early traditions in the later post-exilic period. We survey here the works devoted to the exile itself, both the complexities of historical, political, and sociological circumstances, and those that look more directly at the theological issues related to exile.

### The History of Studies on the Exile

In the twentieth century and on through the present, one of the primary scholarly debates has been to assess the influential significance of the Babylonian exile; that is, does the biblical account of a major catastrophe fit the modern historical reconstruction of the data?[53] Many have expressed ambivalent opinion concerning the conditions of exile.[54] John Bright, for example, gives seemingly opposing pictures within three pages: "Although we should not belittle the hardships and the humiliation that these exiles endured, their lot does not seem to have been unduly severe." But then he states, "When one considers the magnitude

---

50. Whybray, *Introduction to the Pentateuch*, 91.

51. Wellhausen, *Prolegomena*, 362. On the character of the Deuteronomic law as a blueprint, see Blenkinsopp, *Pentateuch*, 233–37.

52. In his foreword to Smith-Christopher, *Biblical Theology of Exile*, vii.

53. For a helpful summary, see Smith-Christopher, *Biblical Theology of Exile*, 30–54.

54. The following exhibit mixed opinions: Bright, *History of Israel*; Foster, *Restoration of Israel*; Klein, *Israel in Exile*; Ackroyd, *Exile and Restoration*; Scott, *Exile*; idem, *Restoration*; Grabbe, *Leading Captivity Captive*; Oded, "Observations on the Israelite/Judean Exiles," 205–12.

of the calamity that overtook her, one marvels that Israel was not sucked down into the vortex of history along with the other little nations of western Asia."[55] The classic work of Peter Ackroyd shows the same ambiguity on the same page; he writes that indications "are of reasonable freedom, of settlement in communities—perhaps engaged in work for the Babylonians, but possibly simply engaged in normal agricultural life—of the possibility of marriage, of the ordering of their own affairs, of relative prosperity," but also that the "uncongenial nature" of the situation should not be "understated."[56]

There have been those who have totally de-emphasized the exile. As early as 1910, C. C. Torrey commented that the exile, "which was in reality a small and relatively insignificant affair, has been made, partly through mistake and partly by the compulsion of a theory, to play a very important part in the history of the Old Testament."[57] This more radical skepticism has appeared from time to time,[58] but recent work has gone further in discounting the possibility of confidently reconstructing historical events before, and even during, the exile. The works of Thomas L. Thompson, John Van Seters, Philip R. Davies, and others, suggest that "post-exilic Judaism" created, virtually *ex nihilo*, the entire biblical pre-exilic tradition.[59] The so-called Heidelberg School (including Peter Frei, Klaus Koch, and Erhard Blum) even claims that the Pentateuch itself is an invention of the Persian court.[60] Though extreme, these positions

55. Bright, *History of Israel*, 345, 347.
56. Ackroyd, *Exile and Restoration*, 32.
57. Torrey, "Exile and the Restoration," 285.
58. On Torrey's views and a resurgence of his skepticism, see Barstad, *Myth of the Empty Land*, 21–23; cf. Carroll, "Exile! What Exile," 62–79. Barstad concludes that while there were deportations from Judah, the bulk of the population remained in the land; the archaeological record shows no significant break in settlement or culture, and although there was a return, it was not nearly as large as depicted in Ezra–Nehemiah. See also Donner, "Separate States of Israel and Judah," 421, 433: "It is easy . . . to overemphasize the drastic and debilitating consequences of the fall of Jerusalem and the triumph of Babylonian forces. Various aspects of life certainly were greatly modified, but Babylonian policy was not overly oppressive. The exiles were not forced to live in inhuman conditions . . . [and] remained free and certainly should not be understood as slaves. They would have been under no overt pressure to assimilate and lose their identities."
59. For the works of Thompson, Van Seters, and Davies, see n. 41. Others include Lemche, *Ancient Israel*; idem, *Early Israel*; Whitelam, *Invention of Ancient Israel*; cf. the important collection of essays in Grabbe, ed., *Can a "History of Israel" Be Written?* Among the most polemical responses is Dever, *What Did the Biblical Writers Know*.
60. The position is summarized and critically reviewed in Watts, *Persia and Torah*.

are outgrowths of the assumption of most modern scholars that Jewish attitudes toward Persian rule were generally positive.[61]

Alongside, and in reaction to, the ambiguous and skeptical pictures is the view that the exile was indeed catastrophic and transformative for Hebrew existence. This position finds more evidence than the others for severe treatment during and after the exile. Important at the methodological level (of assessing evidence), James C. Scott shows that "resistance" usually does not take the form of outright revolution or open warfare in history, so one should look for more discrete human responses to oppression and suppression.[62] John M. Wilkie challenges assumptions about the generally light treatment of exiles by looking at Isaiah's concept of the "suffering servant": "There is independent evidence to suggest that Second-Isaiah's language is neither metaphorical nor at variance with the actual conditions, but is an accurate description of conditions which he knew only too well."[63] Daniel L. Smith-Christopher draws on these and other sources, concluding that "the assessment of the impact of the Babylonian exile must make far more use of nonbiblical documents, archaeological reports, and a far more imaginative use of biblical texts read in the light of what we know about refugee studies, disaster studies, postcolonialist reflections, and sociologies of trauma."[64]

## Theology of Exile in Old Testament Studies

The reason for summarizing the historical debate above is that attempts to write about theological aspects of exile are influenced heavily by each writer's understanding of its historical, political, and sociological contexts. In other words, one's interpretation of the text is somewhat determined by one's reconstruction of history. To be sure, all recognize "exile" to be a major theological construct in which to interpret the biblical

---

61. The biblical data used to support this positive stance includes (1) the bestowal of the term "Messiah" on Cyrus in Isa 45:1; (2) the existence of Jewish names among the Murashû documents; and (3) the book of Daniel's benign view of Darius. For summary and references, including a critique, see Smith-Christopher, *Biblical Theology of Exile*, 36–38.

62. Scott, *Dominion and the Arts of Resistance*.

63. Wilkie, "Nabonidus and the Later Jewish Exiles," 36–44.

64. Smith-Christopher, *Biblical Theology of Exile*, 33. He refers to several works, most notably Speckermann, *Juda unter Assur in der Sargonidenzeit*, who counters Morton Coogan in a similar debate concerning the Neo-Assyrian conquest of the Northern Kingdom in 722 BC.

data; the Old Testament has even been referred to as "the foundational metanarrative of exile."[65] But often the emphasis is on "exile" as an ideological *Leitmotif* involved in the self-understanding of Second Temple Judaism—the primary setting for various reflections on exile. This, in turn, has generated close focus on the concepts of exile and restoration in the extra-biblical literature of the period, often in conjunction with the growing interest of exile-restoration theology in New Testament studies.[66]

The remainder of this section is limited to a brief examination of six books that explicitly attempt a theological investigation of exile in Old Testament literature.[67] At the risk of oversimplification, we will synthesize these theologies with respect to some of the more relevant issues that relate to our study. In chronological order, these books are those of Peter Ackroyd (1968), Thomas Raitt (1977), Ralph Klein (1979), Donald Gowan (1998), Daniel Smith-Christopher (2002), and C. Marvin Pate et al. (2004). It is helpful to keep the dates of publication in mind, for these studies display some of the methodological, ideological, and epistemological trends in biblical studies generally. While all note that the Old Testament texts offer varying responses to the exile, they account for the differences based on their various methods and presuppositions. We will

---

65. Hatina, "Exile," 348. See n. 3.

66. See especially the collections of essays in Scott, *Exile*; idem, *Restoration*; Carson et al., eds., *Justification and Variegated Nomism*; idem, *Paradoxes of Paul*. We will address NT concerns below.

67. To my knowledge these are the only full monographs with such a theological focus: Ackroyd, *Exile and Restoration*; Raitt, *Theology of Exile*; Klein, *Israel in Exile*; Gowan, *Theology of the Prophetic Books*; Smith-Christopher, *Biblical Theology of Exile*; Pate et al., *Story of Israel*.

We do not include here the work by Newsome, *By the Waters of Babylon*. Despite the subtitle, no real theological discussion is apparent in the book. In Newsome's words, "This volume attempts to tell the story of the Jewish people during those years before the destruction of Jerusalem in 587 BC, to profile the Jewish experience under Babylonian rule, and to sketch the shape of those hopes which led to Jerusalem's restoration under the Davidic princes Sheshbazzar and Zerubbabel" (ibid., 7). For Newsome, exile and restoration are facts of history; Newsome provides a synthesis of biblical and extra-biblical material to reconstruct the major events of Jewish history between 625 and 500 BC. Only in a concluding reflection for contemporary application does Newsome consider the symbolic nature of Judah's experience, which is simply a realization that God often fulfills his promises in ways that may not be to our satisfaction or according to our expectations (ibid., 152–54).

summarize their similarities and differences after looking at each work individually.

*Peter Ackroyd (1968)*

Ackroyd's *Exile and Restoration: A Study of Hebrew Thought of the Sixth Century B.C.* concentrates on problems of the sixth century BC in order to define the theological mindset of the time. Ackroyd's thesis is that the thinking of the period must be seen as a creative response to the tragedy of the exile. In depicting the events of the exile, Ackroyd admits to "historical uncertainties," but that "there is no real doubt about the main outlines."[68] The main problem is not in historical reconstruction but in discerning the various attitudes toward the exile itself and what the future might hold in terms of restoration. He clarifies these attitudes as found in Jeremiah, the Deuteronomic History, the Priestly work, Ezekiel, Second Isaiah, and the postexilic prophets.

Ackroyd concludes that the exile was a genuine catastrophe. The effect it had on the interpretation of religion in the national literature was two-fold: first, older material was reinterpreted in light of the new setting; second, new lines of thought emerged. On this latter point, the exile was accepted as the proper judgment of a just God; also, there would be a new act of God, a new age, a renewed and purified Israel. Exile, then, becomes a basis of ideology rather than a simple fact of history. The idea of restoration is centered on three aspects: first, the temple as a place where all the world may go to worship; second, the new community and the new age as constituting a complete renewal of the life of the whole world, though tensions exist concerning the Davidic hope as universalistic or nationalistic, and in that the new age is both unrealized and present; and third, the people's response as characterized by an emphasis on piety, the evolution of law, and the production of a large amount of wisdom material.

Though Ackroyd discerns differences among the biblical writers, it seems that the differences can be credited more to historical vantage point than ideological competition. For example, the Deuteronomic History is one of the earliest responses to the exile.[69] It therefore is focused on getting the community to accept God's judgment, for such ac-

---

68. Ackroyd, *Exile and Restoration*, 232.

69. The "Deuteronomic History" (as Ackroyd calls it) is discussed in Ackroyd, *Exile and Restoration*, 83.

ceptance is preliminary to any possible forgiveness and restoration. As it stands, the Deuteronomic History presents an oversimplification of the human situation, though it hints at the need for a new act of God—an idea that finds full expression only later.[70] At this early stage, restoration can be no more than shadowy, which explains why the emphasis of hope is found in the old patterns of divine election and covenant theology. Later writers have felt free to progress from (but not necessarily contradict) this outlook.[71]

## Thomas Raitt (1977)

Raitt's *A Theology of Exile: Judgment/Deliverance in Jeremiah and Ezekiel* is a form-critical and tradition-historical study of the oracles of judgment and the oracles of deliverance in Jeremiah and Ezekiel. Raitt attempts a "systematic analysis of the tension between those two theological poles [of judgment and deliverance], their relationship, and their historical and theological roots" as expressed in the two prophets who interpreted the onset of the Babylonian exile.[72] The heart of the issue with which Raitt deals is the surprising shift from a predominating message of doom to a dominant emphasis on salvation. The fundamental point of his study is that the two types of oracles are carried by totally different speech forms. Though Raitt does not rehearse the historical events of the exile, he argues that the form-critical distinctions presume external political changes and shed light on an actual theological shift that took place when Judah went into exile.

The oracle of judgment has a covenantal frame of reference. In this framework, blessing and curse are dictated by human response (see Deut 28). The failure to produce repentance, however, created a "radicalization" of the judgment message.[73] This entailed a heightening of the prophetic pronouncement of the people's sinfulness and God's wrath against their sin, resulting in his rejection of his people. This rejection motif, considered a new element in the prophets, creates questions of

---

70. Ibid., 235.

71. See, e.g., the discussion concerning the exodus tradition in Ackroyd, *Exile and Restoration*, 239. While Jeremiah and Second Isaiah speak of restoration as a "new exodus," others (e.g., Nehemiah and Judith) abandon the deliverance motif in favor of a stress on God's continuing mercy and grace in spite of his just punishment.

72. Raitt, *Theology of Exile*, 3.

73. Ibid., 35–58.

theodicy that the old covenant structure could not answer. Therefore, the oracle of deliverance in Jeremiah and Ezekiel is motivated by, and presented as, a vision totally different from the Deuteronomistic promises (Deut 4:26–31; 30:1–10; 1 Kgs 8:46–53).[74] The three major elements of this oracle are deliverance, transformation, and relationship. Unlike the oracle of judgment, the oracle of deliverance "has no 'reason' to explain or justify it."[75] It depicts God's grace as "arbitrary, illogical, and unfathomable." In contradistinction to the judgment oracle, for the prophets "an eschatological model of interpreting God's activity in history superseded covenant theology throughout their salvation preaching."[76]

Exile demarcates two eras. The oracles of judgment and the oracles of deliverance in the two prophets show the discontinuity between the two eras. The two oracle forms also help hold the tension between divine justice and divine love. Ultimately, for Raitt, the tension is rooted in God himself.

### Ralph Klein (1979)

In *Israel in Exile: A Theological Interpretation*, Klein contends that the exile had significant socioeconomic and psychological impact: "Exile meant death, deportation, destruction, and devastation."[77] The burning of the Jerusalem temple, the end of the Davidic dynasty, the loss of land, and the decimation of the priesthood and sacrificial system—all these posed great theological challenges, for they rendered useless the old symbols and created uncertainty about hopes for the future. The various responses included doubt (Ezek 20:32; 37:11), frustrations (Lam 2:4–5; Ps 44:3–4), protestations of one's own innocence (Jer 31:29; Ezek 18:2; cf. Pss 44:17–18; 79:8), appeals to return to the oldest promises and the Mosaic ideal (Priestly writing), calls to brand new saving acts of Yahweh (Second Isaiah), confessions of guilt and acknowledgement of the justification of Yahweh's actions (the Deuteronomistic History; cf. Lam 1:18),

---

74. See especially Raitt, *Theology of Exile*, 120–21. For Raitt, the Deuteronomistic vision of restoration is conditional upon obedience and tied to the patriarchal promise; neither of these concerns are of interest in the original oracle of deliverance (Jer 24:4–7; 29:4–7, 10–14; 32:6–15, 42–44; 31:31–34; 32:36–41; 33:6–9; Ezek 11:16–21; 20:40–44; 34:11–16; 34:20–24; 34:25–31; 36:8–15; 36:22–32; 36:33–36; 37:11–14; 37:19–23; 37:24–28).

75. Ibid., 145.

76. Ibid., 207.

77. Klein, *Israel in Exile*, 2.

a renewed stress on God's forgiveness (Jer 31:34; Ezekiel; Second Isaiah; P; cf. Mic 7:7–20), and uncontrollable grief (Lam 2:18–21).

Klein argues that the exile shaped the entire message and outlook of certain exilic authors. He describes six literary works from the exilic period and their respective responses. These are regarded as contemporaneous, competing voices in the biblical text. Three are products of the Palestinian community and offer little hope for the future. Exilic laments (Lamentations; Pss 44; 74; 79; 102) consider the exile to be a time to pray to Yahweh as both king and enemy. The Deuteronomistic History, which must be read as a "rhetorical whole,"[78] offers a detailed explanation as to why the people are in exile; the exile, therefore, is a time of confession and repentance. Jeremiah pleads that the people accept the inevitable and not be overcome by the events.[79]

According to Klein, three other literary works emerged in Babylon and give explicit descriptions of the future. Ezekiel claims that, although the exile is just and shows that corruption had polluted Israel almost from the beginning, Yahweh would still be faithful to his promises; his complete scheme for a "new Israel" offered hope. Second Isaiah concentrates on the establishment of Yahweh's control over the world and history; while waiting for a "new exodus," Israel is called on to take the role of the Suffering Servant. The Priestly writing concludes that since Yahweh's promises were trustworthy in the past, they should be trusted in exile; hope, then, is in the memory of God's graciousness.

## Donald Gowan (1998)

Gowan claims, in *Theology of the Prophetic Books: The Death and Resurrection of Israel*, that the prophetic books in the Latter Prophets of the canon are works of theology that came into existence because of three major historical turning points: the destruction of the kingdoms of Israel and Judah, respectively, and the beginning of the Judean restoration. This appears to influence Gowan's method. At one level, he pays particular attention to parts of prophetic texts that appear contemporary to the catastrophic events. Overall, he takes a conservative approach to the biblical account about the events themselves. At another level, Gowan

---

78. Ibid., 24.

79. When Klein speaks of "Jeremiah" as a distinct voice, he has in mind an earlier corpus derived from source criticism. A later Deuteronomic redaction of Jeremiah is more hopeful.

focuses on the final canonical form of the books, considering them to be mature reflections of the historical experiences.[80] The unifying theme of the corpus is the death and resurrection of Israel.

The structure of the book is straightforward. Chapter 1 sets forth introductory and methodological issues. Here he includes a helpful discussion of Deuteronomy, which he considers to be a late-eighth-century reaction to the Assyrian deportation of the northern kingdom in 722 BC.[81] He notes that Deuteronomy betrays ambiguity about the nature of exile and restoration, and tension concerning the conditionality of the patriarchal land promise. Except for Deuteronomy 30, there is little evidence in the book that it is influenced by restoration promises of the prophets. Chapters 2–4 of Gowan's book examine the prophets in turn, with brief historical introductions to each chapter and intermittent sections about each prophet's unique messages and how each prophet fits within the context of the whole prophetic message. The "death" of the northern kingdom is the message of Amos, Hosea, Micah, and Isaiah 1–39; the "death" of the southern kingdom is the message of Zephaniah, Habakkuk, Jeremiah, Obadiah, Ezekiel, and Jonah. The "resurrection" of the southern kingdom is the message of Isaiah 40–55, Haggai and Zechariah, Isaiah 56–66, Malachi, and Joel. A final chapter briefly discusses the continuing influence of Old Testament prophecy.

### Daniel Smith-Christopher (2002)

Smith-Christopher's *A Biblical Theology of Exile* is an explicitly postmodern attempt to

> ... establish ways that the biblical literature arises from the experience of these events, as well as being deeply influenced by these social, economic, and political contexts. I maintain that the critical point is that the ancient Hebrew 'theology of exile' arose from these circumstances, and therefore any modern 'theology of exile'

---

80. Gowan is a somewhat inconsistent, however, for he does not deal with Isaiah as a canonical book, but considers chaps. 1–39, chaps. 40–55, and chaps. 56–66 separately. Also, though explicitly citing Brevard Childs' canonical approach as a major influence (Gowan, *Theology of the Prophetic Books*, 6; cf. Childs, "Retrospective Reading of the Old Testament Prophets," 362–77), the canonical order of the prophets is not a major part of Gowan's work.

81. Gowan, *Theology of the Prophetic Books*, 18–21.

must carefully recall their context, as well as our own context, for any theological reflection on the biblical experience.[82]

Smith-Christopher is ultimately concerned with contemporary concerns and interests, and so attempts to "defend a view of diasporic theological identity that is not based on a concept of 'temporary loss of stature' and thus a ruse for triumphalist calls for 'restoration.'"[83]

Using an "exilic theology" as a useful device to construct a modern Christian ideology/theology involves two controlling themes throughout the book. First, the Babylonian exile was an historical human disaster. This disaster gave rise to various social and religious responses, which can now be arranged into a coherent socio-theological picture that can serve as a response to the transhistorical conditions of diaspora. Since the reality of the exilic events are crucial for Smith-Christopher's position, he gives much attention to refuting recent attempts to dismiss or mitigate the trauma of the experience. He draws on extra-biblical documents, archaeological reports, and a reader-oriented approach to the biblical data. On the latter point, biblical texts are read in light of contemporary refugee studies, disaster studies, postcolonialist reflections, and sociologies of trauma.[84] He also argues that stereotypical language, such as that found in Deuteronomy 28, need not be evidence against historical reality.[85]

Second, since biblical texts constitute various, even contradictory, responses to exile, not all of them are positive models for today. It is the perspective of the victims—in the community of transmission that produced the biblical books—that controls the examination of the texts. He gives, for example, a psychological reading of Ezekiel and Lamentations; a sociological reading of the Deuteronomistic History and postexilic prayers; an examination of universalism in late Isaianic texts and Jonah; and competing ethical considerations of priestly theology, wisdom texts, Daniel, and Tobit. In the end, Smith-Christopher supports a diasporic Christian theology that does not seek "restoration" in terms of the nation-state model, but rather critiques the structures of power and oppression. No static model fits every context, but each exilic model would

---

82. Smith-Christopher, *Biblical Theology of Exile*, 73.
83. Ibid., 12.
84. Ibid., 33.
85. On Deut 28, see Smith-Christopher, *Biblical Theology of Exile*, 96–103.

be in "a process of constant negotiation with the realities thrown against it in a secular context."[86]

### C. Marvin Pate et al. (2004)

*The Story of Israel: A Biblical Theology* is a biblical theology centered on the story of Israel. By "the story of Israel," the authors mean the pattern of sin–exile–restoration described in the Deuteronomistic History.[87] This theme is traced through OT, Second Temple, and NT literature in a straightforward manner: Pentateuch; Deuteronomistic history; the Psalms and Wisdom literature; Prophets; Second Temple Judaism; Synoptic Gospels; John; Acts; Paul; General Epistles and Hebrews; and Revelation. The authors, who write from an expressly Evangelical perspective, are concerned to show that the theme of the story of Israel allows for both unity and diversity in the Bible, for this one story is interpreted in a variety of ways.

The chosen theme allows Deuteronomy a prominent position. Though only seven pages are devoted to Deuteronomy in particular,[88] the book is referred to throughout the survey of biblical texts. Deuteronomy serves "as a hermeneutical key to the entire Pentateuch,"[89] and "is a critical book, exerting a strong influence throughout much of the rest of the Old Testament."[90] The Deuteronomic curses, including and especially exile, are thought to "portray an ominous future for the nation—it will be the undoing of a nation and the blessings of its God."[91] The Deuteronomic vision of restoration includes repentance, return to the land, and transformation of the people.

In discussing the story of Israel in Second Temple literature and the NT, Pate et al. interact with recent discussions on the importance of exile to Second Temple Judaism. The authors side with those (especially N. T. Wright) who maintain that many Second Temple Jews still considered themselves to be living in the exile awaiting God's full restoration.[92] From this stance, NT authors appropriate the key elements of

---

86. Ibid., 195.
87. Pate et al., *Story of Israel*, 18–27.
88. Ibid., 42–48.
89. Ibid., 42.
90. Ibid., 50.
91. Ibid., 47.
92. Ibid., 17, 20, 106–18, 169–72, 235. The dependence on N. T. Wright (see below)

the sin–exile–restoration paradigm to Jesus' identity and mission, and to understanding the trials of this life for the Christian.

## Summary

The theologies of exile surveyed above differ in scope, methodology, and conclusions. The major object of investigation in developing a theology of exile varies: Smith-Christopher approaches the historical events as the primary object, with biblical texts aiding in the reconstruction of those events; the others primarily intend to develop a theology of the text, which happen to give witness to the events. While all note that the Old Testament texts offer varying responses to the exile, some account for the differences as a matter of historical development, and emphasize more overall unity (Ackroyd, Raitt, Gowan, Pate et al.); the others interpret differences as competing voices, and stress disunity (Klein, Smith-Christopher).

The first five works (excluding the one by Pate et al.), however, show some commonalities. First, they all give some attention to historical and diachronic issues. For these works, historical reconstruction is possible, and biblical texts give positive evidence concerning actual events.[93] One might have expected a strict text-immanent approach, given the growing skepticism about historical reconstruction. But the realities of the exile make it difficult to ignore history altogether.[94] Second, all five writers presuppose critical conclusions concerning the dating and setting of certain biblical texts. This is clear in their common use of "Deutero-/Second Isaiah" and "Deuteronomistic History." All accept Deuteronomy as part of the Deuteronomistic History, and date the book no earlier than the late eighth century. Third, though some attention is given to parts of

---

is explicit on all these pages.

93. In depicting the events of the exile, Ackroyd, for example, admits to "historical uncertainties," but that "there is no real doubt about the main outlines" (*Exile and Restoration*, 232). Smith-Christopher devotes an entire chapter (*Biblical Theology of Exile*, chap. 2) to establishing the horrific reality of the events.

94. Cf. the inconsistency in the methodology in Brueggemann, *Theology of the Old Testament*. Though Brueggemann explicitly brackets out all questions of history and ontology—repeatedly stating that it is impossible to know what "really happened" (e.g., pp. 118, 125 n. 206, 708, 714)—Brueggemann cannot escape the exile. He considers it the matrix for Israel's faith; it is the turning point for Israel and produced different perspectives on interpreting the exile itself for Israelite religion (see pp. 74–78).

Deuteronomy specifically,[95] it is not found to give a distinct voice to the theology of exile.

The theology by Pate et al. is distinct from the others in several respects, including its Evangelical stance and its incorporation of the whole Bible plus intertestamental literature. The most significant difference for our purposes is the great attention given to Deuteronomy, both as a distinct voice and as having major influence on much of the rest of the Bible.

### Theology of Exile in New Testament Studies

N. T. Wright is at the center of a major debate in NT studies. He argues that many or most of first-century Jews considered themselves still in exile.[96] According to the Gospel writers, Jesus picked up this worldview and transformed it. He understood himself to be the Messiah who had come to liberate Israel from its continuing state of exile ("the present evil age") and bring the nation into a state of restoration ("the age to come"). On the cross, he embodied Israel, suffering the exile; his resurrection was the true return from exile, achieving victory over Satan and inaugurating the fulfillment of God's promises to the nation. The result is a renewal of the covenant, the forgiveness of sins, the coming of the kingdom of God, and the fulfillment of Israel's mission to the world.

Supporters and detractors alike base their arguments on extra-biblical and New Testament evidence.[97] Few, however, have given as much

---

95. Raitt (*Theology of Exile*, 35–58) finds Jeremiah and Ezekiel opposing the simple formula offered by Deuteronomy. Gowan (*Theology of the Prophetic Books*, 18–21) stresses the ambiguity of the book, considering the date of most of it prior to the prophets considers Deuteronomy to be a late–eighth-century reaction to the Assyrian deportation of the northern kingdom in 722 BC. He notes that Deuteronomy betrays ambiguity about the nature of exile and restoration, and tension concerning the conditionality of the patriarchal land promise. Except for Deut 30, there is little evidence in the book that it is influenced by restoration promises of the prophets. Smith-Christopher (*Biblical Theology of Exile*, 96–103) finds that chap. 28 uses stereotypical language, but still points to historical reality behind the text.

96. See Wright, *New Testament and the People of God*, 152–66, 268–79, 299–301; idem, *Jesus and the Victory of God*, 126–27, 203–04. For a helpful summary of Wright's thesis, see Blomberg, "The Wright Stuff," 20.

97. Three collections that offer varying responses are Newman, *Jesus and the Restoration of Israel*; Scott, *Exile*; idem, *Restoration*. For the extra-biblical (mainly intertestamental) evidence in support of the thesis, see Knibb, *Qumran Community*, 20; idem, "Exile in the Literature of the Intertestamental Period," 253–72; Neusner, *Self-Fulfilling Prophecy*; Thielman, *From Plight to Solution*; Scott, "Exile and the Self-

attention to the Old Testament, particularly Deuteronomy (especially chaps. 27–32), as N. T. Wright.[98] Wright cites Deuteronomy in at least five contexts. First, Wright is aware that the New Testament writers draw on Deuteronomy in significant texts (e.g., Matt 28:16-20; Rom 10:6f.).[99] Second, Deuteronomy 27–30 is viewed as dealing with the establishment of the covenant, as well as a summary of the whole Pentateuch as covenant; the section is all about exile and restoration, understood as covenant judgment and covenant renewal.[100] Third, noting the logic of exile as the ultimate curse since the land is the place of blessing, Wright explains the covenantal links between Adam and Abraham and between Abraham and Moses.[101] Fourth, Wright gives much attention to the place of Torah as a symbol in the Jewish worldview; there are bonds

---

Understanding of Diaspora Jews," 173–218; Sanders, *Judaism*. The relevant texts from Second Temple Judaism include Sir 36:8; *T. Mos.* 10:1-10; *1 Enoch* 85–90; *T. Levi* 1–18; *Apoc. Abr.* 15–29; *T. Jud.* 24:1–3; *Jub.* 1:15–18, 24; *T. Naph.* 4:2–5; *T. Asher* 7; *T. Benj.* 9; 2 Macc 1:27–29; 1 Esdr 8:73–74; 2 Esdr 9:7; cf. Hatina, "Exile," 348–49.

Against the thesis on the basis of extra-biblical evidence, see the collection of essays in Carson et al., *Justification and Variegated Nomism*, esp. 546–47 n. 158; Bryan, "Jesus and Israel's Traditions"; Kraabel, "Unity and Diversity," 49–60. Two of the main points made against the thesis are (1) just because an ancient writer uses "exile" as a motif does not mean it should be considered a literal, ongoing experience, and (2) restoration should not be equated with "return to land."

For support from the Gospels and Paul, see Thielman, *Paul and the Law*, 46–68; Evans, "Jesus and the Continuing Exile of Israel," 77–100; idem, "Aspects of Exile and Restoration," 299–328; Hafemann, "Paul and the Exile of Israel," 329–71; Bauckham, "Restoration of Israel in Luke–Acts," 435–87; Meier, "Jesus, the Twelve, and the Restoration of Israel," 365–404; Verseput, "Davidic Messiah and Matthew's Jewish Christianity," 102–16; Reid, "Jesus: New Exodus, New Conquest," 91–118; cf. Hafemann, "Paul and the Exile of Israel," 329–71.

For the New Testament evidence against the thesis, see Marsh, "Theological History," 77–94; Casey, "Where Wright Is Wrong," 95–103; Johnson, "Historiographical Response to Wright's Jesus," 210–16; Seifrid, *Christ Our Righteousness*, 17–25; idem, "'New Perspective' on Paul and Its Problems," 4–18; idem, "Blind Alleys in the Controversy," 73–95; Carson et al., *Paradoxes of Paul*.

98. See also Scott, "Paul's Use of the Deuteronomic Tradition," 645–65; cf. Bauckham, "Restoration of Israel in Luke–Acts," 435–88.

99. Wright, *New Testament and the People of God*, 388–89; idem, *Climax of the Covenant*, 146.

100. Wright, *New Testament and the People of God*, 261, 387; idem, *Climax of the Covenant*, 140–41.

101. Wright, *New Testament and the People of God*, 262–63; idem, *Climax of the Covenant*, 22–23. Of course, these connections set up the link between Jesus and the Old Testament figures. The texts in Deuteronomy that are cited are 1:10f.; 7:13f.; 8:1; 28:63; 30:5, 16.

between Torah and Temple, and Torah and Land. In exile, only Torah remained, and so it became the substitute for Temple and Land.[102] Fifth, Wright draws on Deuteronomy in discussing the spiritual aspects of forgiveness, the heart, and the Spirit. Restoration is part of a matrix that includes covenant renewal, circumcision of the heart, return to the land, and perfect keeping of Torah.[103]

The controversy over exile in New Testament theology is not whether or not it is a motif used by the New Testament writers; all agree that it is. The debate centers on at least three issues. First, do the people *really* (i.e., literally) view themselves in exile, or is exile simply a helpful image? Second, does the hope for "restoration" assume that the return from exile has not taken place? Third, how logically necessary are the implications Wright draws from his thesis, especially those that challenge traditional views regarding the gospel of Christ?[104] These issues take us beyond the scope of the present project, but they indicate the importance of understanding the Deuteronomic picture of exile and restoration.

## METHODOLOGY

If we have learned anything from the present state of biblical studies concerning both Deuteronomy and exile, it is that there are fewer scholarly conclusions today that can claim the status of "consensus." One aspect of contemporary consensus, however, is that the final form of Deuteronomy as a book arose intentionally. This supports our focus on this book alone. Beyond this, the general lack of consensus in most other areas allows new studies more freedom to choose among approaches. One must be aware, however, of the limitations of a given approach, as well as the tentative and provisional nature of any conclusion. Given these realities, it seems best to make explicit certain presuppositions that also influence our methodology, whether or not they agree with the presuppositions of most scholars.

This is a work in the realm of "Old Testament theology," by which we mean several things. First, as a writer of Old Testament *theology*, I

---

102. Wright, *New Testament and the People of God*, 228. Cf. Deut 9:4–5; 18:12.

103. Wright, *Jesus and the Victory of God*, 126, 248, 282–87.

104. E.g., the doctrine of justification, Paul's sense of guilt in his conversion, and the role and/or importance of the individual in salvation. We will touch on this last issue in chap. 5.

hold to divine inspiration.[105] Predictions and/or allusions to future exile and/or restoration in Deuteronomy are not, therefore, automatic indicators of prophecy *ex eventu*. Arguments for later redactional activity must be based on actual textual evidence, not mere suppositions about which context a given statement—or entire narrative—"fits best with."[106] The focus on theology also entails, in my mind, a primary concern with issues regarding God and his relationship to his creation, instead of historical, anthropological, or sociological foci.

Second, as a writer of *Old Testament* theology, I am more concerned with the present shape and canonical position of Deuteronomy than its prehistory. Since the text is what we have, our investigation must begin with and focus on it. This certainly will not preclude diachronic considerations, both at the exegetical level and the level of theological investigation. Particularly when considering Deuteronomy's outlook on exile in connection with other texts, a simple "final form" approach will not handle all the questions that need to be answered.[107] I will consider significant theological differences depending on the varying horizons one may legitimately take into account. In principle, this is also true with respect to canonical horizons.[108] Even the recent critical reconstructions of the Pentateuch, as described above, support the possibility of analyzing Deuteronomy either as an independent corpus or as a transitional link between the Pentateuch and the Former Prophets.

Finally, as a writer of *Old* Testament theology, I assume that there are further horizons beyond the Old Testament that must at least be broached.[109] I no doubt bring certain Christian biases (of a Protestant

---

105. Cf. the similar stance taken in Gowan, *Theology of the Prophetic Books*, 9.

106. Particularly, references to exile do not automatically mean that the event had already taken place. Deportation was a fact of life generally, and was always a threat to smaller nations. See Kitchen, "Ancient Orient," 5. Cf. the statement concerning Deut 28 in McCarthy, *Treaty and Covenant*, 124: "The element of disaster and its consequences, hunger, slavery, exile . . . is common in the curse literature. Hence we cannot reject out of hand any reference to exile as a secondary addition. Why must Deuteronomy be denied the right to use it as a threat as did the composer of Esarhaddon's treaty and of the Sfire text, cases where there is no question of *vaticinium ex eventu*, but only knowledge of the probable result of ancient warfare? Hence, a simple reference to exile like that of 28:36–37 is hardly a sign that the passage is a later addition."

107. So also McConville, "Restoration in Deuteronomy," 12.

108. On which, see Childs, *Introduction to the Old Testament as Scripture*; idem, *Old Testament Theology in a Canonical Context*.

109. In practice, most large-scale OT theologies interact with NT texts.

and Reformed persuasion) to the Old Testament text, but the admission here goes beyond mere intellectual honesty.[110] This work is written, in large part, as a preliminary step later to engage the ongoing debate in New Testament theology described in the previous section.[111] Issues in that debate provoke initial questions to which I will be seeking answers in Deuteronomy.[112] These questions include: What is the relationship between the patriarchal and Sinai (Horeb) covenants? What is the relationship between the exodus and exile? How certain are exile and/or restoration from a Deuteronomic standpoint? Does restoration necessarily include return to the land? Is there any indication of a "remnant theology"? What is the relationship between the individual and corporate identities? What is the relationship between human obedience/repentance and divine blessing/grace? These questions, and others that are sure to arise, may not all be answerable from our study, but they will at least be asked.

---

110. Though I appreciate the cautions and awareness about limitations given us by postmodern thinkers, I still maintain that determinate meaning can be approximated in interpretation.

111. It is beyond the scope of the present work to actually enter this debate here. In chap. 5, however, we do make reference to the discussion.

112. Given my stance in the previous note, I, of course, am not suggesting a reader-response approach here. One of my reasons for choosing Deuteronomy, however, is that some of the issues are central to its own horizon. As has already been explained, this seems to be why the New Testament—and, thus, New Testament scholars like N. T. Wright—point to Deuteronomy with respect to the exile motif.

2

## The Vocabulary of Exile

BEFORE VENTURING INTO THE Deuteronomic vocabulary of exile we briefly need to address and alleviate the concerns of such a methodology. A major challenge to word study was posed by James Barr in his *The Semantics of Biblical Language*.[1] Barr denies that a study of a writer's terminology will reveal anything significant about the way the author thinks:

> In general the idea that differences of thought structure will correspond to differences of language structure seems to be contradicted by facts.[2]

> It is the sentence (and of course the still larger literary complex such as the complete speech or poem) which is the linguistic bearer of the usual theological statement, and not the word (the lexical unit) or the morphological and syntactical connection.[3]

> The distinctiveness of biblical thought and language has to be settled at sentence level, that is, by the things the writers say, and not by the words they say them with.[4]

For Barr, studies of individual words are valuable only to the degree to which the words have become technical terms.

The present study is sensitive to this critique and will in some ways validate its concerns, but we believe word study can be an important

---

1. Barr, *Semantics of Biblical Language*. For a summary of the initial debate, including criticisms and responses, see Price, "Lexicographical Study," 5–11. On typical word-study fallacies, see Carson, *Exegetical Fallacies*, chap. 1 (see especially references in p. 27 n. 1).

2. Barr, *Semantics of Biblical Language*, 42.

3. Ibid., 263.

4. Ibid., 270. Cf. pp. 265, 269.

starting point in our study for at least three reasons.[5] First, as will become clear, Deuteronomy avoids the normal terms for exile, while employing unexpected terms. Second, a study of the vocabulary will assist in highlighting the major texts that need to be the foci of theological investigation, as well as mark some minor texts that may prove more relevant than they may have previously. Third, the terminology itself may, in fact, aid the discernment of the author's thought patterns and theological understanding of exile.

## THE VOCABULARY OF EXILE

Exile language is divided into three categories. The first category discusses the major Hebrew roots used for exile. The second category details eleven roots that are considered the closest synonyms and/or parallels to the major roots. The third category explores the distinctive Deuteronomic terminology for exile.

### Major Roots

The two main roots for exile are גלה, "go into exile"; and שבה, "take captive." These will be discussed in turn.

### גלה

According to Price, גלה has four principal meanings across its 250 instances in the Hebrew Bible: (1) uncover; (2) reveal; (3) depart; and (4) go into exile. The first two meanings have to do with perception; the last two are concerned with motion.[6] Corresponding with this simpler division, most scholars[7] reduce the range to two basic meanings: גלה$_\text{I}$ carries a general sense, "to uncover, open, remove, reveal"; גלה$_\text{II}$ represents a verb of motion, "to emigrate, go away, go into captivity," including references to exile.[8] Scholars debate whether we are dealing with two distinct

---

5. Note the statement by Price ("Lexicographical Study," 8) after reviewing the initial criticisms of Barr: "It is clear ... that he has not succeeded in wielding a death blow to the process of word study."

6. Ibid., 20. See pp. 20–35 for his discussion of the relationship between these meanings. According to Howard, "גלה," 861, the verb occurs 187 times, with 74 of these corresponding to the second sense of motion..

7. See Howard, "גלה," 861–64; Zobel, "גָּלָה," 476–88; Westermann and Albertz, "גלה," 314–20; Waltke, "גָּלָה," 160–61.

8. I will follow the simpler division; however, it should be noted that not every in-

roots or if the second meaning is an etymological derivation of the first; but all tend to treat them separately.⁹ The only caveat with respect to this sharp division is that גלה$_I$ may, at times, be used figuratively in context to offer an allusion or echo of exile.¹⁰ גלה$_{II}$ is utilized in specific predictions of exile for those of both the Northern Kingdom of Israel and the Southern Kingdom of Judah.¹¹ It is also used in historical retrospect of the exiles of Israel and Judah, and even of foreigners.¹²

In the Pentateuch, גלה is used 33 times, but none with an exilic sense. It usually denotes the uncovering of the human body (cf. Gen 9:21; Lev 18:6–19; 20:11–21); we will consider later the connection between nakedness and exile (cf. Deut 28:48).¹³ Two of the three instances of גלה in Deuteronomy are found in legal prescriptions concerning forbidden sexual relations; in both cases a man having sexual intercourse with his stepmother is considered to have "uncovered his father's skirt" (23:1[22:30]; 27:20). The third reference uses a substantive form in a theologically charged context important to exile and restoration: "The hidden things belong to Yahweh our God, but the revealed things (וְהַנִּגְלֹת) belong to us and to our children forever ..." (29:28[29]).¹⁴

---

stance of גלה in the second sense (i.e., motion) means exile in a technical sense. For the root as a verb of motion, the basic meaning of גלה can be found in Ezek 12:3(2x), where the prophet receives the commission "go forth," and the lament in 1 Sam 4:21, "the glory has departed from Israel." Cf. also Isa 24:11; Prov 27:25. It becomes the dominant term for exile—including the nominative forms—specifically in prophetic judgments, the Deuteronomistic History, and later historical books.

9. For a brief discussion, see Westermann and Albertz, "גלה," 314–15; cf. Howard, "גלה," 861; Zobel, "גָּלָה," 478. The two meanings are usually related by assuming an elliptical omission of the object "land," resulting in the meaning "to go forth, to emigrate = to lay (the land) bare." Westermann and Albertz, however, question this relationship and assume two different verbs for semasiological purposes.

10. A clear example is the divine threat to "uncover" the foundations of Samaria (Mic 1:6). Cf. the possible figurative use of גלה$_I$ in Isa 22:8; 23:1; Jer 13:22; Hos 2:12; 10:5; Nah 2:8 (which might be גלה$_{II}$); 3:5. See Price, "Lexicographical Study," 201, 208, 220, 224–28, 231–32.

11. For the Northern Kingdom, see Amos 5:5[2x], 27; 6:7[2x]; 7:11[2x], 17[2x]. For the Southern Kingdom see Isa 5:13; Jer 13:19; 20:4; Ezek 12:11; Mic 1:16.

12. For Israel, see, e.g., 2 Kgs 17:23; Obad 20. For Judah, see, e.g., Isa 45:13; 49:21; Jer 29:4, 7, 14; Ezek 39:28; Obad 20; Esth 2:6; Lam 1:3, 5, 18; 4:22; 1 Chr 5:41[6:15]. For foreigners, see 2 Kgs 15:29; 16:9; 17:11; Isa 20:4; Amos 1:5, 6; Nah 3:10.

13. See Klingbeil, "Exile," 246.

14. See Zobel, "גָּלָה," 486, for theological considerations concerning revelation. One could ask whether or not there is a wordplay here with the following restoration text of 30:1–10.

As stated, גלה‏_II is absent in Deuteronomy. With the exception of Amos (where the term is used 12 times),[15] rarely is it employed before the early sixth century (2 Kings, Jeremiah, and Ezekiel use it frequently).[16] Several historical explanations for this phenomenon have been offered. Westermann and Albertz, along with Price, argue that גלה became specialized to mean, "be taken into exile," when mass deportations as a means of conquest entered Israel's historical experience, such as during the time of the Neo-Assyrian Empire. Even so, this specialized meaning did not gain universal popularity until later.[17] Gowan, however, argues that the root had no special reference to exile even in Amos' time, and that the modern term "exile" is a slightly misleading term to use in translating Amos since it was simply his word of choice for the fate of deportation. It is the author of 2 Kings 17, with his intent to describe the fulfillment of Amos' prophecies in the Babylonian exile (2 Kgs 17:21, 23; cf. Amos 7:17), that imposes theological significance on the term.[18]

These proposals, however, do not explain the absence of an exilic sense of גלה in Deuteronomy—at least with respect to the modern consensus of the date of the book (see chap. 1). Deuteronomy 4, one of the foundational texts on exile and restoration (vv. 25–31), is considered one of the latest layers in the book (see chap. 3). One could argue, then, that the absence of the term is more consistent with a relatively early date of the book, but this would entail an argument from silence, and need not be pursued. Instead, a theological explanation is suggested at the conclusion of this chapter.

שבה

While גלה specifically denotes the forcible removal of individuals or nations to a foreign land, the other major lexeme for exile (שבה) involves a

---

15. Verbal forms are used to predict exile for different groups: Syria (1:5); Gaza (1:6); Gilgal (5:5[2x]) Israel (5:27; 6:7[2x]; 7:11[2x], 17[2x]). A nominal form depicts the exile of the Ammonite king (1:15). גלה is used once in the sense of "reveal" (3:7).

16. It appears once in Judges in a description of Jonathan and his sons serving as priests to the tribe of the Danites "until the day of the captivity of the land" (18:30). See also the references above in 1 Samuel, Isaiah, and Micah.

17. Price, "Lexicographical Study," 33, 184ff. (with respect to his fourth category, "go into exile"); Westermann and Albertz, "גלה," 316; cf. Smith-Christopher, "Engendering Exile," 15–16. For a thorough study of Assyrian deportation practices, see Oded, *Mass Deportations*.

18. Gowan, "Beginnings of Exile," 204–7.

broader range of contexts of capture, including an individual seizing another person, an army taking of booty, and a nation's capture of another nation.[19] A survey of the Pentateuch recognizes non-exilic uses (but see below on Deut 28:41).[20] שבה occurs 20 times in more general contexts: in reference to capture of property (Exod 22:9) and individuals (Gen 14:14; 31:26; Exod 12:29); captives in general (Gen 34:29; Deut 32:42); capture of non-Israelites by non-Israelites (Num 21:19; 24:22); capture of Israelites by non-Israelites (Num 21:1); and capture of non-Israelites by Israelites (Num 31:9, 19, 21, 26; Deut 21:10, 11, 13).

As one might expect, שבה often denotes exile in the Prophets. It occurs six times in Solomon's dedicatory prayer of the temple—a significant passage for the theology of exile (note also the use of שוב):

> If they sin against you—for there is no one who does not sin—and you are angry with them and give them to an enemy, so that they are *carried away captive* (וְשָׁבוּם שֹׁבֵיהֶם) to the land of the enemy, far off or near, yet if they turn (וְהֵשִׁיבוּ) their heart in the land to which they have been *carried captive* (נִשְׁבּוּ), and repent (וְשָׁבוּ) and plead with you in the land of their captors (שֹׁבֵיהֶם), saying, "We have sinned and have acted perversely and wickedly," if they repent (וְשָׁבוּ) with all their mind and with all their heart in the land of their enemies, who *carried them captive* (שָׁבוּ), and pray to you toward their land, which you gave to their fathers, the city that you have chosen, and the house that I have built for your name, then hear in heaven your dwelling place their prayer and their plea, and maintain their cause and forgive your people who have sinned against you, and all their transgressions that they have committed against you, and grant them compassion in the sight of *those who carried them captive* (שֹׁבֵיהֶם), that they may have compassion on them (for they are your people, and your heritage, which you brought out of Egypt, from the midst of the iron furnace). (1 Kgs 8:46–51)[21]

---

19. See Cohen, "שָׁבָה," 895–96; Howard, "שבה," 18–19. As a verb, שבה occurs 47 times in the OT, with God as the subject only once: "you [God] led captives in your train (שָׁבִיתָ שֶּׁבִי)" (Ps 68:19[18]). The verb is used most often in historical narrative books (33 times), especially 2 Chronicles (12 times). Three nominative cognates to שבה, meaning "captivity, captives," are שְׁבִי (49 times), שִׁבְיָה (9 times), and שְׁבִיָּה (1 time). The most common term in the LXX for the words related to שבה is αἰχμαλωτίζω, "capture." As such, the LXX does not always clearly distinguish between גלה and שבה.

20. See Price, "Lexicographical Study," 131–32, 154.

21. Cf. four occurrences in the parallel passage in 2 Chr 6:36ff. See also 2 Chr 30:9.

Jeremiah and Ezekiel seem to use שבה synonymously with גלה (e.g., Jer 13:17, 19; 15:2; 20:4, 6; Ezek 12:11). Isaiah uses the root in passages of restoration (61:1: "proclaim liberty to the captives") and reversal (14:2: "They will take captive those who were their captors"), including the "exile" of idols (46:2).

Deuteronomy uses the root six times: once as a verb (21:10) and five times as a nominative (שְׁבִי in 21:10, 13; 28:41; שִׁבְיָה in 21:11; 32:42). Deuteronomy 21:10–13, concerning the treatment of female prisoners of war, contains most of these references:

> "When you go out to battle against your enemies, and Yahweh your God gives them into your hands and you take captive its captives (וְשָׁבִיתָ שִׁבְיוֹ), and see among the captives (בַּשִּׁבְיָה) a beautiful woman, and have a desire for her and would take her as a wife for yourself....She shall also remove the clothes of her captivity (שִׁבְיָהּ) and shall remain in your house...."

In the so-called "Song of Moses" (Deut 32), Yahweh speaks of intoxicating his arrows with the blood of his enemies, described as "the slain and the captives" (32:42). Only in the final reference, Deuteronomy 28:41, does שבה refer to the captivity of Israelites. As part of the covenant curses, Israel is warned, "You shall have sons and daughters but they will not be yours, for they will go into captivity (יֵלְכוּ בַשֶּׁבִי)."

Thus, with the sole exception of a substantive use, whatever Deuteronomy has to say about exile it does so without reference to the major (later) terminology for the topic. It remains to be seen how the book employs secondary and alternative vocabulary.

## Closest Synonyms and Parallels

The Hebrew Bible employs several terms that often carry an exilic meaning in context and/or parallel either גלה or שבה: ברח, "go through, flee"; דבר, "turn, drive away; subjugate";[22] זרה, "scatter, fan, winnow"; טול, "hurl, cast"; נדד, "retreat, flee, depart, wander"; נדח, "impel, thrust, banish"; נהג, "drive"; נתץ, "pull down, break down"; פוץ, "be dispersed, scattered"; רדף, "pursue, chase, persecute"; and רחק, "be far."[23] Table 1 gives

---

22. This is דבר₂, "turn/drive away, persecute (Pi.); subjugate (Hi.)." See Howard, "דָּבַר," 912. The root is used approximately 12 times, with Ps 18:48[47] as the clearest example: "...the God who gave me vengeance and subdued (וַיַּדְבֵּר) peoples under me...."

23. Howard ("שבה," 19) lists the closest synonyms to ברח₁, דבר, and רדף. The other

the distribution of these terms in Deuteronomy. The six roots found in Deuteronomy will be discussed in turn.

### נדח, "Impel, Thrust, Banish"

This verb is usually used in reference to the forceful movement of individuals, such as the banishment of Absalom from David (2 Sam 14:14) and the expulsion of legitimate priests from Israel (2 Chr 13:9).[24] It can thus be employed within the context of exile (19 of the verb's 55 occurrences are found in Jeremiah, often with Yahweh as the subject).[25] Three significant points can be made from an observance of the data. First, some cases of the root lack the idea of force, particularly with respect to straying animals (e.g., Deut 22:1). This sense is picked up in exilic contexts in the metaphor of God's people as sheep. For instance, Yahweh condemns the "shepherds of Israel" for neither caring for the sheep nor bringing back "the strayed," and promises himself to be the shepherd who brings them back (Ezek 34:4, 16). Second, when נדח refers to exile, it often occurs in contexts that also offer or promise restoration.[26] Both of these observations help balance divine judgment with emphasis on divine mercy and faithfulness—grace that will eventually extend to the nations (cf. Isa 16:3–4; Jer 49:5, 36). Third, the "force" is not always physical, but includes the enticement into idolatry. It appears, for instance, in the theological explanation for the destruction of Israel: "When he had torn Israel from the house of David, they made Jeroboam the son of Nebat king. And Jeroboam drove (וַיַּדַּח; following *Qere*) Israel from following Yahweh and made them commit great sin" (2 Kgs 17:21).

Deuteronomy uses נדח in a variety of ways. General usage includes references to straying animals (22:1) and the wielding of an axe (19:5;

---

eight are customary terms accompanying the exilic use of שבה in pre-exilic texts, according to Gowan, "Beginnings of Exile–Theology," 204. For other terms that are used with respect to exile in context, see Price, "Lexicographical Study."

24. Carroll R., "נדח," 34–35; Coppes, "נָדַח," 556–57; Driver, "Hebrew Roots and Words," 406–15 (esp. 408–9); Kronholm, "נָדַח," 235–41.

25. This latter point is especially true of the Hiphil forms (Jer 8:3; 24:9; 27:10, 15; Ezek 4:13; cf. Jer 16:15).

26. This is true of participle forms denoting "the scattered/the exiles (of Israel)" (Isa 11:12; Jer 30:17; Zeph 3:19; Ps 147:2; Neh 1:9). Restoration is foreseen as a reality subsequent to the people's repentance and calling upon Yahweh (Deut 30:1–4; Jer 23:3, 8; 29:14; 32:37; 46:28).

20:19).²⁷ It also is used in decrees of harsh penalties for those who have "drawn away" individuals or the nation into idolatry (13:6[5], 11[10], 14[13]). In this sense, the root does appear in exilic contexts. Moses warns, "Beware lest... you be drawn away (נדח) and bow down to them [sun, moon, and stars] and serve them" (4:19). Likewise, "if your heart turns away, and you will not hear, but are drawn away (נדח) to worship other gods and serve them, I declare to you today, that you shall surely perish" (30:17–18a). Finally, the root itself refers to exile in the restoration text of 30:1–10. Israel will recall the blessing and the curse "among all the nations where Yahweh your God has driven (הדיח) you" (30:1). Yahweh promises to gather his people, even "if your outcasts (Ni. ptc. נדח) are in the uttermost parts of heaven" (30:4).

Table 1. Synonyms and Parallels

נהג, "Drive"

| Root | Basic Meaning | Deuteronomic Use |
|---|---|---|
| חרב | go through, flee | — |
| רבד | turn, drive away; subjugate | — |
| הרז | scatter, fan, winnow | — |
| לוט | hurl, cast | — |
| דדנ | retreat, flee, depart, wander | — |
| נדח | impel, thrust, banish | 4:19; 13:6, 11, 14; 19:5; 20:19; 22:1; 30:1, 4, 17 |
| נהג | drive | 4:27; 28:37 |
| נתץ | pull down, break down | 7:5; 12:3 |
| פוץ | be dispersed, scattered | 4:27; 28:64; 30:3 |
| רדף | pursue, chase, persecute | 1:44; 11:4; 16:20; 19:6; 28:22, 45; 32:30 |
| רחק | be far | 12:21; 14:24; 30:11 |

The basic use of the verb describes the (forceful) leading of animals (e.g., Gen 31:18; Exod 3:1) or people (e.g., 1 Sam 30:22) from one place to another.²⁸ This can include the movement of prisoners of war, often in contexts also employing שבה (e.g., Gen 31:26; 1 Sam 30:2; Isa 20:4).

27. I am assuming that the references in 19:5 and 20:19 actually derive from נדח. Some scholars consider the possibility of another root, either דחה, "push (down)" or דחח, "push." But even these roots would be variations or derivatives of נדח. See the discussion in Carroll, "נדח," 34–35.

28. See Baker, "נהג," 42–43; Coppes, "נָהַג," 558–59; Gross, "נָהַג," 255–59.

Drawing from the metaphor of a shepherd, an extended use of the verb describes Yahweh as one who leads his people: "Then he led out his people like sheep and guided them in the wilderness like a flock" (Ps 78:52; cf. Ps 80:2[1]; Isa 49:10; 63:14). Combining both senses, it is perhaps with biting irony that Deuteronomy employs נהג with respect to exile (4:27; 28:37 [both Pi.]). Yahweh will "lead" his people, but it is through scattering them "among the peoples" (4:27), resulting in their public scorn (28:37) and service of foreign gods (4:28; 28:36).

### נתץ, "Pull Down, Break Down"

This verb denotes the destruction of various structures, including altars (Exod 34:13; Judg 6:28, 30-32), high places (2 Chr 31:1), city walls (2 Kgs 25:10), houses (Lev 14:45), and even ovens or stoves (Lev 11:35).[29] It is used figuratively for God's destruction of life. Job laments, "He breaks me down (נתץ) on every side, and I am gone, and my hope has he pulled up like a tree" (Job 19:10). The psalmist warns the mighty man, "But God will break you down (נתץ) forever; he will snatch and tear you from your tent; he will uproot you from the land of the living" (Ps 52:7[5]). Jeremiah extends this figurative sense to God's actions toward nations—whether his own people (Jer 1:10; 31:28) or other nations (18:7)—including plucking up (נתש), breaking down (נתץ), overthrowing (הרס), and destroying (Hi. אבד).[30] But what God tears down, he will also build up—at least with respect to his own people (Jer 1:10; 31:28).[31] The last reference comes just before the pronouncement of restoration that involves a new covenant, with language reminiscent of Deuteronomy 30:1–10 (Jer 31:31–37).

נתץ occurs twice in Deuteronomy (7:5; 12:3). Both describe the destruction of Canaanite altars, therefore not contributing to the discussion of exile.

### פוץ, "Be Dispersed, Scattered"

פוץ usually carries the sense of scattering,[32] whether with respect to a farmer and his seed (Isa 28:25), God and the lightning (Job 37:11), wick-

---

29. See Barth, "נָתַץ," 108–14; Van Dam, "נתץ," 212–13; Fisher, "נָהַג," 609–10.

30. Interestingly, the final term, אבד, is used in Deuteronomy for exile. See the next section of this chapter.

31. On Jer 31:28, see Brueggemann, *To Build, To Plant*, 67–69.

32. Though it can be used more generally, such as referring to overflowing water

ed "shepherds" and the effect of their leadership on their "flock,"[33] or in military campaigns (e.g., 1 Sam 11:11; 13:8; 2 Kgs 25:5[=Jer 52:8]; Jer 40:15).[34] In this latter sense, Yahweh aids his people in scattering their enemies; פוץ is found in parallel with נוס, "flee" (Num 10:35; Ps 68:2[1]), and זרה, "disperse" (Ezek 29:12; 30:23, 26). Though concentrated in the prophets (especially Jeremiah and Ezekiel), the theological use of this root denoting an act of judgment goes back to the Tower of Babel, when God scattered arrogant humanity "over the face of all the earth" (Gen 11:8-9).

The connection with the exile theme involves a natural transition to a focus on God's judgment and/or chastisement of his own people. Jeremiah uses several qualifying phrases to describe Yahweh's scattering of his people because of their disobedience: "among the nations" (Jer 9:15[16]); "like chaff driven by the wind" (Jer 13:24); and "like the east wind ... before the enemy" (Jer 18:17). In Ezekiel, we find the repeated phrase, "I will scatter (Hi. פוץ) them among the nations and disperse (Pi. זרה) them through the countries."[35]

The root is also found in more "positive" contexts. Yahweh assures his people of his divine presence during the exile: "Though I removed them far off (Hi. רחק) among the nations, and though I scattered (Hi. פוץ) them among the countries, yet I have been a sanctuary to them for a while in the countries where they have gone" (Ezek 11:16). It is found in contexts that lead into promises of restoration: "For I am with you to save you, declares Yahweh; I will make a full end of all the nations among whom I scattered you, but of you I will not make a full end" (Jer 30:11; cf. Ezek 36:19). The promise of restoration often utilizes קבץ, "gather," as the opposite to פוץ:

> Therefore thus says Yahweh, the God of Israel, concerning the shepherds who care for my people: "You have scattered (Hi. פוץ) my flock and have driven (Hi. נדח) them away, and you have not attended to them. Behold, I will attend to you for your evil deeds,"

(Prov 5:6) or the extension of a battle (2 Sam 18:8).

33. E.g., Jer 10:21; 23:1-2 (note parallel with אבד; Ezek 34:5, 21). Yahweh himself promises to take up the shepherding tasks (Jer 23:3-4; Ezek 34:7-16).

34. See Carroll R., "פוץ," 585-89; Hamilton, "פוץ," 719-20; Ringgren, "פוץ," 509-12.

35. Ezek 12:15; 20:23; 22:15; cf. 29:12; 30:23, 26 (referring to Egyptians); cf. 36:19 (precedes restoration text starting in v. 22).

declares Yahweh. "Then I will gather (Pi. קבץ) the remnant of my flock out of all the countries where I have driven (Hi. נדח) them, and I will bring (Hi. שוב) them back to their fold, and they shall be fruitful and multiply." (Jer 23:2-3)[36]

Deuteronomy uses פוץ only three times, but each reference occurs in the most important passages for the theology of exile. These will occupy much of the present study:

> And Yahweh will scatter (Hi. פוץ) you among the peoples, and you will be left few in number among the nations where Yahweh will drive you. (Deut 4:27)

> And Yahweh will scatter (Hi. פוץ) you among all peoples, from one end of the earth to the other, and there you shall serve other gods of wood and stone, which neither you nor your fathers have known. (Deut 28:64)

> Then Yahweh your God will restore your fortunes and have compassion on you, and he will gather (Pi. קבץ) you again from all the peoples where Yahweh your God has scattered (Hi. פוץ) you. (Deut 30:3)

As will be explained in greater detail, Yahweh's scattering of his people is grounded in covenant warnings. Still, the covenant relationship is also the basis for the restoration hope of the in-gathering of the dispersed.

### רדף, "Pursue, Chase, Persecute"

Utilized more than 150 times, this term usually refers to the pursuit of individuals or groups for the purpose of warfare or taking revenge.[37] As such, it is found most frequently in Joshua and the Psalms. In more theological contexts, God pursues the wicked (e.g., Isa 41:3; Jer 29:18; Nah 1:8; Lam 3:66; cf. Ezek 35:6). He enables his people to pursue their enemies (e.g., Lev 26:7, 8[2x]; Ps 18:38[37]). In a twist, the psalmist claims that, as "the hounds of heaven," goodness and mercy shall pursue him all the days of his life (Ps 23:6).

The root appears in a few exilic contexts. Leviticus' list of covenant curses includes an overwhelming fear that will drive the people to flight

---

36. See also Ezek 11:17; 20:34, 41; 28:25; 29:13; 34:12–13; cf. Neh 1:8-9; Isa 11:12.

37. See Dumbrell, "רדף," 1057–62; White, "רָדַף," 834. In 1 Sam 26:20, it refers to the hunting of a partridge. It can be extended to the pursuit of abstract concepts, such as evil (Prov 11:19), righteousness (Prov 15:9; 21:21), or knowledge (Hos 6:3).

even "when none pursues" (Lev 26:17, 36, 37), leading to exile (vv. 38–39). Hosea warns that Israel's enemies shall pursue her (Hos 8:3). The poet of Lamentations repeatedly mourns that Judah's pursuers have overtaken her (Lam 1:3, 6; 4:19; 5:5). God himself is described as the adversary: "You have wrapped yourself with anger and pursued us, killing without pity" (Lam 3:43). But there is hope for reversal, including God's pursuit of Judah's oppressors: "You will pursue them in anger and destroy[38] them from under your heavens, O Yahweh" (Lam 3:66). In Jeremiah 29, the prophet gives instructions to the exiles in Babylon on how they ought to conduct themselves (vv. 4–9), and predicts Yahweh's future restoration of them (vv. 10–14). He then reports God's coming judgment on the self-deceived back in Jerusalem, including, "I will pursue them with sword, famine, and pestilence, and will make them a horror to all the kingdoms of the earth, to be a curse, a terror, a hissing, and a reproach among all the nations where I have driven them" (Jer 29:18).

Deuteronomy utilizes רדף in a variety of contexts. Others have pursued Israel in her trek to the land, including the Egyptians during the exodus (11:4) and the Amorites in the wilderness (1:44). The so-called "lawcode" (chaps. 12–26) uses the term in abstract notions: judges are exhorted to pursue justice (16:20); cities of refuge curb the pursuit of revenge (19:6). רדף approaches an exilic sense twice in the covenant curses of chapter 28. In both cases, the curses themselves are personified as the agents of God's judgment.

> Yahweh will strike you with wasting disease and with fever, inflammation and fiery heat, and with drought and with blight and with mildew. They shall pursue (רדף) you until you perish (אבד). (28:22)

> All these curses shall come upon (בוא) you and pursue (רדף) you and overtake (Hi. נשג) you till you are destroyed (Ni. שמד), because you did not heed the voice of Yahweh your God, to keep his commandments and his statutes that he commanded you. (28:45)

Finally, one can possibly detect an exilic nuance in the Song of Moses: "How could one have chased (רדף) a thousand, and two have put ten

---

38. The word "destroy" translates the Hiphil of שמד, one of the major roots used in exile contexts in Deuteronomy.

thousand to flight, unless their Rock had sold them, and Yahweh had given them up?" (32:30).

## רחק, "Be Far"

This root is used more than fifty times in all types of contexts with reference to either spatial or temporal relationships.[39] In ethical and religious contexts, the people are urged to stay "far away" from wicked people and alien cults (e.g., Exod 23:7). In more theological contexts, God's activities, attributes, or presence is the concern. The psalmist, for instance, cries, "My God, my God, why have you forsaken me? Why are you so far from saving me, from the words of my groaning?" (Ps 22:2[1]). Or conversely, "You know when I sit down and when I rise up; you discern my thoughts from afar" (Ps 139:2; cf. Job 36:3). The same concept of Yahweh's transcendent knowledge is applied to Judah's sinfulness, which ultimately leads to exile:

> "Am I a God at hand (קָרוֹב)," declares Yahweh, "and not a God afar off (רָחוֹק)? Can a man hide himself in secret places so that I cannot see him?" declares Yahweh. "Do I not fill heaven and earth?" declares Yahweh. (Jer 23:23-34)

The Hiphil of the verb itself connotes Yahweh's exile of his people: "For it is a lie that they are prophesying to you, with the result that you will be removed far (Hi. רחק) from your land, and I will drive you out (Hi. נדח), and you will perish (אבד)" (Jer 27:10). Even so, the same word is used in the promise of restoration, emphasizing that there will be ample space for the restored people: "A day for the building of your walls! In that day the boundary shall be far extended (רחק)" (Mic 7:11). In the latter half of Isaiah, Yahweh announces that his righteousness will not "be far" (Isa 46:13); instead it will be Israel's enemies who shall be "far away" (49:19), and oppression itself shall be removed "far off" (54:14). But reversion to sin causes the people to lament that God's justice and salvation are "far from us" (Isa 59:9, 11).

Deuteronomy does not use רחק in exilic contexts, per se. It is used twice in reference to exigencies when an individual is "too far" from the "place" of divine choice, either to slaughter animals (12:21) or to

---

39. See Kühlewein, "רחק," 1230-32; O'Connell, "רחק," 1099-1103; White, "רָחַק," 843-44.

pay the tithe (14:24). Still, the adjective is used in the significant text of 30:11–14, speaking of the accessibility of God's revelation:

> For this commandment that I command you today is not too hard for you, neither is it far off (רָחוֹק). It is not in heaven, that you should say, "Who will ascend to heaven for us and bring it to us, that we may hear it and do it?" Neither is it beyond the sea, that you should say, "Who will go over the sea for us and bring it to us, that we may hear it and do it?" But the word is very near you. It is in your mouth and in your heart, so that you can do it.

This text is found in an interesting position. It immediately follows the promise of Israel's future restoration after exile (30:1–10), yet it precedes a present call to choose life with the ominous threat of destruction for disobedience lingering on the surface (30:15–20).

## Conclusion

In summary, this section shows that, though the quantity is not overwhelming, Deuteronomy does use some of the secondary vocabulary for exile. The clearest instances include 30:1) נדח; cf. v. 4), 28:37; 4:27) נהג), and 30:3; 28:64; 4:27) פוץ). Apart from these specific references to exile, most of the terms studied in this section occur in contexts of exile. They are also found in several other contexts, especially various historical stages of Israel's movement to the land. These points suggest that a study of the exile theme in Deuteronomy will have to (1) look for alternative terminology for exile, and (2) set exile within the broader context of Israel's historical experiences.

### *Other Deuteronomic Terms*

How else does Deuteronomy speak of exile? We can begin with the programmatic statement in chapter 4:

> When you father children and children's children, and have grown old in the land, if you act corruptly by making a carved image in the form of anything, and by doing what is evil in the sight of Yahweh your God, so as to provoke him to anger, I call heaven and earth to witness against you today, that you will soon utterly perish (אָבַד (תֹּאבֵדוּן)) from the land that you are going over the Jordan to possess. You will not live long in it, but will be utterly destroyed (הִשָּׁמֵד תִּשָּׁמֵדוּן). And Yahweh will scatter (פוץ) you among the peoples, and you will be left few in number

among the nations where Yahweh will drive (נהג) you. And there you will serve gods of wood and stone, the work of human hands, that neither see, nor hear, nor eat, nor smell. (Deut 4:25–28)

Other than the use of פוץ and נהג, which we have examined above, the concept of exile is driven here by two nearly synonymous terms of destruction and annihilation: אבד and שמד. These are two dominant roots in Deuteronomy, especially with respect to our theme. They deserve special attention.

Two Main Terms: אבד and שמד

Tables 2 and 3 provide all the references in Deuteronomy to אבד and שמד, respectively. The tabulation includes each reference's location;[40] its parsed form;[41] the general theme of its immediate context; the agent who performs the action, whether or not it is the actual subject of the verb; the patient who receives the action of the verb; and a list of other terms and phrases in close proximity to the reference.

אבד can refer to straying animals[42] and therefore may have originally meant, "be lost, to wander about, to run away."[43] In most cases, however, it carries a basic idea of destruction:

---

40. The combination of an infinitive absolute and finite verb of the same root is considered as one reference.

41. Except Deut 22:3 (where "nfs" = noun, feminine, singular), all the references are verbal forms. The first capital letter refers to the stem: (Q)al, (P)iel, or (H)iphil. For finite verbs, the second capital letter refers to the tense/aspect: (P)erfect, (I)mperfect, or I(M)perative. This is followed by person, gender, and number (e.g., "3ms" = third-person, masculine, singular). Infinitives are indicated either by "i.a." (absolute) or "i.c." (construct). Participles are indicated by "ptc" and include gender and number. If a preposition fronts the verb, it is given in parentheses.

42. Either literally or figuratively; see 1 Sam 9:3, 20; Jer 50:6; Ezek 34:4, 16; Ps 119:176.

43. See Van Dam, "אבד," 23–25; Harris, "אָבַד," 3–4; Jenni, "אבד," 13–15; Otzen, "אָבַד," 19–23. Otzen notes that the meaning of "wander off, run away" is more widespread in other Semitic languages. The nominative אֲבֵדָה is a general term indicating something lost, including whether animals, clothing, and money (Exod 22:9[8]; Lev 5:22[6:3]; Deut 22:3). However, the nominative אֲבַדָּן means "destruction" or "annihilation" (Esth 8:6; 9:5; cf. 3:5–11).

## Table 2. אבד in Deuteronomy

| Text | Form | Context | Agent | Patient | Parallel Terms |
|---|---|---|---|---|---|
| 4:26 | Q i.a. + QI2mp | Exile of Israel | Yahweh (implied) | Israel | –שמד (v. 26)<br>–פוץ (v. 27)<br>–נהג (v. 27)<br>–not lengthen days (v. 26)<br>–left few in number (v. 27) |
| 7:10 | H i.c. (ל) | Covenant Relationship (Conquest) | Yahweh | Israelite (potential) | –שלם (2x) repay<br>–not be slack |
| 7:20 | Q i.c. (עד) | Conquest (encouragement in) | Yahweh (hornets) | Nations (left) | (see on v. 24) |
| 7:24 | HP2ms | Conquest | Israel (Yahweh) | Nations' Name | –נשל (v. 22)<br>–make an end (כלה) (v. 22)<br>–give over (v. 23)<br>–throw into confusion (v. 23)<br>–שמד (v. 23)<br>–שמד (v. 24)<br>–give kings into hand (v. 24)<br>–burn images (v. 25) |
| 8:19 | Q i.a. + QI2mp | Covenant Fidelity | Yahweh (implied) | Israel | (cf. v. 20) |
| 8:20a | H ptc ms | Covenant Fidelity (comparison) | Yahweh | Nations | (cf. v. 19) |
| 8:20b | QI2mp | Covenant Fidelity (comparison) | Yahweh (implied) | Israel | (cf. v. 19) |
| 9:3 | HP2ms | Conquest (Reason for success) | Israel (Yahweh, v.3a) | Nations | –שמד (Yahweh)<br>–כנע (Yahweh)<br>–ירש (Israel) |
| 11:4 | PI3ms | Covenant Fidelity (recalling Yahweh's acts) | Yahweh | Egyptian army, etc. | –made water flow over them |
| 11:17 | QP2mp | Covenant Fidelity (blessings/curses) | Yahweh (implied) | Israel | stock curse phrases |
| 12:2 | P i.a. + PI2mp | Chosen Place | Israel | Nations' cult sites | –tear down altars (Pi נתץ)<br>–shatter pillars<br>–burn Asherim<br>–hew down images |
| 12:3 | PP2mp | Chosen Place | Israel | Nations' name | (cf. v. 2) |
| 22:3 | nfs + QI3mf | Laws concerning brother ("lost") | | | |
| 30:18 | Q i.a. + QI2mp | Choice of Life/Death | Not stated (Yahweh implied?) | Israel | –not lengthen days |
| 32:28 | Q ptc ms | Song of Moses (meaning "void") | | | |

## Table 3. שמד in Deuteronomy

| Text | Form | Context | Agent | Patient | Parallel Terms |
|------|------|---------|-------|---------|----------------|
| 1:27 | H i.c. (ל) | Wilderness Wandering (murmuring) | Yahweh | Israel | –brought out of Egypt<br>–to give us to Amorites |
| 2:12 | HI3mp | Wilderness Wandering (parenthetical note) | Sons of Esau | Horites | –dispossessed (ירש) and settled |
| 2:21 | HI3ms | Wilderness Wandering (parenthetical note) | Yahweh (before Ammonites) | Rephaim | –dispossessed (ירש) and settled<br>–cf. vv. 22, 23 |
| 2:22 | HP3ms | Wilderness Wandering (parenthetical note) | Yahweh (before people of Esau) | Horites | –dispossessed (ירש) and settled<br>–cf. vv. 21, 23 |
| 2:23 | HP3cp | Wilderness Wandering (parenthetical note) | Caphtorim | Avvim | –settled in their place<br>–cf. vv. 21, 22 |
| 4:3 | HP3ms | Command of obedience (recall Baal-peor) | Yahweh | Followers of Baal | |
| 4:26 | N i.a. + NI2mp | Exile of Israel | Yahweh (implied) | Israel | –אבד (v. 26)<br>–פוץ (v. 27)<br>–נהג (v. 27)<br>–not lengthen days<br>–left few in number |
| 6:15 | HP3ms | Call to fear Yahweh | Yahweh | Israel | –Yahweh's anger kindled (note: "from off the face of the earth") |
| 7:4 | HP3ms | Conquest (no inter-marriage/covenant) | Yahweh | Israel | –Yahweh's anger kindled |
| 7:23 | N i.c. (עד) | Conquest | Yahweh (confusion) | Nations | –נשל (v. 22)<br>–make an end (כלה) (v. 22)<br>–give over (v. 23)<br>–throw into confusion (v. 23)<br>–אבד (v. 24)<br>–give kings into hand (v. 24)<br>–שמד (v. 24)<br>–burn images (v. 25) |
| 7:24 | HP3ms (עד) | Conquest | Israel | Nations' kings | (see above on v. 23) |
| 9:3 | HI3ms | Conquest (Reason for success) | Yahweh | Nations (Sons of Anakim) | –כנע (Yahweh)<br>–ירש (Israel)<br>–אבד (Israel) |
| 9:8 | H i.c. (ל) | Conquest (Recall stubbornness at Horeb) | Yahweh | Israel (almost) | –Yahweh was angry |
| 9:14 | HI1cs | Golden Calf | Yahweh | Israel | –blot out name from under heaven |
| 9:19 | H i.c. (ל) | Golden Calf (Moses intercedes) | Yahweh | Israel | –bore anger and hot displeasure |
| 9:20 | H i.c. (ל) | Golden Calf (Moses' intercession) | Yahweh | Aaron | |

## Table 3 (continued). שמד in Deuteronomy

| Text | Form | Context | Agent | Patient | Parallel Terms |
|---|---|---|---|---|---|
| 9:25 | H i.c. (ל) | Initial call to conquest (Moses' intercession) | Yahweh | Israel | -שחת (not שמד) in prayer (v. 26) |
| 12:30 | N i.c. | Warning against idolatry following conquest | Yahweh (implied); "before you" | Nations | -כרת (v. 29)<br>-dispossess (ירש) and dwell (v. 29) |
| 28:20 | N i.c. (עד) | Covenant Curses | Yahweh (implied; using curses) | Israel | -many more curses<br>-אבד (vv. 20, 22)<br>-כלה (v. 21)<br>(cf. v. 24) |
| 28:24 | N i.c. (עד) | Covenant Curses | Yahweh (implied; using dust from heaven) | Israel | (see v. 20 above) |
| 28:45 | N i.c. (עד) | Covenant Curses | Yahweh (implied; using "all these curses") | Israel | -come upon (בוא)<br>-pursue (רדף)<br>-overtake (נשג) |
| 28:48 | HP3ms (עד) | Covenant Curses | Yahweh | Israel | -send enemies against (v. 48)<br>-put yoke of iron on neck (v. 48)<br>-bring nation against (v. 49) |
| 28:51 | N i.c. (עד) | Covenant Curses | not stated (foreign nation sent by Yahweh) | Israel | -several curses<br>-אבד |
| 28:61 | N i.c. (עד) | Covenant Curses (Exile of Israel) | Yahweh (using "every sickness and every affliction") | Israel | -several curses<br>-אבד (v. 63)<br>-plucked off land (jsn) (v. 63)<br>-פוץ (v. 64)<br>-brought back to Egypt (v. 68) |
| 28:63 | H i.c. (ל) | Covenant Curses (Exile of Israel) | Yahweh | Israel | (see v. 61 above) |
| 31:3 | HI3ms | Succession of Joshua (encouragement in conquest) | Yahweh | Nations | -give them over (v. 5) |
| 31:4 | HP3ms | Succession of Joshua (recall Sihon and Og) | Yahweh | Land of Sihon, Og | |
| 33:27 | HMms | Moses' final blessing (God's protection of Israel) | Israel | "the enemy" | -he thrust out (גרש) |

"perish, to be destroyed" (Qal); "destroy" (Piel); and "cause to be destroyed" (Hiphil).[44] This destruction can involve inanimate objects,[45] animals,[46] individuals,[47] or even abstract concepts.[48] But nations are often the object of the judgment depicted by אבד, including Egypt (Exod 10:7), the Canaanites (Deut 7:20), the Philistines/Cherethites (Amos 1:8; Zeph 2:5[Hi.]), Tyre (Ezek 26:17), Ammon (Ezek 25:7[Hi.]), Moab (Num 21:29–30), Babylon (Jer 51:55[Pi.]), and Israel.[49] Not surprisingly, the transitive forms usually occur in contexts dealing with military and political situations, often with Yahweh as the direct or indirect agent of the destruction.

Though a close synonym, שמד appears more straightforward than אבד. שמד is consistently used for destruction or annihilation of (groups of) persons for the purpose of vengeance or divine judgment.[50] Because of its use in contexts of the conquest, it comes close to attaining the technical sense of חרם, "devote to the ban."[51] Yahweh is usually the im-

---

44. In the OT, אבד occurs more than 100x in Qal, about 40x in Piel, and about 25x Hiphil. On the difference between the Piel and Hiphil—in which the latter is used mostly with persons and with respect to future—see Jenni, "Faktitiv und Kausativ von אבד," 143–57.

45. E.g., images (Num 33:52; Ezek 30:13), weapons of war (2 Sam 1:27), a harvest (Joel 1:11), a plant (Jonah 4:10), and the law (Jer 18:18; Ezek 7:26).

46. E.g., Ps 49:21[20].

47. E.g., Ps 49:11[10]. Yahweh destroys transgressors of the law (Lev 23:30; Deut 7:10).

48. E.g., one's name (Deut 7:24), memory (Ps 9:7[6]), truth (Jer 7:28), righteousness (Mic 7:2), courage (Jer 4:9), wisdom (Isa 29:14), and counsel (Jer 18:18; 49:7; Ezek 7:26).

49. We could include the more general description of Israel's enemies (Ps 2:12; 83:18[17]; cf. Esth 9:6, 12). Apart from the references in Deuteronomy, the destruction directed against Israel can be found in Lev 26:38; Jer 15:7[Pi.]; 25:10[Hi.]; 27:10, 15 (cf. Jer 31:28[Hi.]; Esth 3:9[Pi.], 13[Pi.]).

50. Hall, "שמד," 51–52; Vetter, "שמד," 1367–68; Austel, "שָׁמַד," 935. Of its 90 occurrences, only four have objects that are not personal: metal images (Num 33:52); high places (Lev 26:30; Hos 10:8); and a plain (Jer 48:8). Rarely is the term used with respect to the killing of a single person (but 2 Sam 14:7, 11, 16). Inexplicably, Austel ("שָׁמַד," 935) only notes 63 occurrences. Vetter ("שמד," 1367) correctly notes 21 Niphal and 69 Hiphil forms.

51. According to Naudé ("חרם," 276–77), the verb (always causative) "involves consecration of something or someone as a permanent and definitive offering for the sanctuary; or in war, the consecration of a city and its inhabitants to destruction and the carrying out of this destruction. The vb. denotes also the total annihilation of a population in war." חרם is used several times in Deuteronomy (verb in 2:34; 3:6[2x];

plicit or explicit agent of the destruction,[52] often in "holy war" contexts, wherein Yahweh himself executes the ban commandment.[53] In general, the destruction described by שמד is permanent.

In Deuteronomy, אבד and שמד are used in a variety of contexts. The following analysis will trace the terms with respect to the various stages of Israel's journey.[54]

### Patriarchal Era

The first reference is both significant and obscure. Toward the conclusion of the "lawcode," instruction is given concerning offerings of firstfruits, including the following confession recalling Jacob's position:

> And you shall make response before Yahweh your God, "A wandering (אֹבֵד) Aramean was my father. And he went down into Egypt and sojourned there, few in number, and there he became a nation, great, mighty, and populous." (Deut 26:5)

The translation of the phrase אֹבֵד אֲרַמִּי as "a wandering Aramean" is supported by most modern translations,[55] but the older translations have "a Syrian ready/about to perish."[56] Many scholars render it "an Aramean on the point of destruction."[57] Based on the Akkadian, others prefer the nu-

---

7:2[2x]; 13:16; 20:17[2x]; noun in 7:26[2x]; 13:18). But other words, including שמד, are used with the same effect. See the discussions in Austel, "שָׁמַד," 935; Vetter, "שמד," 1368. See the general statement in Austel "שָׁמַד," 935.

52. Hall ("שמד," 151) notes that this is the case in nearly 80 percent of the occurrences. In non-theological texts, it refers to destruction of a family (Gen 34:30), a national group (2 Sam 21:5; Esth 3:6, 13), or many nations (Isa 10:7).

53. For the use of the verb in "holy war," see von Rad, *Holy War in Ancient Israel*, 49f., 57, 115ff. The phrase "holy war" is an unfortunate term and is increasingly growing out of favor. However, because we often refer to the classical literature (which uses "holy war") on the subject, we reluctantly retain the traditional term.

54. The focus on Israel's "journey" is drawn from McConville and Millar, *Time and Place*. A couple of references in poetic texts do not easily fit into this scheme. In the Song of Moses, Yahweh describes Israel's enemy as a nation "void (אבד) of counsel" (32:28). In Moses' final blessing on Israel, Moses encourages the people: "The eternal God is your dwelling place, and underneath are the everlasting arms. And he thrust out (גרש) the enemy before you and said, Destroy (שמד)" (33:27).

55. ESV, NASB, NJB, NIV, NLT, NRSV, RSV.

56. ASV, AV, NKJV.

57. See the discussion in Otzen, "אָבַד," 20f.

ance of "fugitive" or "refugee."[58] Given both the immediate and broader contexts, the latter option has much to commend it. As Millard states,

> To the Israelite settled in his Promised Land, who came with his firstfruits to God, the contrast of his 'confession' would be all the greater. His ancestor was a political refugee and a social misfit; he, the descendant, was cultivating his own land as a citizen of an established nation.[59]

With the connection between אבד and exile in Deuteronomy, this text may support the idea that exile involves a reversal—a reversal of history, a reversal of promise.

## The Exodus

Throughout Deuteronomy, Moses calls on the people to recall the events of the exodus as a motivation for covenant fidelity.[60] What God actually did to Egypt is described in 11:4: "... what he did to the army of Egypt, to their horses and to their chariots, how he made the water of the Red Sea flow over them as they pursued after you, and how Yahweh has destroyed (Pi. אבד) them to this day." The exodus is an outworking of divine sovereignty (4:34) and election (4:20, 37), and fulfillment of the promise to the fathers (7:8). Because of what Yahweh did for Israel in bringing them out of Egypt, they should fearlessly engage the nations in the conquest (7:18–19), keep his commandments (5:6), and instruct their children (6:21–23). They are warned not to forget the exodus, lest they be led into idolatry (4:20; 6:12; 8:14).

## Sinai/Horeb

שמד occurs four times in Moses' recalling of the golden calf incident at Horeb (Deut 9:6-21). In each case Yahweh is the agent of the (potential) destruction of his people. The first reference is a sort of summary statement of the account: "Even at Horeb you provoked Yahweh to wrath, and Yahweh was so angry with you that he was ready to destroy (Hi.

---

58. Cf. Albright, *From the Stone Age to Christianity*, 238; Millard, "Wandering Aramean," 153–55. Millard says that Jacob's actions with respect to Laban "put himself into the class of people called *'apiru*, those who have no roots in the recognized social order" (ibid., 155). The choice of "fugitive/refugee" is not inconsistent with "wandering," but it adds a nuance not necessarily felt in the more neutral sense of "wandering."

59. Millard, "Wandering Aramean," 155.

60. E.g., 4:20, 34, 37; 5:6; 6:12, 21–23; 7:8, 18–19; 8:14; 11:4; cf. 9:7; 10:22.

שמד) you" (9:8). It soon becomes clear that the destruction envisioned is nothing short of annihilation. Atop the mountain, Yahweh exclaims to Moses, "Let me alone, that I may destroy (Hi. שמד) them and blot out (מחה) their name from under heaven. And I will make of you a nation mightier and greater than they" (9:14). The fear of such divine anger causes Moses to intercede both for the people in general and for Aaron in particular, both of whom Yahweh "was ready to destroy (Hi. שמד)" (9:19, 20). The use of שמד in this account is typical of its biblical usage, but it creates a tension with other references that do not envision such permanence.

## The Wilderness Experience

This basic pattern—human recalcitrance provoking divine wrath—is the norm for Israel in the wilderness.[61] In his first speech, Moses recalls the faithlessness of the nation at the point of entry into the land, Kadesh-barnea:

> Yet you would not go up, but rebelled against the command of Yahweh your God. And you murmured in your tents and said, "Because Yahweh hated us he has brought us out of the land of Egypt, to give us into the hand of the Amorites, to destroy (Hi. שמד) us." (Deut 1:26–27)

The refusal to take possession of the land at Kadesh-barnea is but one of various points along the way that Moses highlights following the golden calf incident; Israel also provoked divine wrath at Taberah, Massah, and Kibroth-hattaavah (9:22–23). As at Horeb, Moses intercedes, "because Yahweh had said he would destroy (Hi. שמד) you" (9:25). There does not appear to be a special nuance to the term here. In his actual prayer, Moses uses the synonym שחת, "corrupt, ruin, destroy" (9:26[Hi.]), and the result of the action is viewed as "putting to death" (9:28).

Our terms also show up in more positive memories in the wilderness, particularly with respect to the successful conquests in the Transjordan, which provide a paradigm for the coming conquest of

---

61. Moses says as much at the beginning of the golden calf account: "Know, therefore, that Yahweh your God is not giving you this good land to possess because of your righteousness, for you are a stubborn people. Remember and do not forget how you provoked Yahweh your God to wrath *in the wilderness*. From the day you came out of the land of Egypt until you came to this place, you have been rebellious against Yahweh. Even at Horeb..." (9:6–8a).

the land. Moses seeks to motivate the people to obedience, reminding them that "Yahweh your God destroyed (Hi. שמד) from among you all the men who followed the Baal of Peor" (4:3b). The conquests of Sihon and Og are initially described without use of אבד and שמד (2:26—3:11). Rather, on Yahweh's initiative,[62] Israel "takes possession" (ירש) of land (2:31; cf. לקח in 3:8), "defeats/strikes down" (Hi. נכה) the people (2:33; 3:3), "captures" (לכד) cities (2:34; 3:4) and "devotes to destruction" (Hi. חרם) their inhabitants (2:34; 3:6). This activity was thorough, leaving no survivors (2:34; 3:3; but 3:11). In the narrative describing Joshua's succession of Moses, the same events are recalled with the use of שמד as Moses encourages Joshua in the coming conquest:

> Yahweh your God himself will go over before you. He will destroy (Hi. שמד) these nations before you, so that you shall dispossess them, and Joshua will go over at your head, as Yahweh has spoken. And Yahweh will do to them as he did to Sihon and Og, the kings of the Amorites, and to their land, when he destroyed (Hi. שמד) them. And Yahweh will give them over to you, and you shall do to them according to the whole commandment that I have commanded you. (Deut 31:3–5)

Finally, four occurrences of שמד are found in parenthetical comments that deal with certain battles between foreign nations. The people of Esau "dispossessed (ירש) and destroyed (Hi. שמד)" the Horites (2:12). The next two explicitly name Yahweh as the subject: "Yahweh destroyed (Hi. שמד) [the Rephaim] before the Ammonites, and they dispossessed (ירש) them and settled in their place" (2:21); and "he destroyed (Hi. שמד) the Horites before [the people of Esau] and they dispossessed (ירש) them and settled in their place" (2:22). Finally, the Caphtorim "destroyed" the Avvim "and settled in their place" (2:23). In these cases, it is not clear whether the "destruction" is annihilation or mere removal.

## The Conquest of the Land

Because Deuteronomy is set forth primarily as Moses' speeches on the brink of entering the land, the ensuing conquest is a major part of the broader context in which everything is set. Even so, certain texts refer specifically to conquest, and several use the vocabulary under analysis. In

---

62. Israel's activity is consistently preceded by Yahweh "giving" (נתן) something or someone into their hands (2:30, 31, 33, 36; 3:2, 3). In 2:30, the giving of Sihon is even preceded by divine hardening of the heart.

Deuteronomic fashion, the conquest is conceived as both command and promise, and recognizes both divine and human agency. Deuteronomy 9:1–3 is typical:

> Hear, O Israel: you are to cross over the Jordan today, to go in to dispossess (ירש) nations greater and mightier than yourselves, cities great and fortified up to heaven, a people great and tall, the sons of the Anakim, whom you know, and of whom you have heard it said, "Who can stand before the sons of Anak?" Know therefore today that he who goes over before you as a consuming fire is Yahweh your God. He will destroy (Hi. שמד) them and subdue (Hi. כנע) them before you. So you shall drive them out (Hi. ירש) and make them perish (Hi. אבד) quickly, as Yahweh has promised you.

The initial call to wipe out the land's inhabitants in chapter 7 uses the language of the ban: "... and when Yahweh your God gives them over to you, and you defeat them, then you must devote them to complete destruction (Hi. חרם). You shall make no covenant with them and show no mercy to them" (7:2).[63] But Moses also employs several other terms in his emotional appeal. Divine activity is spoken of in terms of נתן "give (over)" (vv. 2, 23) and נשל "clear away" (vv. 1, 22). Israel's activity toward the nations includes נכה, "strike, defeat" (v. 2[Hi.]), אכל, "consume," (v. 16), ירש, "dispossess" (v. 17[Hi.]), and כלה יכל, "make an end" (v. 22). Both אבד and שמד are used this way in the summary statement of verse 24: "And he will give their kings into your hand, and you shall make their name perish (Hi. אבד) from under heaven. No one shall be able to stand against you until you have destroyed (Hi. שמד) them."

The language of absoluteness and triumph in the passage is tempered by two significant issues. First, the "destruction" of the nations will not be punctiliar. God will clear them away "little by little," and Israel "may not make an end of them at once" (7:22). There will clearly be survivors from the initial warfare, for God "will send hornets among them, until those who are left and hide themselves from you are destroyed (אבד)" (v. 20). Through the process, he "will give them over to you and throw them into great confusion, until they are destroyed (Ni. שמד)" (v. 23). Thus, the "destruction" variously spoken of in this passage carries different nuances; sometimes it refers to complete annihilation,

---

63. The root חרם forms an inclusio around the whole passage. The noun, חֵרֶם, appears twice in v. 26.

and other times to something less final. One must pay close attention to contextual indicators of how terms are being used (here and elsewhere in the book).

Second, the fate of the nations can become Israel's fate. Failure to fulfill the commandment of the ban presents the danger of Israel falling into wholesale idolatry, which in turn would provoke divine anger leading to Israel's quick destruction (Hi. שמד in 7:4) and her own placement under the ban (7:26). Far from being a random or unexpected response, this is consistent with the divine nature; not only is Yahweh "the faithful God who keeps covenant and steadfast love with those who love him and keep his commandments" (7:9), but he is also the one who "repays to their face those who hate him, by destroying (Hi. אבד) them" (7:10). What this destruction would entail is not spelled out here, but we must allow the overall context of the book to assist our reading and imagination. Namely, since these terms are used with respect to exile elsewhere, it is possible that exile is suggested here as well. Conversely, the discussion of conquest may aid in our grappling with the reason why words of destruction are being used for exile.

## The Future: Life in the Land and Warning

The laws put forth in Deuteronomy are given in light of the next stage in Israel's journey: life in the land.[64] Still, the laws themselves are subsumed under a call to Israel's complete fidelity to her covenant partner, Yahweh. This is clear in the beginning of chapter 6, where the call to keep the statutes and judgments "in the land to which you are going over" (v. 1) is followed by the Shema and "greatest commandment" (vv. 4ff.). The great danger of gifted land is for the occupants to forget the giver (v. 12), and instead turn to "the gods of the peoples" (v. 14). The result of such covenant breach would be utterly devastating: "lest the anger of Yahweh your God be kindled against you, and he destroy (Hi. שמד) you from off the face of the earth (אדמה)" (v. 15).

---

64. The "lawcode" uses אבד and שמד only a few times, and the references do not add much to our discussion. At the very beginning, Israel is commanded to "surely destroy (Pi. אבד) all the places where the nations whom you shall dispossess served their gods . . . You shall chop down the carved images of their gods and destroy (Pi. אבד) their name out of that place " (12:2, 3). The nations themselves are again described as those who "have been destroyed (Ni. שמד) before you" (12:30). Deut 22:3 refers to "lost" (אבד) animals and/or items that should be returned. The final reference (26:5) has already been discussed.

Similar warnings arise in chapters 8, 11, and 30:

> And if you forget Yahweh your God and go after other gods and serve them and worship them, I solemnly warn you today that you shall surely perish (אבד). Like the nations that Yahweh makes to perish (Hi. אבד) before you, so shall you perish (אבד), because you would not obey the voice of Yahweh your God. (Deut 8:19–20)

> Take care lest your heart be deceived, and you turn aside and serve other gods and worship them; then the anger of Yahweh will be kindled against you, and he will shut up the heavens, so that there will be no rain, and the land will yield no fruit, and you will perish (אבד) quickly off the good land that Yahweh is giving you. (Deut 11:16–17)

> But if your heart turns away, and you will not hear, but are drawn away to worship other gods and serve them, I declare to you today, that you shall surely perish (אבד). You shall not live long in the land that you are going over the Jordan to enter and possess. (Deut 30:17–18)

An immediate tension is felt in trying to discern the exact meaning of אבד in these references. That Israel would perish "like the nations" (8:20) seems to imply annihilation. But we have seen that the destruction of the nations is not always envisioned as total and final. Moreover, certain qualifying phrases add to the ambiguity: Israel will perish "off the good land" (11:17); she will not live long "in the land" (30:18). The emphasis here on the covenantal relationship between the people and the land opens up interpretive possibilities. Specifically, Israel is said to "perish/be destroyed" when there is a rupture in the people-land bond, which is central to the concept of exile.

These warnings set the stage for the long list of covenant curses in Deut 28:15–68 in which אבד and שמד appear 11 times and can be considered in three different clusters:

> Yahweh will send on you curses, confusion, and frustration in all that you undertake to do, until you are destroyed (Ni. שמד) and perish (אבד) quickly on account of the evil of your deeds, because you have forsaken me. Yahweh will make the pestilence stick to you until he has consumed you off the land that you are entering to take possession of it. Yahweh will strike you with wasting disease and with fever, inflammation and fiery heat, and with drought and with blight and with mildew. They shall pursue

you until you perish (אבד). And the heavens over your head shall be bronze, and the earth under you shall be iron. Yahweh will make the rain of your land powder. From heaven dust shall come down on you until you are destroyed (Ni. שמד). (vv. 20–24)

All these curses shall come upon you and pursue you and overtake you till you are destroyed (Ni. שמד), because you did not obey the voice of Yahweh your God, to keep his commandments and his statutes that he commanded you. They shall be a sign and a wonder against you and your offspring forever. Because you did not serve Yahweh your God with joyfulness and gladness of heart, because of the abundance of all things, therefore you shall serve your enemies whom Yahweh will send against you, in hunger and thirst, in nakedness, and lacking everything. And he will put a yoke of iron on your neck until he has destroyed (Hi. שמד) you. Yahweh will bring a nation against you from far away, from the end of the earth, swooping down like the eagle, a nation whose language you do not understand, a hard-faced nation who shall not respect the old or show mercy to the young. It shall eat the offspring of your cattle and the fruit of your ground, until you are destroyed (Ni. שמד); it also shall not leave you grain, wine, or oil, the increase of your herds or the young of your flock, until they have caused you to perish (Hi. אבד). (vv. 45–51)

Every sickness also and every affliction that is not recorded in the book of this law, Yahweh will bring upon you, until you are destroyed (Ni. שמד). Whereas you were as numerous as the stars of heaven, you shall be left few in number, because you did not obey the voice of Yahweh your God. And as Yahweh took delight in doing you good and multiplying you, so Yahweh will take delight in bringing ruin (Hi. אבד) upon you and destroying (Hi. שמד) you. And you shall be plucked off (Ni. נסח) the land that you are entering to take possession of it. And Yahweh will scatter (פוץ) you among all peoples, from one end of the earth to the other, and there you shall serve other gods of wood and stone, which neither you nor your fathers have known. (vv. 61–64)

The entire text will be examined in more detail further into our study, but we can make a few observations about the use of our vocabulary here.

First, the destruction is consistently described as the termination point—even goal—of divine judgment. The first nine references occur in phrases introduced by עַד ("until").⁶⁵ The last two references picture God's destruction of his people as the antithesis and reversal of covenant blessings (v. 63). Various other curses in the list might occur intermittently in the nation's history, but when Israel experiences what is depicted by אבד and שמד, she is at her end.

Second, despite much of the language used in the chapter, Yahweh's destruction of his people is not a once-for-all annihilation. The stock language and progression of the text will be examined later, though it seems that the reader must avoid an overly literalistic reading of the curse list. One need only observe the means by which Yahweh will "destroy" his people: frustrated human activity (v. 20); disease and illness (vv. 21-22, 60-61); meteorological activity (vv. 22-24); foreign invasion and conquest (vv. 48-51); and direct divine activity, including exile (vv. 63-64). There is also the more comprehensive statement, "All these curses shall come upon you ... till you are destroyed" (v. 45; cf. v. 20). It is difficult to imagine all of this happening at one time, but if Israel were to be wiped out by one means, why are several additional means listed? The rhetoric of the text must be kept in mind.

Third, this destruction clearly involves exile. Exile is mentioned for the first time explicitly in the curse list in verses 36-44, using more conventional language:

> Yahweh will bring (Hi. הלך) you and your king whom you set over you to a nation that neither you nor your fathers have known. And there you shall serve other gods of wood and stone. And you shall become a horror, a proverb, and a byword among all the peoples where Yahweh will lead (Pi. נהג) you away. (vv. 36-37)

> You shall father sons and daughters, but they shall not be yours, for they shall go (הלך) into captivity (שְׁבִי). (v. 41)

In context, these are part of "all these curses" that lead to destruction (v. 45). More particularly, the final references to אבד and שמד are juxtaposed to exile terminology: "... so Yahweh will take delight in bringing ruin (Hi. אבד) upon you and destroying (Hi. שמד) you. And you shall be plucked off (Ni. נסח) the land ... And Yahweh will scatter (Hi. פוץ) you among all peoples ..." (vv. 63-64). It is not necessary to equate the

---

65. עד is only used in the chapter in these phrases. Similar usage is found with אבד in 7:20 and שמד in 7:23[Ni.] and 7:24[Hi.].

destruction vocabulary with exile, only to recognize the very close connection. The parallels with 4:26–28 are clear:

> ... you will soon utterly perish from the land that you are going over the Jordan to possess (4:26)

> ... you shall be plucked off the land that you are entering to take possession of it (28:63)

> And Yahweh will scatter you among the peoples (4:27)

> And Yahweh will scatter you among the peoples (28:64)

> And there you will serve gods of wood and stone (4:28)

> ... and there you shall serve other gods of wood and stone (28:64).

### Five Minor Terms

In examining the texts, several words were used in conjunction with those discussed above. It seems that at least five other terms at least approximate an exilic sense in Deuteronomy: שאר, "remain, be left over"; כלה, "be complete, spent"; נסח, "pull, tear away"; נתש, "pull up, pluck up, root out"; and שלך, "draw out, draw off."[66]

שאר, "remain, be left over," is the central Hebrew term to express the remnant motif.[67] Thus, it carries significant theological weight for the theme of exile and restoration in the Old Testament. It is striking, then, that its use in Deuteronomy is primarily negative.[68] In battles against the armies of Sihon and Og, Israel "left" no survivors (2:34; 3:3), other than Og himself (3:11). In the conquest, Yahweh will make sure that even "those who are left" will be destroyed (7:20). As for Israel, the destruction leading up to, and including, exile consists of the nation being "left few in number" (4:27; 28:62). Though שאר more specifically expresses

---

66. A sixth term used for exile is שוב (17:16[2x]; 28:68), but I will reserve this discussion for the next section. More general terms, such as the Hiphil of הלך, "go," could also be added.

67. Sang Hoon Park, "שאר," 11. For a thorough study of the remnant motif, see Hasel, *Remnant*.

68. Apart from the more theological references mentioned here, שאר is used in a few more general contexts. In a legal setting, a malicious witness is brought to justice in such a way that "the rest shall hear and fear" (19:20). In the covenant curses, Israel is warned that a nation "shall not leave you grain" (28:51), and that a man shall not share his children as food to his brother "because he has nothing else left" (28:55).

the result of other activity, it is an important term for the discussion of exile. Negatively, it clearly speaks to the reversal of the Abrahamic blessing of being "as numerous as the stars of heaven" (28:62). Nevertheless, there is a hint of hope in the fact that there will be a surviving remnant after Yahweh's destruction of his people in exile (note "among the nations" in 4:27).

The root כלה, "be complete, spent," occurs seven times in Deuteronomy. Five of these are general references and irrelevant for our discussion.[69] It occurs once in a conquest passage, where Israel is told, "you may not make an end of them at once" (7:22). The final reference is in the curse list of chapter 28:

> Yahweh will make the pestilence stick to you until he has consumed (כלה) you off the land that you are entering to take possession of it. (28:21)

Several factors make this a possible reference to exile. First, as we have seen, verses 20–24 is a paragraph with several occurrences of אבד and שמד (אבד, vv. 20, 22; שמד, vv. 20, 24). These terms are clearly associated with exile later in the chapter (v. 63), and may be so here as well. Second, כלה is in a similar construction—as the object of the preposition עד "until"—that we witnessed with אבד and שמד throughout chapter 28 (see also 7:23, 24). Third, the qualification, "off the land," is similar to other phrases in statements of exile (e.g., "perish from the land" in 4:26; "plucked off the land" in 28:63).

The other three roots appear quite infrequently in Deuteronomy, but each clearly refers to exile.[70] In one of the main exilic passages, we find the phrase, "And you shall be plucked (נסח) off the land" (28:63b). This immediately follows the double note of destruction (אבד and שמד in v. 63a) and immediately precedes Yahweh's "scattering" of his people (פוץ in v. 64). The final two terms parallel each other in a statement from foreigners who observe the destruction of Israel: "Yahweh uprooted (נתש) them from their land in anger and fury and great wrath, and cast (Hi. שלך) them into another land, as they are this day" (29:27[28]).

---

69. It is used with respect to someone "finishing" something: speaking (20:9; 32:45); paying a tithe (26:12); and writing (31:24). In a poetic text, it refers to arrows that are "spent" (32:23).

70. נסח and נתש only occur once each. שלך appears two other times, referring to Moses' handling of the Decalogue tablets (9:17[Hi.]) and his handling of the golden calf (9:21[Hi.]).

One additional common root in Deuteronomy may be mentioned: ירשׁ, "take possession, inherit, dispossess." Taking possession of the land is often commanded as an act of obedience or asserted as a fact (often as a result of obedience).[71] The closest ירשׁ comes to exile-like actions is in contexts where Israel dispossesses the inhabitants of the land during the conquest,[72] but Israel is never herself said to be dispossessed by another.[73] This word, however, does help temper the destruction language it often parallels. Dispossession can carry a wider range of applications than annihilation.

## THE VOCABULARY OF RETURN

The vocabulary of return in Deuteronomy is not nearly as complicated as that of exile. Therefore, we will reserve much of the discussion for the exegetical and theological analyses in subsequent chapters. Nevertheless, an examination of certain terms will be helpful to set the stage. Restoration is explicitly encountered in two texts; both correspond to the main texts for exile (4:25–28; 28:63ff.).

> But from there you will seek (Pi. בקשׁ) Yahweh your God and you will find (מצא) him, if you search (דרשׁ) after him with all your heart and with all your soul. When you are in tribulation, and all these things come upon you in the latter days, you will *return* (שׁוב) to Yahweh your God and obey (שׁמע) his voice. For Yahweh your God is a merciful God. He will not leave (Hi. רפה) you or destroy (Hi. שׁחת) you or forget (שׁכח) the covenant with your fathers that he swore to them. (4:29–31)

> And when all these things come (בוא) upon you, the blessing and the curse, which I have set before you, and you call (Hi. שׁוב) them to mind among all the nations where Yahweh your God has driven (Hi. נדח) you, and *return* (שׁוב) to Yahweh your God, you and your children, and obey (שׁמע) his voice in all that I com-

---

71. Imperatives: 1:8, 21; 9:23. Assertions/promises (with no explicit condition): 1:39; 4:22; 5:31, 33; 9:4, 5; 11:31[2x]; 15:4; 17:14; 25:19; 26:1; 28:21, 63; 30:5[2X]. As a result of obedience: 4:1; 6:18; 8:1; 10:11; 11:8; 16:20. With respect to taking possession of land in the Transjordan, there are imperatives (2:24, 31), and unconditional assertions/promises (3:18; 4:38).

72. Deut 7:17[Hi.]; 9:1; 11:23[1x Qal; 1x Hi.]; 12:29[2x]; 18:12[Hi.], 14; 19:1; 31:3; cf. 12:2 (destruction of cultic sites).

73. Foreigners only dispossess other foreigners (2:12, 21, 22). Remarkably, ירשׁ is not even used this way against Israel in the curse list of Deut 28, where we might expect it.

mand you today, with all your heart and with all your soul, then Yahweh your God *will restore your fortunes* (וְשָׁב ... אֶת־שְׁבוּתְךָ) and have compassion on you, and he will *gather* (Pi. קבץ) you again from all the peoples where Yahweh your God has scattered (פוץ) you. If your outcasts (Ni. ptc. נדח) are in the uttermost parts of heaven, from there Yahweh your God will *gather* (Pi. קבץ) you, and from there he will *take* (לקח) you. And Yahweh your God will *bring* (Hi. בוא) you into the land that your fathers possessed (ירש), that you may possess (ירש) it. And he will make you more prosperous (Hi. יטב) and numerous (Hi. רבה) than your fathers. And Yahweh your God will circumcise (מול) your heart and the heart of your offspring, so that you will love Yahweh your God with all your heart and with all your soul, that you may live. And Yahweh your God will put all these curses on your foes and enemies who persecuted (רדף) you. And you shall again (שוב) obey (שמע) the voice of Yahweh and keep all his commandments that I command you today. Yahweh your God will make you abundantly prosperous (Hi. יתר) in all the work of your hand, in the fruit of your womb and in the fruit of your cattle and in the fruit of your ground. For Yahweh will again (שוב) take delight in prospering you, as he took delight in your fathers, when you obey (שמע) the voice of Yahweh your God, to keep his commandments and his statutes that are written in this Book of the Law, when you turn (שוב) to Yahweh your God with all your heart and with all your soul. (30:1–10)

Though there is a wealth of terminology in these texts that will need to be considered later, four terms specifically refer to return from exile: שוב, "turn back, return" (4:30; 30:2, 3[2x]); קבץ, "gather, collect" (30:3, 4); לקח, "take" (30:4); and בוא, "come (in), go (in), bring [Hi.]" (30:5).

### שׁוּב, *"Turn, Return"*

The verb is usually rendered as "turn," "return," or "repent" in the Qal stem and "bring back" or "restore" in the Hiphil stem.[74] שוב is a basic verb of motion, and is used with reference to various contexts involving persons, creatures, and things. It also is used in reference to changing directions, recurrent motion, and as an auxiliary verb (meaning "again")

---

74. Though a bit dated, the main work to which scholars still refer is Holladay, *Root šûbh*. For a helpful study that interacts heavily with Holladay see Price, "Lexicographical Study," 87–129. See also Hamilton, "שוב," 909–10; Soggin, "שוב," 1312–17; Thompson and Martens, "שוב," 55–59. Holladay (*Root šûbh*, 59ff.) divides the uses in Qal into ten different meanings, with subdivisions with each.

to convey repetition of another verb. It is common in both a physical and religious sense; it exhibits a flexibility to speak both of "turning to" and "turning from."⁷⁵ These factors make שׁוּב a central and powerful term for restoration, which involves (1) a return to God and a return to land, and (2) a turning to God and a turning away from evil/idols.⁷⁶

Not surprisingly, the prophets especially employ שׁוּב in its various religious senses. First, Israel is accused of moral and spiritual lapses—for turning from God (e.g., Jer 8:5; 34:16), for turning to evildoing (e.g., Jer 11:10), for refusing to turn from its evil ways (e.g., Jer 15:7), or for not returning to God (e.g., five times in Amos 4:6–11). The noun מְשׁוּבָה (or שׁוֹבָב), "apostasy," is also prominent,⁷⁷ often accompanying the verb.⁷⁸ Second, through the prophets, God calls his people to return to him. This usually involves repentance,⁷⁹ but not always (e.g, Isa 44:12).⁸⁰ Third, God promises to turn to the person seeking forgiveness and reconciliation, often in the sense of turning away his anger (e.g., Hos 14:5[4]).⁸¹

---

75. The root occurs over 1050 times total. Price ("Lexicographical Study," 88–89) breaks down the "non-exilic" religious usage as follows: "return to God" (62x); "turn from evil" (38x); "withdraw from God, become apostate" (10x); and "turn back from good to evil" (11x). To the 38 exilic references of שׁוּב counted by Holladay, Price adds 30 passages "in which there seems to be some influence by the thought of exile and return" ("Lexicographical Study," 89). Price includes the 27 occurrences of שׁוּב שְׁבוּת (see the discussion below).

76. The use of שׁוּב for discussions about death and life may strengthen the thesis of our study. The word is used for return to ground (Gen 3:19), return to dust (Eccl 12:7), and, most intriguingly, return from death to life (2 Sam 12:23).

77. E.g., Isa 57:17; Jer 2:19; 3:14, 22[2x]; 5:6; 8:5; 14:7; Hos 11:7; 14:5[4]).

78. Note the wordplay in Jer 3:22a: "Return (שׁוּבוּ), O faithless (שׁוֹבָבִ) sons; I will heal your faithlessness (מְשׁוּבֹתֵיכֶם)." Cf. Jer 8:5.

79. The historian remarks, "Yet Yahweh warned Israel and Judah by every prophet and every seer, saying, 'Turn from your evil ways and keep my commandments and my statutes, in accordance with all the Law that I commanded your fathers, and that I sent to you by my servants the prophets'" (2 Kgs 17:13). See especially the sustained appeals in Jer 3:22—4:2 and Hos 14:2–4[1–3]). Cf. Ezek 14:6; Joel 2:12–13; Mal 3:7.

80. Some prophets (e.g., Isaiah and Amos) rarely, if ever, appeal for repentance.

81. 2 Chr 30:6 shows the reciprocity: "O people of Israel, return (שׁוּבוּ) to Yahweh, the God of Abraham, Isaac, and Israel, that he may turn again (וְיָשֹׁב) to the remnant of you who have escaped from the hand of the kings of Assyria." Conversely, Yahweh often refuses to turn away his anger or punishment (e.g., 2 Kgs 23:26); cf. Amos' repetitive use of the phrase, "For three transgressions of XXXX, and for four, I will not revoke (Hi. שׁוּב) it [i.e. wrath or the punishment]" (Amos 1:3, 6, 9, 11, 13; 2:1, 4, 6).

Finally, the prophets use שׁוב to speak of return to the land as central to restoration. Jeremiah and Ezekiel can serve as examples.[82] The announcement of return may accompany an announcement of exile (e.g., Jer 12:14–15; 16:13–15; cf. Deut 4:25–31) or be freestanding (e.g., Jer 31:16; Ezek 29:26–28; cf. Deut 30:1–10):

> Thus says Yahweh concerning all my evil neighbors who touch the heritage that I have given my people Israel to inherit: "Behold, I will pluck (נתשׁ) them up from their land, and I will pluck (נתשׁ) up the house of Judah from among them. And after I have plucked (נתשׁ) them up, I will again (שׁוב) have compassion on them, and I will bring (Hi. שׁוב) them again each to his heritage and each to his land. (Jer 12:14–15)

> Therefore I will hurl (Hi. טול) you out of this land into a land that neither you nor your fathers have known, and there you shall serve other gods day and night, for I will show you no favor. Therefore, behold, the days are coming, declares Yahweh, when it shall no longer be said, "As Yahweh lives who brought up the people of Israel out of the land of Egypt," but "As Yahweh lives who brought up the people of Israel out of the north country and out of all the countries where he had driven (Hi. נדח) them." For I will bring (Hi. שׁוב) them back to their own land that I gave to their fathers. (Jer 16:13–15)[83]

> Thus says Yahweh: "Keep your voice from weeping, and your eyes from tears, for there is a reward for your work, declares Yahweh, and they shall come back (שׁוב) from the land of the enemy. (Jer 31:16)

> They shall forget their shame and all the treachery they have practiced against me, when they dwell securely in their land with none to make them afraid, when I have brought (שׁוב) them back from the peoples and gathered (Pi. קבץ) them from their enemies' lands, and through them have vindicated my holiness in the sight of many nations. Then they shall know that I am Yahweh their God, because I sent them into exile (Hi. גלה) among the na-

---

82. These two prophets focus on the theme more than any other, but שׁוב as "return from exile" does appear elsewhere: Isa 10:22; Zech 10:9 (note "shall live and return"); cf. 1 Kgs 8:34 (uses Hiphil like Jer 12:15); Ezra 2:1; Neh 7:6. Cf. the absence of the promise in Jer 22:10: "Weep not for him who is dead, nor grieve for him, but weep bitterly for him who goes away, for he shall return (שׁוב) no more to see his native land."

83. See also the metaphor of good and bad figs in Jer 24:1–10, which has several verbal links with Deuteronomy.

tions and then assembled (Pi. כנס) them into their own land. I will leave none of them remaining among the nations anymore. (Ezek 39:26–28)

Thompson and Martens pinpoint three motivations for the return to the land: (1) Yahweh's compassion (cf. Jer 29:10–11; 31:16, 20); God's own reputation (Ezek 36:22–24); and (3) return to the land represents a return to the place of blessing (Jer 31:10–14).[84]

שוב is the focal term in the Deuteronomic vision of restoration. It is the only word of return used in 4:29–31 (v. 30), and functions as a *Leitwort* in 30:1–10 (vv. 1, 2, 3[2x], 8, 9, 10).[85] A similar use appears in three phrases:

> When you are in tribulation, and all these things come upon you in the latter days, you will return (וְשַׁבְתָּ) to Yahweh your God and obey his voice. (4:30)

> [And when all these things come upon you ... and [you] return (וְשַׁבְתָּ) to Yahweh your God, you and your children, and obey his voice in all that I command you today, with all your heart and with all your soul.... (30:1a, 2)

> ... when you obey the voice of Yahweh your God, ... when you turn (כִּי תָשׁוּב) to Yahweh your God with all your heart and with all your soul. (30:10)[86]

The emphasis of שוב is clearly on the restoration of the relationship between the people and Yahweh. In each instance, the return is specifically "to Yahweh your God," and set in conjunction with obeying (שמע) Yahweh's voice. In fact, the promise of return to land is only explicit in Deuteronomy 30:5 (see below on בוא).

In Deuteronomy 30:3 we encounter the idiom שׁוּב שְׁבוּת, usually rendered "restore the fortunes of."[87] The phrase can either refer generally

---

84. Thompson and Martens, "59–58", שוב.

85. In 30:1–10, only some of the references deal with restoration (vv. 2, 3, and probably v. 10). In v. 1, שוב + אֶל + לֵבָב forms an idiom meaning "call to mind" or "lay to heart" (also in 4:39). In vv. 8 and 9, שוב functions as an auxiliary verb (= "again") to repeat the action of another verb (שמע, v. 8; עשׂה, v. 9; cf. 24:4).

86. We will reserve the syntactical and exegetical details for chap. 3. Though the statements have striking linguistic and conceptual similarities, there are important differences (such as the construction of the temporal clauses [the "when" statements are more similar in English than Hebrew], and the protasis/apodosis constructions).

87. Sometimes the nominative is שְׁבִית. There are 25 to 27 occurrences of this idiom

to an overall spiritual covenantal restoration (e.g., Job 42:10) or specifically to physical restoration to land (e.g., Jer 30:3; 32:44).⁸⁸ But this may be a distinction without a difference when it comes to our passage. The restoration includes return to the land (Deut 30:5) as part and parcel with the covenantal blessings of divine compassion (v. 3), prosperity (vv. 5, 9), progeny (vv. 2, 5), and heart circumcision (v. 6).

Several of the other Deuteronomic references of שוב deserve attention as well.⁸⁹ It is used in a few general contexts with Yahweh as subject. He will "turn" from his anger if the people do not handle a city's spoil that is under the ban (13:18[17]; חרם used for city in v. 16[15] and for the spoil in v. 18[17]). He will "turn" away from those who defile the camp (23:15[14]). He will "return" vengeance on his enemies (32:41; parallels Pi. שלם, "repay").

More significant is the use of שוב in the curse list. One of the final curses is that Yahweh "will bring (Hi. שוב) upon you again all the diseases of Egypt" (28:60). With interesting wordplay, the direction is soon reversed: "And Yahweh will bring (Hi. שוב) you back in ships to Egypt, a journey that I promised that you should never make again" (28:68a). The irony inherent in this statement is heightened when read in light of the actual "promise," which occurs within the context of the king law:

> Only he [i.e., the king] must not acquire many horses for himself or cause the people to return (Hi. שוב) to Egypt in order to

---

in the Old Testament (the discrepancy in number depends on *Ketib-Qere* problems). Though debated in the past, it is now known that the nominative is a cognate of שוב rather than שבה. For a summary of the material see Holladay, *Root šûbh*, 110–14. Cf. the lengthy discussion in Price, "Lexicographical Study," 89–123. For a briefer discussion accompanied by a helpful bibliography see Soggin, "שוב," 1314–15.

88. Price ("Lexicographical Study," 102, 122–23) considers an historical development of the idiom. He concludes that the original sense of "restore the fortunes" underwent a theological reinterpretation and came to be used for restoration of Israel to the land. In the postexilic period it was re-generalized to describe a general restoration of paradisal conditions in the apocalyptic visions of the period.

89. The root occurs a total of 35 times in the book. The other references reveal all types of general activities. In Qal: return from battle (1:45); return to land (3:20; Reubenites and Gadites); return to one's house (20:5, 6, 7, 8); turn back (to cover excrement, 23:14[13]; to gather a sheaf, 24:19); return a donkey (28:61); cf. the sense of taking "again" (24:4). In Hiphil: report (1:22, 25); lay (to heart)/call (to mind) (concerning divine sovereignty, 4:39; concerning the blessing and the curse, 30:1); return a brother's animal (22:1[2x], 2); restore a pledge for a loan (24:13[2x]).

acquire many horses, since Yahweh has said to you, "You shall never return (שׁוב) that way again." (17:16)[90]

As will be seen in detail later, exile is clearly pictured as a reversal of the exodus from Egypt. But the important (and ironic) point at this stage is that the major term for return from exile is being used for exile itself!

### קבץ, "Gather, Collect"

This root can be used for the gathering of plunder,[91] but usually conveys the gathering of people into one place.[92] People are gathered for social gatherings, the mustering of troops, religious functions, corporate judgment, and restoration. It is this last use that concerns us. Even before exile, David looks forward to God's restoration in order to give him thanks:

> Save us, O God of our salvation,
> and gather (קבץ) and deliver (נצל) us from among the nations,
> that we may give thanks to your holy name,
> and glory in your praise. (1 Chr 16:35; cf. Ps 106:47)

This prayer is transformed into a promise by the prophets. The primary metaphor is of a shepherd gathering his lambs.[93] Exiled Judah will be brought back to the land.[94] The prophets go further still; this divine gathering will take place around the world, and will result in a unified Israel and the inclusion of Gentiles.[95] After the return from exile, God tells the people to remember his promise (Neh 1:9; cf. Ps 107:3).

---

90. See Reimer, "Concerning Return to Egypt," 217–29.

91. Besides the references in Deut 30:3, 4, the only other reference of קבץ in the book deals with gathering the spoil of a city under the ban in order to burn it as an offering (13:17[16]).

92. See Coppes, "קָבַץ," 783–84; Rogers and Cornelius, "קבץ," 862–65; Sawyer, "קבץ," 1099–1101. Cf. Widengren, "Yahweh's Gathering of the Dispersed," 227–45. The root occurs 127 times in the OT.

93. Isa 40:11; Jer 31:10; Ezek 34:13; Mic 2:12. Isaiah also uses the image of a husband who gathers back his wife with compassion (54:5–7).

94. קבץ appears in the restoration promises of Isa 43:5; 54:7; 56:8; Jer 31:8, 10; Ezek 11:17; 34:13; 37:21; Mic 4:6; Zeph 3:20; cf. Isa 49:18; 60:4.

95. On gathering from around the world, see Isa 11:12; 43:5 (cf. Ps 107:3). On a unified Israel, see Ezek 37:11; Mic 2:12. On the inclusion of Gentiles, see Isa 11:12; 66:18.

The use of קבץ in Deuteronomy 30 is consistent with its biblical usage.[96] The gathering, which is explicitly based on divine compassion, is "from all the peoples where Yahweh your God has scattered you" (v. 3). The scope is universalized in verse 4 ("the uttermost parts of heaven").

## לקח, "Take"

לקח is a common term used in a variety of contexts in the Bible, but we are concerned with its theological usage.[97] On rare occasions, persons experience bodily assumption into heaven as God "takes" them.[98] More frequently, God "takes" a person in the sense of selecting or summoning him: Abraham (Gen 24:7; Josh 24:3), Jeroboam I (1 Kgs 11:31), Nebuchadnezzar (Jer 43:10), Amos (Amos 7:15), Zerubbabel (Hag 2:23), David (2 Sam 7:8; 1 Chr 17:7; Ps 78:70), and Levites (Num 3:12, 41, 45; 8:16, 18). In this manner, לקח is used to describe the exodus:

> I will take (לקח) you to be my people, and I will be your God, and you shall know that I am Yahweh your God, who has brought you out from under the burdens of the Egyptians. (Exod 6:7)

> But Yahweh has taken (לקח) you and brought you out of the iron furnace, out of Egypt, to be a people of his own inheritance, as you are this day. (Deut 4:20)

> Or has any god ever attempted to go and take (לקח) a nation for himself from the midst of another nation, by trials, by signs, by wonders, and by war, by a mighty hand and an outstretched arm, and by great deeds of terror, all of which Yahweh your God did for you in Egypt before your eyes? (Deut 4:34)

---

96. On Deut 30:1-10 as forming the basis for the prophetic proclamation, see Weinfeld, *Deuteronomy and the Deuteronomic School*, 345-61, 366-70.

97. The root appears about 1000 times, but only about 50 times with God as the subject. See Els, "לקח," 812-17; Kaiser, "לָקַח," 481-82; Schmid, "לקח," 648-51; Seebass, "לָקַח," 16-21. There are 45 references in Deuteronomy. General references include the following: general "taking" of an object (1:25 [fruit]; 7:25 [idols]; 9:9 [tablets]; 9:21 [golden calf]; 21:3 [heifer]; 22:6, 7 [bird]; 24:19 [sheaf]; 26:2 [firstfruits]; 26:4 [basket]; 31:26 [Book of the Law]); selection of leaders (1:15, 23); capture of cities and land (3:4, 8, 14; 29:7[8]); taking a wife (i.e., marriage; 7:3; 20:7[2x]; 21:11; 22:13, 14; 23:1[22:30]; 24:1, 3, 4, 5[2x]; 25:5, 7, 8); (not) taking a bribe (10:17 [God as subject]; 16:19; 27:25); arresting an offender (19:12; 22:18); establishing evidence (22:15); grasping revelation (30:12, 13); teaching (noun לֶקַח; 32:2); and the spreading of wings (32:11).

98. Gen 5:24; 2 Kgs 2:3, 10-11; cf. Ps 49:16[15]; 73:25[24].

## The Vocabulary of Exile   71

לקח parallels קבץ in Deuteronomy 30:4 (and Hi. בוא in v. 5) to refer to restoring the people from exile. The prophets of exile can speak the same language:

> Return (שוב), O faithless children, declares Yahweh; for I am your master; I will take (לקח) you, one from a city and two from a family, and I will bring (Hi. בוא) you to Zion. (Jer 3:14)

> I will take (לקח) you from the nations and gather (Pi. קבץ) you from all the countries and bring (Hi. בוא) you into your own land. (Ezek 36:24)

> ... then say to them, "Thus says Yahweh Elohim: 'Behold, I will take (לקח) the people of Israel from the nations among which they have gone, and will gather (Pi. קבץ) them from all around, and bring (Hi. בוא) them to their own land.'" (Ezek 37:21)

Interestingly, and perhaps with bitter irony, Jeremiah can also use this language for exile:

> Therefore thus says Yahweh of hosts: "Because you have not obeyed my words, behold, I will send for (= שלח and לקח) all the tribes of the north, declares Yahweh, and for Nebuchadnezzar the king of Babylon, my servant, and I will bring (Hi. בוא) them against this land and its inhabitants, and against all these surrounding nations. I will devote them to destruction (Hi. חרם), and make them a horror, a hissing, and an everlasting desolation." (Jer 25:8–9)

> I will take (לקח) the remnant of Judah who have set their faces to come to the land of Egypt to live, and they shall all be consumed. In the land of Egypt they shall fall; by the sword and by famine they shall be consumed. From the least to the greatest, they shall die by the sword and by famine, and they shall become an oath, a horror, a curse, and a taunt. (Jer 44:12)

These passages support the notion that exile is a reversal of prior history and promise—an anti-exodus. Restoration is a reversal of the reversal—perhaps a new exodus.

### בוא, "Come, Go"

בוא, the fourth most frequent word in the Hebrew Bible, is the most common verb of motion.[99] Martens identifies four major aspects in

---

99. Arnold, "בוא," 615–18; Jenni, "בוא," 201–4; Martens, "בּוֹא," 93–95; Preuss,

which the term appears in varied but significant theological contexts: (1) it is found with reference to Yahweh as one who comes to his people; (2) it is associated with the promise-fulfillment motif; (3) it refers to the coming Messiah; (4) and it is used with respect to people coming to the sanctuary.[100]

Three of these four aspects are attested in Deuteronomy,[101] but only the second one is most immediately relevant at this point. The use of בוא with respect to the promise-fulfillment motif concerns several issues: God's word "coming to pass"; God's judgment or salvation "coming upon" Israel (or God's "bringing upon" Israel his judgment/salvation);

---

"בוֹא," 20–49. Jenni ("בוֹא," 201) notes that 106 of the over 2500 references are found in Deuteronomy.

100. Martens, "בוֹא," 94–95.

101. The third aspect is missing. Deuteronomy does not appear to present any messianic expectation (the "prophet like Moses" passage of 18:15–22 is not strictly messianic). בוא is used in connection with this theme in Gen 49:10; Ezek 21:32[27]; Zech 9:9f.; cf. the NT appropriation to Jesus Christ of Ps 118:26: "Blessed is he who comes in the name of Yahweh."

The first aspect is highlighted in the very beginning of Moses' final blessing on Israel: "Yahweh came (בוא) from Sinai and dawned from Seir upon us; he shone forth from Mount Paran; he came from the ten thousands of holy ones, with flaming fire at his right hand" (Deut 33:2; cf. Hab 3:3). This coming established the kingship of Yahweh—"Thus Yahweh became king in Jeshurun . . . " (v. 5)—and recalls Yahweh's initial coming in thick clouds to Mount Sinai (Exod 19:9; 20:20) and his promise that he would come to every place he chose to cause his name to be remembered (Exod 20:24; cf. Ps 24:7, 9). Moses' words find fulfillment as Yahweh comes to fight for Israel throughout the nation's history (Isa 30:27) and in the future (Isa 66:15). Though God also comes to judge sinful Israel (Ps 50:3; Mal 3:1), he will come with salvation (Hos 6:3; Mic 4:8); he will come to bring back his people from the ends of the earth (Isa 41:9–11), and will come and dwell in Jerusalem (Zech 2:14[10]). God also comes in various modes of revelation: in a dream (Gen 20:3); through messengers (Judg 6:11; 13:6–10); in connection with the ark (1 Sam 4:6–7); and in the prophetic word (Num 22:38; 1 Sam 2:27).

The fourth aspect—worshipers coming to the sanctuary—is based on the assurance that Yahweh's presence can be encountered (recall Exod 20:24). (For a convincing argument that, against the scholarly consensus, Deuteronomy promotes the personal presence of Yahweh, see Wilson, *Out of the Midst of the Fire*. Thus, the lawcode begins with a call to "go" (Qal) to the chosen place of worship (Deut 12:5) and "bring" (Hiphil) sacrifices, offerings, and tithes (12:6, 11). (See also 2 Sam 7:18; Isa 30:29; Jer 7:2, 10; Ps 5:8[7]; 42:3[2].) Deut 17:9 states that the people also went to the priests when they came to the sanctuary (cf. going to the prophet for a divine word; e.g., 1 Kgs 14:3, 5; 2 Kgs 4:42; Ezek 14:4, 7). When Israel comes to the chosen place, the leaders are to read the Torah in their hearing (31:11). Though foreigners could come to pray (1 Kgs 8:41), eunuchs were excluded from entering the cultic community (Deut 23:2[1]).

and God's "bringing" Israel back to himself and to the land. Note the wordplay as Joshua brings together the first two points:

> And now I am about to go the way of all the earth, and you know in your hearts and souls, all of you, that not one word has failed of all the good things that Yahweh your God promised concerning you. All have come (בוא) to pass for you; not one of them has failed. But just as all the good things that Yahweh your God promised concerning you have been fulfilled for you (lit., "come [בוא] upon you"), so Yahweh will bring (Hi. בוא) upon you all the evil things, until he has destroyed (Hi. שמד) you from off this good land that Yahweh your God has given you, if you transgress the covenant of Yahweh your God, which he commanded you, and go and serve other gods and bow down to them. Then the anger of Yahweh will be kindled against you, and you shall perish (אבד) quickly from off the good land that he has given to you. (Josh 23:14–16)

So the "coming" of judgment (= exile?; note אבד and שמד) will testify that God's word has "come to pass."

Joshua does not have a corresponding word of salvation; thus, his pronouncement lacks the third point of God bringing Israel back. But the prophets speak clearly:

> And the ransomed of Yahweh shall return (שוב) and come (בוא) to Zion with singing; everlasting joy shall be upon their heads; they shall obtain gladness and joy, and sorrow and sighing shall flee away. (Isa 35:10 [= 51:11])

> "Return (שוב), O faithless children," declares Yahweh; "for I am your master; I will take (לקח) you, one from a city and two from a family, and I will bring (Hi. בוא) you to Zion." (Jer 3:14)

> "And I will bring (Hi. יצא) them out from the peoples and gather (Pi. קבץ) them from the countries, and will bring (Hi. בוא) them into their own land. And I will feed them on the mountains of Israel, by the ravines, and in all the inhabited places of the country." (Ezek 34:13)

> "I will take (לקח) you from the nations and gather (Pi. קבץ) you from all the countries and bring (Hi. בוא) you into your own land." (Ezek 36:24)

> Thus says Yahweh Elohim: "Behold, I will take (לקח) the people of Israel from the nations among which they have gone, and will

gather (Pi. קבץ) them from all around, and (Hi. בוא) bring them to their own land." (Ezek 37:21)

"At that time I will bring (Hi. בוא) you in, at the time when I gather (Pi. קבץ) you together; for I will make you renowned and praised among all the peoples of the earth, when I restore your fortunes (שׁוּב + שְׁבוּת) before your eyes," says Yahweh. (Zeph 3:20)[102]

With these pronouncements, the reputation of God (and each of the prophets) is put on the line; for the word to "come to pass" Israel must "come/be brought" back to the land.

These connections help us understand the use of בוא in Deuteronomy. Though the term is used only once for return to the land (30:5), the discussion above may reveal greater thematic connections than first anticipated. First, the "coming to pass" of the prophetic word can be connected with God "bringing" his people back from exile. The identification of a true prophet, based on the veracity of his word, is fundamental for the ongoing welfare of the nation (18:15–22; note בוא in v. 22; but see 13:3) and if subsequent prophets are to be "like Moses," then Moses' own words—including those in 30:1–10—must be fulfilled. Second, Yahweh will "bring" his people into the land (30:5) only after the blessing and the curse have "come" upon them (30:1; cf. 28:2, 15). Third, Israel's re-entry into the land via restoration should be considered in light of the initial entry via conquest.[103] בוא (Hi.) is also used of God bringing Israel into the land in the first place (e.g., 4:38).[104]

## CONCLUSION

The purpose of this chapter was to examine the language of exile used in Deuteronomy, and to compare it to the witness of the rest of the Old

---

102. Cf. Ezekiel's use of בוא for exile: "Therefore say, 'Thus says Yahweh Elohim: Though I removed them far off (Hi. רחק) among the nations, and though I scattered (פוץ) them among the countries, yet I have been a sanctuary to them for a while in the countries where they have gone (בוא)'" (Ezek 11:16).

103. On Deut 30:5, Price ("Lexicographical Study," 158) comments that "the influence of the 'D' vocabulary used in describing the conquest on the vocabulary describing the restoration is obvious."

104. Note also the stereotypical phrase "go and take possession" (e.g., 1:8; 4:1; 6:18; 8:1) during the conquest, where בוא becomes a technical term for land inheritance. On the gift of land as past, present, and future in Deuteronomy and the Deuteronomistic History, see Preuss, "בּוֹא," 27–30.

Testament. We anticipated that such a study might assist further investigation of the exile theme in specific ways: by aiding the prioritization of texts related to our theme; by highlighting the relevance of other texts to the discussion that might have been underestimated; by suggesting methodological strategies by which exile can appropriately be read and understood within the theological contours of the book; and by raising certain exegetical, literary, and theological questions that must be addressed.

We found a rather limited use of the normal vocabulary for exile in Deuteronomy. The primary roots גלה and שבה are all but absent with no simple explanation as to why. Several of the secondary terms are found in the book, but their application to exile is selective.[105] In stark contrast, Deuteronomy's choice and use of return language appears quite consistent with the rest of the Hebrew Bible. This further underscores the variance with respect to exile terminology.

An investigation into alternative Deuteronomic terminology for exile centered on two words: אבד and שמד. At least two factors with respect to these terms complicate our study. First, there is a fundamental tension between the basic meaning of these words and the notion of exile. אבד and שמד are words of extermination—"perish," "destroy," "annihilate," and the like. This "no-survivor" thought world is clearly different from that of exile, which, by definition, necessitates survival (however unpleasant it might be). Two, while these terms serve the exile theme in Deuteronomy, they also serve several other themes. We find these terms in contexts reflecting on covenant relationship in general and various historical situations in particular.

The complexity of the situation may also be the way forward. The data analyzed in this chapter suggests certain perspectives for a theological reading of exile in Deuteronomy. One focus is to reflect on the equation that exile is death. It is no surprise to find devastation and loss associated with the experience of exile; corporate land loss and deportation inevitably involves the destruction of homes and businesses, the breakdown of political and religious institutions, and even the death of individuals. But more seems to be going on in the text: exile constitutes the death of Israel as a nation in covenant—a covenant comprised of a symbiotic relationship between Yahweh, the nation, and the land. Whatever existence continues, it is discontinuous with the past.

---

105. The clearest examples are 30:1) נדח; cf. v. 4), 28:37; 4:27) נהג), and פוץ (4:27; 28:64; 30:3).

A second, but related, focus is to consider exile as a stage in Israel's journey. The vocabulary of exile is also the vocabulary of several important historical moments and periods. Exile, then, cannot be viewed in isolation from the past, but as the end of the nation's journey. This yields a sense of continuity, which must balance the sense of discontinuity discussed above.

These points demand that we pay close attention to the details of, and connections among, various texts. It is important to set the primary and secondary references within their broader, shared literary and theological contexts. For this reason, chapters 3 and 4 examine the themes of exile and restoration in the texts themselves and the location of these texts within the structure of the book.

Theologically, exile creates several problems that must be handled with care: the problem of history, the problem of covenant, the problem of land, the problem of human ability, and the problem of the individual. These problems are interrelated. The problem of history refers to the perceived tension found when examining factors related to the stage of exile as compared to previous stages in the journey; same factors show continuity, others show discontinuity. The problem of covenant involves the fact that exile seems to both substantiate and nullify the covenant between Yahweh and Israel. The problem of land is a subplot of the problem of covenant and raises questions about the nature of God and his word. The problem of human ability asks why the prospect of life is couched in a sentence of death. The problem of the individual deals with the concept of the remnant. Chapter 5 addresses these problems and explores what possible resolutions the theme of restoration offers them.

3

## The Texts and Contexts of Exile, Part 1

CHAPTERS 3 AND 4 build upon the examination of the Deuteronomic vocabulary for exile and restoration in chapter 2. That study confirmed the three major texts for the exile theme (4:25–31; 28:58–68; 30:1–10), but also showed that other texts contain hints and echoes of the theme. The task here is to focus on the primary texts in order to place the exile theme within its literary and theological contexts. The next chapter will focus on the secondary texts as well as a consideration of all the texts within the macrostructure of the book of Deuteronomy. The present chapter is divided into seven main parts. The first part is a prologue that surveys the relevant contents and themes in Deuteronomy 1–3. The final six sections alternate between analyses of immediate contexts and specific texts: Deuteronomy 4:1–40 functions as the context for 4:25–31; Deuteronomy 27–28, for 28:58–68; and Deuteronomy 28:69—30:20, for 30:1–10. The end of each section will provide theological considerations for the theme of exile.

### PROLOGUE: DEUTERONOMY 1-3

In chapter 1, we rehearsed the history of scholarship for Deuteronomy. The only real consensus concerning Deuteronomy 1–3 is that these chapters do not belong to the rest of the book. This view became popular at the end of the nineteenth century,[1] but Noth's paradigm shift gave a rationale for the inclusion of chapters 1–3 within the book of Deuteronomy:

---

1. It started with a suggestion by Kleinert, *Untersuchungen zur alttestamentlichen*, 6, 31, 36. It was adopted by Wellhausen and Steuernagel; Wellhausen, *Die Composition des Hexateuchs*; Steuernagel, *Der Rahmen des Deuteronomiums*; idem, *Deuteronomium und Josua*. One of the few to maintain that chaps. 1–11 were a unity was Driver, *Critical and Exegetical Commentary on Deuteronomy*, lxvii.

> One quickly finds persuasive evidence that 1:1—4:43 has nothing in common with the Deuteronomic law but is directly related to the Deuteronomistic history. From this we conclude that Deuteronomy 1-3(4) is not the introduction to the Deuteronomic law but the beginning of the Deuteronomistic historical narrative and that this narrative begins therefore at 1:1.[2]

Our stated methodology is to deal with the text in its present form and context, so we will not attempt a critique of this position.[3] Chapters 1-3 fit well the theological concerns of Deuteronomy, as will be demonstrated. We agree with Millar's assessment on chapters 1-3: "It is *here* that the journey of Israel begins . . . . Without this material, what follows scarcely makes sense."[4]

In Deuteronomy 1-3, Moses rehearses selective incidents in the wilderness years. The combination of military successes and defeats functions to identify Israel's life with God as an ongoing journey and to bring her to the place of decision on the edge of the land.[5] As we look at various episodes and highlight themes relevant for the theology of exile, we will note when the vocabulary studied in chapter 1 occurs. It should become clear that Israel's future exile and return should be considered in light of the descriptions of removal and occupation during the wilderness years.

In chapter 1, Moses recounts how Israel had previously failed to heed the command to take possession of the land. At both ends of the eleven-days' journey from Horeb to Kadesh-barnea (v. 2), the command comes with great encouragement and motivation to obey:

---

2. Noth, *Deuteuronomistic History*, 29. The vast majority of scholars have followed Noth, with only some tinkering of his conclusions. See Preuss, *Deuteronomium*, 77.

3. Noth's scheme is critiqued at least implicitly by those who find strong conceptual and rhetorical links between chaps. 1-3 and the rest of the book. The first to recognize that the literary characteristics of these chapters contain a definite theological agenda is Lohfink, "Darstellungskunst und Theologie," 105-34. This is developed more fully in Moran, "End of the Unholy War," 147-55; and Plöger, *Literarkritische, formgeschichtliche und stilkritische Untersuchungen*, 20-22. These scholars argue that old stories are retold to make theological points.

4. Millar, *Now Choose Life*, 68. Millar claims that Noth is reductionistic in his characterization of alternative views (ibid., 68 n. 3).

5. On the concepts of journey and decision in Deuteronomy, see McConville and Millar, *Time and Place*.

> See, I have set the land before you. Go in and take possession of the land that Yahweh swore to your fathers, to Abraham, to Isaac, and to Jacob, to give them and to their offspring after them. (v. 8)
>
> You have come to the hill country of the Amorites, which Yahweh our God is giving us. See, Yahweh your God has set the land before you. Go up, take possession, as Yahweh, the God of your fathers, has told you. Do not fear or be dismayed. (vv. 20–21)

The emphasis throughout the passage is that this land is a divine gift.[6] It was a central part of Yahweh's promise to the patriarchs (vv. 8, 35; cf. Gen 12:7); that he had already begun to fulfill this antecedent promise—such as the multiplication of the people (v. 11; cf. Gen 15:5; 17:2)—should have provided impetus for heeding his call. Moreover, "the God of your fathers" (vv. 11, 21) is also "our/your God";[7] his presence and assistance in the more recent past—in Egypt and in the wilderness (vv. 30–33)—underlies his repeated promise to give the land. He has given every reason for them not to fear (vv. 21, 29), but, for all this, the people refused to obey. Their initial stalling via their request for an exploration of the land appeared like wise strategy, even to Moses (v. 23). Their hearts were exposed, however, in their response to the report of the scouts;[8] instead of taking encouragement that "it is a good land that Yahweh our God is giving us" (v. 25), they focused on the size and strength of the land's inhabitants (v. 28). They also offered a twisted interpretation of Yahweh's intentions in the past and present: he executed the exodus out of hatred rather than love; now he wants to "give" Israel to the land's occupant rather than the land to Israel; and he seeks to "destroy" (Hi. שמד) his people rather than aid his people in destroying her enemies (v. 27). Moses describes such response as rebellion (v. 26), murmuring (v. 27), and a lack of faith (v. 32).

Yahweh's response is more active than descriptive. Because Israel failed to prosecute the "holy war," Yahweh institutes a series of reversals. First, instead of leading the Horeb generation into the land, only a rem-

---

6. נתן, "give," is used no fewer than six times with reference to the land (vv. 8[2x], 20, 21, 25, 29).

7. Verses 6, 10, 19, 20, 21, 25, 30, 31, 32, 41. It is interesting that Moses reverts to the simpler "Yahweh" in describing the penalty for Israel's rebellion in vv. 34–46 (vv. 34, 37, 41, 42, 43, 45[2x]).

8. A more general use of שוב occurs in 1:22, 25, when the scouts "bring back" their report after exploring the land.

nant will be allowed to enter with a later generation (vv. 35–39). Second, Moses must soon relinquish his leadership to Joshua (vv. 37–39). Third, the nation is called to head back toward Egypt on an "anti-exodus" journey (v. 40; cf. v. 7).[9] Fourth, Yahweh withdraws his presence and commands the nation *not* to wage war in the land (v. 42). Thus, the faithlessness of the people turned an immanent entry into the land into many years of restless wandering. The purpose is to show that disobedience leads to exclusion from the land: "Not one of these men of this evil generation shall see the good land that I swore to give to your fathers" (1:35).

In the final episode of chapter 1 (vv. 41–45), Israel showed that the one thing that had not changed was her stubborn heart (and ears). Though Israel confesses her sin and commits herself to follow God's word in waging war (v. 41), it seems she falls short of a full change of heart. There are initial hints: Israel claims, "We *ourselves*[10] will go up and fight" (v. 41); and she "deemed it easy" to execute the war (v. 42). But it becomes crystal clear when she refuses to listen to Yahweh's command, which is based on the lack of his presence: "for I am not in your midst" (v. 42). The result was that the Amorites "chased" (רדף) them away (v. 44), causing them to "return" (שוב) and weep before Yahweh (v. 45). The defeat is attributed to the recalcitrance of the people; Moses rebukes them for not listening, for rebelling against God's command, and for acting presumptuously (v. 43). Yahweh's refusal to respond to the people (v. 45) implies that their weeping was mere whining rather than cries from a repentant heart.

In chapters 2–3, Moses recalls the positive moments in the wilderness that "describe the journey that was necessary to bring Israel back to the place where it all went wrong."[11] Moses is virtually silent about the thirty-eight years following the events of chapter 1, stating only that the people set out in a southeasterly direction and traveled around Mount Seir (2:1),[12] and that the entire Horeb generation had perished

---

9. On the anti-exodus theme, see n. 3 above.
10. This reading interprets the pronoun אֲנַחְנוּ emphatically.
11. Millar, "Chapters 1–3—Introduction of the Journey," in *Time and Place*, 27.
12. I follow Christensen, *Deuteronomy 1—21:9*, 33–34, who takes the notices to Kadesh-barnea in 1:46 and Mount Seir in 2:1 as parallel references to the same period of time and the same general region (cf. 2:14), against Tigay, *Deuteronomy*, 22, who argues that the stay at Kadesh (1:46) was no more than a few months.

(2:14–16).¹³ He does, however, offer a brief, theocentric interpretation of this time period, which balances the reminder that the generation perished with a note of divine care:

> For Yahweh your God has blessed you in all the work of your hands. He knows your going through this great wilderness. These forty years Yahweh your God has been with you. You have lacked nothing. (2:7)

Whether or not Israel would have shared this assessment, she perhaps had learned something of the necessity of divine sponsorship. Yahweh, at least, thought it was time to move them (2:2), as he had at Horeb (1:6). It is the motif of being "on the move" towards the land in chapters 2–3 that signals an obedient people.¹⁴ With a new generation, Israel is given a second chance to make the right decision.

In the first part of chapter 2, Israel's renewed journey begins with some irony.¹⁵ The lens is broadened as Israel's activity is viewed in the larger context of Yahweh's involvement with other nations with whom past promises had been made. He has given other lands to the descendants of Lot—namely, Seir (v. 5), Moab (v. 9), and Ammon (v. 19). Therefore, Israel is commanded not to contend with these peoples. Parenthetical details describe how these other peoples replaced the former occupants in each location (vv. 12, 21, 22, 23).¹⁶ The formula employed is as follows: X "destroyed" (Hi. שמד) and "dispossessed" Y and "settled" in their place.¹⁷ That Yahweh is the ultimate agent of these actions is clear from the introductory note that he himself has "given" these lands to Lot's descendants "for a possession" (vv. 5, 9, 19), and specifically using Yahweh as the subject of שמד in two references (vv. 21, 22). Ironically, Israel initially failed where other nations succeeded. God had become Israel's enemy in chapter 1; in chapter 2, God is a friend

---

13. Perhaps significant, in 2:14–16 the words for "perish" (תמם; vv. 14, 15, 16) and "destroy" (חמם; v. 15) are not אבד and שמד.

14. For the contrast between the static situation of chap. 1 and the beginning of chap. 2 and the journey language in chaps. 2–3 ("sets out," "moves on," "turns back," "crosses over"), see McConville and Millar, *Time and Place*, 27; Millar, *Now Choose Life*, 71–72.

15. See Olson, *Deuteronomy and the Death of Moses*, 27–29; cf. McConville and Millar, *Time and Place*, 72.

16. For a discussion of the identity and origin of the Caphtorim in v. 23, see the literature cited in Craigie, *Book of Deuteronomy*, 113 n. 10.

17. ירש, "possess, dispossess," is absent in v. 23.

and ally to other peoples. This section urges Israel to consider herself in broader scope, not only because Yahweh is the Creator of all, but also because Israel's ultimate mission is for the sake of the world.[18]

In 2:26—3:22, Moses describes the defeat of two Amorite kings, Sihon and Og, and the subsequent occupation of their lands. Four points are emphasized. First, from the beginning to the end, Yahweh was at work and in charge. He hardened Sihon's heart (2:30); he issued the command (2:31; 3:2); he encouraged Israel to not fear (3:2); and he "gave" these kings and their lands into Israel's hands.[19] Second, Israel demonstrated meticulous obedience to Yahweh's command (2:33-37; 3:3-8). Moses notes that there were no survivors (2:34; 3:3), for every city was devoted to destruction (Hi. חרם; 2:34; 3:6); but the people were mindful not to encroach on the land of Ammon, which Yahweh had forbidden (2:37). Third, Israel must maintain a sense of corporate solidarity despite the reality of inner distinctions. The tribes who were apportioned the land in Transjordan must assist their "brothers" (3:18, 20) in occupying their land (3:18-20); only then can they "return" (שוב) to their possession (3:20). This inter-generational unity is only part of the much larger reality that, from the patriarchs on, Israel is essentially one. Though the "fathers" are not explicitly mentioned here, the antecedent promise underlies the phrases "sons of Israel" (3:18) and "the land that Yahweh your God gives" (3:20) and the theme of Yahweh giving rest (3:20). Fourth, the occupation of Transjordan should serve as a prelude to and a blueprint for success in the conquest proper. Moses encourages Joshua,

> Your eyes have seen all that Yahweh your God has done to these two kings. So will Yahweh do to all the kingdoms into which you are crossing. You shall not fear them, for it is Yahweh your God who fights for you. (3:21-22)

---

18. Cf. Olson, *Deuteronomy and the Death of Moses*, 28: Deut 2 "reminds the community of God that it exists for the sake of the larger community and in fact depends on it." This point will be reinforced in Deut 4:5-8.

19. With Yahweh (or equivalent) as subject, נתן is used with respect to Sihon and Og and their lands in 2:30, 31, 33, 36; 3:2, 3, 18, 19, 20. Moses (literally, "I") is the subject of נתן only when he describes the apportionment of the lands (already given fundamentally by Yahweh) to the Reubenites, Gadites, and the half-tribe of Manasseh (3:12, 13, 15).

In other words, the immediate past holds the key to enjoyment of the covenant relationship in the future.[20] The main lesson in this section is that Israel—all Israel—is to act only on the command and in the strength of her God. In so doing, success is guaranteed.

The optimism of chapters 2-3 is tempered by Yahweh's refusal of Moses' request to enter the land (3:23-29).[21] As promised, only Caleb and Joshua would escape the judgment of the rebellious generation (1:36-38; 3:28; cf. Num 14:30). Ironically, Moses seems to indict the present generation for his failure to enter the land: "Even with me Yahweh was angry *on your account* and said, 'You shall not go in there'" (1:37); "But Yahweh was angry with me *because of you* and would not listen to me" (3:26).[22] Whatever else may be said of this, Moses' exclusion due to the people's disobedience shows that the decision of Kadesh is yet to be reversed. This sets the stage for Moses' exhortation in chapter 4.

### Theological Considerations

Several themes from Deuteronomy 1-3 must be taken into account as we consider the theme of exile in the rest of the book. First, Israel is continually depicted as being on a journey. The major stopping points have included Horeb, Kadesh, and Moab. Though Israel is about to enter the land, her journey continues: "The journey to the land becomes a model for ongoing life in the land."[23] In other words, Israel's history shows that, to be faithful, she must always be "on the move," submitting to Yahweh's initiative (cf. 2:2) and acknowledging the need for his presence and sustenance (cf. 2:7). That Israel's journey will eventually include exile and return implies, then, that Israel would forget and then relearn this lesson and posture. The wilderness experience, therefore, serves as a basic example of how land can be lost and gained.

Second, Yahweh has been described in chapters 1-3 as very involved in and concerned with human affairs. His voice issues law (נתן;

---

20. Millar, *Now Choose Life*, 73.

21. See Olson, *Deuteronomy and the Death of Moses*, 28-29.

22. Cf. 4:21-22: "Furthermore, Yahweh was angry with me *because of you*, and he swore that I should not cross the Jordan, and that I should not enter the good land that Yahweh your God is giving you for an inheritance. For I must die in this land; I must not go over the Jordan. But you shall go over and take possession of that good land."

23. Millar, *Now Choose Life*, 76.

1:3), speaks (Pi. דבר; אמר),²⁴ commands (Pi. צוה; 1:19, 41; 2:37), swears (Ni. שבע; 1:8, 34, 35; 2:14), promises (Pi. דבר), and blesses (Pi. ברך; 2:7). His presence with his people is demonstrated as he goes before them (הלך; 1:30, 33), fights for them (Ni. לחם; 1:30; 3:22), carries them (נשא; 1:31), and hears them (שמע; 1:34). In fulfilling his promises, he gives land to Israel and others (נתן),²⁵ multiplies his people (Hi. רבה; 1:10), and gives them rest (נתן; 3:20). In judgment, he defeats kings (Hi. נכה; 1:4), and gives them to Israel (נתן; 2:30, 31, 33; 3:2, 3); destroys nations (Hi. שמד; 2:21, 22; cf. 1:27), including Israel (המם; 2:15); becomes angry (קצף in 1:34; Hith. אנף in 1:37; Hith. עבר in 3:26); and refuses to listen (שמע in 1:45; 3:26; Hi. און in 1:45). His power extends to operating on human hearts: he puts fear and dread into Israel's neighbors (נתן; 2:25); he hardens (Hi. קשׁה) Sihon's spirit and makes obstinate (Pi. אמץ) his heart (2:30). Israel should expect that Yahweh's nature and heart will continue to be on display in the future. The thought that "all that Yahweh your God has done . . . thus will Yahweh do" (3:21) could serve as a great encouragement in the face of foreign kingdoms, but the concept of exile turns this promise into an ominous threat from the sovereign suzerain.

Third, the wilderness experience shows that "land" takes on heightened significance for Israel. Though "land" is indeed turf, it also has become a rubric for "life" itself. Israel's identity and health depend on her possession of land; the gift of land is the gift of rest (3:20), but denial or loss of land means destruction and death (see 1:35; 2:14-16). This suggests that exile, the ultimate loss of land, should be interpreted as the ultimate death for Israel. In anticipation of the use of destruction terminology for exile later (as we have shown in chapter 1), it is noteworthy that שמד, "destroy, annihilate," was used in parallel with the dispossession of land (2:12, 21, 22, 23).

Fourth, Israel was repeatedly called to understand her intergenerational and trans-generational unity. Thus, the fate of a given generation rose or fell together (see 1:35; 3:18-20), though there were exceptions (1:36-39). The greater emphasis was on the coalescence between past Israel and present Israel. This explains the repeated references to the "fathers" and allusions to the patriarchal promise, and helps clarify why Moses at times seems to speak anachronistically (e.g., the identity of

---

24. דבר in 1:6, 21, 43; 2:1, 17; אמר in 1:29, 42; 2:2, 9, 31; 3:2, 26.

25. Concerning land in Transjordan: 1:8[2x], 20, 21, 25, 36, 39; 2:12, 29; 3:20; concerning land in Cisjordan: 2:5, 9, 19, 24, 31, 36 (cities); 3:2, 18, 20.

"you" in 1:37; 3:26). Given all this, the present generation should be quite concerned with the threat of a future exile. No matter which generation would receive immediate impact, ultimately the identity and mission of all Israel is at stake.

Two major questions still remain, however. One, if Israel is Israel, will the nation as a whole ever be able to obey Yahweh in the long run?[26] Though the nation showed promise in the conquests of Sihon and Og (2:26—3:22), it is provocative that these episodes are bracketed by negative memories (1:19-46; 3:23-29). This anticipates the question of why Moses would predict exile when the nation has not even entered the land. And if Israel does prove in any way unable, why would a future return to the land fare any better? Two, what is the relationship between the various covenants Yahweh has made—and is making—with Israel? Particularly, it is not clear in chapters 1–3 how Horeb corresponds with the patriarchal covenant; whatever Moses is doing at Moab in "expounding this Torah" (1:5), he chooses to bring these two alongside each other. Moab does appear to be construed as a re-actualization of past moments. It parallels Kadesh as a place of decision on the edge of the land; as a place of giving law and making or renewing covenant, it functions as a new Horeb. This "new" covenant does not replace the "old" one; rather, Moab takes Horeb as its foundation and adds application and nuance that are needed for a new context (i.e., life in the land). Whether this sense of progression clarifies or exacerbates the confused relationship between the patriarchal covenant and Horeb remains to be seen.

## FIRST CONTEXT: DEUTERONOMY 4:1–40

While Deuteronomy 4 is a significant text with respect to the exile theme in particular, it is also a crucial part of the whole book.[27] The chapter both anticipates and summarizes the scope and themes of the book; it is "the theological heart of Deuteronomy."[28] Unfortunately, the theological

---

26. I say "the nation as a whole" because Caleb (and, implicitly, Joshua) is singled out for having "wholly followed Yahweh" (1:36). This raises a further question of the relationship between the individual Israelite and corporate Israel: why was Caleb able to be faithful amidst an evil generation? We will see that the concept of individualism is a concern in Deuteronomy.

27. By "Deuteronomy 4" we are speaking only of vv. 1–40 (v. 40 ends Moses' speech). On the widely accepted delimitation of vv. 1–40 from vv. 41–49, see Braulik, "Review of Mittmann," 351–78; Holter, *Deuteronomy 4 and the Second Commandment*, 2 n. 1; 6–13.

28. Tigay, *Deuteronomy*, 41, who is referring to the fundamental precepts of mono-

grandeur of the chapter has too often been overshadowed by literary-critical conundrums.²⁹ Therefore, we will begin this section with a brief review of some points of debate. Then, an examination of the chapter itself will follow.

## History of Interpretation

In chapter 1 we detailed the history of interpretation for Deuteronomy. No portion of the book has been more scrutinized and debated in recent years than chapter 4.³⁰ The discussion concerns three central issues: the relationship of chapter 4 to chapters 1–3 and 5–11; the date of chapter 4; and the literary coherence of chapter 4.

The first two issues are interrelated. Before Noth, commentators were uncertain as to whether chapter 4 functions as a conclusion to chapters 1–3 or an introduction to chapters 5–11. While Noth included it as part of the "outer frame" (with chaps. 1–3, 31–34) that he considered to be the introduction to the Deuteronomistic History, he also was uncertain and called chapter 4 a "special case."³¹ It seems that Noth's decision (albeit tentative) was driven less by stylistic and thematic issues and more by a prior decision that chapter 4 belongs to the latest strata in the redactional history of the book.

The relative late date and insertion of chapter 4 is now assumed by almost all critical scholars.³² The mention of exile and restoration in 4:25–31 presupposes, for many, an exilic (or postexilic) setting.³³ Others

---

theism and the prohibition of idolatry; cf. McConville, *Deuteronomy*, 102. McConville and Millar (*Time and Place*, 49) go even further: "When the theological coherence of the text is uncovered, it appears that this chapter can lay a substantial claim to being the hermeneutical key to Deuteronomic theology as displayed in the book as a whole."

29. Cf. McConville and Millar, *Time and Place*, 32: "Chapter 4 is probably the most complex chapter in the whole book of Deuteronomy. It is laden with theological meaning, though critical problems have hindered every attempt to interpret the text."

30. The research history of chap. 4 has been well rehearsed. See Begg, "Literary Criticism," 10–55; Knapp, *Deuteronomium 4*, 3–20; and Mayes, "Deuteronomy 4," 23–51. For a more recent, but briefer, article on literary critical studies of chap. 4, see Holter, "Literary Critical Studies of Deut 4," 95–98.

31. Noth, *Deuteronomistic History*, 14. Noth's uncertainty is shown in putting the number "4" in parentheses as he refers to the unit: "Deut 1–3(4)"; see *Deuteronomistic History*, 13–14, 27–29, 38–39.

32. Mayes, "Deuteronomy 4," 35.

33. See references in Begg, "Literary Criticism," 12. In a broader scope, the (post)exilic dating of chap. 4 is also due to its supposed association with a stream of

point to the developed monotheism and divine transcendence.[34] With an exilic *Sitz im Leben*, the impetus for its inclusion would be to address the question of obeying the law in Babylon given the destruction of the temple. God's presence is relocated in heaven, and wisdom replaces the law as the key to obedience. Millar summarizes the critical stance:

> Chapter 4 then functions as a hermeneutical key for the rest of the book in its final Deuteronomistic form. A fresh interpretation of the Horeb theophany enables a redefinition of Yahweh's covenant demands in terms of exclusive worship in a pluralistic environment, preaching the *Hauptgebot* to the exile.[35]

Scholars continue to debate the literary coherence of the chapter.[36] Proponents of the non-unitary view have traditionally emphasized the so-called *Numeruswechsel*—the frequent change between second-person singular and second-person plural.[37] The change in number is taken as evidence of various redactional hands and layers. However, some of the more recent proponents of the composite view downplay the criterion of the *Numeruswechsel* and focus more on thematic changes in the text.[38] Scholars who argue for the unity of authorship base their case on the language, form, and content of chapter 4.[39] They contend that the

---

Deuteronomistic redaction (including Deut 30:1–10; 1 Kgs 8:46–53; Jeremiah's new-covenant theology) and similar thematic connections with Isa 40–55. See Wolff, "Kerygma," 83–100.

34. See, e.g., Moshe Weinfeld (*Deuteronomy 1–11*, 212), who claims that absolute monotheism is of late (exilic) origin (he references Deut 4:35, 39; 7:9; 10:17; Isa 45:5, 6, 14, 18, 21, 22; 46:9; 1 Kgs 8:60; Joel 2:27). For a critique of the position that Yahweh is not really present, see Wilson, *Out of the Midst of the Fire*, esp. 45–53.

35. In McConville and Millar, *Time and Place*, 34. Millar goes on to critique this stance. Specifically, he argues that presence in chap. 4 is dependent on the concept of presence associated with the Exodus/Wilderness traditions in chaps. 1–3 "in contrast to the capricious Canaanite deities tied to their sanctuaries, rather than a firmly developed temple ideology" (p. 35). Cf. Millar, *Now Choose Life*, 73.

36. For a full discussion, see Begg, "Literary Criticism"; Mayes, "Deuteronomy 4," 23–51.

37. Major changes occur in vv. 3–4, 19–20, 21–22, 23–26, 34–35. For the relatively recent promotion of this criterion see Cazelles, "Passages in the Singular," 213–14 (which is an extension of the study on chaps. 5–11 by Tillesse, "Sections," 29–87); Mittmann, *Deuteronomium 1:1—6:3*, 1–6, 15–28.

38. Most notably, Knapp, *Deuteronomium 4*, 21–25, 112–14, 205–6. See also Begg, "Literary Criticism," 23–27, 55, who considers the change in number to be a literary-critical indication only in v. 29.

39. The unity view is best represented by Braulik, *Die Mittel*, esp. 91–100, 146–49;

change in number represents stylistic concerns, including the desire to mimic earlier Deuteronomic–Deuteronomistic texts and/or show a shift of emphasis between a more collective and more individual view of the audience.[40] Despite all the ink spilled in the debate, it is relativized by the fact that most concede the conceptual unity of the chapter.[41]

While our stated methodology is to deal with the text in its present form and context, this brief summary of some of the major issues particularly related to Deuteronomy 4 highlights the need to give due attention to this chapter for understanding the book as a whole. As we shall see, even from a rhetorical standpoint, chapter 4 is a "special case." Formally, Deuteronomy 1–4 constitutes Moses' first discourse; however, chapter 4 is markedly different in style and tone from the preceding chapters,[42] and introduces themes that occupy chapters 5–11 and the rest of the book.[43] Thus, chapter 4 clearly marks a transition—even a

---

Lohfink, "Auslegung deuteronomischer Texte," 247–56; and Mayes, "Deuteronomy 4." The recognition of an inclusio with vv. 1–8 and 32–40 strengthens this position (see on vv. 32–40 below). Unity of authorship is also argued by the prosodic analysis of Christensen, *Deuteronomy 1—21:9*, 73.

40. For critiques of using *Numerweschel* as a criterion, see Braulik, *Die Mittel*, 146–49; Levenson, "Who Inserted the Book of the Torah?" 204–7; Lohfink, *Das Hauptgebot*, 30–31, 239–58. Christensen ("*Excursus:* The Numeruswechsel in Deuteronomy," in *Deuteronomy 1—21:9*, xcix–ci) contends that most of the instances of the *Numeruswechsel* in the book function as structural markers—usually boundaries between rhythmic units of a text, or sometimes indicating the center or turning point within a structure. McConville ("Singular Address in the Deuteronomic Law," 19–36) argues that Deuteronomy adapts the use of the singular address in the laws to support its theology of responsibility of the people as such for the keeping of Torah (in contrast to the ANE idea of the king as sovereign).

41. For example, though Holter takes a principally diachronic approach, he still concludes that "Deut 4 simply justifies being approached as a literary unity" (*Deuteronomy 4 and the Second Commandment*, 10).

42. Tigay, *Deuteronomy*, 40, notes two differences: (1) while chap. 4 is historical (like chaps. 1–3), it is not narrated consecutively; and (2) the object of obedience shifts from military directives (chaps. 1–3) to permanent laws (chap. 4). On the change of narrative technique, Polzin (*Moses and the Deuteronomist*, 40) remarks, "Chapter 4 stands off from the first three chapters not only by its references to future rather than past events and utterances, but also by the fact that its reported speech is predominantly in indirect discourse, whereas the reported speech in chaps. 1–3 was overwhelmingly in direct discourse." Weinfeld (*Deuteronomy 1–11*, 214) adds "Unlike Deut. 1–3, which uses past events and historical facts in order to educate the people, this chapter uses, for the same purpose, religious ideology on the one hand and rhetorical media on the other."

43. Tigay, *Deuteronomy*, 40, views chap. 4 as a "précis" of chaps. 5–11, and that together, "chapters 4 and 5–11 present the historical experiences that establish the va-

pause—in the flow of the book (see below on 4:1). We will return to the place of Deuteronomy 4 within the whole book in chapter 4 of the present study.

### Text

Deuteronomy 4 is concerned with Israel's response to Yahweh, both before and after the entry into the land. With great urgency and passion, Moses sets before the nation the revelation of God in order to motivate them to faithful obedience. Within the flow of the book, chapter 4 interprets the past story (chaps. 1–3) for the sake of the future.[44] The opening ועתה, "and now," signals this transition to application.[45] The call to obedience in chapter 4, then, should be seen as the implication of past history and the necessity for future life.[46] We will summarize the main themes of the chapter to provide a sense of the immediate context for exile in verses 25–31.

Scholars have divided 4:1–40 into subunits in various ways, as Table 4 exemplifies.[47] The subunits tend to be grouped together to form

---

lidity of the laws and the attitudes that are basic to their observance, and they appeal for obedience to the laws."

44. See Block, *Gospel according to Moses*, 128–29. Block notes that the transition is both physical (move to the other side of the Jordan) and thematic (introducing many of the theological issues that are of major concern in subsequent chapters).

45. Cf. Deut 10:12; Gen 3:22; 21:23; Judg 9:16; 10:23, 25; 1 Sam 12:13. See Tigay, *Deuteronomy*, 351 n. 14; Weinfeld, *Deuteronomy 1–11*, 199. Tigay (*Deuteronomy*, 42) identifies several thematic and verbal links between chaps. 1–3 and chap. 4: Beth-peor (3:29) and Ball-peor (4:3); basis of "seeing/not seeing" throughout chap. 4 echoes 1:19, 30–31, 35–36; 3:21, 25, 27, 28; rhetorical questions of God's uniqueness in 4:6–7, 32–39 is echoed in 3:24; God's anger with Moses and refusal to let him enter the land (3:26–27; 4:21–22); the Hebrew of "do not add . . . command you" (4:2) is similar to "never speak . . . again" (3:26); and "the land . . . occupy" (4:14, 26) echoes Moses' request (3:25; cf. vv. 27, 28 and 4:21–22).

46. Miller, *Deuteronomy*, 53.

47. The table is adapted from the table in Christensen, *Deuteronomy 1—21:9*, 75, which is an expansion from Labuschagne, *Deuteronomium*, 227. Other outlines could be added: Block (*Gospel according to Moses*, 130) finds three major units (vv. 1–8, 9–31, 32–40); Knapp (*Deuteronomium 4*, 112–14) finds three major units, each enlarged by a later hand: vv. 1–14 (1–4 + 9–14, enlarged by 5–8); vv. 15–28 (15–16a + 19–28), enlarged by 16b–28); vv. 29–40 (29–35, enlarged by 36–40); McConville (*Deuteronomy*, 101–2) finds five units (vv. 1–8, 9–14, 15–24, 25–31, 32–40); Miller (*Deuteronomy*, 54–63) finds 3 units (vv. 1–8, 9–31, 32–40) ; Nielsen (*Deuteronomium*, 54–68) finds three units, each reflecting various layers (vv. 1–8, 9–24, 25–40) ; Tigay (*Deuteronomy*, 41) finds four units (vv. 1–4, 5–8, 9–31, 32–40) ; Weinfeld (*Deuteronomy 1–11*, 199–214)

larger units as well. For our purposes, it seems best to consider the appeal to obedience in chapter 4 as it is developed in four major units: verses 1–4, 5–8, 9–31, 32–40. Along with many common thematic and verbal features,[48] each unit opens with an appeal to the mind—"hear" (v. 1), "see" (v. 5), "do not forget" (v. 9), and "inquire" (v. 32)—and offers several types of motivation for obedience.

Table 4. Division of Deuteronomy 4.

|  | Steuernagel | Krämer | Ridderbos | **Lohfink** | Braulik | Labuschagne | Christensen |
|---|---|---|---|---|---|---|---|
|  | 1–4 | 1–8 | 1–8 | 1–4 | 1–4 | 1–4 | 1–4 |
|  | 5–8 |  |  | 5–8 | 5–8 | 5–8 | 5–8 |
|  | 9–14 | 9–14 | 9–14 | 9–14 | 9–14 | 9–10 | 9–10 |
|  |  |  |  |  |  | 11–14 | 11–14 |
|  | 15–20 | 15–24 | 15–24 | 15–22 | 15–22 | 15–19 | 15–18 |
|  |  |  |  |  |  |  | 19 |
|  | 21–24 |  |  | 23–24 |  | 20–24 | 20–22a |
|  |  |  |  |  |  |  | 22b–24 |
| Exile | 25–28 | 25–28 | 25–28 | 25–31 | 23–31 | 25–28 | 25–28 |
| Restoration | 29–31 | 29–31 | 29–31 |  |  | 29–31 | 29–31 |
|  | 32–40 | 32–40 | 32–35 | 32–40 | 32–40 | 32–35 | 32–34 |
|  |  |  | 36–40 |  |  | 36–40 | 35–38 |
|  |  |  |  |  |  |  | 39–40 |

### Deuteronomy 4:1-4

Moses' call to obedience in verses 1–4 introduces a shift in focus from the preceding chapters. In particular, the object of obedience is no longer military orders but והמשפטים החקים, "the statutes and judgments" (v. 1; also vv. 5, 8, 14, 45).[49] There is some ambiguity as to the precise meaning of the phrase here,[50] though it seems flexible enough to refer both gener-

---

finds six units (vv. 1–4, 5–8, 9–14, 15–22, 23–31, 32–40).

48. Tigay, *Deuteronomy*, 41–42, notes the following repeated features in chap. 4: (1) the linking of laws taught/commanded and the land (vv. 1, 5, 14, 21, 26, 40); (2) argument based on history; (3) seeing and hearing—what Israel saw/did not see with her own eyes (vv. 3, 9, 12, 15, 34–36); the impression observance will make in the eyes of the nations (v. 6; cf. vv. 5, 19, 28); hearing (vv. 1, 6, 10, 12, 28, 30, 32, 33, 36); (4) teaching and learning (למד in vv. 1, 5, 10, 14); (5) knowing and making known (ידע in vv. 9, 35, 39); and (6) forgetting (vv. 9, 23, 31). The repetition of these features reflects the sermonic, didactic character of Deuteronomy as a whole.

49. Other crucial references of this phrase include 5:1, 31; 6:1, 20; 7:11; 11:32; 12:1; 26:16–18. Several of these indicate points of transition; cf. McConville, *Deuteronomy*, 103.

50. A lot has been written on the phrase. For a brief summary and discussion see McConville and Millar, *Time and Place*, 38–40; Millar, *Now Choose Life*, 36–40. Millar

ally to Moses' whole preaching in Deuteronomy 4–30 (esp. chaps. 5–26) and more specifically to the Decalogue. What is clear is the immediacy and urgency of the present decision to obey ("hear" and "do" in v. 1), especially noted by the emphasis on "now" (v. 1) and "today" (vv. 4, 8).[51]

Three motivations can be delineated in this initial appeal. One is that strict adherence to Moses' teaching will result in entry into the land (v. 1). What had been the initial command itself (1:8, 21; cf. 2:31) now becomes the purpose or result of obedience to God's laws. The fact that this is juxtaposed with the description of the land as that which "Yahweh, the God of your fathers, is giving you" (v. 1) shows the interdependence of gift and duty. A second motivation is based on a past experience. Israel is called to remember the incident at Baal-peor in which Yahweh "destroyed" (Hi. שׁמד) idolaters from among the people (v. 3), but spared those "who clung to Yahweh" (v. 4). This should remind Israel that Yahweh is not a God to be trifled with, and that, in spite of the introduction of laws, loyalty to Yahweh himself remains the focus. As the rest of chapter 4 will show, idolatry—technically, the violation of the First and Second Commandments[52]—is the root sin behind any disobedience. This incident also reveals that, though Israel is usually consid-

---

thinks the prominence of the phrase in chap. 4 makes it probable that the intention of the chapter is to introduce the idea of החקים והמשׁפטים in order to begin to provide the content of the decision facing Israel in the present.

51. The powerful repetition of "today" plays a key role in Deuteronomy. On its recurrence, von Rad (*Deuteronomy*, 26) notes, "It is the common denominator of the Deuteronomic homiletic as a whole . . . .It cannot be maintained that this is merely an effective stylistic device which the Deuteronomist has chosen to make more vivid what he has to say. On the contrary, it is a quite fundamental feature of Deuteronomy."

52. For convenience, I am using the standard numeration in the literature, which follows the Reformed list of the Decalogue. I actually think it is difficult to separate the First and Second Commandments (which would support the Catholic/Lutheran list). Deut 4:28 is a clear example, which makes אלהים, "gods," (from the First Commandment in 5:7) the object of עבד, "serve," (from the Second Commandment in 5:9) rather than "carved images" or the like. Miller (*Deuteronomy*, 58) notes the close tie of the prologue and first two commandments of the Decalogue: the prologue is echoed in v. 20; the First Commandment in v. 19; the Second Commandment in references to graven image (vv. 16, 23), what is on earth (v. 17), what is in heavens (v. 19), bowing down (v. 10), and jealous God (v. 24). The Deuteronomic version of the Decalogue particularly seems to view the prohibition of images as an interpretation or expansion of 5:7, "You shall have no other gods before me," which was noted and popularized in Zimmerli, "Das Zweite Gebot," 234–48. See Block, *Gospel According to Moses*, 250–52; Holter, *Deuteronomy 4 and the Second Commandment*, 72–77 (74 n. 164 lists scholars who follow Zimmerli); Olson, *Deuteronomy and the Death of Moses*, 43.

ered as a whole, Yahweh is able to distinguish between individuals. The third motivation arises in the emphasis on life and death. Moses begins his appeal with, "Israel, hear the statutes and judgments ... that you may live" (v.1), and ends this section with describing the faithful as "alive" (v. 4). The alternative is death, as witnessed in the immediate context with the account of Baal-peor (v. 3), but also with the preceding prediction of Moses' death and exclusion from the land (3:23–26). By couching land entry in terms of life and death, Moses is seeking to make Israel realize that immediate and uncompromising obedience is absolutely critical.

Deuteronomy 4:5–8

The appeal in verses 5–8 begins with "see" (cf. "hear" in v. 1), perhaps because Moses now looks forward to life in the land. In verse 5, he emphasizes that the reason for having taught the people the statutes and judgments was that they would be obeyed after they enter and occupy the land. Coming on the heels of verse 1, where obedience would result in entering the land, we may detect a presumption of continuity: what got them there will keep them there.[53] As we noted in the discussion of the victories in Transjordan, Israel must never rest on prior obedience. The blessings of the past—whether at Horeb, in Moab, or in the land of promise—are always contingent on the actions of the ever-present "today" (cf. v. 8).

The motivation to obedience in this section focuses on the nature of Yahweh, Israel, and the law when considered in an international context (vv. 6–8). If Israel keeps the law, she will be considered by other peoples to be "wise and understanding" (v. 7), an epithet with which Moses (and, thus, Yahweh) would agree (v. 6). The law itself will be recognized as "righteous" (v. 8). Perhaps above all, the nations will recognize something of the uniqueness of Yahweh. Particularly, they will marvel at his presence among his people: "a god so near ... as Yahweh our God" (v. 7). Interestingly, it is not the law itself that is the stated locus of divine presence (however true this may be); keeping the law is merely the means by which the nations realize that Israel's God is present "whenever we call

---

53. Mayes ("Exposition of Deuteronomy 4:25–31," 71) contends that the themes of obedience as condition for land entry and obedience in the land are not "two quite different views; basic to both is that obedience to the law of God is necessary for life (see 4:4), but 'life' for Israel usually means living in the land (see 4:26, 40)."

upon him" (v. 7).[54] Thus, the law is subsumed under the larger and more fundamental reality of covenant (embodied in worship and prayer), and not simply to be equated with it. Given the international context—both the existence of law codes that boast of "just laws"[55] and the absence of covenants between gods and nations—a clear polemic is introduced here. Israel, then, should obey because nothing less than the glory of Yahweh is at stake. Having God's presence and having God's word rather than size and strength will comprise her being a "great" nation (v. 6).[56]

## Deuteronomy 4:9–31

The emphases shift in the core of the chapter (vv. 9–31) as the paranesis becomes a meditation on the events of Horeb, with a narrowing focus on the Second Commandment's prohibition of images. While Horeb is dominant, Moses also alludes to other historical contexts, including creation (vv. 16–19), the division of the nations (v. 19), the patriarchal covenant (v. 31; cf. v 21), the exodus (v. 20), the wilderness (v. 21), and future exile and return (vv. 25–31). This combination of various events of the past reinforces the historical continuities (and discontinuities) in which Israel must consider herself. The oneness of Israel, as we shall see, is predicated upon the oneness of God: "the oneness of God implies a consistency in the way in which God's people experience life under

---

54. Against Miller, *Deuteronomy*, 56, who focuses only on the idea that God draws near in his law. Ironically, Miller states this in the context of countering the normal understanding that the ark (see 10:1–5) assumes the absence of God: "If the law in some way embodies the presence and nearness of God, then the ark continues to function in some fashion as the vehicle for God's presence in the midst of the people." While I share Miller's rejection of the majority view on divine presence in Deuteronomy, identifying God's presence with his law *alone* could still be used to deny an ontological presence of Yahweh with his people.

55. Most notably the Code of Hammurabi (CH 1:30–31; 4:9–10; 24:1–5, 26–31). See McConville, *Deuteronomy*, 104–5; Weinfeld, *Deuteronomy 1–11*, 202. McConville adds that the anti-Canaanite polemic implicit here is consistent with the program of Deut 16:18—18:22 that downplays the role of the king in Israel's constitution.

56. Cf. 7:6–8, wherein Moses capitalizes on Israel's smallness to magnify the grace and power of Yahweh in choosing Israel and redeeming her from Egypt. Weinfeld (*Deuteronomy 1–11*, 202) is mistaken to consider this idea of "greatness" to be at odds with texts that do signal the increase of numbers (Gen 12:2; 17:5–6; etc.). He claims that Deut 26:5—"he became [in Egypt] a nation, great, mighty, and populous—draws on the "old tradition" of Exodus 1, as if Deut 4:6 (and 7:7) is a newer and different tradition. The point of 4:6 and like texts is to highlight the uniqueness of the relationship between Yahweh and Israel *as witnessed by others*. There is no claim in these texts that Israel would remain insignificant and in more normal ways.

this one God."⁵⁷ Also, the appeal to obedience becomes personalized; whereas before the people are to "keep" (שמר) the commandments (vv. 2, 6; cf. v. 40), now they are to "keep" (i.e. guard, watch) themselves:

> Only guard (Ni. שמר) yourself and keep (שמר) your soul diligently, lest (פן) you forget the things that your eyes have seen, and lest they depart from your heart all the days of your life. (v. 9)

> Therefore guard (Ni. שמר) yourselves very carefully, since you saw no form on the day that Yahweh spoke to you at Horeb out of the midst of the fire—lest (פן) you act corruptly ... and lest (פן) you raise your eyes to heaven .... (vv. 15–16, 19)

> Guard (Ni. שמר) yourselves, lest (פן) you forget the covenant of Yahweh your God. (v. 23)

The irony is that most of the present audience had not experienced the Horeb theophany (see 1:35; 2:14).⁵⁸ With an intentional anachronism, Moses is calling Israel to what Brueggemann calls "an act of corporate imaginative remembrance."⁵⁹ Similar to the use of "today," this conflation of generations is rhetorically effective because Yahweh has chosen his word to be the manner of his presence in Israel. As McConville reflects,

> The primary speech-act of God is not left in the past as a single event, but is made present by its representation in the laws and instruction given by Moses.... The essence of the Moab covenant is to assert that the decisive encounter with God can be continuously repeated.⁶⁰

Verses 9–31 urge obedience to the prohibition of idolatry based on the nature of Israel's encounter with God at Horeb, and backed up with the threat of exile. We can subdivide this unit into four sections (vv. 9–14, 15–21, 22–23, 25–31); as listed above, the first three begin with a warning employing שמר, "keep," and פן, "lest."⁶¹ In verses 9–14, Israel is warned

---

57. Olson, *Deuteronomy and the Death of Moses*, 34.

58. Tigay, *Deuteronomy*, 46, reasons that only about a third of the audience was actually at Horeb.

59. Brueggemann, "Imagination as a Mode of Fidelity," 1. The singular "you" in vv. 9–10 may highlight the theme of generational unity.

60. McConville, *Deuteronomy*, 115–16. McConville adds that the death of Moses (4:21–22) also shows this.

61. It is clear from the previous table that scholars disagree about these divisions. Only the break after v. 14 is fairly consistent. We will argue more fully for the break

about forgetting her experience at Horeb (v. 9). Though there is mention of the Decalogue (v.13), and an allusion to the Second Commandment by the introduction of the term תמונה, "form," (v. 12; cf. 5:8), the experience itself is emphasized over the content of what God said. Moses repeatedly recalls the people's personal encounter with Yahweh:

> that your eyes have seen (v. 9)
>
> on that day that you stood before Yahweh (v. 10)
>
> you came near and stood at the foot of the mountain (v. 11)
>
> Yahweh spoke to you out of the midst of the fire (v. 12a)
>
> you heard the sound of words, but saw no form (v. 12b)
>
> he declared to you his covenant (v. 13)[62]

The description of the theophany emphasizes the mode of revelation and begins to expound upon its consequences. Though the warning begins with "lest you forget the things that your eyes have seen" (v. 9), it is also a matter of remembering what they did *not* see. What they saw was "the mountain burned with fire to the heart of heaven, wrapped in darkness, cloud, and gloom" (v. 11). What they did not see was a "form"; instead they only heard a sound of words (v. 12). The visual aspect, with the double motif of fire and cloud, highlights something of Yahweh's complex nature, for he is both transcendent and immanent.[63] Given the anti-Canaanite polemic behind verses 6–8, there is also an implication that Israel must approach Yahweh in a unique way.[64] The verbal character—which is clearly the emphasis—specifies how Israel should

---

before v. 25 below. On the frequent combination of שמד (Ni.) + פן in Deuteronomy (4:9, 23; 6:12; 8:11, 16; 12:13, 19, 30; 15:9), see Weinfeld, *Deuteronomy and the Deuteronomic School*, 357.

62. Cf. v. 15: "you saw no form on the day that Yahweh spoke to you at Horeb out of the midst of the fire."

63. As Miller (*Deuteronomy*, 59) so aptly puts it, "The Hebrew simply juxtaposes in stark fashion as if to state a vivid paradox that cannot be explained: on the one hand, bright burning fire; on the other hand, the thickest black darkness. Thus are held together, as one, hiddenness and revelation, mystery and accessibility, transcendence and immanence."

64. Cf. McConville and Millar, *Time and Place*, 45: "Yahweh is the God who is accessible but not confined, who communicates but cannot be comprehended." The key symbol of fire (7 times in chap. 4: vv. 11, 12, 15, 24, 33, 36[2x]) itself symbolizes God as being both illuminating and consuming, as one who both draws and repels.

and should not approach (i.e., worship) the God who is in her midst.⁶⁵ As at Horeb, Israel's ongoing relationship with Yahweh will be centered on things audible and written rather than visual.⁶⁶ The rest of the passage will spell out the practical implications of this in the focus on the prohibition of images (cf. vv. 15–18, 23, 25, 28). Here, there is a concern for an attitude of reverence: "so that they may learn to fear me" (v. 10). The goal of "fear" points to the necessity of having an internal posture, which corresponds to the command to "keep your *soul* diligently, lest you *forget* the things that your eyes have seen, and lest they depart from your *heart*" (v. 9).

The description also reinforces the archetypical nature of Horeb. First, by stressing the presence of the assembled nation at Horeb—though most were not actually there—we can discern a rhetorical identification between Horeb and Moab; there is no difference between the "you" at Horeb and the "you" in Moab.⁶⁷ Second, there is a distinction between the "law" of Horeb and subsequent "law" in Deuteronomy. The

---

65. The major critical position claims that Deuteronomy never speaks of God's presence on earth (cf. 4:36); see Weinfeld, *Deuteronomy and the Deuteronomic School*, 190–209; cf. Tigay, *Deuteronomy*, 36. For an excellent response, see especially Wilson, *Out of the Midst of the Fire*, 45–53. As McConville (*Deuteronomy*, 106) states, "Invisibility does not mean absence." The critical position is not able, in my opinion, to account adequately for statements in chap. 4 like "a god so near to it as Yahweh our God is to us" (v. 7); "on the day that you stood before Yahweh your God at Horeb" (v. 10); "'Gather the people to me'" (v. 10); "Yahweh spoke to you out of the midst of the fire (which blanketed the mountain)" (v. 11); "you heard his words out of the midst of the fire" (v. 36); and "Yahweh is God in heaven above and on the earth beneath" (v. 39). Accordingly, it is not accurate to view divine presence in Deuteronomy as shifting from vision to word (as is commonly done); "word and actual encounter with Yahweh belong inseparably together" (McConville, *Deuteronomy*, 107). The concept of divine presence continues to be an important theme in Deuteronomy (cf. 10:8; 12:7; 18:7; 29:14; 31:11–13).

66. As signaled by several roots employed: דבר ("things," v. 9; "spoke," v. 12; "words," vv. 12, 13); ידע ("make known," v. 9 [Hi.]); אמר ("say," v. 10); שמע ("hear," vv. 10, 12); למד ("learn," v. 10; "teach," vv. 10, 14 [Pi.]); קול ("voice," v. 12); נגד ("declare," v. 13 [Hi.]); צוא ("command," vv. 13, 14 [Pi.]); כתב ("write," v. 13).

67. McConville and Millar, *Time and Place*, 44. This fits with the retrospective focus of chaps. 1–3, which aims to confront the present generation with the binding reality of past events: "This method aims to draw the whole experience of Israel from Egypt to Horeb to Moab (via the diversions of Kadesh) into the environment of the ethical decisions facing every individual. The ethical history of a nation coalesces into the series of 'ethical moments' which constitute the life of the individual. Each Israelite in effect was present every step of the way from Egypt, and each decision should be informed by the richness of his or her tradition" (ibid.).

Decalogue is equated with Yahweh's, ברית, "covenant,"⁶⁸ and was declared by Yahweh himself (v. 13); the "statutes and judgments"—further explanation and application of the Decalogue—were to be taught by Moses (v. 14). The relevant point is that the covenant made in Moab (cf. 28:69[29:1]) should not be viewed as an altogether distinct one; Horeb, especially the Decalogue, is still the base.⁶⁹ Third, having God's word in written form (v. 13) and teaching it (v. 14; cf. v. 10) enables future generations to identify themselves with their predecessors. In sum, "The Horeb event thus becomes a model for all time of Israel's position before God, at the place of decision."⁷⁰

In verses 15–22, Moses spells out a logical consequence of the Horeb theophany: idolatry, in any form, is forbidden. In verse 15, the command of verse 9 is repeated, now grounded in the reality of verse 12: "Therefore guard yourselves very carefully, since you did not see any form on the day that Yahweh spoke to you at Horeb out of the midst of the fire." The warning involves two פן-clauses (vv. 16–18, 19) that speak of idolatry from different angles. The first warns Israel of "acting corruptly" (Hi. שחת) by violating the Second Commandment—by making a carved image in the form of any figure, including humans and animals (vv. 16–18).⁷¹ Such images would serve to represent Yahweh in a

---

68. On the meaning of ברית, see Weinfeld, "*Berit*—Covenant vs. Obligation," 120–28; cf. Tigay, *Deuteronomy*, 48. The term ברית has various meanings or nuances, including (1) promise (i.e., obligation imposed on oneself); (2) stipulation (i.e., obligation imposed on another); and (3) compact (reciprocal obligations accepted by two parties). All three meanings are operative in the formal relationship between Yahweh and Israel, though references can focus on one of these. In Deuteronomy 4, ברית is used for the Decalogue (v. 13) and the patriarchal promise (v. 31).

69. This conclusion is reinforced by the many echoes and allusions to the rest of the Sinai revelation (especially the Book of the Covenant in Exod 21–24) in Deut 12–26.

70. McConville, *Deuteronomy*, 107. Cf. McConville and Millar, *Time and Place*, 32–49.

71. Verses 16–18 follows the Second Commandment almost verbatim. Holter (*Deuteronomy and the Second Commandment*, 35–46) discusses three textual differences. The change in number (plural in 4:16f; singular in 5:8) is insignificant and easily accounted for by other factors involving the *Numeruswechsel*. The change of negation between 4:12 ("you saw no form") and 4:15 ("you did not see any form") is probably due to a contextual shift from the general (the Decalogue) to the particular (the Second Commandment). Holter considers the change in order of כל, "any," and תמונה, "form," between 4:16 ("a carved image in the form of any figure") and 5:8 ("a carved image of any form") to be significant, for it allows for chap. 4's interpretation of the prohibition to include images of non-yahwistic deities.

wholly inadequate and manipulative way. The second warns against being enticed to worship (supposed) astral deities in violation of the First Commandment (v. 19).[72] These "gods" would replace or compete with Yahweh. Both categories of objects (images of Yahweh and others) pose a threat because of their visibility, tangibility, and attractiveness.[73] But both forms of idolatry would be a rejection of Horeb, where no form was seen; even the heavenly bodies were blotted out by darkness and clouds.

The motivation for obedience in this section, however, involves a wider scope than Horeb. First, there are several echoes to creation. The use of שׁחת (Hi.), "corrupt, destroy," to describe making a carved image as "acting corruptly" in verse 16 (cf. "act corruptly" in v. 25; "destroy" in v. 31), recalls the "corruption" and subsequent "destruction" of humanity in Genesis 6:11-12, 17.[74] The word pair "male/female" (זכר/נקבה) and the four kinds of living beings in verses 16-18 are taken from Genesis 1:20-27.[75] The heavenly bodies in verse 19 are creations of God in Genesis 1:14-19. When all these are taken together, idolatry can be viewed as nothing less than an anti-creational act: instead of recognizing the sun, moon, and stars as temporal boundary markers established by God (Gen 1:16), man worships them in place of God; instead of ruling over the creatures (Gen 1:26), man makes images of the creatures and worships them as gods; instead of reflecting that man was made in the image and likeness of God (Gen 1:26-27), man makes God in his own image and likeness.[76] In short, idolatry is a rejection of God as Creator, and is worthy of his own anti-creational response.

Second, in the climax of the section, Moses recalls the exodus, reminding Israel of her special status: "But Yahweh has taken you and

---

72. This is a clear example why the First and Second Commandments ought to be considered together.

73. On the two categories, see Miller, *Deuteronomy*, 60.

74. McConville, *Deuteronomy*, 107.

75. This was cited as an example of "inner-biblical exegesis" in Fishbane, *Biblical Interpretation*, 321-22. Though the connection is ignored in some recent commentators, others have noted it: Knapp, *Deuteronomium 4*, 88-91, 112-14; Labuschagne, *Deuteronomium*, 262-66; McConville, *Deuteronomy*, 108; Otto, *Das Deuteronomium*, 168-69. For discussion and references, see Holter, *Deuteronomy 4 and the Second Commandment*, 55-63.

76. As Holter (*Deuteronomy 4 and the Second Commandment*, 70) remarks, "the making of images reflects a destruction of the triangular relationship between God, humankind, and the rest of creation. Humanity's relationship to God is destroyed.... But also humanity's relationship to the rest of creation is destroyed."

brought you out of the iron furnace, out of Egypt, to be a people of his own treasured possession, as you are this day" (v. 20). The juxtaposition of verses 19–20 shows the unique way Yahweh has treated Israel in comparison to other nations. Yahweh is sovereign over all people simply by being their Creator, but his sovereignty over Israel includes a personal attachment to them, as suggested by the use of the familial term, נחלה, "special possession."[77] The exodus is the central example that exhibits both realities: Yahweh is stronger than other peoples and their gods; and Yahweh has acquired Israel for himself. On the surface, Yahweh's allotment of the heavenly hosts to other peoples in verse 19 (cf. 32:8–9) appears to endorse non-Yahwistic religion,[78] but, in context, this is unwarranted.[79] Given the underlying polemic that we have already noted in chapter 4, as well as the anti-polytheistic polemic in Genesis 1,[80] there is an implicit criticism of pagan worship. Through the exodus experience, Israel was set apart from the rest of humanity, not simply to be free, but to be enabled to represent God in the world—to bear the image of God.[81] In order to do this effectively, her worship of Yahweh must differ from the way others worship. Idolatry, then, is a rejection of the very purpose of the exodus, which provided Israel with her special status and would invite Yahweh's own anti-exodus response.

Third, Moses' ban from the land recalls the wilderness years (vv. 21–22). At first glance, this appears to be a digression from the immediate context and has invited speculation.[82] We can compare and contrast

77. Israel as Yahweh's נחלה is most often found in the framework (e.g., 9:26, 29; 32:8–9; but 14:2), while the land as Israel's נחלה is usually found in chaps. 12–26 (e.g., 12:9; 15:4; 19:10; but 4:21, 38). See von Rad, "Promised Land and Yahweh's Land," 29–93; Diepold, *Israels Land*, 83ff.; Wright, *Deuteronomy*, 52. Block (*Gods of the Nations*, 78–79) argues that the term is more appropriately drawn from a feudal social context than inheritance terminology. On the term in 4:20, see Block, *Gospel according to Moses*, 174–77.

78. E.g., Tigay, "Excursus 7: The Biblical View of the Origin of Polytheism," in *Deuteronomy*, 435–36. Tigay thinks this began when God divided humanity into separate nations after it built the Tower of Babel.

79. With Holter, *Deuteronomy and the Second Commandment*, 79–80; McConville, *Deuteronomy*, 108.

80. See Wenham, "Genesis 1–11 and the Ancient Near East," in *Genesis 1–15*, xlvi–l.

81. Cf. Olson, *Deuteronomy and the Death of Moses*, 34: v. 20 suggests "that the closest one can get to the image of God in the world is to look at the people of Israel."

82. Ibid. Cf. Tigay, *Deuteronomy*, 51. Does it seek to prevent the posthumous wor-

this reference with the first two accounts of Moses' ban (1:37f.; 3:23f.). The central motive is the same in all three texts: Yahweh is angry with Moses "because of you" (1:37; 3:26; 4:21). The motive is used differently in each: the first is in a narrative about the people's rebellion against Yahweh, with the result that no one will see the land (1:35); the second is in a narrative of Moses questioning Yahweh's decision of not letting him (alone) enter the land (3:23-25); the third (4:21-22) involves a theological re-orientation, and must be seen in light of its context.[83] In chapter 4, Moses is portrayed as a mediator of the word of Yahweh (cf. vv. 1, 2, 5, 8, 14, 40). In verses 21-22, his role as mediator takes on a new dimension: "Moses is not only Yahweh's representative versus Israel, he is now also portrayed as Israel's representative versus Yahweh, who is made responsible for the sins of the people as a whole."[84] In its immediate context, then, the ban on Moses is transitional. The main textual connection with the preceding discussion is the reference to the land as Israel's נחלה (v. 21); Moses reminds Israel that what they are about to possess is a good gift from Yahweh. The exclusion of Moses, however, makes this more of a warning than an encouragement, indicating that idolatry can undo the promise. If the greatest individual among them could die outside the land due to the sins of others, how much more could an idolatrous nation draw divine anger and lose the blessing of life in the land.[85] The ban, therefore, looks backward and forward, providing logic for the connection between idolatry and loss of land.

Another transitional section comes in verses 23-24. It is connected with the preceding by the use of a similar introductory warning with שמר plus פֶּן: "Guard yourselves, lest you forget the covenant of Yahweh your God, which he made with you, and make a carved image..." (v. 23).

---

ship of Moses? Does it suggest that the land had become Moses' idol? Has Moses forgotten the covenant (cf. v. 23)? Does his death act as a vicarious atonement for the people (note "because of you" in v. 21)? Does it strengthen the upcoming threat of exile (vv. 25-28)? Or is Moses simply a bitter old man?

83. See Braulik, *Die Mittel*, 46; Holter, *Deuteronomy 4 and the Second Commandment*, 87-89.

84. Holter, *Deuteronomy 4 and the Second Commandment*, 88.

85. The theme of "anger" is often used in the Deuteronomistic History for divine anger against "images" and "other gods." Of the five references besides Deut 1:37 and 4:21, four are in these contexts: Deut 9:8, 20 (calf); Deut 9:20 (calf); 1 Kgs 11:9 (Solomon's wives); 2 Kgs 17:18 (judgment over Northern king [exile]); 1 Kgs 8:46 (prayer of dedication [which also mentions exile]). See Weinfeld, *Deuteronomy and the Deuteronomic School*, 346.

With the following section (vv. 25–31), it establishes a contrast between Israel and Yahweh: Israel may "forget the covenant" (v. 23), but Yahweh will not "forget the covenant" (v. 31). Yahweh's character is also contrasted as "an impassioned God" (v. 24) versus "a compassionate God" (v. 31). The keywords, "carved image" (v. 23) and "fire" (v. 24), appear in the preceding and following verses. The warning itself crystallizes the progression and logic of the passage thus far. For the first time, the twin themes of chapter 4—covenant and idolatry—are explicitly combined; idolatry *is* forgetting the covenant. The Second Commandment (with the First) is offered as the sum of the whole.[86] The substance of covenant commitment, therefore, continues to be loyalty to Yahweh alone, as it had been before Moses began his instruction in Moab (cf. vv. 3–4).

The motivation for obedience is explicit and direct: "For Yahweh your God is a consuming fire, an impassioned God" (v. 24). Both terms אש אכלה, "a consuming fire," and אל קנא, "an impassioned God," preeminently recall events at Horeb and describe God as an agent of destruction. The first term applies one of the keywords of chapter 4 to Yahweh himself; elsewhere, "fire" is the agent that burned the mountain (v. 11; cf. 5:23; 9:15) and the source out of which Yahweh spoke.[87] In Exodus 24:17, the full term "consuming fire" describes "the appearance of the glory of Yahweh" on Sinai. Israel's response to the theophany shows they rightly interpreted the theological implication:

> Behold, Yahweh our God has shown us his glory and greatness, and we have hear his voice out of the midst of the fire. This day we have seen God speak with man and man still live. Now therefore why should we die? For this great fire will consume (אכל) us. If we hear the voice of Yahweh our God any more, we shall die. (Deut 5:24–25)

Moses would later capitalize on this understanding as he encourages Israel to dispossess the nations of the land:

> Know therefore today that he who goes over before you as a consuming fire (אש אכלה) is Yahweh your God. He will destroy

---

86. The NT writers totalize the law in similar ways. Paul focuses on the Tenth Commandment that prohibits coveting (Rom 7:7–12). James declares that violation of the Fifth (murder) or Sixth (adultery) Commandment translates into violation of the whole law (Jas 2:8–11). Following the Jesus tradition (cf. Matt 22:34–40), they also see the sum of the law in loving God and loving neighbor (e.g., Rom 13:9–10; Jas 2:8).

87. Verses 12, 15, 33, 36; cf. 5:4, 22, 24, 26; 9:10; 10:4.

(Hi. שמד) them and subdue them before you. So you shall drive them out and make them perish (Hi. אבד) quickly, as Yahweh has promised you. (Deut 9:3)

In its other four references, Yahweh as "an impassioned God"[88] functions as a deterrent to idolatry (i.e., worshiping gods other than Yahweh). The Second Commandment conjoins it with the idea of Yahweh as a punisher of iniquity (Exod 20:5; Deut 5:9). With particular focus on life in the land, the descriptions in Exodus 34:14 and Deuteronomy 6:15 parenthetically underscores warnings with respect to Israel's encounter with the inhabitants of the land:

> Guard yourself, lest you make a covenant with the inhabitants of the land to which you go, lest it become a snare in your midst. You shall tear down their altars and break their pillars and cut down their Asherim (for you shall worship no other god, for Yahweh, whose name is Passion, is an impassioned God), lest you make a covenant with the inhabitants of the lad and whey they whore after their gods and sacrifice to their gods and you are invited, you eat of the his sacrifice, and you take of their daughters for your sons, and their daughters whore after their gods and make your sons whore after their gods. (Exod 34:12-16)[89]

> And when Yahweh your God brings you into the land ... guard yourself lest you forget Yahweh, who brought you out of the land of Egypt, out of the house of slavery. It is Yahweh your God you shall fear. Him you shall serve and by his name you shall swear. You shall not go after other gods, the gods of the peoples who are around you (for Yahweh your God in your midst is an impassioned God), lest the anger of Yahweh your God be kindled against you, and he destroy (Hi. שמד) you from off the face of the earth. (Deut 6:10, 12-15)

The identification of Yahweh as "a consuming fire" and "an impassioned God" in Deuteronomy 4:24, then, is a warning that the nation that is about to take possession of the land (cf. vv. 22, 26) could suffer a reversal

---

88. I prefer "impassioned" to the more traditional "jealous" for קנא because of some unfortunate connotations usually associated with the latter term. Cf. Block, *Gospel according to Moses*, 179-78; Weinfeld, *Deuteronomy 1-11*, 295-96.

89. Given the reference in Exod 34:14, it is possible to take קנא אל (here and in 4:24) as a name for Yahweh. Either way, the theological point remains the same. Both Exod 34 and Deut 6 show how the First and Second Commandments are closely connected.

of the land's conquest and occupation if they take a different posture toward Yahweh and his covenant.

In verses 25–31, Moses turns to the future rather than drawing on past history. We will soon examine this passage in greater detail; for now, we can overview how verses 25–31 fit within its context thus far. Though lacking the שמר-plus-פן introduction, as a subunit of verses 9–31, this passage is clearly a warning against violating the prohibition of images. The possibility of future exile is a motivation to obey God in Moab. Several terms and themes from chapter 4 re-emerge: land possession and occupation (v. 25; cf. vv. 1, 5, 14, 22); acting "corruptly" by making a carved image (v. 25; cf. vv. 16, 23); provoking divine anger (v. 25; cf. v. 23); "today" (v. 26; cf. vv. 4, 8, 10, 20); exclusion from land (v. 26; cf. v. 21); judgment of "being destroyed" (Hi. שמד in v. 26; cf. v. 3; cf. Hi. שחת in v. 31); other peoples (v. 27; cf. vv. 6–8, 19); "heart" and "soul" (v. 29; cf. v. 9); "hear" (v. 30; cf. vv. 1, 10, 12); "forget" (v. 31; cf. vv. 9, 23); "covenant" (v. 31; cf. vv. 13, 23); and "fathers" (v. 31; cf. v. 1). Still, the theme of restoration in verses 29–31 raises elements of discontinuity with the rest of chapter 4: obedience appears to be the result rather than prerequisite of the move home; judgment is a foregone conclusion rather than a motivation and refers instead to the "covenant with your fathers" rather than the covenant made at Horeb. These continuities and tensions with the rest of chapter 4 will need to be explored further.

## Deuteronomy 4:32–40

These verses conclude the exhortation of chapter 4 as well as Moses' first major discourse in the book. This liturgical conclusion[90] balances the prologue (vv. 1–8) in a chiastic pattern:

A  Law and Land (1–2)
    B  Israel's experience of judging acts of Yahweh in the past (3–4)
        C  Israel's incomparability with respect to observing Yahweh's law (with two rhetorical מי-questions) (5–8)

---

90. Weinfeld, *Deuteronomy 1–11*, 211, is right to see this liturgical pattern as a proper introduction for the Decalogue and Shema.

C' Yahweh's incomparability with respect to handling Israel (with four rhetorical ה-questions) (32–35)

B' Israel's experience of saving acts of Yahweh in the past (36–39)

A' Law and Land (40)[91]

At the same time, it builds upon the argument of verses 9–31, which established the primacy of the First and Second Commandments by referring to various historical experiences. Here, Moses' lesson for Israel is that no other God—and thus, no other law than the one he gives—should be obeyed because of what Yahweh has done for Israel.

In verses 32–35, history demonstrates the truth of monotheism. Since no other god has done what Yahweh has done for Israel in the exodus (v. 34) and at Horeb (v. 33), "there is no other besides him" (v. 35b). As Tigay remarks, "For Moses, the *sine qua non* of divinity is effectiveness."[92] There is an immediate link with the preceding section by the contrast between looking into "the latter days" (v. 30) of the future and recalling "the former days" (v. 32) of God's acts in the two seminal experiences.[93] The argument is prefaced by placing these events in the context of a vast history that begins at creation (v. 32).[94] The heaven–earth dimension puts the salvific acts in a cosmic setting, highlighting that the

---

91. Adapted from Holter, *Deuteronomy 4 and the Second Commandment*, 102–7; cf. Mayes, "Deuteronomy 4," 26. Terminological links include "statutes," "judgments," "commandments" (vv. 1–2, 5, 40); "which I command you" (vv. 2, 40); "in order that" as introduction to a promise (vv. 1, 40); witness of "eyes" (vv. 3, 34); and "great" (vv. 6, 7, 8, 32, 34, 36, 37, 38).

92. Tigay, *Deuteronomy*, 55. Cf. Isa 41:23–24; 2 Chr 25:15b.

93. The function of the opening כי ("*For* ask now of the former days . . .") in v. 32 is debated. Tigay (*Deuteronomy*, 432) considers it an indication that vv. 29–31 is a literary (exilic) interpolation, since the point of vv. 32ff. is that Yahweh is the only true God and thus justify vv. 25–28; they have nothing to do with the promise of restoration in vv. 29–31. Tigay does acknowledge that several scholars see a link between vv. 32ff. and the note of a compassionate God in v. 31 (see references in Tigay, *Deuteronomy*, 528–29 n. 3). Cf. Driver, *Deuteronomy*, lxxvi; Wolff, "Kerygma," 83–100. An emphatic sense—"indeed"—fits the context better than a causal reading. See Block, *Gospel According to Moses*, 200–201. On a similar construction, cf. Job 8:7–8: "And though your beginning was small, your latter days will be very great. *For* inquire, please, of bygone ages . . . ."

94. As McConville (*Deuteronomy*, 112) notes, by looking back to creation, all history is bracketed between that day and "today" (vv. 39, 40). This is the only reference to ברא, "create," in the Deuteronomistic History. אדם, "man," is only used rarely in Deuteronomy (4:28; 5:24; 8:3; 20:19; 32:8).

God of history is also the (only) God of creation (cf. v. 36). Unlike the corresponding section of rhetorical questions about the uniqueness of Israel in verses 5–8, which considers Israel's possession of just laws and divine presence in an international context, the uniqueness of Yahweh is presented here solely for Israel's sake: "To *you* it [i.e., Horeb and the exodus] was shown, that *you* might know that Yahweh is God; there is no other besides him" (v. 35). The focus on the uniqueness of Yahweh explains why such emphasis is put on *how* he rescued his people—"by trials, by signs, by wonders, and by war, by a mighty hand and an outstretched arm, and by great deeds of terror" (v. 34)—and *how* the just laws were revealed (v. 33). With these verses, the argument has certainly moved beyond the practical concerns of the Second Commandment to fixing Israel's eyes on the God with whom she has to do.

The same themes recur in verses 36–39, but with Yahweh's own motivations behind his salvific acts made more explicit. First, Yahweh allowed the hearing of his voice at Horeb "that he might discipline you" (v. 36).[95] Like Moses (cf. vv. 5, 14), Yahweh will teach his laws to the people; like a father (cf. v. 10), Yahweh will instill a proper reverence in them.[96] Second, Yahweh's acts of deliverance in Egypt and the wilderness (vv. 37–38) are predicated upon the idea that "he loved your fathers and chose their offspring after them" (v. 37). Israel's love for Yahweh essentially entails heartfelt obedience (cf. chap. 6). Yahweh's "obligation" toward Israel, however, derives from a self-imposed attachment. Third, Yahweh's stated purpose is to give Israel the land "for an inheritance" (v. 38), of which we have already noted the backdrop of adoption language. Thus, the driving metaphor for Yahweh seems to be that of father to his adopted son, Israel. As in verses 32–35, historical experience rather than philosophical argumentation leads to the conclusion that "Yahweh is God in heaven above and on the earth beneath; there is no other" (v. 39).

95. Tigay (*Deuteronomy*, 56) contends that v. 36—with God speaking "out of heaven" and Israel hearing his words "out of the midst of the fire"—resolves the apparent inconsistency in Exodus, which reports that God spoke from Sinai (Exod 19:11, 18, 20) and from heaven (Exod 20:19). However, as we have already intimated with respect to divine presence in Deuteronomy, there is no reason to distinguish too sharply between God's voice from heaven or from the fire.

96. Driver (*Deuteronomy*) states that the term יסר denotes "the discipline or education of the moral nature: the spectacle was one adapted to quell waywardness and pride, to generate in Israel's heart a temper of submissiveness and reverence." For a reading of the book that sees it as a program of catechesis, see Olson, *Deuteronomy and the Death of Moses*, 7–14.

The concluding command in verse 40 sets the stage for the delineation of the "statutes and commandments" that will commence with the Decalogue in chapter 5. The appeal to obedience includes motivations of self-interest and divine gift: "that it may go well with you and with your children after you, and that you may prolong your days in the land that Yahweh your God is giving you forever." As has been the case all along, the aspect of grace—through a presentation of the person and work of Yahweh—tends to heighten rather than diminish the aspect of demand, but also puts the demand in its proper context, as a response to grace.

## *Theological Considerations*

Deuteronomy 4 is not a statement of God's laws *per se*, but a sustained exhortation to Israel to obey them. Various types of arguments are set forth, including lessons from history, logic, and promised effects of obedience. Observing the laws—which represent the will of the only true God—allows entry into the land, enables well-being in the land, makes Israel unique, earns the admiration of others, secures God's presence, and unites present and future generations of Israel with those who have witnessed divine blessings in the past. The obedience must be thorough, from the heart, and with knowledge of who God really is.

Several theological issues are raised here that have some bearing on a full understanding of exile in Deuteronomy. First, possession of land is both gift and duty. Neither legalism nor cheap grace will do. The necessity of obedience is predicated upon and subsequent to the gracious acts of Yahweh on Israel's behalf. The call to obey, then, is a call to trust God to fulfill his promises. Exile will be the result of forgetting this connection. Conversely, restoration must involve a re-establishment of it.

Second, this passage demonstrates a close connection between Horeb and Moab. This will be a dominant feature in chapters 27–30. Such a connection re-emphasizes the historical continuity of God's people—one that extends as far back as the patriarchs. The stress on the word written will enable this perspective to continue, as it also ensures that Israel is without excuse as to what Yahweh expects of them— "expectation" both in terms of requirements and future prospects.

A tension arises, however, with the singling out of individuals within the nation (4:3, 21–22). Despite the generational conflation, even within a generation, Yahweh can act differently toward specific individuals. It is unclear how this tension is played out in a national catastrophe like exile.

Third, the law and its violation are put within the framework of concern for Yahweh's reputation. The emphasis on monotheism underlies the focus on idolatry as the supreme transgression. Related to this is Yahweh's purpose for Israel in an international context, which is both polemical and missiological (4:5-8, 33-35). These broader concerns should not be lost in the discussion of exile. As chapter 29 especially will show, the foreign reaction to God's dealings with his own people is of special concern.

## FIRST TEXT: DEUTERONOMY 4:25-31

The penultimate paragraph of Moses' first speech constitutes the book's overture to the theme of exile. Having examined its immediate context, it is necessary to look at the text in more detail. The present author's own translation is given below, followed by some observations on formal and stylistic features.[97] The exposition of the text will focus on theological questions and considerations, many of which have already arisen in this study.

> **25** "When [כי][98] you beget children and grandchildren and grow old[99] in the land, and you act corruptly by making a carved image in the form of anything—by doing what is evil in the sight of Yahweh your God, so as to provoke him to anger—**26** I call heaven and earth to witness against you today, that you will soon utterly perish from the land that you are going over the Jordan to possess. You will not live long in it, but will be utterly destroyed. **27** And Yahweh will scatter you among the peoples, and you will be left few in number among the nations where Yahweh will drive you. **28** And there you will serve gods of wood and stone, the work of human hands, that neither see, nor hear, nor eat, nor smell. **29** But from there you will seek Yahweh your God and you will find him, when [כי][100] you search after him with all your heart and with all your soul. **30** When you are in tribulation, and all these things come upon you in the latter days, you will return to Yahweh your God and heed his voice. **31** For Yahweh your God is a compassionate God. He will neither leave you nor destroy

---

97. The MT is relatively sound and need not be emended. The variants are minor and easily accounted for; none affect the overall interpretation of this study.

98. See discussion on temporal reading of כי.

99. See discussion on possible translation of "become complacent."

100. See the discussion on temporal reading of כי.

you nor forget the covenant with your fathers that he swore to them." (Deut 4:25-31)

## Form, Structure, and Style

We discussed the breakdown of Deuteronomy 4 into subsections in the previous section. As with the chapter as a whole, there is no consensus about this particular unit. Most recognize a clear break at the end of verse 31.[101] Some argue, however, that the section should begin at verse 23 rather than verse 25.[102] This would allow these verses to be tied to a warning headed by שמר ("keep, watch"), which begins vv. 9, 15, and 23. It also highlights the contrasts between Israel forgetting Yahweh's covenant (v. 23) and Yahweh's refusal to forget his covenant with the patriarchs (v. 31), and between the divine attributes of passion (v. 24) and compassion (v. 31).[103] But the distinct temporal reference of verses 25-31—the distant future—argues strongly for treating verses 25-31 as a separate paragraph. Both the MT and SP support this break.[104] If one considers the *Numeruswechsel* as a structural indicator,[105] then this phenomenon offers further support of this delineation. We already noted the phenomenon in verses 25 and 29: the singular תוליד, "(when) you beget," in verse 25 is followed in verses 25-28 by nine second-person verbs and three second-person suffixes, all (except אֱלֹהֶיךָ, "your God," in v. 25) in the plural; conversely, וּבִקַּשְׁתֶּם ("but . . . you [pl.] will seek")

---

101. But see Christensen, *Deuteronomy 1—21:9*, 90-98, who divides the text based on a prosodic analysis, finding vv. 25-40 as a major subunit (by examining the *Numeruswechsel*, he divides the passage into four parts: vv. 25-26, 27-28, 29-34, and 35-40); Knapp, *Deuteronomium 4*, 112-14, who considers vv. 29-40 as a subunit; Nielsen, *Deuteronomium*, 54-68, who considers vv. 25-40 to be a third layer (after vv. 1-8 and 9-24).

102. Braulik (*Die Mittel*, 91-100) gathers together the features of the language that indicates a single linguistic unit. For Braulik, each of his 6 sections for the chapter (vv. 1-4, 5-8, 9-14, 15-22, 23-31, 32-40) is considered self-contained and all but the last begin with a warning to obey the law, which is then reinforced through reference to history. Braulik is followed by Weinfeld *Deuteronomy 1-11*, 199-214; Mayes, "Deuteronomy 4"; and Tigay, *Deuteronomy*, 51. In another work, however, Mayes divides the text into vv. 25-31 ("Exposition of Deuteronomy 4:25-31").

103. Weinfeld, *Deuteronomy 1-11*, 207.

104. Tigay, *Deuteronomy*, 51.

105. See Christensen's excursus on "The *Numeruswechsel* in Deuteronomy," in *Deuteronomy 1—21:9*, xcix-ci. On 4:25-31, see Christensen, *Deuteronomy 1—21:9*, 94.

in verse 29 is followed in verses 29–31 by five second-person verbs and eleven second-person suffixes, all in the singular.[106]

Deuteronomy 4:25–31 can be outlined as a two-stage process:

Stage 1: Exile from the Land (vv. 25–28)
    Temporal Indicators: distant future (25aα)
    Spatial Referent: *in the land* (25aβ)
Apodosis: *when you act corruptly* (25bα)
    Manner of corruption (25β–γ)
        Act: *by making a carved image* (25bβ)
        Theological Evaluation: *doing what is evil in Yahweh's eyes* (25bγ)
    Result: *to provoke him to anger* (25bδ)
Protasis (26–28)
    Invocation of Divine Witnesses: *heaven and earth* (26a)
    Temporal Reference: *today*
    Consequences of idolatry (26b–28)
        *Utterly perish* (אבד) (26bα)
            Temporal Reference: *soon*
            Spatial Reference: *from the land you are going over . . . to possess*
        *Not live long* (26bβ)
            Spatial Reference: *in* (*the land*)
        *Be utterly destroyed* (Ni. שמד) (26bγ)
        *Will be scattered* (Hi. פוץ) (27a)
            Explicit Agent: *Yahweh*
            Spatial Reference: *among the peoples*
        *Be left few in number* (27b)
            Spatial Reference: *among the nations*
        *Will be driven* (Pi. נהג) (27c)
            Explicit Agent: *Yahweh*
            Spatial Reference: *where* (i.e., among the nations)
        *You will serve gods* (28)
            Spatial Reference: *there* (i.e., among the nations)
            Disparaging Description of Gods
                *of wood and stone*

---

106. The change in number in v. 29 indicates that vv. 25–28 and 29–31 are the two main subsections within the paragraph. See the outline below.

> *the work of human hands*
> *that neither see nor hear nor eat nor smell*

    Stage 2: Restoration to Yahweh (vv. 29–31)
        Description #1: Seek (Pi. בקשׁ) and Find (מצא) (29)
            Spatial Reference: *from there* (i.e., among the nations)
            Explicit Object: *Yahweh your God*
            Circumstantial/Temporal Reference: "full" search (דרשׁ)
            (*with all your heart and with all your soul*)
        Description #2: Return (שׁוב) and Heed (שׁמע) (30)
            Circumstantial/Temporal References
                *when you are in tribulation*
                *and all these things* (i.e., vv. 25–28) *find you*
                *in the latter days*
            Explicit Objects
                (you will return) to *Yahweh your God*
                (and heed) *his voice*
        Theological Basis (31)
            Yahweh's Nature: *a merciful God* (31a)
            Yahweh's Promises (31b)
                Concerning His Future Presence: *He will not leave you*
                Concerning His Future Activity: *He will not destroy*
                (Hi. שׁחת) *you*
                Concerning His Past Commitment: *He will not forget*
                *the covenant with your fathers that he swore to them*

This outline provides the basis for the exposition of the text below.

Various stylistic features will be raised throughout the exposition, but a few observations be can be pointed out up front that show that this passage is "at home" in Deuteronomy 4.[107] First, the style of 4:25–31 fits within Moses' paranesis. The sermonic style is felt by the direct, urgent,

---

107. We have already noted one feature, the *Numeruswechsel*. Besides being a structural marker, it also may highlight other things: rhetorically, it may serve to emphasize especially important content in a passage; theologically, it may note the dual corporate and individual constitution of the audience. For example, McConville (*Deuteronomy*, 110) calls the isolated plural in v. 29 "an arresting rhetorical feature, indicating a significant new turn in the argument."

and vivid appeal of the text.¹⁰⁸ A sense of simplicity is felt, alongside a repetitiveness of themes, such as act corruptly//do evil (v. 25), perish//not live long//be destroyed (v. 26), scatter//be left few in number//be driven (v. 27), seek//search (v. 29), and find//find (vv. 29, 30). Hyperbolic language occurs in the use of אבד and שמד for exile. There is moral evaluation (to make a graven image is to "act corruptly" and "do what is evil" [v. 25]) and intellectual evaluation (to serve gods that are human-made, but cannot even perform basic human functions [v. 28], is foolishness).

Second, this text is carried by temporal and spatial indicators. The passage moves from one future time period to another—from an initial time in the land (v. 25a), to a time of rebellion (v. 25b), to a time of dispersion (vv. 26b–27), to a time in exile (v. 28), to a time of repentance in "the latter days" (v. 30a), to a time of return (v. 30b). This sequence is broken by a reference to "today" (v. 26a) and a recalling of the distant past ("fathers" in v. 31). The spatial expressions include "in the land" (v. 25), "from the land (that you are going over the Jordan to possess)" (v. 26), "among the peoples" (v. 27a), "among the nations" (v. 27b), and three references of שׁם, "there" (i.e., place of exile)—"to there" (v. 27c), "there" (v. 28a), and "from there" (v. 29). These temporal and spatial features keep Israel on the move in her ongoing journey.¹⁰⁹

Third, this passages exhibits aspects of the covenant formula. The word "covenant" (ברית) appears here with respect to the patriarchal covenant (v. 31; see discussion below). The focus on judgment for violating the prohibition of idols (v. 25) recalls the equation of "covenant" with the Decalogue earlier in 4:13. The notion of covenant is further highlighted by several elements that are common to the ANE covenant/treaty form: stipulations (v. 25); divine witnesses (v. 26a); a list of curses, including destruction and exile (vv. 26b–28); and a list of blessings (vv. 29–31). At the same time, these parallels help emphasize the uniqueness of Yahweh and his relationship with Israel. However, in contrast to ANE treaties, "heaven and earth" in verse 26 are clearly metaphorical witnesses rather than actual deities.¹¹⁰ Also, the treaties that include blessings do so to

---

108. Mayes, "Exposition of Deuteronomy 4:25–31," 70.

109. Concerning the focus on temporal and spatial features in Deuteronomy, I am indebted to McConville and Millar, *Time and Place*.

110. On "heaven and earth" being included in the list of deities cited as witnesses to a treaty, see Craigie, *Book of Deuteronomy*, 139.

motivate obedience rather than repentance, and never offer hope of restoration beyond judgment.

*Exposition*

By this point in the discourse, Moses has already referred to several key moments in Israel's journey to the land, but now he focuses on a time and place in and beyond the land. Looking to the distant future, he considers the worst prospect imaginable for the nation—removal from the land of promise (vv. 25–28); he then considers the unimaginable—restoration beyond exile (vv. 29–31).

Stage 1: Exile from the Land

Despite the future outlook of the passage, the manner in which Moses addresses his present audience urges them to take the message to heart (note "today" in v. 26). Thus, while he speaks of a time after future generations have been born and the nation has existed for some length in the land (v. 25a), the address is consistently to "you." This orientation forces the reader to consider up front the identity of the "you." Given the discussion of chapter 4 and the note in verse 26, it must include Moses' contemporaries. Still, it is hard to imagine that the present audience alone could experience all the events envisioned, both stated and implied: enter and occupy the land, produce children and grandchildren, sin to such a degree that Yahweh takes drastic action, be violently removed from the land, travel to foreign territory, endure exile, come to one's senses, repent and seek after Yahweh, return to the land, and live a life of obedience. Additionally, the themes of the passage speak to more than a single generation. Therefore, the addressee ("you") must be flexible—every future generation that dwells in the land is a potential candidate to experience the things described here. Even so, if the future is, in a sense, open, it is also clear that no generation or individual is entirely "free." The actions of the nation and and/or its members mutually affect each other, both contemporaneously and trans-generationally. Whatever else the alternation of singular and plural "you" may signal, it highlights this sense of corporate solidarity. The fact that Israel is also in covenant relationship with Yahweh adds a further, complicating dimension, and only increases the urgency for each age to consider what God says "today" (cf. v. 26a) to "you."

This reality of solidarity is a double-edged sword. On the positive side is the notion of election. It is because of Yahweh's gracious choice of Abraham that his descendants have been rescued from Egypt and now stand ready to enter the land, fulfilling an ancient promise (Gen 12:1; cf. Deut 4:1). In the end, this established relationship and commitment will ensure the nation's future security and blessing (v. 31). But between these poles Israel is confronted with the conditionality of the divine commandment and the potential of failure. The relationship is covenantal, which forges election with obligation. The problem facing future generations is that they are cut from the same cloth as past generations—a reality that, as we have seen and shall further explore, is far from encouraging.

A difficult but crucial matter of interpretation is whether to read the introductory כי in verse 25 as conditional or temporal (see below on v. 29).[111] Syntactically, the כי governs the entire verse (the apodosis does not begin until v. 26):

כי־תוליד . . . ונושנתם . . . והשחתם ועשיתם פסל. . . ועשיתם הרע . . .

> If/When you beget . . . and grow old . . . and act corruptly and make an image . . . and do what is evil . . . .

The problem cannot be solved on formal grounds.[112] In a study of כי in Biblical Hebrew, Aejmelaeus claims that a conditional sense rarely occurs outside of legal texts; a temporal reading is preferred "when our understanding of the context suggests a higher probability that the contents of the כי clause will actually occur."[113] Even so, she offers a conclusion quite apropos for our passage:

> The border line between conditional and temporal is, however, extremely vague—particularly in cases referring to the future. In

---

111. A survey of English translations shows that this is not an idle debate. A conditional sense is witnessed in ESV, NIV, NRSV, and RSV (all put the "if" immediately before "act corruptly"; they begin the sentence with "when" or "after"). A temporal sense is witnessed in ASV, AV, NASB, NJB, and NKJV. LXX is no help since it translates כי with ἐάν, "if, since, when."

112. See Aejmelaeus, "Function and Interpretation of כי," 193–209. Cf. Schoors, "Particle כִּי," 240–76. Aejmelaeus ("Function and Interpretation of כי," 196) notes that while a כי-clause that preceeds the main clause (as in v. 25) is normally conditional, temporal, or causal, there is no formal distinction between these cases.

113. Aejmelaeus, "Function and Interpretation of כי," 197.

several cases, the interpreter may freely choose either interpretation according to one's own consideration of the wider context.[114]

The present task, then, is to seek contextual indicators that help us decided whether the envisioned exile and restoration is merely potential or, in fact, inevitable.[115]

We could compare the use of כי in verse 25 with its use in verse 29, though the situations are not exact parallels.[116] If verse 29 is considered alone, a conditional reading makes sense: "you will seek Yahweh your God and you will find him *if* you search after him with all your heart...." But a temporal (or circumstantial) understanding makes better sense when one considers the parallel phrase in verse 30: "*when* (ב preposition) you are in distress ... you *will* return (*waw*, consecutive plus perfect) to Yahweh your God and obey his voice."[117] However, this does not completely settle the meaning of the reference in verse 25 since the restoration of verses 29–31 presumes that the events of verses 25–28 have taken place (explicit in v. 30a). Therefore, the actuality of restoration is dependent upon what one decides about the conditionality or eventuality of apostasy and exile. In other words, a "when" in verse 29 does not necessarily mandate a "when" in verse 25. This question can only be answered fully after examining other arguments.

If the כי in verse 25 is interpreted conditionally, the main protasis-apodosis reads, "*if* you act corruptly by making a carved image ... *then* I call heaven and earth ..." (vv. 25–26). This fits well with the warning of the surrounding context. We have seen that chapter 4 functions as a sustained appeal against committing idolatry. The threat of exile *if* the nation violates the prohibition would be a great deterrent. Conversely, would not a temporal reading undercut the warning? Why should

---

114. Ibid. Deut 6:20 is given as an example.

115. The question of inevitability is actually a better way of posing the question. Idolatry is clearly a "condition" of exile, for the latter will not happen without the former. We will use "conditional," then, in the sense of merely potential.

116. Aejmelaueus ("Function and Interpretation of כי," 207–8) notes that v. 29 is an example of a conditional or temporal כי following a main clause. Further, "it is only in Deuteronomy that כי is found introducing a condition after the main clause" (ibid., 207). This always occurs in a context of Israel's obedience as a condition for promises concerning the future (e.g., Deut 12:25, 28; 19:9; 28:22, 9, 13; 30:10).

117. Interestingly, of the translations that read a temporal כי in v. 25, only ASV reads it temporally in v. 29. All the other translations read a conditional כי in v. 29—despite the fact that LXX reads ὅταν, which is usually temporal.

Israel seek to avoid something that will eventually take place anyway? Also, the curses in ANE treaties, which certainly serve as a backdrop to Deuteronomy and, as we have noted, parallel language in the present text, are always strictly conditional rather than prophetic. We will explore the connection further when we analyze the covenant curses in Deuteronomy 28, but it is clear that one could argue that intentional allusion to this treaty tradition assumes conditionality. If one follows this line of reasoning, then the destruction and exile envisioned in verses 26–28 is merely a threat. Following this line of argument, of course, the restoration in verses 29–31 would also be purely hypothetical.

Several factors, however, favor a temporal reading, and thus speak to the certainty of exile in Israel's future. First, the כי-clause in verse 25 clearly includes other temporal indicators. The first two verbal acts—begetting offspring and growing old—are assumed to take place.[118] If כי is conditional, it is strictly so only for the third verbal act of acting corruptly.[119] One might expect a different construction in this case, such as fronting the first two verbs with a preposition (ב or כ) to indicate "when" (cf. initial ב in v. 30) and fronting the last three verbs with the כי to indicate "if."

Second, the inclusion of the promise of restoration in verses 29–31 raises a major difficulty if the threat of exile is merely a threat. Whatever apparent difficulty there is with a temporal reading within the context of warning, it pales in comparison to the difficulty in seeing the logic of including the promise in the course of threatening exile, for the promise could weaken the effectiveness of the warning.[120] So, while we have not yet provided a satisfactory reason for the inclusion of verses 29–31, it is easier to see it as the second stage of a prophetic foresight of the future.

This yields a third factor favoring a temporal reading: the text's use of the Second Commandment. The Second Commandment is clearly in view in verse 25 with the combination of "children" (4:25a; cf. 5:9) and

---

118. At this point, we are considering the second verb, Ni. ישׁן(II) "be old," as a temporal marker. We will suggest a more subtle reading later.

119. The last two verbs—making an image and doing what is evil—should clearly be taken as the manner of acting corruptly (thus, "*by* making an image . . .") and, thus, would be part of the condition.

120. See Ginsberg, *Israelian Heritage in Judaism*, 80. This is one of the arguments for considering Deut 4:29–31 and 30:1–10 as literary interpolations during the time of the exile; cf. Tigay, *Deuteronomy*, 432.

"make a carved image in the form of anything" (4:25b; cf. 5:8).[121] In verse 28, the experience of exile includes the fact that what the commandment forbids—to "serve" (עבד) idols (5:9)—actually constitutes part of the curse itself. Holter explains the complex relationship:

> The exile is a result of Israel breaking the Second commandment, and the exile is also a context of continued breaking of the commandment; nevertheless, at the same time the exile is a context from which Israel will repent from her breaking the commandment....[122]

The innovation in our text changes curse and blessing from being exclusive alternatives for a given individual (as in 5:9, 10) to chronologically subsequent periods in the history of the nation (4:25-28, 29-31). When interpreting the exile in light of the commandment, the surprising optimism at the end of our text becomes a natural consequence; the three or four generations of exilic punishment are overshadowed by a thousand generations of post-exilic mercy.[123] This helps counter the treaty parallels. If our text can offer a surprising twist in its use of another Deuteronomic text, it certainly is free to alter the ANE treaty tradition and need not follow the latter's requirement of strict conditionality with respect to the curses. The simple fact is that blessing following curse is unique to Yahweh's covenant with Israel.

We will witness other hints of inevitability in the book. For the time being, the tension in chapter 4 suggests that we may need to view the theme of exile here from multiple levels, including both conditional and temporal senses. Within the immediate argument, the daunting possibility (*if*) of future exile serves as one of the major motivations for heeding

---

121. Three main differences can readily be observed. First is the difference in order (4:25a//5:9; 4:25b//5:8). Second, whereas 4:25a expands "children" by adding "and children's children," 5:9 qualifies "children" with "to the third and fourth generation." Third, there is a syntactical difference in the place of כל ("any"): 4:25b reads ועשיתם פסל תמונת כל, "and make a carved image in the form of anything"; 5:8 reads לא־תעשה־לך פסל כל־תמונה אשר, "You shall not make for yourself a carved image of any form that (is in heaven above ... )." For a full treatment, see Holter, Deuteronomy and the Second Commandment (pp. 93-100 for allusions in 4:25).

122. Holter, *Deuteronomy and the Second Commandment*, 96.

123. Ibid., 99. The three or four generations of the commandment (5:9) is most likely a reference to the size of the extended family in ancient Israelite society (so, the thousand generations is a hyperbolic contrast). Cf. Weinfeld, *Deuteronomy 1-11*, 296-97. The interpretation for 4:25-31 assumes a switch to consecutive stages.

the call to faithfulness and obedience, but the fact (*when*) of future exile and restoration points to broader issues that transcend the immediate context. The interface between the exile theme and the theological subtext of Deuteronomy represents the focus of this whole study.

Verses 26–28 describe exile. In chapter 2 of this study, we examined the relevant vocabulary for exile in this text. To rehearse, exile is described in verse 27 by the more common exilic terms פוץ (Hi.), "scatter," and נהג (Pi.), "drive," and the phrase ונשארתם מתי מספר, "and you shall be left few in number." This terminology helps contextualize and qualify the language of verse 26. Specifically, the notions of "utterly perishing" (אבד), "not living long," and being "utterly destroyed" (Ni. שמד) cannot mean total annihilation.[124] The parallel qualifying phrases in both verses support this interpretation: verse 26 describes the point of departure—"you will soon utterly perish *from the land*," and, "you will not live long *in it*"; verse 27 describes the destination—"Yahweh will scatter you *among the peoples*, and you will be left few in number *among the nations where* Yahweh will drive you" (cf. "there" in v. 28 and "from there" in v. 29). A final note of interest with respect to this issue is the distinction made in verse 31; the promise that Yahweh "will not destroy you" uses a different term for "destroy" (Hi. שחת), which is not contextualized like the terms in verse 26. Nonetheless, with death language being conjoined with more usual exile terminology, what looms over Israel goes beyond a devastating event in the life of the nation; it is the nation's "life" itself that is at stake.

The agent of this destruction is Yahweh himself and Yahweh alone. It is Israel's covenant partner, "Yahweh your God," who is provoked to anger. It may be significant that in describing exile Moses uses the shortened "Yahweh" as the subject of "scatter" and "drive" (v. 27). The other curses use "you" as the subject, though Yahweh is the most natural implied agent of the passives "be utterly destroyed" (v. 26) and "be left few in number" (v. 27), and the ultimate cause of the nation perishing (v. 26), not living long in the land (v. 26), and serving foreign gods in foreign nations (v. 28). The absence of mediate agents does not preclude them being used by Yahweh (cf. 2:12, 22, 23), but, in final analysis, the fate of Israel is in the hands of her God. His creation will stand as witness (v.

---

124. Both אבד and שמד occur within an infinitive absolute–plus–imperfect construction.

26). This emphasis is consistent with the polemical nature of other parts of chapter 4 and its monotheistic claims.

Exile entails the reversal of covenant blessings, which is why verses 26-28 read like curses of a covenant. The blessings are summarized in Yahweh's initial call of Abram:

> Go from your country and your kindred and your father's house to the land that I will show you. And I will make of you a great nation, and I will bless you and make your name great, so that you will be a blessing. I will bless those who bless you, and him who dishonors you I will curse, and in you all the families of the earth shall be blessed. . . . To your offspring I will give this land. (Gen 12:1-3, 7)

Deuteronomy alludes to several of these promises: the special presence of God (4:7); increase in numbers (1:10-11); Israel as a "great" nation (4:6-8); curse of enemies (2:26—3:11); and land possession (e.g., 4:1, 25). Deuteronomy highlights the land as the chief covenantal blessing—the one upon which all the others are dependent. Therefore, exile, which is the undoing of this chief blessing, is a theological rubric for covenant reversal. This perspective explains why exile in our passage includes the dramatic decrease in numbers (4:27) and the irony of forced worship of artificial gods (4:28).[125] It also explains why such emphasis is placed on the conditionality of God's promises in Deuteronomy.[126] The conditional character of land possession itself has already been expressed in several ways: the Exodus generation was prevented entry because of rebellion (1:19-46); Moses was denied entry because of Yahweh's anger against him (1:37; 3:26-27; 4:21-22); and present entry into the land is dependent on obedience to the commandments (4:1). If Israel's health and witness in the world are tied to the land, as Deuteronomy argues, then

---

125. Some reject the claim of "forced" worship because religious coercion was not typical in the ancient near East; rather, Moses is thinking of religious assimilation. See Tigay, *Deuteronomy*, 53. Cf. Kaufmann, *From the Babylonian Captivity*, 498. In support of my interpretation see Olson, *Deuteronomy and the Death of Moses*, 35. The emphasis on the divine agency of exile means we must interpret the passage in light of Deuteronomic theology and not merely historical parallels.

126. This is not to suggest that Deuteronomy denies the priority of grace or that conditionality of covenant blessings is unique to Deuteronomy. In Genesis several responses are expected in light of the promise: faith (15:6); specific obedience (12:1, 4; 22:1); entrance into God's presence (17:1); a blameless life (17:1); and circumcision (17:9-14, 22-27).

all the blessings appear to be contingent on maintaining the land, which itself involves fidelity to the covenant.

All this adds further support to our repeated contention that we must look beyond the physical experience of exile and consider its theological dimension and connections. Moses is not simply reporting future events, but historically applying the consequences of the covenant relationship. We will raise the pertinent theological questions after discussing verses 29–31.

Stage 2: Return to Yahweh

As the outline of the passage shows, verses 29 and 30 give two parallel descriptions of this predicted return. The first description focuses on the process: "But from there you will seek Yahweh your God and you will find him, when you search after him with all your heart and with all your soul" (v. 29). The second description focuses on the result: "When you are in tribulation, and all these things come upon you in the latter days, you will return (שׁוּב) to Yahweh your God and heed his voice" (v. 30). Moses predicts a day when Israel fully and wholly (i.e., as a whole) will inwardly turn and externally return to the one who had sent her into exile. The explicit theological basis is given in verse 31 which begins with an explanatory כִּי ("for"). The promise of restoration in verses 29–30 is grounded in Yahweh himself—his nature ("a compassionate God"), his persevering presence ("will not leave you"), his commitment to life ("will not destroy you"), and his memory and fidelity ("will not forget the covenant with your fathers that he swore to them").

As might be expected, verses 29–31 present several reversals and contrasts. First, Israel undergoes a change in position and disposition, yielding the wholehearted obedience for which Moses had preached. Second, Yahweh's response to Israel changes, noted by the contrast of descriptions of Yahweh as "a consuming fire, an impassioned God" (v. 24) and "a compassionate God" (v. 31). Of course, Yahweh's change is not as fundamental as Israel's, which highlights another contrast between Yahweh and Israel. The basic constancy of Yahweh differentiates him from Israel: unlike Israel, he will not forget the covenant (vv. 23, 31); in contrast to Israel who would "act corruptly" (Hi. שׁחת; v. 25), he will not "destroy" (Hi. שׁחת; v. 31) Israel.

The text exhibits a couple of contrasts, however, that are more surprising and pose interpretive difficulty. One is the absence of any explicit reference to return to the land. The return is simply "to Yahweh your God" (v. 30). This is particularly noteworthy given the emphasis on the land in the Mosaic preaching, and not least the spatial references in verses 25–28. The passage, instead, is fixed on the divine-human relationship, including the relational verbs in verse 29 (all of which have Yahweh as the explicit object), the fresh heeding (שׁמע) of Yahweh's voice in verse 30, and the emphasis on Yahweh's nature and enduring presence in verse 31. We follow the vast majority of commentators who assume that return to the land is implicit. This can be argued from the reference in verse 31 to the patriarchal covenant (see below), the central tenet of which (in a Deuteronomic perspective) is the land. Nonetheless, the lacuna is noteworthy.

Another contrast is that restoration is based explicitly on Yahweh's remembrance of the "covenant" with the patriarchs (v. 31) rather than the Horeb covenant (cf. ברית in v. 13). This reading assumes that "fathers" in verse 31 refers to the patriarchs.[127] We will see in the next chapter that the identity of "fathers" is a matter of some debate for several texts in Deuteronomy (see discussions on 5:3; 7:12; and 8:18 in chap. 4). Though some have argued that the Horeb generation is in view in 4:31,[128] the other five references to "fathers" in Moses' first discourse all appear to refer to the patriarchs:

> Go in and take possession of the land that Yahweh swore to your fathers—Abraham, Isaac, and Jacob—to give to them and to their offspring after them. (1:8)

> May Yahweh, the God of your fathers, make you a thousand times as many as you are and bless you, as he has promised you. (1:11)

> Go up, take possession [of the land set before you], as Yahweh, the God of your fathers, has told you. (1:21)

> And now, O Israel, listen ... that you may live, and go in and take possession of the land that Yahweh, the God of your fathers, is giving you. (4:1)

---

127. The patriarchs are assumed to be in view in, e.g., Mayes, *Deuteronomy*, 157; Merrill, *Deuteronomy*, 129; Weinfeld, *Deuteronomy 1–11*, 210; Tigay, *Deuteronomy*, 53–55.

128. E.g., Block, *Gospel according to Moses*, 190–93. Block argues that the introduction of another covenant into a context about Horeb is unnecessary (ibid., 192). However, this pales in comparison to the intrusiveness felt by the introduction of the theme of restoration itself into the context.

> Because he loved your fathers and chose their offspring after
> them and brought you out of Egypt .... (4:37)

Though only one of these is explicit (1:8), the others involve patriarchal blessings: multiplication (1:11; cf. 7:13), land (1:21; 4:1), and election (4:37; cf. 7:6–8). Additionally, in the perspective of chapter 4, the present generation *is* the Horeb generation (see 4:9–20), which is distinguished from the "fathers" (4:37). Therefore, the covenant "with your fathers" in 4:31 most naturally refers to an antecedent covenant made prior to Horeb. Moreover, the two covenants (patriarchal and Horeb) appear to be contrasted in some way, though the exact nature of their relationship cannot be determined at this point. We will consider these issues further as we examine the rest of the book.

We have argued already for a temporal or circumstantial reading of the כי ("when") in verse 29 based on the parallel structure. While the "full" search—"with all your heart and with all your soul"—is a condition, it is an inevitable condition. The only question is how such a condition can be guaranteed. We begin to get an answer by observing the explicit theological basis in verse 31, which sets forth Yahweh's nature and commitment. On one level, verse 31 answers the simpler question, why would Yahweh receive Israel back? At a deeper level, it also suggests that, in some way not explicated, Yahweh himself will be the cause of Israel's spiritual resuscitation. If so, this would be consistent with the Yahweh-centeredness of verses 26–27.

## Theological Considerations

Exile is highly theological. Yahweh is intimately involved in the prospect. He is the source of the threat. He is the agent of destruction. He is the way of escape. And, he himself is the point of return. The combination of his passion (4:24) and compassion (4:31) shows that Yahweh is deeply interested and invested in Israel's future. Because her fundamental identity is as Yahweh's covenant partner, Israel is portrayed singularly. A word spoken to one generation affects all. While she is on the verge of embracing the long-standing promise of land, she now faces the threat of losing it. Thus, Israel should be as concerned as Yahweh about her future.

However, the description of exile and restoration in Deuteronomy 4:25–31 raises more questions than it answers concerning several theological issues. Is Israel even able to obey in the present? What is the relationship between the commandment and the promise in the covenant relationship? What is the real significance of the land? What is the relationship between the covenants Yahweh has established with this one covenant partner? We will consider these and other questions as we examine the rest of the book.

## SECOND CONTEXT: DEUTERONOMY 27–28

The themes of exile and restoration reappear in the latter chapters of the book. These themes are recapitulated and expanded especially in Deut 28:58–68 and 30:1–10, respectively. Deuteronomy 27–28, which serves as the context for the first passage, forms a concluding unit to Moses' second speech (4:44—28:68) around the themes of the potential blessings and curses facing Israel in the land.[129] After making some introductory observations on structure, this section will discuss the significant issues that pertain to our theme in each of the two chapters.

To discuss structure, we must make some comments on chapter 26, which is a transitional text. It forms an inclusio with chapter 12 as part of the framing structure around the specific laws of the so-called "lawcode."[130] Both texts deal with instructions to the people to go the place "that Yahweh your God will choose" and bring offerings (12:5–7; 26:1–2). Deuteronomy 26:16 also contains the phrase "laws and statutes," which occurs as a transitional marker at other points (5:1; 11:32; and 12:1).[131] Chapter 26 presents a series of declarations by Israelites on given occasions.[132] In the third and final declaration (vv. 16–19), Moses states that both Yahweh and Israel have declared themselves willing covenant partners. Israel commits to obey the laws wholeheartedly (v. 17); Yahweh declares that "today" Israel is his "treasured possession,"

---

129. Deuteronomy 27 is not actually part of the speech. See the discussion below on why chap. 27 was incorporated into the speech and can be considered with it.

130. See McConville, *Deuteronomy*, 376–77. The last of the specific laws ends at 25:16, and is followed by a command to destroy Amalek (25:17–19).

131. Lohfink, "Die '*huqqîm umispātîm*," 1–27. Cf. Christensen, *Deuteronomy 21:10—34:12*, 646; McConville, *Deuteronomy*, 382.

132. Note אמר in vv. 3, 5, 13, 17, 18. The first declaration deals with the bringing of firstfruits; the worshipers shall rehearse their ancestors' journey into and out of Egypt (vv. 3, 5–10). The second deals with the bringing of the triennial tithe; the worshiper affirms that he has obeyed the related commands (vv. 13–15).

and that she will have an esteemed reputation above all the nations and will be a sanctified people (vv. 18–19).[133]

As several scholars have recognized, this last affirmation serves as a transition to the following section of the book. Christensen and McConville,[134] for example, arrive at similar structures paralleling 11:26–32 and chapters 27–28, centered around 26:16–19:

A Blessing and curse in a covenant renewal under Moses (11:26–28)
  B Blessing and curse in a covenant renewal at Shechem (11:29–32)
    X Mutual commitments between Yahweh and Israel (26:16–19)
  B' Blessing and curse in a covenant renewal at Shechem (chap. 27)
A' Blessing and curse in a covenant renewal under Moses (chap. 28)

The logic of such a structure is to show a parallel between the future covenant at Shechem and the covenant at Moab, which, as we have seen, parallels the covenant at Horeb. This observation will help explain and relativize some of the conundrums of the text (especially with respect to chap. 27).

## Deuteronomy 27

Deuteronomy 27 prescribes three rituals to take place in the land as a form of covenant renewal: inscribing the law on stones (vv. 2–4), building an altar (vv. 5–7), and proclaiming blessings and curses (vv. 11–13). Notwithstanding some scholarly dissent,[135] these events come about in Joshua 8:30–35. Deuteronomy 27 has been puzzling to scholars for several reasons, including the seeming tension of chapter 27 in its context, the time and location of the first ritual (vv. 2–4), the identification of the stones in verse 8, and the relationship of the envisioned ceremony of blessings and curses in verses 11–13 and the declaration of curses in verses 14–26.[136] Though we will touch on these issues, the important

---

133. For a recent study on 26:16–19, see Block, "Privilege of Calling," 387–405.

134. Christensen, *Deuteronomy 21:10—34:12*, 644; McConville, *Deuteronomy*, 387. Similar structures are found earlier in Craigie, *Book of Deuteronomy*, 212; Lohfink, *Das Hauptgebot*, 233–34.

135. See the discussion in Tigay, *Deuteronomy*, 486–89.

136. Besides the commentaries, for helpful discussions of the main issues, see

theological point was stated above: future covenant renewal is an extension of the present covenant at Moab, which is an extension of Horeb.

With respect to the context, chapter 28 could naturally and easily follow chapter 26 as the conclusion to Moses' second speech in Moab. The "interruption" of chapter 27 is noted by the reversion to third-person address in 27:1 and the combination of speakers in the chapter (Moses and elders in v. 1; Moses and Levitical priests in v. 9; Moses alone in v. 11). While some use this to show literary discontinuity,[137] we have seen that larger structural factors can account for the position of chapter 27. The paralleling of covenants is a point shared by scholars who disagree about the literary continuity of the text.[138] Despite his critical stance, Tigay argues that the ceremonies in chapter 27 "constitute a third covenant, and it seems likely that they are interpolated here to make it clear that they are a reaffirmation of the one being made in Moab, and therefore of the earlier one concluded at Horeb as well."[139]

Deuteronomy 27 breaks naturally into three sections: verses 1–8, 9–10, 11–26.[140] The theme of covenant ceremony unites these sections to each other and to the surrounding context. An examination of each

---

Anbar, "Story of the Building of an Altar," 304–10; Barker, "Theology of Deuteronomy 27," 277–303; Bellefontaine, "Curses of Deuteronomy 27," 256–68; Buis, "Deuteronome XXVII 15–26," 478–79; Lewy, "Puzzle of Dueteronomy 27," 207–11; Lohfink, *Das Hauptgebot*, 233–34; Seebass, "Garazim und Ebal als Symbole," 22–31; Tigay, "Excursus 25: Deuteronomy 27," in *Deuteronomy*, 486–89; Weinfeld, "Emergence of the Deuteronomic Movement," 79–83.

137. For a summary of this position, see Anbar, "Story of the Building of an Altar," 304–10.

138. Note Millar's reference (in *Time and Place*, 70) to Anbar ("Story of the Building of an Altar"), suggesting that the construction of the altar in Deut 27:5–7 is interpolated to show a parallel between the covenant at Shechem (Josh 24) and Horeb.

139. Tigay, *Deuteronomy*, 246. Cf. Weinfeld, "Emergence of the Deuteronomic Movement," 83. In an excursus, Tigay (*Deuteronomy*, 488) presents a common critical stance, contending that Deuteronomy reconciles once independent traditions of when God established his covenant: Sinai/Horeb in Exod 19–24 and Deut 4–5; Moab in Deut 28:69; 29:9–28; at or near Shechem in Deut 27 and Josh 24.

140. Narrative markers begin each of these sections. The Hebrew texts divide before vv. 1 (MT, SP, 4QDeut$^c$), 9 (MT, SP), and 11 (MT), and after v. 26 (MT, SP, 4QDeut$^c$). MT also breaks before vv. 15, 16, 17, 18, 19, 21, 22, 23, 24, 25, 26. See Tigay, *Deuteronomy*, 393 n. 1. One could argue that vv. 1–10 constitute a unit by recognizing an envelope around the passage, indicated by the shift to first person in v. 10 and the parallel of "all the commandment" (v. 1) and "his commandments and his statutes" (v. 10); cf. Christensen, *Deuteronomy 21:10—34:12*, 652, 655. But vv. 9–10 relates to the Mosaic present, and so should be treated separately.

section will buttress the statement above on the position of chapter 27 in its context. The multiplicity of ceremonies suggests the great importance of Israel's land entry—comparable to the exodus, which also came with several ceremonies (cf. Exod 12–13).

In the first part (vv. 1–8), Moses and the elders[141] command two rituals at Shechem: writing the Torah on steles that will be set up in the land (vv. 2–4; cf. v. 8); and building an altar for sacrifice to Yahweh (vv. 5–7). Theologically, this section supports the basic continuity among the various covenants between Yahweh and Israel (Horeb, Moab, Shechem). The stipulations of the Moab covenant—"all the commandment" (v. 1) and "all the words of this Torah" (vv. 3, 8)[142]—are to be written down on stones, reminiscent of Horeb. The connection is unmistakable when we compare the ceremony in Exodus 24, which also combines the writing down of God's laws, the building of an altar, the offering of sacrifices, and the erection of stones. That all this is to take place at Shechem instead of Moab completes the theological point.

Seen in this light, some of the interpretive difficulties raised above are somewhat mitigated. Scholars have been troubled over the questions about when the stones in verses 2–4 are to be erected and which stones are to be inscribed in verse 8. For the first question, the phrase, "on the day you cross over the Jordan" (v. 2) suggests the erection of the stones would be the first act in the land. It would be impossible, however, for Israel to reach Mount Ebal (v. 4) within twenty-four hours,[143] and we know from the book of Joshua that several other events occur before this command is fulfilled (Josh 8:30f.). This has led many scholars to take verse 4 as a later interpolation.[144] This is an unnecessary step in light

---

141. The elders are added because Moses would not be present at the ceremony of covenant renewal on Mount Ebal (cf. priests in v. 9). See Craigie, *Book of Deuteronomy*, 327. The addition is consistent with the progression of the book towards the death of Moses and the overall Deuteronomic outlook of corporate responsibility of the whole community (cf. the distribution of leadership in 1:9–18).

142. The referent at least includes the laws in chaps. 12–26, but may include parts or all of chaps. 1–11. See Christensen, *Deuteronomy 21:10—34:12*, 653; McConville, *Deuteronomy*, 388; McConville and Millar, *Time and Place*, 71; Tigay, *Deuteronomy*, 247–48.

143. Mount Ebal (v. 4) is 30 miles from Jericho and 4000 feet higher.

144. These scholars argue that a general sense of "day" is not the natural way to construe v. 2 (with definite article and relative particle). The present text, then, is "an intentional conflation of traditions, those of Shechem where Israel's covenant tradition was particularly preserved, and those of Gilgal . . . where memories of Israel's first entry

of what we have already seen with respect to the regular Deuteronomic use of "today" as a call for urgent decision and Israel's ongoing journey, wherein each stage becomes a recapitulation of past events and responses.[145] The juxtaposition of "today" in verse 1 ("Keep all the commandment that I command you today") and "the day (you cross over the Jordan)" in verse 2, therefore, suggests that "[t]he day of Moab and the day of Shechem are brought into unity at the outset."[146]

With respect to the second question, verse 8 repeats the command of verse 3 to inscribe the Torah on stones, but the placement of verse 8 after the building of an altar with (other) stones (vv. 5–6) creates the impression that the stones of verse 8 are the stones of the altar rather than the stones of verses 2–3, leading to further speculation of interpolation and/or textual corruption.[147] Still, if the point of the passage is to highlight the covenant parallels, then it is possible that verse 8 is withheld for rhetorical effect; that is, it comes only after there has been an identification of Ebal and Horeb.[148] Whatever the solution, the text as it stands emphasizes Torah rather than the altar or sacrifice. By having God's revelation in written form, the foundation of Israel's faith and practice is sustained.[149]

The immediate concern of the Moab covenant comes back to the fore in verses 9–10. Moses is joined by the Levitical priests in giving a summary appeal to Israel to "hear" (שמע): "Keep silence and hear, O

into the land were preserved" (Mayes, *Deuteronomy* 341). Cf. Driver, *Deuteronomy*, 295-96, who sees different version of the command underlying the text; and Tigay, *Deuteronomy*, 486-87, who argues that this interpolation was made by the north Israelite circles in which the book developed who believed Mount Ebal was more suitable of a location than Gilgal since Shechem was the first place in the promised land where Abraham built an altar to God. I think the arguments for interpolation and conflation are unconvincing and ultimately unnecessary.

145. So Barker, "Theology of Deuteronomy 27," 277–303; McConville, *Deuteronomy*, 388; Millar, *Time and Place*, 72. Millar describes life in the land as a "settled nomadism."

146. McConville, *Deuteronomy*, 388. Similarly, Millar (*Time and Place*, 72) says the point is that the "day of decision" of Moab becomes the "day of response" in Canaan.

147. See especially the discussion in Tigay, "Excursus 25," 487–88. Tigay makes a good case why the stones of vv. 2–4 are different from the ones in vv. 5–6. He offers various possibilities that have been offered to explain the impression of v. 8.

148. McConville and Millar, *Time and Place*, 72.

149. Like the addition of other speakers (elders in v. 1; priests in v. 9), the focus on writing fits with the narrative's movement toward Moses' death. See Sonnet, *Book within the Book*, 95.

Israel! ... Hear the voice of Yahweh your God!" (27:9b, 10a). The call to "hear" is a call to repeat the Horeb experience (cf. 4:1; 26:16–19). The center of the passage, which comes between these commands, bases the appeal to fidelity (v. 10) in the established covenant relationship: "This day you have become the people of God" (v. 9).[150] Like the conflation of generations at Horeb in 4:10 (cf. 5:2–3), this surprising statement must be viewed more rhetorically than historically. This is not a denial that Israel had already been Yahweh's people. As McConville states, "Rather, the rhetoric illustrates that it must always enter the covenant afresh. That, indeed, is the essence of the idea enshrined in the Moab covenant itself."[151] This interpretation is strengthened by the stress (again) on "this day" (v. 9) and "today" (v. 10). Nevertheless, despite the continuity, Israel is indeed venturing on a new situation (i.e., life in the land)—one that presents greater blessings but also poses greater risks.

Verses 11–26 introduce the third ritual to take place at Shechem: the pronouncement of blessings and curses on Mount Gerizim and Mount Ebal, respectively. Traditionally, the twelve anathemas in verses 15–26 are assumed to constitute the "curse" of verse 13.[152] At least three difficulties must be overcome to retain this position.[153] First, since verse 14 has the Levites speaking, one must understand the subject of the infinitive לְבָרֵךְ, "to bless" (v. 12), to be other than the various tribes. One could translate the phrase, "for the blessing of the people" (cf. "for the curse" in v. 13).[154]

---

150. Cf. the chiastic structure of vv. 9-10, which puts this statement at the center, in Christensen, *Deuteronomy 21:10—34:12*, 652.

151. McConville, *Deuteronomy*, 390. Though Tigay understands the rhetorical nature of the statement, he goes too far in explaining the passage: "At Mount Sinai the people were frightened after hearing the Ten Commandments and asked Moses to receive the rest of God's commandments on their behalf (5:19—6:3). Now, forty years later, Moses is conveying to them the remaining commandments. Only now that they have received all of God's commandments—the full definition of their obligations to Him—are they fully His people" (*Deuteronomy*, 251).

152. This is supported by the Masoretic *parashiyot*, which indicate that vv. 11–26 form a single section, inferring that this is the same ceremony. See Tigay, *Deuteronomy*, 394 n. 33 (though Tigay rejects this interpretation; see pp. 251–53). This view is followed by, e.g., Craigie, *Book of Deuteronomy*, 331; McConville, *Deuteronomy*, 392–93; McConville and Millar, *Time and Place*, 73–74; and Seebass, "Garazim und Ebal," 23.

153. These difficulties are raised by those who consider that different ceremonies are envisioned in vv. 11–13 and vv. 14–26, respectively. See Lewy, "Puzzle of Deuteronomy 27," 207–11; cf. Christensen, *Deuteronomy 21:10—34:12*, 659; Tigay, *Deuteronomy*, 251–53.

154. McConville, *Deuteronomy*, 387 n. 12. Cf. also the blessings in Num 6:22ff.;

Second, one must account for the absence of blessings in verses 14ff. Some try to solve this issue by seeing a connection with chapter 28 and suggesting that the blessings in 28:1–14 were perhaps sufficient to make the point (cf. the structure below).[155] Third, one must deal with the difference between the type of curses one would expect in the covenant ceremony of 27:11–13 and the type we find in verses 15–26. As Buis points out, the connection with 11:27–29 shows that the blessings and curses of the ceremony would seem to be circumstantial descriptions of reward and punishment for obeying or disobeying the laws in general, not a list of curses against specific sins that focus more on the sins than the consequences.[156]

Whatever conclusion one comes to on the matter, it seems that the more significant issue is the function of the litany of curses in the context. Considering verses 11–26 within the structure of chapters 27–28 as a whole emphasizes again the parallel nature of Moab and Shechem. Christensen offers the following structure:

> A Shechem ceremony (27:1–10)
> B Positioning of tribes at Shechem—litany of 12 curses (27:11–26)
> X Six ritual blessings in Moab (28:1–14)
> B' Six ritual curses that echo the old Shechem ceremony (28:15–19)
> A' Moab ceremony (28:20–69)[157]

This shows that covenant reenactment was to be an ongoing part of the worship experience for Israel in the land. The curses in 27:15–26 are set against the mutual commitments in 26:16–19. Israel continually accepts the consequences if she fails to be the "holy people" Yahweh desires (cf. 26:19).

The curses themselves are formally different from those found in 28:15–68; by correlating with particular offences an individual might commit, they resemble laws and commands more than treaty sanc-

---

Deut 10:8ff.

155. E.g., McConville, *Deuteronomy*, 392–93. Craigie (*Deuteronomy*, 331) compares 28:3–6 and 16–19 and suggests that the twelve blessings would have been the exact reverse of the twelve curses. But Barker ("Theology of Deuteronomy 27," 281) thinks such a list would make little sense.

156. Buis, "Deuteronome XXVII 15–26," 478–79; cf. Tigay, *Deuteronomy*, 252.

157. Christensen, *Deuteronomy 21:10—34:12*, 659.

tions.¹⁵⁸ The list of sins includes relations to God (vv. 15, 26), social sins (vv. 16-19, 24-25), and sexual sins (vv. 20-23)—much like other representative lists in the Old Testament.¹⁵⁹ The unique emphasis of this list, however, is the concentration on sins that often escape detection because they are commonly committed in secret.¹⁶⁰ This is declared explicitly with respect to making a carved image and setting it up "in secret" (v. 15), and striking down a neighbor "in secret" (v. 24), but most of the others assume a similar situation. As Bellefontaine notes, "With regard to the curse, only the scrutiny of the deity could assure the execution of justice for secret crimes."¹⁶¹ These statements recognize the limitations of human processes and institutions of justice.

The covenant relationship is also emphasized. The first and last curses deal with relations to God and are the twin principles that sum up the book's teaching (developed in chap. 4): worshiping Yahweh alone and being faithful to his commands.¹⁶² But now the covenant relationship is extended to the individual level—"Cursed be anyone . . . ." This individuation will come up again in 29:17-28. The point seems to be that Yahweh is not willing for the nation to suffer for the sins of some. On the flip side, given the national nature of the curses in chapter 28 that end in exile, it suggests that if and when the nation experiences the curses, they will be the consequence of wholesale and widespread breach of the covenant by individuals.

## Deuteronomy 28

Deuteronomy 28 continues and concludes Moses' second discourse on the plains in Moab. The chapter presents a series of blessings and curses to encourage landed Israel to faithful obedience. The blessings include abundance in crops and food, human and animal fertility, wealth,

---

158. McConville, *Deuteronomy*, 392-93.

159. E.g., the Decalogue, Exod 21-23, Lev 18-20, Ezek 18, Ezek 22, and Ps 15. Cf. Christensen, *Deuteronomy 21:10—34:12*, 660. On the formal and thematic connections with the Decalogue, see the apodictic law argument in Alt, *Essays on Old Testament History and Religion*, 114-16.

160. See Weinfeld, *Deuteronomy and the Deuteronomic School*, 276-78.

161. Bellefontaine, "Curses of Deuteronomy 27," 58.

162. Tigay, (*Deuteronomy*, 253-54) notes that the first and last anathemas are the longest and phrased in a different style (relative clauses rather than participial), which shows that they are the most important. The two sins—making carved images and not fulfilling the words of the Torah—are the most frequent ones cited in Deuteronomy.

surplus, prestige, and military success (vv. 1–14). The curses include drought, disease, crop failure, economic collapse and dependency, military defeat, conquest, oppression, famine, cannibalism, and exile (vv. 15–68). The curses especially appear repetitious and detailed in order to make an impression on the mind and heart of the people.[163] Their comprehensiveness shows that Yahweh is in control of all the contingencies of life.

Much scholarly energy has been spent on the structure, style, and literary background of the chapter, especially with respect to ANE treaty parallels (and the parallels in Leviticus 26).[164] The striking parallels include drought, defeat, plague, illness, blindness, slavery, exile, locusts, the ruin of the city, and cannibalism.[165] While some have used the parallels to argue for dating the material,[166] the most important point is to recognize a common tradition in which to place the blessings and curses in Deuteronomy. This backdrop helps explain some of the data, such as the unequal length between the blessings and curses, and the lack of logical progression in much of the curse section. Unlike the treaties,

---

163. McCarthy, *Treaty and Covenant*, 187, notes that Deut 28 has transformed the mechanical or objective view of blessings and curses—which considers them as automatic consequences of obedience or disobedience—into something more emotive, persuasive, and internal. Olson (*Deuteronomy and the Death of Moses*, 120) adds, "In Deuteronomy this more objective point of view has been covered over by the desire to persuade. Thus the blessings and curses doubtless remain effective in themselves, but the full rhetorical expansion, the vivid picture of the promised good or evil, turns them into a means of convincing, or producing in the hearer or reader the will to obey because he is moved and persuaded.... The desire to produce an internal consent, a conviction which will move one to obedience, has been given an exceptionally important place."

164. Though the sources could be multiplied, the standard works include the following: Frankena, "Vassal-Treaties of Esarhaddon," 122–54; Hillers, *Treaty Curses*; McCarthy, *Treaty and Covenant*, 172–82; Plöger, *Literarkritische, formgeschichtliche und stilkritische*, 130–217; Seitz, *Redaktionsgeschichtliche Studien*, 254–302; Steymans, "Eine assyrische Vorlage," 118–41; Weinfeld, *Deuteronomy and the Deuteronomic School*, 116–29; idem, "Traces of Assyrian Treaty Formulae," 417–27. Tigay (*Deuteronomy*) offers two helpful excurses that summarize the issues ("Excursus 26: The Structure and Style of Deuteronomy 28," pp. 489–93; "Excursus 27: The Literary Background of Deuteronomy 28," pp. 494–97).

165. See especially McCarthy, *Treaty and Covenant*, 172–74.

166. The debate is whether the material is closer to Hittite treaties (second millennium) or neo-Assyrian treaties (seventh century). See the discussion in chap. 1.

however, Yahweh's covenant with Israel is not presented as a means of obliging other agencies to help.[167]

The blessings in verses 1–14 are tied to the land. On its own, this point is hardly remarkable, since the land is where Israel will be living. Still, two further observations add significance to the focus on land. First, this turf is explicitly "the land that Yahweh swore to your fathers to give you" (v. 11; cf. v. 8). Therefore, the land-based blessings point to Yahweh's commitment to his own word. Second, a major subject of the blessings is Israel's standing in relation to other nations (vv. 7, 10, 12, 13). The land becomes a platform for Yahweh to display his own glory in the world: "all the people of the earth shall see that you are called by the name of Yahweh" (v. 10). These factors must be kept in mind in the discussion of the theme of exile. Exile removes Israel from the realm of blessing, but it cannot entail a reversal or undoing of Yahweh's commitments to keep his word and to be glorified among the nations. On the contrary, exile is a fulfillment of the divine word (28:58–68) and will be viewed by foreigners as a demonstration of great power (29:21–27[22–28]).

The structure of the curse list in Deuteronomy 28:15–68 can be broken into three major parts (vv. 15–44, 45–57, 58–68) based on similar introductory verses:

> But if you will not heed the voice of Yahweh your God or be careful to do all his commandments and his statutes that I command you today, then all these curses shall come upon you and overtake you. (v. 15)

> All these curses shall come upon you and pursue you and overtake you until you are destroyed, because you did not heed the voice of Yahweh your God, to keep his commandments and his statutes that he commanded you. (v. 45)

> If you are not careful to do all the words of this Torah that are written in this book,
> ... then Yahweh will bring on you and your offspring extraordinary afflictions.... (vv. 58–59)[168]

---

167. McConville, *Deuteronomy*, 410.

168. See especially Tigay, *Deuteronomy*, 261ff., 489–92. Christensen (*Deuteronomy 21:10—34:12*, 665–66), who calls chap. 28 "the most tightly structured of the entire book," veers from most analyses by putting vv. 15–19 (the curses that begin with "Cursed shall you be") with vv. 1–15 and observing a chiastic pattern for the whole chapter. For the curse list (vv. 20–68), he sees major breaks at vv. 32 and 45, and considers vv. 58–68 as a subunit within vv. 45–68.

In the first section (vv. 15–44), six basic curses (using קלל) in verses 16–19 are expanded—with no logical or cause-and-effect order[169]—in verses 20–44, which threaten natural calamities, disease, and military reversals. In the second and third sections (vv. 45–57, 58–68), the curses have a completely national focus and show a natural sequence of disasters in which each leads to the next. According to verses 45–57, Israel faces utter privation before her enemies as Yahweh sends them into the land to destroy life and besiege the towns. The devastation progresses from foreign oppression (vv. 49–52) to self-destruction (vv. 53–57), and the military siege turns the Israelites into cannibals of their own children. Wrapped in highly charged theological language, the final outcome of military defeat—exile—is described in verses 58–68.

Instead of walking through each section in detail, we will deal with some of the details as they relate to specific theological observations relevant to our theme.[170] First, the blessings and curses display a concern for the triangular relationships of God-people-land. Unlike the typical ANE priority of the deity-land relationship, the relationship between Yahweh and Israel is clearly fundamental here.[171] Yahweh's treatment of the land is part and parcel of his disposition toward the people. As Olson states, the breakdown in the covenant relationship "leads to ecological disaster (drought, diseased crops), the revenge of nature (28:26, 42), political defeat and slavery at the hands of other people, and the loss of personal health, family, and security."[172] The land, therefore, is put in proper perspective: life in the land serves as a tangible display (to Israel and others) of Yahweh's particular concern for and connection with Israel. Israel's response to Yahweh, therefore, affects every sphere and relationship in which Israel finds herself.

Second, Yahweh is portrayed as the ultimate source and cause of the blessings and curses. This is maintained even though there is an al-

---

169. For example, the verses following the curse of exile in v. 36 presume Israel is still in the land. Tigay (*Deuteronomy*, 491) observes a mostly chiastic structure for these verses; exile in vv. 36–37 is matched with defeat before enemies in vv. 25–26 because both lead to Israel becoming a byword.

170. Cf. especially the observations in Olson, *Deuteronomy and the Death of Moses*, 120–22.

171. For a detailed discussion on the different emphases between Israelite and non-Israelite perspectives with respect to deity–people–land relationships, see Block, *Gods of the Nations*, especially 21–33.

172. Olson, *Deuteronomy and the Death of Moses*, 121.

ternation between the direct agency of Yahweh and a more impersonal agency. Yahweh is the direct agent of the blessings of superiority among the nations (v. 1); military victory (v. 7); success in labor (v. 8); sanctification (v. 9); abundance in prosperity, childbearing, livestock and crops (v. 11), and rain (v. 12). Yahweh is the explicit subject in most of the curses in verses 20–29, 35–37, and 58–68. The curses also include the agency of a foreign nation, which will inflict Israel with pain, siege, hunger, and destruction (vv. 48ff.). However, the enemies are explicitly those "whom Yahweh will send against you" (v. 48); the nation is one that "Yahweh will bring . . . against you from far away" (v. 49). On the other hand, explicit references to Yahweh are lacking in the blessings of verses 3–6 and curses of verses 16–19, 30–34, and 38–44. This last category of more impersonal agency displays "a kind of fixed order of correspondence between blessing and obedience, curse and disobedience."[173] Rather than detracting from divine causality and sovereignty, however, it actually supports it. All of life is under the control of the one God, Yahweh—a very different picture than the one represented by ANE parallels that set forth a variety of gods that have limited control of various spheres.

Third, the curses focus primarily on reversals of blessings. This can be noted immediately in comparing the six concise blessings in verses 3–6 with the six concise curses in verses 16–19. For every sphere involving a "blessed shall you be," there is a virtually identical "cursed shall you be": "in the city" (vv. 3a, 16a); "in the field" (vv. 3b, 16b); "the fruit of your womb, . . . ground, . . . and beasts" (vv. 4, 18); "your basket and your kneading bowl" (vv. 5, 17); "you in your coming in" (vv. 6a, 19a); and "you in your going forth" (vv. 6b, 19b). Table 6 reveals numerous other reversals and contrasts.[174]

Table 6. Covenant Reversals in Deuteronomy 28

The last example in table 6 prompts us to reflect further on the theme of covenant reversal. One of the most striking features throughout the curses is the motif of return to Egypt,[175] which echoes the "anti-exodus"

---

173. Ibid.

174. Several of these are pointed out by McConville, *Deuteronomy*, 405–8; and Tigay, *Deuteronomy*, 261–74.

175. See especially McConville and Millar, *Time and Place*, 75–77; Millar, *Now Choose Life*, 90–91. Millar claims that of the commentators only Craigie does justice to the memory of Egypt underlying the curses.

theme we observed in chapters 1–3 (cf. 17:14–20). Expulsion from the land is first mentioned in verse 21, ". . . until he has consumed you off the land."[176] Egypt is first explicitly mentioned in verse 27: "Yahweh will strike you with the boils of Egypt." Memories of the Egyptian experience include the death of livestock (v. 31), anger and anguish under oppression (vv. 32–33), affliction with boils (v. 35), failed harvests due to

| Blessing | | Curse |
|---:|:---:|---|
| Rain (12) | | Drought (23–24) |
| Defeat of enemies (7) | | Defeat before enemies (25a) |
| Respectful fear from nations (10) | | Horror to nations (25b, 37) |
| Protection of the weak (cf. 27:18) | | Blindness, exploitation (27–29) |
| *Shalom*, abundance (4, 8, 11) | | Futility before oppressors (30–34) |
| Exalted status over nations (1, 10) | | Captivity (36–37, 63ff.) |
| Ease and prosperity (11–13) | is reversed by | Economic dependence (38–44) |
| Serve Yahweh in freedom (47) | | Serve enemies in slavery (48) |
| Abundance (47) | | Lack of everything (48) |
| Land possession | | Loss of land possession (49–57) |
| Safety, Protection (4, 7, 10, 11) | | Devastation of foreigners (51) |
| Great numbers (cf. 1:10–11) | | Reduction in numbers (62) |
| Yahweh's joy in blessing (63) | | Yahweh's joy in destroying (63) |
| Rest from enemies (cf. 12:9–10) | | Restlessness in foreign place (65) |
| Terror on nations (7, 10) | | Terror on Israel (67) |
| Salvation from Egypt | | Return to Egypt (68) |

locusts (v. 38), and loss of offspring (v. 41). It seems the plagues Egypt once suffered are now threatened upon Israel. This suspicion is verified in verse 46 as the curses are labeled "a sign and wonder"—a phrase that until now always refers to the plagues (4:34; 6:22; 7:19; 34:11).[177] It is not so surprising, then, to find the final curse of exile to include, "and Yahweh will bring you back in ships to Egypt" (v. 68). We will discuss this verse further as we look in more detail at verses 58–68 and its depiction of the reversal of history.

A final feature to be observed is the sense of inevitability that develops in the description of the curses. The blessings and curses are presented as open possibilities in verses 1–44: the blessings in verses 1–14 are conditioned by אִם שָׁמוֹעַ תִּשְׁמַע, "if you surely obey" (v. 1); the curses in verses 15–44 are conditioned by אִם לֹא תִשְׁמַע, "if you will not obey" (v. 15). But a "key grammatical shift" takes place in verse 45, where "the text shifts abruptly from this conditional mode into a declarative and

---

176. Note the use of שׁמד (Hi.) and אבד in the parallel phrase in v. 20: ". . . until you are destroyed and perish."

177. Cf. Exod 7:3; 8:23; 10:1, 2; 11:9, 10.

narrative mode."¹⁷⁸ Instead of a conditional אם, "if," verse 45 uses a causal or explanatory כי: "All these curses shall come upon you and pursue you and overtake you till you are destroyed, *because* you did not obey . . . ." The referent of "all these curses" is comprehensive; verse 45 functions as a hinge or connecting link between the curses in verses 15-44 and the curses in verses 46-57, which focus more narrowly on military defeat and its consequences.¹⁷⁹ Therefore, what begins as conditional possibilities—as one would expect from ANE curse lists—becomes future actualities. Since this is so, when Israel heard the description of the curse of exile, it is as though she were given her obituary in advance. This is consistent with our analysis of 4:25ff., wherein exile is predicted and not merely threatened.¹⁸⁰ We will seek to explain why the curses are given a sense of inevitability later.

When we look at the theme of exile in Deuteronomy 28:58-68 specifically, it is clear that it is both a part of and a climax to the issues of chapter 28 discussed above. By definition, Israel's exile involves removal from the land. The text describes the Israel-Land separation in graphic terms; the idea of being "plucked off the land" (v. 63) and "scattered" (v. 64) is conjoined by harsh circumstances of afflictions and disease (vv. 59-61), loss of life (v. 63), and psychological trauma (vv. 65-67). Moreover, it is none other than Yahweh who will perform these acts: "Yahweh/he will bring on you . . ." (vv. 59, 60, 61); "Yahweh will take delight in bringing ruin upon you and destroying you (v. 63); "Yahweh will scatter you" (v. 64); and "Yahweh will return you" (v. 68). As we have seen, exile involves a series of reversals: death instead of life; grief instead of *shalom*; loss instead of increase; divine wrath instead of divine pleasure; dispossession of land instead of possession; and Egypt instead of Canaan.

---

178. Olson, *Deuteronomy and the Death of Moses*, 122. Partly due to this shift, some propose that vv. 45-68 may have been added later to conform to Israel's historical experience of exile. See McCarthy, *Treaty and Covenant*, 147 n. 11; Seitz, *Redaktionsgeschichtliche Studien*, 263-64. Tigay (*Deuteronomy*, 491) claims that nothing in the text requires the inference that the Babylonian conquest is in mind.

179. Craigie (*Book of Deuteronomy*, 347) notes the similar introductions in vv. 15, 20, and 45. Both Tigay (*Deuteronomy*, 268) and Christensen (*Deuteronomy 21:10—34:12*) explain how v. 45 looks backward and forward.

180. Commentators do not agree on this point of inevitability. McConville (*Deuteronomy*, 409-10), for instance, discounts any thought of inevitability in the list of curses, though his interest seems to be to counter those who seek to assign the curses to different historical periods.

## SECOND TEXT: DEUTERONOMY 28:58–68

The second major text on exile functions as the climactic paragraph of the covenant curses. In discussing this text, we will follow the same basic format as we did for Deuteronomy 4:25–31.[181] A comparison between 4:25–28 and 28:58–68 concludes this section.

> 58"If you are not careful to do all the words of this Torah that are written in this book, to fear this glorious and awesome name, Yahweh your God, 59then Yahweh will bring on you and your offspring extraordinary afflictions, afflictions severe and lasting, and sicknesses grievous and lasting. 60And he will return upon you every disease of Egypt, of which you were afraid, and they shall cling to you. 61Indeed every sickness and every affliction that is not written in the book of this law, Yahweh will bring upon you, until you are destroyed. 62Whereas you were as numerous as the stars of heaven, you shall be left few in number, because you did not heed the voice of Yahweh your God. 63And as Yahweh took delight in doing you good and multiplying you, so Yahweh will take delight in causing you to perish and destroying you. And you shall be plucked off the ground that you are entering to possess it. 64And Yahweh will scatter you among all the peoples, from one end of the earth[182] to the other end of the earth, and there you shall serve other gods of wood and stone, which neither you nor your fathers have known. 65And among these nations you shall find no respite, and there shall be no rest for the sole of your foot, and Yahweh will give you there an anguished heart and cried-out eyes and a dry throat.[183] 66Your life shall hang in doubt before you, and night and day you shall be in dread and have no assurance of your life. 67In the morning you shall say, 'If only it were evening!' and at evening you shall say, 'If only it were morning!' because of the dread that your heart shall dread, and the sights of your eyes that you shall see. 68And Yahweh will return you in ships[184] to Egypt, a journey that I

---

181. The variants to the MT of Deut 28:58–68 are minor and easily accounted for. Questions of translations will be handled in the discussion.

182. Hebrew ארץ could be "land" or "earth." Context favors the latter rendering.

183. Hebrew נפש could be translated "soul" to correspond to "heart" (cf. ESV, "languished soul"); but "throat" corresponds to the closer parallel, "eyes." On the translation and meaning of the phrase see Gruber, "Hebrew *da'ăbôn nepeš*" 365–69; cf. Tigay, *Deuteronomy*, 273; Christensen, *Deuteronomy 21:10—34:12*, 701.

184. Many follow J. Z. Meklenburg's repointing of MT בָּאֳנִיּוֹת, "in ships," to בַּאֲנִיּוֹת, an abstract plural of בַּאֲנִיָּה, "mourning, lamenting." See Christensen, *Deuteronomy 21:10—34:12*, 697; Tigay, *Deuteronomy*, 397 n. 104.

promised that you would never see again; and there you shall sell yourselves to your enemies as male and female slaves, but there will be no buyer." (Deut 28:58-68)

### Form, Structure, and Style

In the discussion of Deuteronomy 28 as a whole, we noted the transitional nature of verse 45 as the text picks up a sense of inevitability and begins to focus more narrowly on the final curses facing Israel. A different type of transition occurs at verse 58. The reference to "this book" (cf. "the book of this Torah" in v. 61) and the unusual reference to Yahweh's name signal that the curses are coming to an end.[185] Verses 58-68 share the basic stylistic features of the rest of the curse list.[186] Terminological and thematic links include the following: disobedience described as not heeding (שׁמע) Yahweh's voice (v. 62; cf. vv. 15, 45) and not keeping/doing (שׁמר/עשׂה) all his commandments (v. 58; cf. vv. 15, 45); the direct agency of Yahweh; explicit reference to Egypt (vv. 60, 68; cf. v. 27); the destruction terms, אבד (v. 63; cf. vv. 20, 22, 51) and שׁמד (vv. 61, 63; cf. vv. 20, 24, 45, 48, 51); idolatrous worship in exile (v. 64; cf. v. 36); psychological reactions "because of what your eyes shall see" (v. 67; cf. v. 34); and various reversals (see table 6).

Despite these links with the rest of the curse list, verses 58-68 exhibit some distinct features. First, the focus is much narrower. Removing Israel from the land is the primary concern, and is described by a concentration of terms: Hi. אבד (v. 63); Hi. שׁמד (v. 63); Ni. נסח, "pluck off" (v. 63); Hi. פוץ, "be dispersed, scattered" (v. 64); and Hi. שׁוב (v. 68). Second, Yahweh is the sole cause given in these verses. Unlike before, there is no mention of the mediate agency of another nation. Instead, Yahweh is explicitly identified as the one who will "bring upon you" the various afflictions in verses 59-61 and ultimate destruction in verse 62; he will be the cause of exile itself (vv. 63-64, 68) and of the lasting effects while in exile (v. 65). Third, the reversal described moves beyond simple antitheses to specific blessings. As we shall see, it involves a complete reversal of covenant and

---

185. McConville, *Deuteronomy*, 408. The references to "book" and "book of this Torah" in vv. 58 and 61 are the first (but see 17:18) of several in chaps. 28-31 (29:19-20[20-21], 26[27]; 30:10; 31:26; cf. 31:24). This new focus is due to the fact that Moses' address and life are coming to a conclusion.

186. On the style of the curse list, see Hillers, *Treaty Curses*, 12-42; Tigay, *Deuteronomy*, 492-93.

history. Because of this, verses 58–68 really are outside the range of parallels between chapter 28 and the ANE treaty tradition.[187]

The climactic features of verses 58–68 support its consideration as a semi-independent sub-unit. Christensen observes the following concentric structure:

| A  | YHWH will bring back upon you the *"plagues" of Egypt* | 28:58–61 |
| B  | You will be decimated in numbers | 28:62 |
| X  | YHWH takes delight in destroying you | 28:63 |
| B' | YHWH will scatter you among the nations | 28:64–65 |
| A' | YHWH will make you *return to Egypt* | 28:66–68[188] |

This structure is useful in seeing the main theological thrusts of the passage. The outer frame progresses from "Egypt" entering Israel to Israel entering Egypt! With a return to Egypt, Israel's history is undone. The inner frame, with its focus on reduction in numbers and removal from the land, implies the reversal of the patriarchal covenant. The center is the most disturbing as the basis of covenant relationship—Yahweh's election of and commitment to Israel—is overturned. We will discuss the interplay of these themes as we examine the text in detail.

### Exposition

We noted the inherent tension between the conditionality and inevitability of Israel's future in 4:25–31 (especially the use of כי in 4:25 and 29). The same tension exists in the present text. The sense of inevitability that pervades the curse list by this point is supported by the repetition of the causative כי-clause (from v. 45) in verse 62: "*because* you did not heed the voice of Yahweh your God." After all, the requirement is to do "*all* the words of this Torah" with an internal disposition of "fear" toward Yahweh (v. 58). However, Moses begins this last section with a reminder

---

187. The comparisons of curses tend to be limited to vv. 20–57. See Lenchak, *Choose Life*, 23.

188. Christensen, *Deuteronomy 21:10—34:12*, 698. The boundaries of the first three units (vv. 58–61, 62, and 63) are marked by the *Numeruswechsel* at the beginning and end of vv. 62 and 63. The *Numeruswechsel* also occurs at the end of v. 68. Cf. his larger structure of chap. 28 on pp. 664–66, 698–99. Though Christensen considers vv. 45–68 as a unit, he recognizes that vv. 58–68 has its own concentric structure that can be viewed independently (what he calls a "wheel within a wheel").

of the conditionality of the matter (אִם, "if," in v. 58). If Israel is ultimately destroyed, she will have no excuse for she has been sufficiently warned.

In keeping with the nature of the curses in chapter 28, we can approach this text through the lens of covenant reversal. At least six reversals can be observed.[189] The specific terminology used to describe these reversals, however, points to the deeper theological structure in which the theme of exile is embedded. First, a medical reversal focuses on the severity and duration of sickness and disease (vv. 58–61). These afflictions are the natural consequences of the siege in the previous section (vv. 45–57). But the real issue is Israel's identity, not her health. By labeling these afflictions as "every disease of Egypt" (v. 60), Yahweh threatens to expose Israel to the horrifying plagues he once sent upon Egypt. Thus, what is actually at stake is a reversal of the exodus—a reversal of Israel's history of salvation.[190]

Second, a numerical reversal reduces the population to a small remnant (vv. 62–63). Similar to above, however, the issue is more than a matter of numbers. In Deuteronomy, the phrase, "as numerous as the stars of heaven" (28:62), describes the size of the people presently (1:9; 10:22), which is a direct fulfillment of Yahweh's promise to Abraham (cf. Gen 15:5). The root רבה, "be great," used in verse 63 of Yahweh's multiplying the people, parallels the antecedent description that in Egypt Israel became "populous" (adjective רב in 26:5; cf. רבה in Exod 1:7). Conversely, the phrase, "few in number" (v. 62), depicts the size of the people as they first sojourned to Egypt under Jacob (26:5). By using such terminology, therefore, the more significant threat is, again, a reversal of Israel's history. Further, now that the patriarchs are also in view, this reversal of history is simultaneously a reversal of the patriarchal covenant.

Not surprisingly, then, the third reversal is geographic: Israel shall be removed from the land of promise and driven to other nations (vv. 63ff.).[191] Several terms employed highlight similar connections we have seen with respect to the other reversals. אבד and שמד (both Hi. in v. 63),

---

189. See especially Head, "Curse of Covenant Reversal," 218–26.

190. On the anti-exodus theme in the curse list as a whole, see the discussion of chap. 28 above.

191. The use of אדמה rather than ארץ for the land may be influenced by the concreteness of the event—especially with the use of נסח (Ni.), "be plucked off"—but does not diminish the theological point.

as we detailed in chapter 2 of this study, are used in different senses in Deuteronomy. They occur together in four other texts: once in describing exile (4:26), twice in describing the conquest of the land (7:24; 9:3), and once at the front of the curse list (28:20). The conquest passage in chapter 7 (vv. 17ff.) compares Yahweh's destruction of the Canaanites to his judgment of Egypt; in chapter 28, the same fate is reserved for Israel. אבד is used in 26:5 to describe Jacob as "a *wandering* (Qal ptc. אבד) Aramean"; though the meaning is different (see chap. 4), it shows one more link between the two passages. Finally, this land is that which "you are entering to possess it" (v. 63)—the common Deuteronomic reference pointing to the fulfillment of the major tenet of the Abrahamic promise. When these allusions are considered together, exile becomes shorthand for every reversal conceivable for Israel.

Fourth, a national and religious reversal will dissolve Israel's identity as the people of Yahweh since they will be forced to serve foreign gods (v. 64). The description of idolatry in exile is a reversal in at least two interdependent ways. One, it is a reversal of Israel's election. The gods that will be worshiped are explicitly categorized as gods "which neither you nor your fathers have known." Once again, the memory of the patriarchs is invoked in order to demonstrate what such a departure entails. This is strengthened by the language of "scattering" (פוץ) for exile—the same term used in the incident of Babel (cf. Gen 11:8), after which Israel's history began. In other words, Israel will be returned to a pre-Abrahamic state while in exile; that is, she will no longer be Israel. Two, idolatry in exile signifies a reversal of the covenant established at Horeb because it involves a rejection of its most fundamental tenet—exclusive devotion to Yahweh. We saw in chapter 4 that the prohibition of images as the core of obedience is rooted in the person (monotheism) and work (exodus) of Yahweh. This is simply an exposition of the Decalogue, which unites redemption from Egypt and avoidance of idolatry. Therefore, for Israel to be forced into idolatry is a statement of her status and not merely of her condition.

Fifth, a dispositional reversal brings about a lack of security and *shalom* (vv. 65–67). Exilic existence will include the physical and psychological struggles of lack of rest "for the sole of your foot" (v. 65), anguish (adj. רגז, "tremble") and grief over loss (v. 65),[192] doubt (v. 66), and dread (פחד in vv. 66 and 67). These are clearly reversals of specific blessings. Moses equates life in the land with having "rest from all your enemies" and "living in safety" (12:10; cf. 3:20). The thrust of the blessings for obedience in 28:1–14 is that life shall be free of worry; Israel need not fear the elements or tentativeness of nature for these are under the control of Yahweh. Neither would Israel need to fear enemies; rather, they shall flee before Israel (v. 7) and be afraid of her (ירא in v. 10). Even so, a consideration of verbal and thematic connections reveals that more is at stake than the temporal experiences of exile. Three antecedent passages, in particular—one concerning the exodus and two concerning the conquest—speak of similar expressions of fear evoked in peoples by Yahweh:

> The peoples have heard; they *tremble* (רגז)
> pangs have seized the inhabitants of Philistia.
> Now are the chiefs of Edom dismayed;
> trembling seizes the leaders of Moab;
> all the inhabitants of Canaan have melted away.
> Terror and *dread* (פחד) fall upon them;
> Because of the greatness of your arm, they are still as a stone,
> till your people, O Yahweh, pass by,
> till the people pass by whom you have purchased. (Exod 15:14–16)

> This day I will begin to put the *dread* (פחד) and fear (ירא) of you on the peoples who are under the whole heaven, who shall hear the report of you and shall *tremble* (רגז) and be in anguish (חול) because of you. (Deut 2:25)

> Every place on which *the sole of your foot* treads shall be yours. Your territory shall be from the wilderness to the Lebanon and from the River, the river Euphrates, to the western sea. No one shall be able to stand against you. Yahweh your God will lay the *dread* (פחד) and fear (מורא) of you on all the land that you shall tread, as he promised you. (Deut 11:25)

---

192. This appears to be the sense of "cried-out eyes" and "a dry throat." The first idiom is also found in v. 32, which describes one's reaction to having one's children taken away; the second expression is a symptom of grief or depression. On the translation and meaning of these phrases, see Tigay, *Deuteronomy*, 265, 273; Christensen, *Deuteronomy 21:10—34:12*, 685, 701.

Israel will thus not only lose what she had, but will suffer the positive judgment of Yahweh heretofore reserved only for others. Israel's special status will be taken away.

Sixth, a redemptive reversal will force Israel back into Egypt (v. 68). What the text has been driving at all along is now made explicit. Obviously, this is a reversal of the exodus, but it is more than that. It is a reversal of promise: " . . . a journey that I promised that you should never make again."[193] This reverse journey is seemingly final—unlike the one in the wilderness in which Israel was given a second chance (cf. 2:1ff.). The comparison of this trip to Egypt during exile to the original descent to Egypt under Jacob creates a stark contrast. Israel had first traveled to Egypt to escape famine (Gen 45:9-11; cf. Abram's similar circumstances in Gen 12:10); while in Egypt, she was forced into slavery (cf. Exod 1:8-11). Now, Israelites will actually seek the status of slaves in Egypt, "but there will be no buyer." The problem is that the true "famine" for Israel is internal, and there is no escape from it.

These interrelated reversals constitute the theological significance of exile. However horrible the actual experience of exile would be, its symbolism is far worse. Exile stands for a rejection of Israel's history—of election, redemption, and covenant. Yes, Israel's disobedience yielding exile shows that she has rejected these gifts, but exile is also about Yahweh's rejection of Israel. To reiterate the central verse, it is Yahweh himself who "will take delight in causing you to perish and destroying you" (v. 63). When Yahweh sends Israel into exile, he is putting her to death; he is killing his son, divorcing his bride, trashing his treasured possession.

Understanding exile as the death of the nation allows us to address again the use of אבד and שמד in the text. These verbs appear together or in close proximity throughout chapter 28;[194] as Driver says, they are "repeated with knell-like effect."[195] Since these terms are fairly strong words for destruction—which may include complete annihilation (especially

---

193. This is a combination of elements from Exod 14:13 ("For the Egyptians whom you see today, you shall never see again") and a similar phrase in the king law in Deut 17:16. See the discussion in Reimer, "Concerning Return to Egypt, 217-29. In trying to establish a *Sitz im Leben* for the phrase, Reimer unfortunately misses the obvious theological point.

194. אבד in vv. 20, 22, 51, 63; שמד in vv. 20, 24, 45, 48, 51, 61, 63.

195. Cited in Tigay, *Deuteronomy*, 493.

שמד)—commentators typically label their usage as "hyperbolic"[196] and/ or use it as evidence of the non-logical nature of the accumulation of the curses.[197] While either interpretation seems reasonable in most of the eleven occurrences of the verbs in the chapter, neither is sufficient to explain their use in verse 63. Like their combined use in 4:26, אבד and שמד are contextualized by the parallel exilic terms נסח, "be plucked off" (v. 63), and פוץ, "be scattered" (v. 64; cf. 4:27), and the phrase, "be left few in number" (v. 62; cf. 4:27). Our contention, therefore, is that the "destruction" depicted by אבד and שמד is none other than exile—at least in 28:63 (and 4:26), and perhaps elsewhere.[198] Conversely, the connotations of death inherent in these terms help us understand the theological significance of exile (i.e., exile is death of a nation). Having analyzed the various reversals in verses 58–68, this connection appears founded.

Now we must see if any of the other references of אבד and שמד in chapter 28, in fact, connote exile. It is interesting that אבד and/or שמד appear in the three most inclusive or summative verses:

> Yahweh will send on you curses, confusion, and frustration *in all that you undertake to do*, until you are destroyed (Ni. שמד) and perish (אבד) quickly on account of the evil doing in forsaking me. (v. 20)

> *All these curses* shall come upon you and pursue you and overtake you till you are destroyed (Ni. שמד). (v. 45)

> Indeed *every sickness and every affliction* that is not written in the book of this law, Yahweh will bring upon you, until you are destroyed (Ni. שמד). (v. 61)[199]

---

196. E.g., Tigay (*Deuteronomy*, 262) on the use of both terms in v. 20; he also points out that there are still survivors after Israel is "wiped out" in vv. 61ff.

197. E.g., on vv. 62–63, McConville (*Deuteronomy*, 408) states, "The threat of obliteration is nevertheless followed by one that strictly contradicts it, of greatly reduced numbers." According to our study, however, while the order of the curses in vv. 15–44 is non-logical, the ones in vv. 45–68 do seem to offer an overall progression.

198. Of course, the normal sense of destruction that occurs in the events leading up to exile are also in view.

199. We should note, however, that v. 15 does not contain these terms but is similarly inclusive: "If you will not heed the voice of Yahweh your God . . . then *all these curses* shall come upon you and overtake you."

The first two verses occur at significant breaks in the text: verse 20 introduces the curses in verses 21–44;[200] verse 45 both concludes the previous section and introduces the following section. The third verse (v. 61) appears in such close proximity to the theme of exile in verses 62ff. that it is difficult not to include it with the exilic terms. The most suggestive reference occurs in verse 20. While not denying actual destruction and devastation in the use of these terms, one cannot deny a possible hint at exile. In the next verse, destruction terminology is combined with removal from land, as Yahweh causes agricultural disaster to fall "until he has put an end (כלה) to you *from upon the land* that you are entering to possess it" (v. 21). If an exilic connotation for אבד and שמד is at least possible in verse 20, then we must say the same for the references to אבד in verse 22 and שמד in verse 24, which are in such close proximity to verses 20–21. In fact, since verse 20 comes near the beginning of the curses, and verse 63 comes near the end, an exilic connotation of the terms in these verses would suggest that the entire curse list is enveloped in the threat of exile. Though this conclusion is not necessary in order to maintain the theological points made previously, it further emphasizes the importance of the anti-exodus and covenant reversal themes in chapter 28. It also suggests the need to re-evaluate other Deuteronomic references to אבד and שמד (see chap. 4 of this study).

### Comparisons with 4:25–28

We have often alluded to Deuteronomy 4 in our explication of the theme of exile in Deuteronomy 28. It may be helpful to summarize the similarities and note any significant differences. First, the thematic and lexical links are well established. The notion of exile is carried basically by the same terms: אבד (4:26; 28:63); שמד (4:26; 28:63); פוץ, "scatter," (4:27; 28:64); and נהג, "drive" (4:27; 28:37). Chapter 28 adds Hi. הלך, "bring" (v. 36), Ni. נסח, "be pulled, torn away" (v. 63), and Hi. שוב, "return" (v. 68). Both texts utilize the phrase, "be left (Ni. שאר) few in number," but perhaps differently: in 4:27, the remnant is in the exiled land; in 28:62, it is unclear if the remnant described remains in the land or is exiled.[201]

---

200. According to our structure of the text, v. 15 actually introduces vv. 15–44. However, as we noted, vv. 20–44 is an expansion of the קלל curses of vv. 16–19; therefore, v. 20 serves as a secondary introduction. Cf. Christensen (*Deuteronomy 21:10—34:12*, 665, 680), who keeps vv. 15–19 with vv. 1–14 and begins a new section at v. 20.

201. We will discuss remnant theology in chap. 5.

Another difference in terminology is that only chapter 4 emphasizes the immanence of the curse of exile: "you will *soon* (מהר) utterly perish from the land," and "you will not live long in it" (4:26). In chapter 28, מהר is used only in verse 20 (with אבד); it would not seem appropriate, however, to emphasize quickness at the end of such a long list of curses, especially with exile being the final curse after siege and war.

Second, both texts emphasize the direct hand of Yahweh in bringing about Israel's exile. It is interesting that while the curses in chapter 28 alternate between direct, divine agency and the use of mediate agents (whether human or "nature"), in verses 58–68 only Yahweh is given as an agent. This is exactly the same situation in 4:26–27.

Third, both texts present idolatry as an added curse in the place of exile: "there you shall serve (other) gods of wood and stone" (4:28; 28:36, 64). As we observed, 28:64 adds the note that these gods were previously unknown to Israel (including the "fathers").[202] Interestingly, while chapter 4 focuses on idolatry as the fundamental sin that leads to exile, idolatry is never singled out in chapter 28 as a cause for experiencing the curses. The closest the covenant curses come is in the phrase, "because you forsook (עזב) me" (v. 20). Otherwise, Israel's infidelity is described more generally and universally as not "heeding" (שמע) Yahweh's voice (vv. 15, 45), not "serving" (עבד) Yahweh gladly (v. 46), and not carefully "doing" (עשה) Yahweh's law (v. 58).

In chapter 5, we will summarize the description of exile in Deuteronomy in more detail. However, it is already clear with these two main texts that chapter 28 picks up and expands on the details of the theme of exile in chapter 4. We might even say that 28:58–68 is performing a sort of "resumptive exegesis" of 4:25–28. It remains to be seen if the theme of restoration experiences the same thing.

## THIRD CONTEXT: DEUTERONOMY 28:69—30:20

The most significant text on the theme of restoration in Deuteronomy is found in 30:1–10. Comparing 4:25–31, one might expect this text to follow immediately upon the curse of exile in 28:58–68.[203] Instead, the two

---

202. In 28:36, it is the nation to which Israel is exiled that is said to have been unknown to Israel and the "fathers."

203. See Block, "Recovering the Voice of Moses," 391 nn. 35 and 36; 396–97; Driver, *Deuteronomy*, xxiii; Lenchak, *Choose Life*, 36; Alexander Rofé, "Covenant in the Land of Moab," 269–80. Rofé notes that early commentators (A. Dillman, A. Bertholet) detected

texts are "interrupted" by an entire chapter (chap. 29)—one that develops several significant theological themes and further discussion of the theme of exile. Deuteronomy 30:1-10 must be viewed in light of its more immediate context: Moses' third discourse (Deut 28:69—30:20).[204]

Deuteronomy 28:69 reads, "These are the words of the covenant that Yahweh commanded Moses to make with the people of Israel in the land of Moab, besides the covenant that he had made with them at Horeb." It has been notoriously difficult to decide whether the verse functions as a subscription to the preceding chapters, following MT, or a superscription to chapters 29-30 (or chaps. 29-32[205]), following LXX.[206] Despite the detailed arguments for both sides of the debate, it appears that the verse should be viewed as a pivotal text that actually belongs

---

this "problem." He cites as evidence the lack of blessings and curses in chap. 29 and similar terminology between 30:1-10 and chap. 28, but missing in chap. 29: "to obey Yahweh" (30:2, 8, 10; cf. 28:1, 15, 45 [29:17 has a distinct diction: "whose heart turns aside from Yahweh"]; scattering (30:3; cf. 28:64 [29:27 has "uprooting"]); abundance, etc. (30:9; cf. 28:11); and "delighting in" (30:9; cf. 28:63). According to Rofé, the only parallel language with chap. 29 is between 29:20 and 30:7, but he considers 30:7 to be a late interpolation, following several early commentators. He concludes that 30:1-10 was not originally part of the Moab covenant.

204. See below for the delineation of these boundaries. The versification here will follow that of MT, which differs with English translations (based on LXX and Vg) with respect to chap. 29. The variance has to do with different views of 28:69 (Eng. 29:1) (see discussion below). As such, the numbers in the English verses in chap. 29 are one higher than in the Hebrew.

The numeration of "third" discourse is based on incorporating chap. 27 within the second discourse. Deut 28:68 concludes Moses' second speech (introduced in 4:44); 29:1 begins his third speech (ending at 30:20).

205. Some argue from a redaction-critical perspective that the superscription in 28:69 ("These are the words of the covenant") functions to unite all of chaps. 29-32. See Lohfink, "Der Bundesschluß im Land Moab," 32-56; Olson, *Deuteronomy and the Death of Moses*, 126-58. The argument is based on the fact that the next superscription does not appear until 33:1 ("This is the blessing"). Against this view are those that argue on the basis of ANE parallels—i.e., covenants end with blessings and curses—that the covenant of Moab extends only through chaps. 29 and 30. So Rofé, "Covenant in the Land of Moab." Besides this parallel, the reporting speech in 31:1-2a interrupts Moses' speech and introduces another (brief) discourse. See Lenchak, *Choose Life*, 171.

206. See the overview of approaches and arguments in Barker, *Triumph of Grace*, 110-12. Most modern commentators favor the superscription view, primarily based on two factors: "covenant" is not used with Moab in earlier references, but "covenant" occurs seven times in 29:1-24; and the other headings in the book (1:1; 4:44; 33:1) are all clearly superscripts. The subscription view still finds some support (Tigay, *Deuteronomy*, 274; van Rooy, "Deuteronomy 28,69—Superscript or Subscript?" 215-22), based on the argument that "words of the covenant" always refers to covenant stipulations or curses.

to both sections.²⁰⁷ We have already witnessed the transitional nature of other texts (26:16–19; 28:45; cf. 29:28), so it is not surprising to find one here. This verse is significant in establishing a connection between the Horeb and Moab covenants—a connection, in fact, made explicit for the first and only time in the book here in this verse. The important point is that the two covenants are juxtaposed to show continuity. Against those who, from a historical-critical perspective, argue that in Deuteronomistic thought Moab is a replacement of Horeb in light of Israel's disobedience,²⁰⁸ the Moab covenant seems more like an augmentation rather than replacement.²⁰⁹ This is consistent with the paralleling of Moab and Shechem in chapters 27–28. On the front side, the only "newness" (of Moab) includes new conditions related to life in the land of Canaan. However, something altogether new takes place in Israel's future restoration (30:1–10), which will raise the question of covenantal continuity from a different angle.

Moses' third discourse is typically viewed as the Moab covenant proper. It is seen as a kind of covenant document, a covenant sermon, or a text used in a covenant renewal ceremony.²¹⁰ This identification has to do with two main factors: the twofold use of ברית, "covenant," in 28:69;²¹¹ and the recognition of components of the ANE treaty form.²¹²

---

207. So also Christensen, *Deuteronomy 21:10—34:12*, 703–6. Cf. Barker, *Triumph of Grace*, 112, who favors the superscription view, but notes that the presence of the debate shows that the division between chaps. 28 and 29 is not as great as some would make out, and gives further support to the close relationship between Horeb and Moab.

208. So Preuss, *Deuteronomium*, 158; Seitz, *Redaktionsgeschichtliche Studien*, 91; cf. Cholewinski, "Zur theologischen Deutung des Moabbundes," 96–111.

209. Barker *Triumph of Grace*, 112–16; McConville and Millar, *Time and Place*, 78–79. Barker refers to several scholars who see an identity between the two covenants, whether in terms of repetition, renewal, explanation, confirmation, supplementation, or extension.

210. E.g., Buis and Leclerq, *Le Deutéronome*, 181; Wright et al., "Deuteronomy," 317; Thompson, *Deuteronomy*, 279. For a survey of approaches on Moses' third discourse, see Barker, *Triumph of Grace*, 108–10. Few argue for literary unity of the section. Not surprisingly, chaps. 29–30 are typically regarded as late (exilic or post-exilic) and understood as reflections upon the Exile.

211. Lenchak (*Choose Life*, 87) notes that the emphasis in 28:69 is not on the speaker nor the audience, but the message of "covenant" itself.

212. A simple version is given by Wright, *Deuteronomy*, 284: historical prologue (29:1–8); parties to the agreement (29:9–14); basic stipulation (29:17); curses for disobedience (29:18–27); possibility of restoration and blessing (30:1–10); and witnesses (30:19). See especially the discussion and various proposals in Lenchak, *Choose Life*, 34

While the parallels with the treaty tradition here are clear,[213] we have already noted differences with respect to the ANE treaties and chapters 4 and 28. It is difficult, therefore, to separate this text from the preaching of Moses in its entirety in Deuteronomy.[214] The text must be seen in its context within the book and not as an independent treaty document.[215] After all, it is Moses' second speech that provided all the terms of this covenant (4:44—26:19; chap. 28). Furthermore, the future outlook of chapters 29-30 corresponds to 5:22-31, which outlined provisions for Moses' continued mediation of God's word at Horeb into the future.[216]

The connections between this unit and the rest of the book can also be seen from a macrostructural consideration. It was pointed out above that chapters 11 and 27-28 form a frame around the preaching

---

n. 128. While some (e.g., Baltzer, McCarthy, Cholewinski) observe a full-fledged treaty structure in chaps. 29-30, others (e.g., Lohfink) see only traces of the treaty form. Rofé ("Covenant in the Land of Moab") sees parallels with Hittite vassal treaties, but only after he removes the supposed interpolations (especially 29:21-27 and 30:1-10).

213. See Lenchak, *Choose Life*, 21-25, 34; Weinfeld, *Deuteronomy and the Deuteronomic School*, 142.

214. For this reason, McConville (*Deuteronomy*, 413) argues against seeing only chaps. 29-30 as the Moab covenant. For extensive references back to chaps. 1-28 in chaps. 29-30 see discussion and exhaustive list in Lenchak, *Choose Life*, 33, 114-18. Cf. the appendix on deuteronomic phraseology by Weinfeld, *Deuteronomy and the Deuteronomic School*, 320-59. Of the 249 words, expressions, and combinations of expressions that Weinfeld lists as characteristic of Deuteronomy and the Deuteronomistic History, 46 are found in Deuteronomy 29-30. Significant verbal and thematic links include Yahweh's oath to the fathers with respect to the land (29:12; 30:5, 20); "with all your heart and soul" (30:2, 6, 10; cf. 4:29; 6:5; 10:12; 11:13; 13:4; 26:16); and "which I am commanding you today" (30:2, 8, 11, 16; cf. 2[2x], 40; 6:6; 7:11; 8:1, 11; 10:13; 11:8, 13, 22, 27, 28; 12:11, 14, 28; 13:1, 19; 15:5; 19:9; 27:1, 4, 10; 28:1, 13, 14, 15).

215. Therefore, I agree with those who caution against hasty conclusions; see McConville, *Law and Theology in Deuteronomy*, 37, 159; Preuss, *Deuteronomium*, 66. Olson (*Deuteronomy and the Death of Moses*, 128) contends that while chaps. 29-32 are explicitly described as "covenant" in 28:69, it does not fit with the ANE treaty form. Mayes (*Deuteronomy*) contends that in chaps. 29-30 "the only really essential element of such a ceremony (and so also of the form), the stipulations, is missing; furthermore, the chapter in fact fall [sic] into almost self-contained units" (Quoted in Rofé, "Covenant in the Land of Moab," 317). Lenchak (*Choose Life*, 24) comments, "Despite so many contacts with and similarities to the ancient vassal treaty, Dt cannot be seriously considered a treaty document itself. Whoever wrote Dt probably made use of the language, ideas, and even form of the treaties to render Israel's covenant and legal traditions faithful to both past and present. Unlike the treaty, however, Dt is not a legal document but an oration with the style of a sermon. It deviates at times from the treaty form."

216. Olson, *Deuteronomy and the Death of Moses*, 126-27.

of the specific laws of chapters 12–26. Similarly, several have perceived that chapters 4–11 (especially chap. 4) and 29–30 form a frame around the Deuteronomic code of chapters 5–28.[217] The connections between chapters 29–30 and chapter 4 go deeper than references to exile and restoration.[218] Both texts show a treaty scheme of history, law, and sanction serving as background. Both fuse Horeb and Moab. Both engage in generational conflation.[219] Both recognize that blessing and curse are subsequent historical facts rather than mere alternatives (4:29-30; 30:1ff.). Both discuss the nearness of God (4:7-8; 30:11-14). Vocabulary connections include idols of wood and stone (4:28; 29:16) and the triad of trials, signs, and wonders (4:34; 29:2).

Like chapter 4, chapters 29–30 consists of a series of exhortations to observe the covenant made in Moab: "Therefore keep the words of this covenant and do them, that you may prosper in all that you do" (29:8). The motivations include several temporal horizons: recital of God's past actions (29:1-8); confirmation of the covenant "today" (29:9-14), including a sermonic warning to the individual (29:15-20); and consideration of foreign appraisal following the full implementation of the curses in the future (29:21-27). Couched between two statements on the accessibility of the law (29:28; 30:11-14), a future restoration is envisioned (30:1-10). The unit ends with a final exhortation to "choose life" (30:15-20). We will proceed through chapters 29–30 in the same way as we did through chapter 4—by noting the various motivations offered for obedience and highlighting the themes that provide the theological context for exile and restoration.

## Deuteronomy 29

While Deuteronomy 29 and 30 form a unit, they exhibit some significant differences in tone and style. Chapter 29 is more pessimistic; chapter

---

217. See, e.g., Begg, "Literary Criticism," 49; Driver, *Deuteronomy*, lxxvi; Knapp, *Deuteronomium 4*, 129-38; Levenson, "Who Inserted the Book of the Torah?" 212-14; Lohfink, *Höpre Israel*, 119-20; Mayes, "Deuteronomy 4," 44-46; McCarthy, *Treaty and Covenant*, 202-5. For other references see Lenchak, *Choose Life*, 5. All see that this framing surrounds the obligations and curses of the deuteronomic code with a message of hope. In his concentric structure of the book, Christensen unites chaps. 27–30 (with chaps. 4–11) within what he call "the inner frame." See *Deuteronomy 1—21:9*, lviii.

218. See Begg, "Literary Criticism," 13; Lenchak, *Choose Life*, 35-36.

219. The term "today" is used 13 times in the third discourse (29:3, 9, 11, 12, 14[2x], 17; 30:2, 8, 11, 16, 18, 19); cf. "as this day" in 29:27).

30 is more optimistic. With respect to the *Numerusweschel*, the plural predominates in chapter 29, and the singular predominates in chapter 30.[220] Based on what we have observed elsewhere, this variance shows a concern both for individuals and the nation as a whole.[221]

The fundamental continuity of the national experience of covenant is maintained in 29:1–8.[222] Moses begins his third discourse by recalling the mighty acts of Yahweh in Egypt (vv. 1–2), the wilderness (vv. 4–5), and the initial conquests in Transjordan (vv. 6–7). These memories serve as motivation for present obedience: "Therefore keep the words of this covenant and do them, that you may prosper in all that you do" (v. 8). The rest of the speech is dedicated to persuading and convincing Israel to make the right choice to observe the covenant.

Despite the recitation of Yahweh's mighty acts and the clear call to obedience, Moses interjects a puzzling statement about Israel's obtuseness in verse 3: "Yet Yahweh has not given you a heart to understand or eyes to see or ears to hear, until this day." Israel's repeated refusal to trust and obey Yahweh in the wilderness revealed the status of her heart then (see 1:26–43; 9:7–8, 22–24; cf. 8:2–5). The question, then, is how to interpret "until this day." Does it mean that Israel had finally come to a right understanding after forty years, or that Moses' audience is still unable to interpret its past experiences properly?[223] The defeat of Sihon and Og (vv. 6–7; cf. chaps. 2–3) does seem to indicate that some change had taken place in Israel's disposition. But the repeated warnings and, especially, the expectation of future rebellion—leading to the experi-

220. This pattern is broken by references in the singular in 29:2, 4, 10b–12, and references in the plural in 30:18–19.

221. While some consider the plural to emphasize the corporate and the singular to emphasize the individual (cf. Lenchak, *Choose Life*, 196), it seems more likely that the reverse is true. For example, 29:17–20 focuses on the sins of an individual.

222. The subunit is clear marked by the inclusion of את כל־אשר עשה in vv. 1b and 8 (in v. 8b verb form is תעשון).

223. On different ways scholars have interpreted the verse, see Barker, *Triumph of Grace*, 117–19; Tigay, *Deuteronomy*, 275–76. Tigay, along with Begg ("'Bread, Wine, and Strong Drink' in Deut 29:5a," 273–74), think that the charge no longer applies to Moses' present audience because the wilderness brought the understanding that was still lacking after the exodus. For a counter argument, see Barker, *Triumph of Grace*, 117–31. Specifically, Barker notes that the structural parallels between vv. 1–3 and 4–6a suggest a parallel statement on the lack of understanding (rather than a two-stage development). Also, "today" always refers to the present day; "until this day" is used five other times in Deuteronomy (2:22; 3:14; 10:8; 11:4; 34:6), none of which offers a sense of change of situation.

ence of the covenant curses, including exile—hang a pessimistic tone over the appeal. The implication that Yahweh himself must provide the necessary perception to understand sets the stage for the (postexilic) divine circumcision of the heart (30:6), wherein the command of 10:16 ("Circumcise the foreskin of your heart") is turned into a promise. We will consider this verse again as we discuss Israel's ability to keep the law (see chap. 5). What we have, then, is an exigence to the command that must await resolution.[224] What is needed for obedience—a heart to understand, eyes to see, and ears to hear—are presently lacking, but the glimmer of hope arises in the recognition that Yahweh is able to give what is lacking.

In verses 9–14,[225] Moses reminds the people why they are assembled:

> ... to enter into the covenant of Yahweh your God and into his oath, which Yahweh your God is making with you today, that he may establish you today as his people, and that he may be your God, as he promised you, and as he swore to your fathers, to Abraham, to Isaac, and to Jacob. (vv. 11–12)

The familiar language ties this covenant with every earlier expression of Yahweh's commitment to Israel and supports the idea that Moab is not really replacing Horeb at all, for it reasserts the same fundamental basis and demands the same response. The combination of the covenant formula and reference to the patriarchs shows a unity that goes back to Israel's beginnings.[226] This unity is also shown by the fivefold use of "today" in these verses (vv. 9, 11, 12, 14[2x]); as explained elsewhere, the Deuteronomic "today"—besides giving a sense of urgency—is used repeatedly in texts that parallel Horeb and Moab and conflate generations. Moreover, the continuity is extended into the future; the participants in this covenant include future generations—"whoever is not here with us

---

224. See Lenchak, *Choose Life*, 112, 119.

225. The phrase, "standing [Ni. נצב in v. 9; עמד in v. 14] ... before Yahweh our/your God," forms an inclusio around vv. 9–14. Many see a chiasm (whether ABBA, ABA, or ABCBA) in this subunit. See Barker, *Triumph of Grace*, 131–33; Lenchak, *Choose Life*, 174–75; Lohfink, "Der Bundesschluß," 38–39. Within any of the structural alternatives, the covenant formula in v. 12 is clearly central.

226. The patriarchs and "covenant" are found together in 4:31; 7:12; 8:18; 29:11–13. See Driver, *Deuteronomy*, 323. Cf. McConville and Millar (*Time and Place*, 79): "The covenant of Moab is also presented as a fulfillment of the promise to Abram in Genesis 15."

today" (v. 14b).²²⁷ This is in keeping with the concept that covenants "are in principle re-realizable in perpetuity, established in 5:2–3."²²⁸ The new emphasis here is the inclusiveness of every member of society; Moses makes sure that every person is accounted for (vv. 9–10, 14a).²²⁹

Two questions arise from this section. First, how does the seeming optimism square with the problem of verse 3? In response, since this covenant renewal is merely external, the internal problem indicated in verse 3 remains. In fact, the use of אלה ("oath" in v. 11), which also means "curse," may be a play-on wording with chapter 28 and 29:20, thus hinting at the expectation of Israel's failure.²³⁰ Second, what is the place of the individual within a nation in covenant to Yahweh? Specifically, what happens to an individual who is, for better or for worse, not in step with the disposition of the nation? In part, this latter question is answered in verses 15–20, which considers the liability of each individual (see below). There is no mention, however, of what happens to a righteous individual in the midst of a rebellious nation.

The hardest part of the discourse to delineate structurally is 29:15–27.²³¹ The sudden shift from the individual (in vv. 15–20) to corporate in verse 21 is usually taken as grounds for separating verses 15–20 and verses 21–27 into distinct subunits.²³² But verse 18 discusses both individuals and groups, so the shift in verse 21 is not as sudden as might

---

227. Commentators favor a reference to future generations here. This makes sense in a book that often refers to future generations (1:39; 4:9—10:25, 40; 5:14; 6:2, 7, 20-21; 7:3-4; 8:5; 11:2, 19, 21; 12:12, 18, 25, 28; 14:2; 16:11, 14; 18:10; 21:16-17, 18-20; 24:16; 25:5-6; 28:32, 41, 46, 53-57; 29:21; 30:2, 6, 9, 19; 31:12-13, 21; 32:5, 19-20, 46; 34:4). See especially Lenchak, *Choose Life*, 102-3. It also makes sense in the third discourse, which, as Polzin (*Moses and the Deuteronomist*, 69–70) notes, concentrates on the future much more than the first two discourses. Rofé ("Covenant in the Land of Moab," 312) considers the reference here to absentees rather than future generations, but he offers no reasons for his position.

228. Lenchak, *Choose Life*, 104. Tigay (*Deuteronomy*, 398 n. 28) notes ANE treaties that also bind future generations.

229. The enumeration of members in vv. 9-10 is the most inclusive "participant list" in the OT, according to Lenchak, *Choose Life*, 101.

230. So Thompson, *Deuteronomy*, 281; cf. Barker, *Triumph of Grace*, 132.

231. See Lenchak, *Choose Life*, 175-77. I follow Lenchak in viewing vv. 15-27 together.

232. Critical scholars have seen this shift as intrusive and thus consider vv. 21-27 to be an exilic interpolation: Levenson, "Who Inserted the Book of the Torah?" 208; Mayes, "Deuteronomy 4," 50–51; Rofé, "Covenant in the Land of Moab," 313. But see a counter argument in Tigay, *Deuteronomy*, 399 n. 53.

appear. Also, the verses are held together by the keywords "land" (8 times) and "anger" (5 times).²³³ The overall theme (and motivation) is that disobedience brings punishment. The specific warning (vv. 15–17a) is followed by the example of the individual sinner (vv. 17b–20) and the example of the punishment of the land (vv. 21–27).

The warning is given in verses 15–17a. It is prefaced on the memory of life in Egypt and the wilderness (v. 15). Unlike most references in Deuteronomy, however, the focus is neither on Israel's suffering nor Yahweh's deliverance, but on knowledge of the nation's idolatry, which Moses describes as "detestable" (v. 16). This leads into the warning (noted by פֶּן, "lest") concerning Israel's potential idolatry: "lest there be among you a man or woman or clan or tribe whose heart is turning away today from Yahweh our God to go and serve the gods of those nations" (v. 17a). The polemical edge (Yahweh versus other gods) anticipates the clear-cut choice of 30:19 and gets to the heart of the basis of the covenant relationship. The rhetorical use of "today" implies that this choice will always be central and significant for Israel.

In verses 17b–20, Moses warns against a person harboring secret reservations about his or her exclusive commitment to Yahweh and the covenant. The judgment on such a person is decisive; he or she alone will experience the covenant curses (vv. 19–20). Rather than resulting in exile as the ultimate curse, however, the individual and his or her memory will be "blotted out" (מחה; v. 19)—the same fate threatened on worshipers of the golden calf (9:14) and what Israel was to impose on the Canaanites and Amalekites (7:24; 25:19). The focus on individuals makes the overall warning as comprehensive as possible,²³⁴ though there is a note of grace in this willingness of Yahweh to deal with individuals who could affect the community.

Before moving ahead, we should pause to reflect on a couple of key points that emerge from verses 15–20 on the issue of Israel's ability and willingness to obey Yahweh. We had already noted that while Israel presently has a basic heart problem (v. 3), this needs to be qualified by the fact that (1) certain individuals (i.e., Joshua and Caleb) have stood

---

233. אֶרֶץ, "land," is used with respect to Egypt (vv. 15, 24), an unknown faraway land (vv. 21, 27), and the land of Israel (vv. 21, 22, 23, 26); cf. 28:69; 3x in 29:1–9; 3x in chap. 30. The synonym אֲדָמָה, "ground," is also used in v. 27. אַף, "anger," is always combined with other descriptive terms: קנא, "jealousy," (v. 19); חמה, "wrath," (v. 22); חרי, "heat" (v. 23); יחר, "be kindled" (v. 26); חמה and קצף, "wrath" (v. 27).

234. Tigay, *Deuteronomy*, 280.

out from their sinful generation to show wholehearted obedience, and (2) the present generation has shown some measure of fidelity by following Yahweh in the conquest of Transjordan. The tension is maintained in these verses. First, our interpretation of verse 3 is substantiated by the more narrow reading of "today" in verse 17 (i.e., with reference to Moses' present audience in Moab)—there is the real danger of turning away from Yahweh into idolatry, suggesting the presence of a fundamental problem. Second, it is possible for individuals to be set apart from the community; the individuation of sinners shows that the nation is not entirely monolithic at every point. Third, there is an implication that Israel's present obedience may be temporary and fleeting. Verses 17–18 involve a progression of the actions of one's "heart": first, the heart turns away from Yahweh (v. 17a); second, the sinner blesses himself "in his heart" (v. 18a); third, there is the recognition of the "stubbornness of my heart" (v. 18b).[235] The notion of "turning away" suggests that one had begun with a proper disposition, but the decline into a stubborn heart shows that this initial obedience reflects the external nature of the covenant relationship in verses 9–14. It is clear that the use of "see" (v. 16) and "hear" (v. 18) involve weaker senses than having "eyes to see" or "ears to hear" (v. 3). Therefore, by negative example,[236] what is really at stake for Israel is the need for internal participation in the covenant. None of the qualifications above provides confidence that Israel as a whole is at that point.

In fact, the opposite conclusion is implied in verses 21–27, as Moses reverts to the responsibility of the whole people to keep the covenant and the style shifts from contingency to prediction.[237] The temporal perspective changes to the future, after the covenant curses have been meted out, not on an individual (cf. v. 19) but on the whole nation. Interestingly, Moses speaks the perspective of foreign observers of Yahweh's judgment

---

235. Barker, *Triumph of Grace*, 133–35. Barker says that this succession suggests that "sin strengthens its grip and places the person in a position of entrenched opposition to Yahweh" (p. 135).

236. Lenchak, *Choose Life*, 190, calls the individual in v. 18 an "anti-model."

237. Driver (*Deuteronomy*, 326) states that "the dreaded contingency is now pictured as a certainty." Cf. Thompson, *Deuteronomy*, 283. On the shift from individual to corporate in v. 21, Lenchak (*Choose Life*, 192) argues that the rhetorical effect is to attract attention: "the ambiguity here forces the audience to contemplate the prospect that the punishment of the land was associated with the lone individual who had sinned."

against his own people. Because exile is explicitly noted here (v. 27), we should consider the relevance of this section to our theme.

Here, great prominence is given to the land.[238] It is the devastation of the land—rather than the people—that initiates the foreign response: "... when they see the afflictions of that land and the sicknesses with which Yahweh has made it sick—the whole land burned out ..." (vv. 21–22). The nations' initial question also continues this focus: "Why has Yahweh done this to this land?" (v. 23). Their response to their own question, while beginning with reference to the infidelity of the people (vv. 24–25), returns to Yahweh's activity toward the land: "Therefore the anger of Yahweh was kindled against this land, bringing upon it all the curses written in this book" (v. 26). Finally, the nations perceive the finality of the judgment of Yahweh in having "uprooted (נתש) them from their land ... and cast (Hi. שלך) them into another land" (v. 27). The emphasis corresponds to what we noted in chapter 28—that there is a difference between Israel and other nations in the way land is perceived in the triangular relationship of deity-people-land.[239] While land certainly is given much attention from an Israelite perspective in Deuteronomy, we noted (especially in chap. 28) that the relationship between Yahweh and Israel is fundamental. Land serves as an arena in which that relationship can be lived out. The foreign perspective, however, is preoccupied with the condition (including occupation) of the land.

Whether or not such a distinction is intended in this text, we must ask why Moses' rhetoric includes a consideration of foreign response.[240] We saw in chapter 4 that Israel's obedience to God's law had serious ramifications for how other nations would view Israel, Yahweh, and the law (4:6–8). We see something of a reversal of this in chapter 29, but it is only partial. The reputation of Israel certainly has been soiled; instead of praising Israel—"Surely this great nation is a wise and understanding people" (4:6b)—the nations rightly judge that Israel experienced Yahweh's curses "because they abandoned the covenant ... and went and served other gods" (29:24–25). This is a complete reversal of Yahweh's promise to set Israel "in praise and in fame and in honor high above all

---

238. The frequent repetition of "land" makes it a leading motif; see Lenchak, *Choose Life*, 176.

239. Block, *Gods of the Nations*, 21–33.

240. Moses considers hypothetical questions and responses at other points in Deuteronomy (6:20; 7:17; 8:17).

nations" (26:19), but there is no parallel reversal of the foreigners' view of Yahweh or his law. In fact, one senses a healthy fear for Yahweh and the demonstration of his wrath due to covenant breach.[241] They even acknowledge Yahweh's past relationship with the patriarchs (v. 24), his gracious rescue of his people from Egypt (v. 24), and fidelity in carrying out his own word (v. 26). Whatever else may be drawn from this, it at least suggests that Israel should not presume upon Yahweh reneging on his threats out of fear of his own reputation in the world. Far from interpreting exile as the defeat of Yahweh, the nations will have scorn only for Israel; they will recognize that the sovereign Lord that overthrew Sodom and Gomorrah, Admah, and Zeboiim (v. 22) is the same one who will "uproot" and "cast out" his people (v. 27).

The conclusion to Moses' warning in Deuteronomy 29 is enigmatic: "The secret things belong to Yahweh our God, but the things that are revealed belong to us and to our children forever, that we may do all the words of this law" (v. 28). "The secret things" (הנסתרת) and "the revealed things" (הנגלת) have been explained in several ways.[242] Though other interpretations are plausible, the force of the text favors taking the verse as "a wisdom maxim."[243] Accordingly, the "secret things" or "hidden things" constitute, then, all that God knows but has not conveyed to Israel; conversely, the "revealed things" include all the Torah. This verse anticipates the discussion of the availability and comprehensibility of Torah in 30:11–14, forming a frame around 30:1–10.[244] One should also view this wisdom text within the immediate context of Moses' look to

---

241. McConville (*Deuteronomy*, 418) notes that this text offers the most concentrated expression of Yahweh's wrath in the book. He helpfully notes, "In every instance in which Yahweh's anger is in view, the theme is fundamental breach of the covenant."

242. See especially Tigay, *Deuteronomy*, 283, who includes several different interpretations in Jewish tradition. Tigay himself follows the meaning expressed in Targum Jonathan (and is the standard Jewish understanding): "concealed acts (that is, concealed sins) are known to God, and He will punish them, but overt ones are our responsibility to punish ('to apply all the provisions of this Teaching')." Cf. surveys in Barker, *Triumph of Grace*, 139–40; Lenchak, *Choose Life*, 152. The options for the "secret things" include the following: (1) unknown future (usual view); (2) hidden causes that motivate God to discipline his people (Maxwell); (3) a wisdom maxim about the limits of human wisdom (Von Rad, McCarthy, Cairns, Mayes); (4) hidden sins of an individual (cf. vv. 19–20; Rofé, Tigay); and (5) God's copy of the covenant (Weinfeld).

243. Thus, Mayes, *Deuteronomy*, 368. This is basically the view of most modern commentators.

244. Barker, *Triumph of Grace*, 139–40; McConville, *Deuteronomy*, 419.

the future. Moses has just anticipated the potential appraisal of foreign peoples on the implementation of the curses on Israel (29:21–27). In 30:1–10 he will describe the more distant future beyond exile. While the fact of exile and return are now being revealed to Israel, how and when they occur are still a mystery known only to Yahweh. Israel's occupation in the present is to obey and teach those things of which they have full knowledge and possession.

With 29:28, we can perceive a transition from the generally negative attitude of chapter 29 to the more optimistic tone of chapter 30.[245] The verse hints at a solution to the problem of 29:3. It is not the solution itself, but it suggests that the solution will depend on a revelation from God.[246]

## Deuteronomy 30

Though part of Moses' third discourse, it is also possible to view chapter 30 as a sub-unit itself. An inclusio is formed in the combination of the phrases, "the blessing and the curse" and "I have set before you" (vv. 1, 19), and the section is united by several key words and phrases: "give" (vv. 1, 7, 15, 19, 20); "today" (vv. 2, 8, 11, 15, 16, 18, 19)"; "which I am commanding you today" (vv. 2, 8, 11, 16); and "to love Yahweh your God" (vv. 6, 16, 20).[247] According to Millar, chapter 30 "is moving in the same thought-world as chapter 4."[248] Both juxtapose appeals to obedience with prophetic insight into the future, and together they form an inclusio around the book. Chapter 30 moves temporally backward from consideration of future restoration from exile (vv. 1–10) to present appeal to obedience (vv. 15–20). Recalling the difficult question of Israel's ability to obey in 29:3, the juxtaposition of these horizons creates what Olson calls "a delicate dialectic."[249] Future restoration presupposes the

---

245. Lenchak, *Choose Life*, 153, 174.

246. Barker, *Triumph of Grace*, 139–40.

247. Lenchak, *Choose Life*, 177. There are other keywords primarily restricted to vv. 1–10, which we will discuss in the next section.

248. McConville and Millar, *Time and Place*, 82. He continues, "We described chap. 4 as an overture to the rest of the book. Chapter 30 is linked to chap. 4, but only as the finale is linked to the overture—in chap. 30 the themes introduced in chap. 4 reach their dénoument."

249. Olson, *Deuteronomy and the Death of Moses*, 132–33. Interestingly, Olson applies the maxim of 29:28 to this dialectic: how it is resolved is a "secret"; that it happens is "revealed." Of course, critical scholars maintain that 30:1–10 is a digression (like 4:29–31) inserted at a late stage. See Tigay, *Deuteronomy*, 283.

curses; present exhortation assumes the possibility of establishing conditions for the blessings.

We will examine verses 1–10 in detail in the next section, but here we can offer some considerations on its connection to the overall discourse.[250] Though it may appear at first glance that chapter 30 naturally follows chapter 28, in their present position verses 30:1–10 function as the positive aspect of the choice facing Israel (cf. 29:8; 29:15–27, which provided the negative side). As with 4:29–31, it may seem odd to motivate people to obedience by declaring the certainty of future destruction. However, in terms of motivation, this text emphasizes the ultimate source of blessing, even after experiencing the curse. Yahweh is named fourteen times, twelve of which add "your God."[251] In nine of these occurrences, the name functions as the subject of verbs. The same God who will drive Israel into exile (v. 1b) and scatter her (v. 3b) will also restore her fortunes (v. 3a), gather her (v. 4b), return her to the land of promise (v. 5a), circumcise her heart (v. 6a), put the curses on her enemies (v. 7a), prosper her (v. 9a), and delight in doing so (v. 9b). This picture of future divine intervention both confirms the gloomy outlook of 29:3 and offers ultimate hope and resolution to the problem, especially in the divine circumcision of the heart (30:6). For the Moab generation, and each succeeding pre-exilic generation, the glorious prospects presented here ought to motivate the people to devote themselves to Yahweh in the present.

While the circumcision of the heart in 30:6 provides the resolution to the dilemma of 29:3, it appears to be in tension with its most immediate context (29:28; 30:11–14). How to resolve the tension, however, is debated.[252] In verses 11–14, Moses emphasizes that God's command-

---

250. It is helpful to consider this connection due to the prominent critical stance that vv. 1–10 is a later insertion that does not fit with the context. E.g., Rofé, "Covenant in the Land of Moab," 312. Cf. our discussion of 4:29–31. Admittedly, there are features of vv. 1–10 that make it stand apart from the rest of the discourse. כל, "all," occurs 13 times in vv. 1–10 (vv. 1[2x], 2[3x], 3, 6[2x], 7, 8, 9, 10[2x]), but not once in vv. 11–20. Variations of שוב occur 7 times (vv. 1, 2, 3[2x], 8, 9, 10; cf. שבותך in v. 3). The phrases, "with all your heart and soul" (vv. 2, 6, 10) "heed the voice" (vv. 2, 8, 10), are not found in the rest of the discourse.

251. In the rest of the discourse, "Yahweh your God" is only found in 29:11 and 30:16–20.

252. Not surprisingly, some suggest different dates and origins for vv. 1–10 and vv. 11–14. Driver (*Deuteronomy*, 330) says that the two texts are only "loosely connected." McCarthy (*Treaty and Covenant*, 15, 229) considers the optimistic passage (vv. 11–14)

ments[253] are doable.[254] The ability to observe the law is based on three premises:

> ... [this commandment] is not too hard for you (v. 11b)
>
> ... it is not too far away (v. 11c)
>
> ... the word is very near to you, in your mouth and in your heart, to do it (v. 14)

The first statement maintains that God's commandment is intelligible;[255] the second statement maintains that it is accessible. The two spatial metaphors in verses 12–13 ("It is not in the heavens ... and it is not across the sea") support these statements and imply that the Lord of creation has made sure that his law is within Israel's mental and physical grasp.[256] These statements, thus, affirm the maxim in 29:28—that by which Israel is to live has been revealed to her—and is consistent with the inclusiveness of the covenant relationship (cf. 29:9–14).[257]

---

to be early and the pessimistic passage to be later. Payne (*Deuteronomy*, 166) thinks the optimism is even later (so exilic or post-exilic). These positions, in effect, ignore the tension of the text.

253. "This commandment" (v. 11) should be understood as the deuteronomic law as a whole. See Braulik's discussion in relation to chap. 4 in "Die Ausdrücke," 39–66.

254. For vv. 11–14 as a discrete unit, preparing for the parenesis of vv. 15–20, see Lohfink, "Der Bundesschluß," 42; cf. Lenchak, *Choose Life*, 178–79. There is a clear chiastic pattern (ABBA). An inclusio might be recognized in the synonyms "commandment" (v. 11) and "word" (v. 14) and in the contrast between "far" (v. 11) and "near" (v. 14).

255. As Wright (*Deuteronomy*, 291) explains, "To say that the law is not too difficult does not mean that obedience is *easy* but rather that it is *simple*." See also Barker, *Triumph of Grace*, 191–93; Christensen, *Deuteronomy 21:1—-34:12*, 742; Tigay, *Deuteronomy*, 285. The root פלא (Ni.), "to be extraordinary, wonderful," refers in 17:8 to judges who do not know how to decide a legal case. Cf. Prov 30:18: "Three things are too wonderful (Ni. פלא) for me; four I do not understand (ידע) ...."

256. Cf. McConville, *Deuteronomy*, 429: "This metaphor [from v. 11], implying something beyond Israel's capacity, leads into an imaginative expansion of the thought [in vv. 12–13], embracing the whole creation. The hyperbole recalls 4:32, which set the giving of the law in the context of Yahweh's universal dominion in creation (cf. 4:39). Yahweh, who has all heaven and earth under his sway, has given the law to Israel; no other agent need be invoked in order to compel it." Ridderbos (*Deuteronomy*, 271) emphasizes that the word's nearness has to do with it being in the mouth and heart, not because of reflection.

257. On the similarities between 29:28 and 30:11–14, see Braulik, *Deuteronomium*, 219; Craigie, *Book of Deuteronomy*, 365 Kline, *Treaty of the Great King*, 134; Miller, *Deuteronomy*, 212; Thompson, *Deuteronomy*, 286. Both speak of "words" (29:28; 30:14), end with a purpose clause "to do," and are about revelation of the law and its

At first glance, the third statement appears to reiterate positively what has already been stated negatively: "the word is very near to you . . . to do it" (v. 14). Because the law is known and understood, it can be put into practice. This echoes the nearness of God in 4:7. Wright rightly states, "In chapter 4, the nearness of God is the basis of Israel's distinctiveness among the nations. In chapter 30, the nearness of God's word is the basis of their moral response to God, which enables their distinctiveness to be visible."[258] Like the polemical undertones we observed in 4:6–8, the present verses depict a unique quality in Israel's relationship to her God when compared to her neighbors.[259]

But the addition of the internalization of the law ("in your mouth and in your heart") returns us to the tension in the text concerning assumptions about Israel's ability to obey the law. This tension is immediately felt when comparing the need for future, divine circumcision of the heart in verse 6 and the statement that the word is "in your heart" in verse 14. As McConville states, verses 11–14 contain "the most explicit statement in the whole book of *their ability* to obey his commands"[260]—thus affirming the opposite of verses 1–10. How one harmonizes the two paragraphs in large part hinges on the temporal horizon of verses 11–14. It is difficult to determine whether the reference to "this commandment that I command you today" (v. 11) is the Mosaic present or the future (following heart circumcision in v. 6).[261] The ambiguity is sustained in part to the fluidity

---

purpose (i.e., obedience).

258. Wright, *Deuteronomy*, 291.

259. Several have pointed out the contrasts between these verses and common ANE views. See especially Craigie (*Book of Deuteronomy*, 365), who discusses the phrase, "who ascended into heaven," in the Sumerian King List, as well as the epic quests (e.g., Gilgamesh) for inaccessible knowledge, which including crossing the sea. Cf. Christensen, *Deuteronomy 21:10—34:12*, 743; McConville, *Deuteronomy*, 429.

260. McConville, *Grace in the End*, 137. Cf. Schenker, "Umwiderrufliche Umkehr und neuer Bund," 99.

261. McConville (*Deuteronomy*, 29) recognizes that vv. 11–14 is in a "curious position," but maintains (as most commentators do) that Moses here reverts to the present time in Moab. He does, however, think it is essential to recognize that the time distinction between present and future has already been blurred in v. 8. For the position that maintains a future day of decision is in view see Braulik, *Deuteronomium*, 218–19; Barker, *Triumph of Grace*, 182–87. Millar seems to have shifted his own position. In one work (*Now Choose Life*, 94 [though published in 1998, this is a revision of his doctoral thesis, and probably represents an early position]), Millar tentatively supports Braulik's position; in a second work (*Time and Place*, 82 [published in 1994]) he takes "today" in v. 11 to be the Mosaic present. His discussions in both works are helpful on the issues

of the Deuteronomic "today," which can refer to both the Mosaic present and subsequent days of decision. This is heightened by the blurring of temporal horizons in similar phrases in verses 2 and 8.

If the "today" of verse 11 refers to the Mosaic present, the tension is real and a resolution must be sought. One could argue that the present generation is viewed more optimistically than future generations, but this would require a position that the heart problem of 29:3 does not apply to the present generation. This would also run counter to the strong corporate solidarity that runs through Deuteronomy. A more plausible explanation would be to understand the contrast with verse 6 in terms of the quality of obedience, i.e., consistent versus immediate obedience.[262] On this reading the nearness of God is viewed primarily in terms of possession. The phrase, "in your mouth and in your heart" (v. 14), must refer to recitation and memorization, recalling 6:6-7.[263] Therefore, the grounds for Israel's capacity to obey are external. Given our interpretation of 29:3, verses 11-14 would say nothing of Israel's ability in terms of heart motivation, but only that Israel could not claim ignorance of God's revealed will.[264]

On the other hand, a case can be made for taking verses 11-14 as referring to the future (so with vv. 1-10), thus taking the common relative clause, "which I am commanding you today" (vv. 2, 8, 11), consistently.[265] Thematically, verses 1-14 are united by the idea of God's revealed words leading to obedience. Terminologically, several common words include the following: לקח, "to take" (vv. 4, 12, 13); עשה, "to do" (vv. 8, 12, 13, 14); שמים, "heaven(s)" (vv. 4, 12[2x]); מצוה, "commandment" (vv. 8, 10, 11); לבב, "heart" (vv. 1, 2, 6[3x], 10, 14); and שמע, "to hear, heed" (vv. 2, 8, 10, 12, 13).[266] Structurally, verses 1-14 link two main arguments. First, verses 9-11 contain a sequence of כי-clauses (vv. 9b, 10a, 10b, 11a). We

involved.

262. So McConville and Millar, *Time and Place*, 82 n. 120.

263. McConville, *Deuteronomy*, 429.

264. Lenchak (*Choose Life*, 200, 205) considers vv. 11-14 to be a refutation of a possible objection that, given vv. 1-10, the law is not even possible. Cf. Craigie (*Book of Deuteronomy*, 365), who sees the quotations in vv. 12-13 as excuses for not keeping the law.

265. This is argued most forcefully by Barker, *Triumph of Grace*, 182-87. He states, "Verses 11-14 extrapolate on vv1-10 showing how the obedience expected in v8 may happen" (ibid., 184). Cf. Braulik, *Deuteronomium*, 218.

266. These connections are considered accidental by Vanoni, "Der Geist und der Buchstabe," 71. Barker *Triumph of Grace*, 183-84), however, considers the common vocabulary to be a considerable factor in assigning vv. 11-14 to the future.

will discuss the meaning of כי in the first three clauses in the next section (whether each is causal, temporal, or conditional); it is clear, though, that the כי in verse 11 must be taken as emphatic or asseverative (cf. NIV, "Now") if verses 11–14 refers to the present—a completely different rendering from the other three occurrences in context. If verses 1–14 are united, the כי in verse 11 can be taken as causal or evidential, which maintains the sequence.[267] Second, verses 1–14 can be structured on the basis of the references to "heart":

    A take the word to heart (v. 1)
        B return and obey with all your heart (v. 2)
            C heart circumcision and subsequent love (v. 6)
        B' return with all your heart (v. 10)
    A' the word is in your heart (v. 14)[268]

On this reading, then, the grounds for Israel's capacity to obey in verses 11–14 are internal and assumes the heart circumcision of verse 6 has already happened. The commandment is "not too hard" (v. 11) because the necessary miracle has already been performed. The word is "in your mouth and in your heart" (v. 14) because Yahweh has put it there. The optimism of verses 11–14, therefore, is derived from—rather than in contrast to—the reality of verses 1–10.

    Despite the contrasting positions, it is not clear to the present writer that one must necessarily choose between them. A "delicate dialectic" is evident throughout the discourse. We have seen that words like "see," "hear," and "heart" can have both weaker and stronger senses (i.e., external versus internal). We have repeatedly noted the rhetorical use of "today," which often blurs the time distinction between the present and the future. The proposal here, then, is that both positions are valid. On the one hand, verses 11–14 speak to the present (and every pre-exilic) generation as a motivation for obedience. They have God's word and it is clear what he wants of them. The only obstacle they face is themselves! On the other hand, verses 11–14 proleptically describe the striking reality resulting from the circumcision of the heart, in which this one obstacle has been removed.[269] As McConville states, "The exhortation

---

267. Barker, *Triumph of Grace*, 185.

268. This is the structure given in Braulik, *Deuteronomium*, 218. It is reproduced in Barker, *Triumph of Grace*, 186.

269. This seems to be the angle Paul takes in Romans 10, where he cites portions of Deut 30:11–14. See Seifrid, "Paul's Approach to the Old Testament," 3–37. Cf. Barker,

remains absolute, though we know that it can only ever have validity in a new arrangement that lies beyond both sin and judgment."²⁷⁰

The summary appeal in verses 15–20 serves as a powerful climax to Moses' exhortation.²⁷¹ It reiterates the basic demands and consequences set forth elsewhere: wholehearted obedience leads to blessing in the land of promise (vv. 16, 20); idolatry leads to destruction (vv. 17-18). But there is a heightened awareness of the significance of the choice facing Israel "today" (vv. 15, 16, 18, 19).²⁷² In fact, this is the only occurrence in Deuteronomy where Israel is the subject of בחר, "to choose."²⁷³ The choice is put in the starkest terms: life versus death (vv. 15, 19), good versus evil (v. 15), blessing versus curse (v. 19).²⁷⁴ This clear-cut bifurcation of options is a logical consequence of the previous paragraph (vv. 11–14); given the clarity and nearness of God's word, only willful and wanton disobedience would explain making the wrong decision. This is supported by two emphases of the text.

The first emphasis is the focus on the heart. Israel's "heart" has already played a significant role in the chapter: positively, it is the seat of God's word (v. 14); negatively, it is in need of repair (v. 6). The purpose and result of its circumcision is "love" toward Yahweh, which in Deuteronomy includes a fearful disposition and internal resolve to covenant fidelity (cf. 6:5; 10:12–13).²⁷⁵ In the present exhortation, loving

---

*Triumph of Grace*, 194–98; Wright, *Climax of the Covenant*, 245.

270. McConville, *Grace in the End*, 229.

271. An inclusio to these verses is found in the double offer of life and death in vv. 15 and 19. Lenchak (*Choose Life*, 180) finds an ABBA chiastic arrangement in vv. 15, 18, 19aa, 19ab.

272. The choice in Deuteronomy is corporate and national. See Weinfeld, *Deuteronomy and the Deuteronomic School*, 308; Thompson, *Deuteronomy*, 288. This supports the view that the singular address (which predominates vv. 15–20) focuses on the corporate rather than individual.

273. Of the 31 Deuteronomic references of בחר, Yahweh is the subject 29 times; Yahweh chooses "the place" (21 times), "you" (7:6, 7; 10:15; 14:2), priests (18:5; 21:5), descendants (4:37), and the king (17:15). In 23:17, a refugee slave is the subject of the verb. See Barker, *Triumph of Grace*, 201–2. On the imperative force of the verb form in 30:19 (Qal Perfect) see Craigie, *Book of Deuteronomy*, 366; Lenchak, *Choose Life*, 219.

274. On the alternatives, see Thompson, *Deuteronomy*, 287. Christensen (*Deuteronomy 21:10—34:12*, 747) notes that v. 15 forms an inclusion with 11:26–28, which sets forth the alternatives of blessing and curse. The additions of life/death and good/evil sustains our contention that the tone and ethos have been intensified here at the conclusion of Moses' speeches.

275. On the meaning of love for God in Deuteronomy, see McKay, "Man's Love for

Yahweh heads the description of the condition of obedience to the commandments: "If you obey the commandments ... by loving Yahweh your God ... " (v. 16).[276] In the call of verse 20, "loving Yahweh" is paralleled with "obeying his voice" and "clinging to him." Conversely, disobedience is defined as idolatry, but it begins in the internal operations of the heart: "If your heart turns away, and you will not hear, but are drawn away to worship other gods and serve them ..." (v. 17). The importance of all this is that the decision Israel makes about her fidelity to Yahweh cannot be anything but considered, deliberate, and intentional.

The second emphasis is the reasonableness of the appeal. The key words in the passage are the noun החיים, "life" (vv. 15, 19[2x], 20; cf. "length of days" in v. 20) and the verb חיה, "live" (vv. 16, 19; cf. "lengthen days" in v. 18). Moses does not conclude his discourse with some esoteric or complicated rationale in order to persuade Israel to obey; rather, he speaks to the most primal human desire—existence. Having been given the true definition of life and the means necessary to sustain it, Israel's "death" would clearly be an act of suicide. For rhetorical purposes, perhaps this is why the direct agency of Yahweh is mentioned only in terms of the blessing and not the curse (vv. 16–17).

Given the inevitability of the curses, one may ask why the final exhortation returns to posing blessing and curse as alternatives.[277] A simple (and true) response is that it shows that human responsibility is never denied.[278] The text does not, however, assume a positive picture of Israel's future. Unlike other covenant ceremonies (cf. Exod 19:3–9; 24:3, 7; Josh 24:16–18, 21, 24), we are not privy to Israel's response here.[279] There are hints at the expectation of failure when the threat of rebellion in verses 17–18 is compared to chapter 29 (cf. the combination of "heart" and "turn away" in 29:17 and 30:17; "bow down" and "serve" in 29:25 and 30:18). The appeal to Israel is to choose Yahweh and his

God," 426–35. See also Moran, "Ancient Near Eastern Background of the Love of God," 77–87.

276. This reading takes the infinitive לאהבה circumstantially (i.e., "by loving [Yahweh your God]").

277. See the discussion in Barker, *Triumph of Grace*, 170–81.

278. Cairns, *Deuteronomy*, 266.

279. Miller (*Deuteronomy*, 215) suggests that the reason for the silence is so that the exhortation can be contemporized or existentialized; i.e., the "today" is for the current reader. This may surely be an effect of the silence, but we would not expect Israel's response within the paranesis in Deuteronomy.

grace (cf. v. 20), implicitly acknowledging her own inability. When seen in light of the context of chapter 30, the people of Israel are not asked to "rely on their own effort but to entrust themselves to the grace and faithfulness of Yahweh who has promised that he will enable the obedience which Israel requires."[280]

The language of death and life in this passage is very relevant for some of the emphases of this present work. First, we have maintained that exile constitutes Israel's "death." This finds support in the curse's juxtaposition of "perish" (אבד) and "not lengthen days *in the land*" (v. 18). Conversely, "life" for Israel is necessarily life in the land; the commandments, the divine blessing, and the nation's future are all explicitly qualified by reference to the land of promise (vv. 16, 19–20). As Barker states, "Death is not necessarily destruction but life outside the land which is thus not real life."[281] Second, this text reaffirms the doctrine of corporate solidarity through the generations. Israel's choice to live "today" has bearing on the life of her future offspring (v. 19); and the life of each generation is delineated as dwelling in the land sworn to the fathers (v. 20). Third, this passage continues the Deuteronomic tendency to unite the patriarchal promise and the covenant given through Moses. Enjoyment of the blessings of the patriarchal promise, including increase in numbers (v. 16) and possession of the land (vv. 16, 20), is preconditioned upon obedience to Moab's requirements. Conversely, in being called to obey the demands, Israel is being called to trust the ancient promise.

## THIRD TEXT: DEUTERONOMY 30:1–10

Deuteronomy 30:1–10 is the final major text on exile in the book. Just as 28:58–68 is a kind of expansion of 4:25–28 on the theme of exile, so 30:1–10 is an expansion of 4:29–31 on the theme of restoration. Difficulties in the translation of 30:1–10 center around the various meanings of שׁוּב in the passage and the potential renderings of כִּי (cf. 4: 25, 29).[282] Both issues will be considered in the exposition below.

---

280. Barker, *Triumph of Grace*, 213. Ibid., 209–13, gives all the terminological links between vv. 15–20 and the rest of chap. 30.

281. Ibid., 254.

282. Variants to the MT are minor and do not affect overall interpretation.

1 "When [כִּי]²⁸³ all these words come upon you, the blessing and the curse, which I have set before you, and you take them to heart among all the nations where Yahweh your God has driven you, 2 and you return to Yahweh your God and heed his voice in all that I command you today—you and your children—with all your heart and with all your soul, 3 then Yahweh your God will restore your fortunes²⁸⁴ and have compassion on you, and he will turn [שׁוּב]²⁸⁵ and gather you from all the peoples where Yahweh your God has scattered you. 4 If your banished ones are in the uttermost parts of heaven, from there Yahweh your God will gather you, and from there he will take you. 5 And Yahweh your God will bring you to the land that your fathers possessed, that you may possess it. And he will make you more prosperous and numerous than your fathers. 6 And Yahweh your God will circumcise your heart and the heart of your offspring, so that you will love Yahweh your God with all your heart and with all your soul, that you may live. 7 And Yahweh your God will put all these curses on your enemies and foes who persecuted you. 8 And you shall return [שׁוּב]²⁸⁶ and heed the voice of Yahweh and do all his commandments that I command you today. 9 Yahweh your God will make you abundantly prosperous in all the work of your hand, in the fruit of your womb and in the fruit of your cattle and in the fruit of your ground. For Yahweh will return [שׁוּב]²⁸⁷ to delight in you for good, as he delighted in your fathers, 10 when [כִּי]²⁸⁸ you heed the voice of Yahweh your God, by keeping his commandments and his statutes that are written in this book of the Torah, when [כִּי]²⁸⁹ you return to Yahweh your God with all your heart and with all your soul.

283. On temporal meaning of כִּי, see discussion below.

284. The phrase, "restore your fortunes," is the traditional rendering for the idiom, שׁבות שׁב. For a discussion of the idiom, see chap. 2.

285. The meaning for שׁוּב here is debated. Older translations (e.g., ASV, AV) assume it refers to the return of Yahweh. This sense is still held by, e.g., Christensen (*Deuteronomy 21:10—34:12*, 738). The more common rendering is "again" (cf. ESV, NASB, NIV, NKJV, NRSV, RSV, and most commentators). See discussion below.

286. Cf. n. 67. The rendering of שׁוּב here as "return" agrees with ASV and AV. Most translations (e.g., ESV, NASB, NIV, NJB, NKJV, NRSV, RSV) translate it as "again." See discussion below.

287. Unlike vv. 3 and 8, all English translations render שׁוּב here as "again." See discussion below.

288. On the temporal reading of כִּי, see discussion below.

289. On the temporal reading of כִּי, see discussion below.

## Form, Structure, and Style

A major theological issue in this passage is "the relationship between Yahweh's decision to restore Israel and Israel's willingness to repent and be redeemed."[290] This question cannot be considered apart from the structure and syntax of the text. There is no disagreement that 30:1–10 is structured concentrically (i.e., chiastically). The text begins and ends, in reverse order, with protasis-apodosis constructions: "When (כי) all these things come upon you ... then Yahweh your God will restore your fortunes and ..." (vv. 1, 3);[291] "Yahweh your God will make you abundantly prosperous ... when (כי) you heed the voice of Yahweh your God ..." (vv. 9, 10). The protases that frame the unit are both כי-clauses that contain references to "(re)turning" and "with all your heart and soul" (vv. 2, 10).

The debate concerns the center of the text. Table 5 presents the two basic structural options.[292]

Table 5. Structural Options for Deuteronomy 30:1–10

The real issue is whether the divine heart circumcision in verse 6 is part of the center. The second option is based on easily recognizable features. The series of *waw*-consecutives that resumes at verse 5 (after the "interruption" of a secondary-level apodosis in v. 4) does not end until the ואתה ("and you") in verse 8. Also, apart from Israel possessing the land as a result of Yahweh's actions in verse 5, Yahweh is the only subject of the mainline verbs in verses 3–7. In verse 8, however, the subject shifts emphatically to Israel. These considerations suggest a break at verse 8. This structure is further supported by the alternations of the subject of שוב in the text:

---

290. McConville, *Deuteronomy*, 423–24.

291. Technically the first apodosis could begin at several places, but the change in subject in v. 3 probably indicates the shift to apodosis. Cf. Barker, *Triumph of Grace*, 142. I have found no translation that disagrees with this decision.

292. Taken from McConville, *Deuteronomy*, 423–25. There are, of course, various nuances and expansions. The first option is supported by, e.g., Barker, *Triumph of Grace*, 141; Mayes, *Deuteronomy*, 367; Vanoni, "Der Geist und der Buchstabe," 74; Wright, *Deuteronomy*, 289. Cf. Christensen (*Deuteronomy 21:10—34:12*, 736), who observes a seven-part menorah pattern that places vv. 6–7 at the center. The second option is supported by, e.g., Lohfink, "Der Bundesschluß," 41, though more complicated than presented here; cf. Lenchak, *Choose Life*, 178, who has vv. 8b–9 in the center; McConville, *Deuteronomy*, 424; Schenker, "Umwiderrufliche," 100–103; Tigay, *Deuteronomy*, 283–84. In this scheme, v. 4 is considered a secondary-level qualification of the main apodosis.

| Option 1 | | Option 2 | |
|---|---|---|---|
| A | Protasis (vv. 1–2) | A | Protasis (vv. 1–2) |
| B | Apodosis (vv. 3–5) | B | Main apodosis (vv. 3–5) |
| C | Center (vv. 6–8) | C | Central exhortation (vv. 6–8) |
| B' | Apodosis (v. 9) | B' | Apodosis (v. 9) |
| A' | Protasis (v. 10) | A' | Protasis (v. 10) |

   A you *take* [Hi. שוב] them to heart . . . and you *return* to Yahweh
   . . . and heed his voice (vv. 1–2)
      B then Yahweh will *restore your fortunes* [שב שבות] . . . and he
      will *turn* [שב] and gather you (v. 3)
         C You shall *return* [תשב] and heed the voice of Yahweh (v. 8)
      B' Yahweh will *return* [ישוב] and delight in you (v. 9)
   A' when you heed the voice of Yahweh . . . when you *return* to
   Yahweh (v. 10)²⁹³

Support for the first option includes several detailed syntactical considerations, including third-person pronominal suffixes, links of dependent clauses, demonstrative elements, and *waw*-consecutives with the same subjects of the verbs.²⁹⁴ The most decisive criterion for determining the structure, though, is thought to be the distribution of vocabulary.

Several words and phrases only occur in certain subsections (e.g., only in ACA' or only in BB').²⁹⁵ For Barker, the occurrences of "heart" in verse 6, which occurs elsewhere in the passage only in the AA' (i.e., the protases) subsections of the structure (the same is true of "today"), is decisive. He states,

> This points to the fact that v6, and not v8, is the centre of vv1–10. Within v6 the subject changes from Yahweh to Israel. לֵבָב ties the two subjects together, uniting the action of Yahweh with the action of Israel throughout all of vv1–10. . . . [The] inclusion of v6 in the central section, vv6–8, indicates the priority of Yahweh's action on Israel's heart to enable Israel's right response.²⁹⁶

---

293. Adapted from Tigay, *Deuteronomy*, 284. I have changed Tigay's renderings of שוב when they differ.

294. See especially the summary table in Vanoni, "Der Geist und der Buchstabe," 74.

295. Ibid., 75–76. Vanoni's arguments are supported and elaborated by Barker, *Triumph of Grace*, 141–44. The main argument is that much of the significant vocabulary only occurs in the AA' and C portions. On close examination, however, the majority of the links between C and AA' are limited to v. 8, a fact admitted by Barker (p. 165).

296. Barker, *Triumph of Grace*, 144.

Despite the details in support of the first option (with v. 6 in the center), the second and simpler option (with v. 8 alone in the center) has more to commend it. As the last statement in the quote above implies, Barker may be allowing his theological presuppositions to drive his formal conclusions.[297] In countering the alternative structure above, he objects that "the effect of this would be to understand the circumcision of the heart as one of a number of blessings given to Israel by Yahweh as a result of Israel's turning and obedience."[298] While I share his theological concerns (against a legalistic reading), it is not clear that putting verse 8 at the center necessitates this unwanted effect. As McConville responds, "the theological balance need not follow the syntactical logic so closely."[299] The allowance for flexibility is supported by the paranetic style of the text. Barker's concerns are further mitigated, as we shall see, by the proper understanding of the כי-clauses in verses 1 and 9–10 and the unconditional nature of verse 8.

### Exposition

The restoration envisioned in this text clearly involves a sense of mutuality. Israel must recall (v. 1), repent (vv. 2, 10), love (v. 6), and obey (vv. 2, 8, 10) before she can be said to be "restored." The actions of Yahweh include showing compassion (v. 3), gathering the scattered (vv. 3–4), bringing Israel into the land (v. 5), prospering her (vv. 5, 9), circumcising her heart (v. 6), and putting the curses on her enemies (v. 7). The meaning of these features is less difficult to determine than how they fit together. As intimated, a major theological question is how this restored relationship is initiated. It is not untypical to find interpreters placing the initiative on Israel.[300] After all, the protases (vv. 1–2, 10) are driven by actions of Israel. But such a view, which reflects a high optimism about Israel's inherent ability to respond and obey, seems at odds with what we

---

297. Barker does something similar with respect to explaining his view of 30:11–14 as future oriented. See the discussion above.

298. Barker, *Triumph of Grace*, 143. Barker recognizes the shift in subject, but he does not account for the break in the series of *waw*-consecutives.

299. McConville, *Deuteronomy*, 425.

300. E.g., Craigie, *Deuteronomy*, 363; Driver, *Deuteronomy*, 328; Levenson, "Who Inserted the Book of the Torah?" 208; Payne, *Deuteronomy*, 164–65; Polzin, *Moses and the Deuteronomist*, 70. Though not in full agreement with Barker, the order of our discussion is similar to his (*Triumph of Grace*, 144ff.).

have encountered before (such as in 29:3). One of the main aims of this section, then, is to see how this text actually promotes the idea of divine priority. We begin with the meaning of שוב and כי in this text.

Rofé rightly calls Deuteronomy 30:1–10 "a majestic fugue on the theme of *šûb*."[301] The root שוב occurs seven times (vv. 1, 2, 3[2x], 8, 9, 10), with various nuanced meanings.[302] We noted above that the text can be structured on the basis of the alternation of Israel and Yahweh as subject of the verb. Three of the four references with Israel as the subject occur in the protases, and therefore deal with preconditions to full restoration and blessing: the first occurs in the phrase, "take (Hi. שוב) them to heart" (v. 1), which refers to Israel's recall of the blessing and the curse in exile; the other two focus on the covenant relationship itself and speak of repentance—"(when) you return to Yahweh your God" (vv. 2, 10). Yahweh appears as the subject for the first time in the idiom, "restore your fortunes" (v. 3a), which describes his restoration of Israel and stands as the initial blessing in the first apodosis.

In the final three references, שוב is often translated as "again," as it is linked to other actions; thus, in the apodoses, Yahweh "again gathers" Israel (v. 3b) and "again delights" in Israel (v. 9); in verse 8, Israel "again heeds" Yahweh. Though "again" is a possible rendering, none of the cases require this reading.[303] They all speak to reversals of previous actions, but not necessarily to a return to former actions. While the idea of repetition fits Yahweh's delight in Israel in verse 9, since Yahweh had delighted in Israel before exile (28:63),[304] Yahweh's gathering of Israel after scattering them in verse 3b does not match a previous experience in the nation's history.[305] It is significant that both of these references appear in the apodoses, and are therefore part of Yahweh's response to Israel's repentance; that is, Israel's turning to Yahweh leads to Yahweh's turning to Israel. Thus, a stronger sense than "again" is favored (such as "turn" or "re-

---

301. Rofé, "Covenant in the Land of Moab," 311.

302. The root has been explored thoroughly in Holladay, *Root šûbh*. But differences of opinion still exist on specific renderings. For the meanings in Deut 30:1–10 see especially Barker, *Triumph of Grace*, 145–50; Rofé, "Covenant in the Land of Moab," 311.

303. This use of שוב is explained in Holladay, *Root šûbh*, 66–70, but none of the references here fit his syntactical structures exactly. Holladay himself acknowledges that there is some doubt with respect to vv. 8a and 9b.

304. So Driver, *Deuteronomy*, 330; Mayes, *Deuteronomy*, 368.

305. McConville (*Deuteronomy*, 422) thinks "again" is an unlikely rendering in v. 3b because the verb is "so marked."

turn"). The final reference in verse 8, at the center of the structure, is in a unique position. Unlike in the apodoses, here Israel's obedience is not a response to anything, though it is a result of Yahweh's actions in verses 3–7. As will be argued below, verse 8 is an unconditional promise. The other occurrences of the phrase, "obey the voice of Yahweh your God," are joined with Israel's repentance (vv. 2, 10), suggesting that verse 8 is also speaking of repentance.[306] שוב might also be referring to return to the land, which is the proper location of keeping God's commandments. Whatever the case, "again" seems wholly inadequate in verse 8, for it is not clear that this description (of Israel's obedience) ever fit Israel in her history up to this point.

The rendering of כי in verses 1, 9, 10a, and 10b is also critical for a proper understanding of this text:

כי all these words come upon you ... (v. 1)

כי Yahweh will return to delight in prospering you (v. 9)

כי you heed the voice of Yahweh your God (v. 10a)

כי you turn to Yahweh with all your heart and all your soul (v. 10b)

The usual response is to take verse 1 as temporal, verse 9 as causal, and verses 10a and 10b as conditional.[307] In discussing the כי-clauses in 4:25 and 29, we noted that the distinction between temporal and conditional כי is not always clear, but that a temporal reading is favored when a high degree of probability may be assigned to the "condition" in question.[308] In verse 1, a temporal reading is clearly favored. כי והיה is temporal in most, if not all, of its other Deuteronomic references.[309] Also, the sequence of

---

306. So Barker, *Triumph of Grace*, 146.

307. Looking at standard English translations (ASV, ESV, JPS, AV, NASB, NIV, NKJ, NRSV, RSV), all take v. 1 as temporal and v. 9 as causal (but NIV leaves כי in v. 9 untranslated). While most translate both references in v. 10 as conditional, ESV translates vv. 10a and 10b as temporal, and NRSV translates v. 10a as temporal but v. 10b as causal. Cf. the references in Barker, *Triumph of Grace*, 154 nn. 289 and 290.

308. Aejmelaeus, "Function and Interpretation of כי," 197. Also see Joüon, *Grammar of Biblical Hebrew*, 621; Schoors, "Particle כִּ֣," 240–76; and Waltke and O'Connor, *Introduction to Biblical Hebrew Syntax*, 637.

309. Deut 6:10; 11:29; 15:16; 26:1; 31:21. In 6:10; 11:29; and 26:1, entry into land is in definite terms. 31:21 speaks of coming disasters. Only 15:16 might be conditional, though a temporal reading is still possible. Diepold (*Israels Land*, 92–93) argues that a temporal reading is proper for a majority of cases of כי in the context of land, but given an assumed reality of Israel already in the land, the sense becomes conditional.

blessing and curse—instead of alternatives—assumes the events will have taken place.[310] All seem to agree that a causal reading in verse 9 is clear.[311] In verse 10, כי is governed by שמע, "heed" (v. 10a), and שוב (v. 10b). If considered alone, a conditional reading makes sense. Given the concentric structure of the whole text, however, the parallel between verses 1–2 and verse 10 (the protases) would favor a temporal reading of the two clauses in verse 10; verses 1–2 also has כי governed by שמע and שוב.[312] A different possibility for verse 10 is to see each כי-clause as a further ground in support of verse 9a.[313] This would stress even more the gracious and promissory nature of the restoration. Either way, given the fact that a strictly conditional reading is unlikely throughout the text, the future hope of restoration should be considered definite. The inevitability of the curses, established in chapters 28–29, is overcome by the inevitability of future blessings.

We are now in a position to discuss the basis or grounds of the restoration. Several factors point to the priority and initiative of Yahweh for return. First is the role of God's word. In verses 1–2, Israel's return to Yahweh is established as a "condition" for Yahweh's return to Israel. However, the very first action is not something that Israel does, but one that comes upon Israel: "When all these words (הדברים) come upon you, the blessing and the curse . . ." (v. 1a). In context, this is a reference both to chapter 28, with the catalogue of blessings and curses, and to 29:28, where יסדבר is in construct with התורה.[314] In chapter 28 and 29:28, God's word is given to promote and enable obedience. Likewise, the purpose of "all these words" in 30:1 is to lead Israel to obedience. This finds a direct parallel in 4:30: "(when) all these things find you . . . you will return to Yahweh your God and heed his voice." When combined with the sense of inevitability already established, it is clear that Israel's "condition" of re-

---

310. See Driver, *Deuteronomy*, 326; Thompson, *Deuteronomy*, 283. McCarthy (*Treaty and Covenant*, 201) notes parallels in Assyrian texts.

311. I have yet to find an alternative reading.

312. Cf. our discussion of 4:29–30.

313. Braulik (*Deuteronomium*, 216–17), for example, translates כי in vv. 10a, 10b, and 11 by "denn" rather than "wenn." Cf. Barker, *Triumph of Grace*, 155–56. Aejmelaeus, ("Function and Interpretation of 8–207 ",כי) says that a כי-clause following the main clause (as in vv. 9–10) is usually causal, though he admits that Deuteronomic use is an exception. Besides, the chiastic arrangement of the text determines the order in this case.

314. See Wolff, "Kerygma of the Deuteronomic Historical Work," 100. Wolff argues that 29:28 introduces 30:1–10.

pentance is first prompted by divine revelation. In fact, Israel's first action is not an "action" at all, but a "taking to heart" the things that have been revealed. Now, what has been revealed includes the call to return.³¹⁵

Second, divine priority is supported by Yahweh's action of gathering (קבץ) Israel in verses 3–4 and bringing (Hi. בוא) her back to the land in verse 5. The picture is not one of Yahweh passively waiting in the land for Israel to run to him. Rather, Yahweh himself travels to every place he had scattered his people (v. 3). The point is so stressed that Moses interrupts the chain of events to highlight the extent Yahweh will go: "If your outcasts are in the uttermost parts of heaven, *from there* Yahweh your God will gather you, and *from there* he will take you" (v. 4). Though divine regathering is a common ANE motif,³¹⁶ this kind of emphasis is rare, if extant at all. This is significantly different even from chapter 4, where "from there" is the stated locale of Israel's seeking and finding Yahweh, not of Yahweh's gathering (4:29). Israel's physical dependence on Yahweh's initiative is continued in verse 5: "And Yahweh your God will bring (Hi. בוא) you into the land . . . ." Elsewhere in Deuteronomy, this combination is always either conditional (expressing obligation through an imperative) or found in a negative clause.³¹⁷ Its unique use here, then, stresses the gifted nature of the land and the gracious nature of the return to it.

Third is the divine circumcision of the heart (v. 6). It is well known that the fact or promise of verse 6 is syntactically different from 10:16, where Israel is commanded, "Circumcise therefore the foreskin of your heart, and stiffen your neck no more." Some, however, do not see a theological difference in the two texts.³¹⁸ But, as 10:16 shows, an uncircumcised heart speaks of a state of hardness and rebellion, not simply a

---

315. Ibid.

316. On the theme of divine gathering in ANE, see Widengren, "Gathering of the Dispersed," 227–45. From the examples supplied, none emphasize the extent factor like Deut 30:3–4.

317. See Barker, *Triumph of Grace*, 156; Vanoni, "Der Geist und der Buchstabe," 90–91. כי-clauses include 6:10; 7:1; 8:7; 11:29; 31:20, 23. Negative clauses include 9:28; 31:21.

318. E.g., Weinfeld, "Jeremiah and the Spiritual Metamorphosis of Israel," 17–56. Giving no reasons, Weinfeld states, "There is apparently no significant difference between God's circumcising the heart of Israel and Israel's circumcising their own heart" (ibid., 35). Cf. Christensen's outline of 30:1–10, where vv. 6–7 is stated as a command (*Deuteronomy 21:10—34:12*, 736). Christensen does the same thing with v. 8 (ibid., 737).

neutral or insensitive position.[319] Israel's uncircumcised heart is the reason she is ultimately unable to be faithful to the covenant. The promise of 30:6 resolves this problem,[320] countering the expectation of Israel's inability in 29:3 and elsewhere.[321] Yahweh will perform for Israel what she is unable to do for herself.[322] This miracle will enable Israel finally to do what she has often been commanded, to love Yahweh with heart and soul (v. 6b; cf. 6:5).

Given that divine circumcision is part of our argument for divine priority and initiative in restoration, we must address Barker's concern stated earlier.[323] He objects to seeing the heart circumcision as the penultimate blessing in the chain of blessings in verses 3-7. Rather, he would argue that the circumcision of verse 6 is the ground of Israel's repentance and subsequent obedience; therefore, the action of verse 6 actually precedes the events of verses 2-5 (and vv. 7-10). In sum, "'the circumcision of the heart through God precedes the conversion of Israel.' It also precedes Israel's ability to obey and heed Yahweh's voice."[324] However, we have opted to take the succession of verbs in the text seriously, while being sympathetic to Barker's theological stance. What Barker (and others) seems to miss is that divine circumcision is held off until Israel is back in the land (v. 5).[325] The line of thought in verse 6 is that divine

---

319. As Weinfeld (*Deuteronomy 1-11*, 428) would explain it. This position is countered by Barker, *Triumph of Grace*, 163ff. Barker states that circumcision "is to remove the state of hardness and rebellion against God. It is to make the heart responsive to God, with a renewed capacity to obey and love, rather than remaining hard" (ibid., 163-64).

320. So Barker, *Triumph of Grace*, 164, 167-68; Freedman, "Divine Commitment and Human Obligation," 419-31; McConville, *Grace in the End*, 137.

321. The standard critical position is to offer a diachronic solution, seeing the early optimism (such as 10:16) outdone by exilic pessimism. Cf. Levenson, "Who Inserted the Book of the Torah?" 212: "certain passages suggest a rewriting from the exilic perspective, stressing the inevitability of sin and perhaps also of destruction."

322. Lenchak (*Choose Life*, 166) states that circumcision expresses "an interior renewal of the people made possible by the power of God" (cf. Deut 10:16; Jer 4:4; 9:24-25; Ezek 44:7, 9; cf. Lev 26:41).

323. See Barker, *Triumph of Grace*, 144, 163-68.

324. Ibid., 197. The first sentence is a quote from Braulik, "Law as Gospel," 14. Cf. Thompson, *Deuteronomy*, 285, on v. 6: "God Himself will carry out the inward renewal of Israel . . . . By His own gracious activity He will reconstitute Israel. Repentance in itself will not suffice. *Perhaps, indeed, the origin of repentance itself lies in the divine activity*" (emphasis added).

325. Ridderbos (*Deuteronomy*, 270) also sees Israel's conversion in v. 2 as preceding circumcision in v. 6, but for him circumcision is "a continual renewal" and not "the

circumcision leads to Israel's love of Yahweh, which leads to life. "Life" in Deuteronomy, we have argued, is life *in the land*. The laws that Israel must obey are intended and designed to be performed in the land. It seems appropriate, therefore, that Yahweh would wait until Israel is in the land to circumcise her heart.[326] If so, we must still address how Israel is able to repent in verse 2 before her heart is circumcised. Though we will have more to say on this later, one could point to the fact that Yahweh is active in the heart in verse 1. It is plausible to posit a divine work of grace in the heart prior to the circumcision.

Fourth, the unconditional nature of verse 8 argues for divine initiative. The verse is a declaration that Israel will one day be faithful: "And you shall return and heed the voice of Yahweh and do all his commandments that I command you today." There is no indication that the verbs should be given an imperatival force,[327] even if there is a "rhetorical force" for the Moab generation in focusing on Israel's obligations.[328] Lenchak is wrong, then, to assume that verse 8 contains "three short conditional clauses" that form a protasis.[329] Rather, the full restoration—including repentance, return to land, and obedience—*is* the blessing itself, and thus part of the promise.[330] As the center of the text, the unconditional statement of v. 8 must be given full consideration, helping to qualify the "conditional" statements of Israel's return in verses 1, 2, and 10. Therefore, no matter how one solves the problem of sequence of events in relation to the divine circumcision in verse 6, Yahweh will ensure that Israel will be obedient in the future.

once-for-all renewal."

326. The same sequence is given in Ezek 36, where Yahweh first gathers Israel and brings her into the land (v. 24), and then gives her a new heart (v. 26).

327. Certainly, the imperfect שובת and the *waw*-consecutive perfect ושמעת could have an imperatival force, but the context does not demand one. Christensen (*Deuteronomy 21:10—34:12*, 737) suggests an imperatival force in his structure of vv. 6–10.

328. See McConville, *Deuteronomy*, 428.

329. Lenchak, *Choose Life*, 198. For Lenchak, v. 9 would be the apodosis.

330. So also Wolff ("Kerygma," 98): "the return is plainly part of the promise. The presupposition in 4:30f. as in 30:2f. is Yahweh's watchful compassion." Olson (*Deuteronomy and the Death of Moses*, 36) adds, "This new hopeful finding and returning to God is not grounded in the people's character and activity but in the character and activity of God." Cf. Sklba, "Call to New Beginnings," 72: "Conversion is in fact promised as a gracious gift of Yahweh, both the spiritual reality of the renewed relationship and the geographical transposition back to the land of promise." All three quotes are given in Barker, *Triumph of Grace*, 148–49.

Fifth, divine priority and grace are established by the grounding of restoration in the patriarchal promises. Though often unrecognized, there are at least seven allusions to these promises in this text: circumcision (v. 6); "your fathers" (vv. 5[2x], 9); land (v. 5); prosperity (vv. 5, 9); progeny (v. 6); divine compassion (v. 3); and love (v. 6).[331] Several of these are linked already in chapter 10: "Yet Yahweh set his heart in love on your fathers and chose their offspring after them .... Circumcise therefore the foreskin of your heart ..." (10:15–16a).[332] The reference to "your fathers" in 10:15 shows that the references in 30:5 and 9 are also to the patriarchs,[333] and that the themes of land, prosperity, and progeny are connected to the patriarchal promises.[334] Circumcision, the physical sign of the Abrahamic covenant (cf. Gen 17:9–12), is now applied symbolically to Israel's heart. The notion of divine compassion in verse 3 is not directly associated with Abraham, but the use of רחם elsewhere in Deuteronomy implies the connection: in 4:31, Yahweh is described as "a compassionate (adj. רחום) God" who will not "forget the covenant with your fathers"; in 13:18[17], if Israel is obedient in dealing with apostates, Yahweh promises to "show you mercy (adj. רחמים) have compassion (Pi. רחם, as in 30:3) on you and multiply you, as he swore to your fathers." With respect to love, in four of the five Deuteronomic occurrences with Yahweh as subject and Israel as object of the verb אהב, the context is the Abrahamic covenant.[335] These allusions suggest that Israel's restoration in the future is ultimately dependent upon Yahweh's faithfulness to the Abrahmic covenant—the

---

331. Barker, *Triumph of Grace*, 169–75. Surprisingly, Braulik ("Deuteronomy and the Birth of Monotheism," 111) states, "not even the covenant with the fathers is mentioned as the reason for the grace granted to Israel."

332. Barker, *Triumph of Grace*, 169–70.

333. Against the common (critical) view that "your fathers" in 30:5 is a reference to the pre-exilic ancestors of the exiles. E.g., Polzin, *Moses and the Deuteronomist*, 70–71; Watts, *Deuteronomy*, 280.

334. Land and progeny in Deuteronomy are clearly connected to the Abrahamic promises. Here, the land is explicitly "the land that your fathers possessed" (v. 5). With respect to progeny, the Hiphil of רבה, "to be many," with Yahweh as subject and Israel as object (as in v. 5), is explicitly linked to the promise to the fathers in 1:10; 7:13; and 13:18 (implicit in 28:63 with the link between 28:62 and Gen 15:5 in the phrase, "numerous as the stars of heaven"). By itself, prosperity is not necessarily Abrahamic. See, however, the discussion and references of recent research on טוב, "to prosper," as deriving from ancient treaty language in Barker, *Triumph of Grace*, 170–71.

335. In 4:37 and 10:15, the object is "the fathers." In 7:8, 13, the object is the current generation. The exception is 23:6[5].

same argument advanced in chapter 4. Israel's fidelity is a means to this end, and one that Yahweh will cause to happen.

Thus, through an analysis of the meanings of שׁוב and כי and an examination of significant features in the text, we conclude that the re-establishment of the covenant relationship is ultimately dependent on Yahweh.[336] This conclusion does not abrogate Israel's responsibility nor eliminate her role in the future restoration. It does, however, partially clarify how the mutual activity of Yahweh and Israel will be conducted. Nonetheless, there are still remaining theological questions that we will seek to address in the following section.

### Theological Considerations

Deuteronomy 30:1–10 adds to the theological topics already raised in this thesis. In the exposition of the text, we labored over the issue of Israel's ability to obey. The fact that Israel is in need of a changed heart that will only come in the future confirms her lack of ability for sustained obedience in the present. Other topics include the issues of historical continuity, covenantal continuity, and the question of the individual. These will be addressed more fully in chapter 5.

The allusions to the partriarchs, especially, express continuity with the past. The "new" Israel of the future is, in fact, a "renewed" Israel; she never loses her identity as the seed of Abraham. But there are also hints at discontinuity, for Israel's restoration is not a return to the *status quo*. The restoration will involve a measurable increase of blessing over the past. Moses declares that Yahweh "will make you *more* prosperous and *more* numerous than your fathers" (v. 5). The most significant change, though, is seen in the metaphorical use of circumcision. In the future, participants in the Abrahamic covenant will be marked by the internal change of a circumcised heart rather than a physical cutting of the flesh. Under the old order, one's spiritual condition was not a determining factor to be among the elect nation. In the new order, God will cause the intent of the symbol to be realized,[337] and the changed heart will be the "symbol" of demarcation. This paves the way for later prophetic

---

336. Against both those who argue that the basis is Israel's obedience (e.g., Schenker, "Umwidernufliche," 98–99) or that Deuteronomy is ambivalent about the matter (e.g., Goldingay, *Theological Diversity*, 145).

337. Cf. Kline, *By Oath Assigned*, 132: "What had been externally symbolized in circumcision ... would be spiritually actualized by the power of God."

promises: through Isaiah, Yahweh promises that all of Israel's children will be taught, protected, and made righteous by Yahweh (Isa 54:13–17); through Jeremiah, Yahweh promises to write his law on the hearts of his people, resulting in universal knowledge of God for every member of the covenant (Jer 31:33–34); through Ezekiel, Yahweh promises to give Israel a new heart that will result in obedience (Ezek 36:26–27). In the New Testament, Paul testifies to this shift of demarcation, identifying a "true" Jew as one that has a circumcised heart (Rom 2:28–29). He explicitly draws a distinction between physical Israel and "true" Israel based on the qualifier of faith (Rom 9:6–8; Gal 3:7). Thus, besides the strong note of corporate solidarity and generational conflation, Deuteronomy proffers an expectation of some discontinuity between the past and future.

Interrelated to the tension between historical continuity and discontinuity is the question of the relationship between the various covenants. We have established a strong connection between Sinai/Horeb, Moab, and Shechem. In 4:29–31 and 30:1–10, Deuteronomy looks to the Abrahamic covenant as the basis of restoration. From one angle, this would appear to pit the Abrahamic covenant against Sinai. Interpreters and theologians often see the former as unconditional and gracious and the latter as conditional and legal. The present text will not allow such a simplistic dichotomy (see the fuller discussion in chap. 5).

A nagging question that must be asked concerns the place of the individual in restoration. The focus in 30:1–10 is on the nation. In particular, the circumcision of the nation's heart (singular) yields corporate obedience (v. 6). This makes sense, since it is the answer to the nation incurring judgment for the outworking of her corrupt heart. However, individuals are distinguished. Those who return to Yahweh include "you and your children" (v. 2). Yahweh's circumcision will extend to "the heart of your children" (v. 6). These references emphasize the permanence of Yahweh's restoration for all future generations, but they also suggest that repentance and regeneration are individuated. Unlike the situation before exile, where the faithful individual was a rarity, a restored Israel will be made up of a people among whom every individual expresses covenant fidelity (see fuller discussion in chap. 5).

## CONCLUSION

The themes of exile and restoration in Deuteronomy are explicated in three main texts. The introduction of these themes in 4:25–31 appears

# 4

# The Texts and Contexts of Exile, Part 2

THE PURPOSE OF THIS chapter is to show that the theme of exile is not found only in the few texts analyzed in chapter 3. This will be argued from two angles. First, we will examine other texts in Deuteronomy that present possible allusions to exile through terminological or thematic connections to the major exile texts. Second, we will see where the texts on exile and restoration fit within the more common macrostructures of the book. Due to the limited purpose of this chapter, the depth of analysis and comment on the texts will be more cursory than in chapter 3.

## OTHER TEXTS

The Deuteronomic texts not examined in chapter 3 fall into three major blocks: Deuteronomy 5–11, 12–26, and 31–34. The following discussion of each section will include a summary of content and a focus on possible references or allusions to exile. This will include a revisiting of the exile vocabulary from chapter 2, especially references to אבד and שמד, as well as a focus on theological themes that were part of the texts analyzed in chapter 3. Little attention will be given to critical debates about textual reconstruction.

### Deuteronomy 5–11

This section is the first part of Moses' second speech (chaps. 5–28), yet, it is usually considered separately from the rest of the speech because of its distinct style and focus. Starting with the repetition of the Decalogue in 5:6–21, chapters 5–11 serve as an introduction to the laws beginning in chapter 12.[1] Almost universally, Deuteronomy 6–11 is held

---

1. While most recognize the introductory or preparatory function of chaps. 5–11, Barker (*Triumph of Grace*, 56) notes that there is no clear consensus on chaps. 5–11 with

to be a reflection on and an interpretation of the First (and Second) Commandment(s).[2] Since so many of the allusions to exile occur in chapters 5-11, it will be convenient to break down this block into subsections. Though this could be done in various ways, we will divide the material based on formal literary grounds into three parts: 5:1—6:3; 6:4—8:20; 9:1—11:32. Each unit begins with שמע ישראל, "Hear, O Israel" (5:1b; 6:4; 9:1).[3]

### Deuteronomy 5:1—6:3

This text focuses on the repetition of the Decalogue and the legitimacy of the intermediation of Moses.[4] Its purpose is to challenge the present generation to grasp what the Horeb generation rejected.[5] It is a central text within the book. First, though it begins a major new section in the book, Deuteronomy 5 has direct connections to chapter 4, which also focuses on the Decalogue and Moses' mission to teach the laws (4:13-14).[6] Second, as stated, this text is a prelude to the single-minded attention given in chapters 6-11 concerning the need for Israel's exclusive wor-

---

respect to form, structure, redaction, coherence, and relationship to rest of book. The classical critical study of Deut 5-11, including its history of formation, is Lohfink, *Das Hauptgebot*. See also Peckham, "Composition of Deuteronomy 5-11," 217-40. Barker (pp. 56-57) notes two other scholars that have influenced critical discussion: Vermeylen, "Les sections narratives de Deut 5-11," 174-207; and García López, "Analyse littéraire," (1977) 481-522; idem, "Analyse littéraire," (1978) 5-49. The view of García López is probably the most common view; cf. Preuss, *Deuteronomium*, 95ff.

2. See the references in chap. 1, n. 1. See also Olson, *Deuteronomy and the Death of Moses*, 49ff.

3. This follows the broad structure in Block, *Gospel According to Moses*, 228-29.

4. On the centrality of Moses' intermediation, see Tigay, *Deuteronomy*, 60.

5. Block, *Gospel According to Moses*, 231.

6. Note especially the similar language between 4:10-14 and 5:22. Tigay (*Deuteronomy*, 60) notes that both chapters concentrate on different aspects of the experience at Mount Horeb: in chap. 4, Israel did not see God but heard his voice; in chap. 5, God spoke to Israel "face to face" but Israel was afraid to hear his voice. Cf. McConville and Millar, *Time and Place*, 53, who note that the "laws and statutes" in 5:1 (cf. 5:31; 6:1, 20; 7:11) shows an obvious link with chap. 4.

ship of Yahweh.[7] Third, chapters 12–28 seem to function in some way as interpretations and extensions of the Ten Commandments.[8]

Exile is not directly mentioned in this text. None of the exile vocabulary appears. However, several related themes arise that show that the concept of exile serves as part of the backdrop. First, the text deals with issues of life and death within the context of land. The Fifth Commandment, which calls for honoring one's father and mother, comes with a promise, "that your days may be lengthened, and that it may go well with you in the land that Yahweh your God is giving you" (5:16). At the end of the unit,[9] this conditional promise is attached to all the commandments: "You shall walk in all the way that Yahweh your God has commanded you, that you may live, and that it may go well with you, and that you may lengthen days in the land that you shall possess" (5:33; cf. 6:2). Tigay rightly notes that this promise can be read as a veiled threat—"otherwise your days will be shortened"—which is consistent with the curse of exile.[10] The connection with exile is strengthened when it is realized that "life" is perceived primarily in corporate and transgenerational terms (e.g., 6:2). Though Israelites can and should hear the commandments as individuals, the focus is on the nation as a unit. Her

---

7. Virtually all agree that 6:4 begins a new section (following the division in MT). See Block, *Gospel According to Moses*, 229; McConville, *Deuteronomy*, 138–39; Weinfeld, *Deuteronomy 1–11*, 327. Chaps. 5 and 6 are also closely related. For an argument to keep the two chapters together, see Lohfink, *Das Hauptgebot*, 66–68, 290–91; cf. McConville (*Deuteronomy*, 138), who states that chaps. 5 and 6 are linked conceptually by the extension of the laws "into the regular lives of the people into future generations."

8. There have been several attempts to account for the sequence of the statutes and ordinances in chaps. 12–26. Recently, it has become increasingly popular (though with several historical antecedents) to recognize a correspondence between the order of the Ten Commandments and the order of the specific laws in the lawcode. See especially the discussion and references in Olson, *Deuteronomy and the Death of Moses*, 63–64 and n. 3. Though I remain unconvinced of the detailed proposals, there is no doubt that there are clear thematic connections between the Decalogue and the laws.

9. McConville (*Deuteronomy*, 134) sees the theme of life as rounding off the unit (cf. vv. 3 and 33), much like chap. 4 (vv. 1, 26, 40). Note also the focus on life and death in 5:24–26.

10. Tigay, *Deuteronomy*, 70. McConville (*Deuteronomy*, 122) asks whether the Deuteronomic addition of the second promise in 5:16, "that it may go well with you," separates the promise of long life from its direct association with the land (contrast Exod 20:12, "that you may live long in the land"), thus anticipating life for Israel outside the land. As McConville himself concludes, this would probably be an overreading of the text; it is best to take the addition as a case of expansionist Deuteronomic style (cf. the same phrase in 4:40; 5:26; 12:25; 22:7).

life in the land, both quantitatively and qualitatively, depends on her fidelity to the covenant presented. This corporate view of "life" is maintained throughout chapters 5–11 (e.g., 6:24; 8:1).

This leads directly to a second major emphasis: corporate solidarity. For the present generation, the corporate sense is emphasized in the initial editorial note that Moses summoned "all Israel" (5:1) and in Moses' recollection that at Horeb Yahweh spoke to "all your assembly" (5:22).[11] Seemingly, however, transgenerational unity is questioned as Moses sharply distinguishes between the past and present generations: "Yahweh our God made a covenant with us in Horeb. Not with our fathers did Yahweh make this covenant, but with us, who are all of us here alive today" (5:2-3). As we discussed with respect to 4:31 ("the covenant with your fathers"), the identity of the "fathers" in 5:3 is a matter of some debate. Though a reference to the patriarchs is not impossible,[12] the force of the rhetoric here favors the more widely held view that "fathers" refers to the Horeb generation.[13] In a forward-looking context, Moses empha-

---

11. McConville (*Deuteronomy*, 131–32) claims that the use of the word "assembly" stresses that the whole people is directly involved in receiving the Decalogue.

12. Not only does this seem to be a common referent to "fathers" in Deuteronomy, the patriarchs are clearly in view in 6:3 (cf. the promise to fathers of multiplication in 6:3; 7:13; 8:1, 13; 13:17; 30:16), the end of our section. Scholars who take "fathers" in 5:3 as the patriarchs do so for various reasons, none of which are ultimately convincing. Tigay (*Deuteronomy*, 61) simply states that "our/your fathers" in Deuteronomy *always* refers to the patriarchs, but he provides no support. Merrill (*Deuteronomy*, 141) assumes the reference, only to use it as supporting an absolute contrast between the patriarchal covenant and the covenant at Horeb—which, even if true (though I would not agree), is hardly Moses' point here. Block (*Gospel According to Moses*, 234–41), who (against Tigay) takes "fathers" to refer to the Horeb generation in other texts (e.g., 4:31; 7:12; 8:18) and (against Merrill) stresses the continuity of the patriarchal covenant and the Horeb covenant, nevertheless takes "fathers" in 5:3 as the patriarchs because he thinks a reference to the Horeb generation creates a misconstrual of the facts, or (if the anachronism is allowed to be rhetorical) it creates "a radical distancing" between Horeb and Moab (see *Gospel According to Moses*, 235). While I share Block's position on the continuity between Horeb and Moab, I do not see how his conclusion is the necessary implication of taking "fathers" as a reference to the Horeb generation. Block's understanding of the contrast between the patriarchal and Horeb covenants is between (1) the place and circumstances in which the covenants were made and (2) the intensity of Yahweh's self-disclosure. We will discuss further the relationship of these covenants in chap. 5.

13. E.g., Craigie, *Book of Deuteronomy*, 148; Mayes, *Deuteronomy*, 165; McConville, *Deuteronomy*, 123–24; Olson, *Deuteronomy and the Death of Moses*, 41; and von Rad, *Deuteronomy*, 55. Labuschagne (*Deuteronomium*, 24) and Wright (*Deuteronomy*, 62) also take "fathers" as a reference to the Horeb generation, but seek to avoid the anachronism by translating כי ... לא as "not only ... but also." This seems unnecessary and

sizes the immediate responsibility of the present generation. Rather than stressing severe discontinuities between past and present (though discontinuities are not absent), the statement actually draws a parallel between the covenant at Horeb and what is taking place at Moab. As Millar states, "the current generation is not to think of the covenant at Horeb as a mere memory, but as *a memory which is actualized in the present at Moab*."[14] Having established the parallel, the unity across generations returns to the surface of the text in 5:29 ("them and their sons") and 6:2 ("you, your son, and your son's son").

A third relevant theme in this text is the question of Israel's ability to be faithful to the renewed covenant at Moab. In many respects, these verses are quite positive and upbeat. The distinction in 5:2–3 between the present generation and the previous one aids this picture. Whereas the "fathers" had rebelled through the idolatry of the golden calf incident (9:7–27) and through a lack of faith at Kadesh-barnea (1:19–40), the "sons" have proven faithful in the Transjordan (2:26—3:17) and at Beth-peor (4:4). The present generation is pictured as demonstrating a healthy fear of Yahweh at Horeb (5:4–5, 23–27). Specifically, Yahweh's evaluation of their request for the intermediation of Moses is clear: "I have heard the words of this people, which they have spoken to you. They are right in all that they have spoken" (5:28).

This bright outlook, however, is clouded by a couple of dark—or at least grey—overtones. First, following on the heels of Yahweh's approving smile comes a wince of pessimism: "Oh that they had such a heart as this always, to fear me and to keep all my commandments, that it might go well with them and with their sons forever!" (5:29) Concern can be sensed by the subtle contrast between one day's demonstration

---

negates the rhetorical point. Given our methodology, we need not discuss a third (critical) option that considers 5:3 to be a late insertion (along with 11:2–9), with "fathers" referring to pre-exilic generations (e.g., Weinfeld, *Deuteronomy 1–11*, 237–39).

14. McConville and Millar, *Time and Place*, 58 (emphasis original); cf. Millar, *Now Choose Life*, 82. Miller (*Deuteronomy*, 67), whom Millar quotes for support, comments, "This verse [5:3] expresses a kind of hermeneutical formula for the book. The time gap and the generation gap are dissolved in the claim that the covenant at Sinai, the primal revelation that created the enduring relationship between the people and the Lord was really made with the *present* generation. The covenant is not an event, a claim, a relationship of the past; it is of the present. The time between the primal moment and the present moment is telescoped, and the two are equated." Cf. McConville, *Deuteronomy*, 124; Tigay, *Deuteronomy*, 74; von Rad, *Deuteronomy*, 55. This also fits with Block's claim that this text should be viewed as a covenant *renewal* text (*Gospel According to Moses*, 231).

of reverence and Yahweh's wish for this disposition כל־הימים, "all the days" (= "always" or "continually"). Several commentators have noted this contrast.[15] With respect to understanding 5:29 as presenting the possibility that, with time, the inclination to obey will weaken, Mayes finds the closest parallel in 4:25, where Israel's failure to keep fresh the memory of the land as gift leads to exile.[16]

Second, and even more subtle, is the negative implication of Israel's acceptance of Moses as mediator.[17] It may seem odd to find anything negative in Moses' role here, but this text must be viewed within the context of the book. Moses is recounting the Horeb experience in his second speech to the Moab generation. In the first speech, the people were reminded three times of Moses' exclusion from the land (1:37; 3:23–29; 4:21). The middle reference is particularly significant, for it, like 5:29, comes as an anticlimactic conclusion to an otherwise positive portrayal of events (i.e., the conquest of Transjordan in 2:26—3:22). In the future, then, how will Israel keep the memory alive when their leader will not be with them? Both issues—Yahweh's wish and the tentative role of Moses—are only suggestive concerning Israel's (in)ability; greater clarity will come in the following chapters.

## Deuteronomy 6:4—8:20

This unit is enveloped by the call to "hear" (6:4; שמע; cf. 5:1; 9:1) and the warning of destruction, "because you would not heed (שמע) the voice of Yahweh your God" (8:20).[18] These chapters display an increasing negativity, showing a connection to the initial doubt raised in 5:29, that

---

15. Block (*Gospel According to Moses*, 292–93) writes, "Even as we hear Yahweh's affirmation of the people's response ... we who read this speech hear an ominous note. It is as if God lacks confidence in his people, that he knows something about the heart of Israel that would prove evanescent." Craigie (*Deuteronomy*, 166) comments, with a reminder of Yahweh's reaction in 1:34 to the people's response in a more mundane setting, that "the attitude expressed in the people's request [in chap. 5] was a proper and a reverential one, but unfortunately it was not a typical attitude." Merrill (*Deuteronomy*, 159) notes, "The very wish, however, implies a lack of confidence in its fulfillment."

16. Mayes, *Deuteronomy*, 173; cf. p. 155 on 4:25. Cf. Tigay (*Deuteronomy*, 73), who already sees in 5:25–26 an implicit concern that as Israel forgets the experience, her reverence will recede.

17. I have not found any commentator to make this point, so I offer it tentatively.

18. See Block, *Gospel According to Moses*, 300ff., who unites these verses under the title, "The Essence of Covenant Relationship."

culminates in overt indictments in chapter 9.[19] Chapter 6 presents the exhortation to exclusive devotion to Yahweh (vv. 4–5),[20] which entails the proper reverence for and transmission of God's word (vv. 6-9, 20–25), as well as warnings of potential dangers to covenant commitment in the land (vv. 10–19). Illustrations of these dangers are developed in chapters 7–8: Israel will be tested externally by the presence of Canaanites in the land (chap. 7; cf. 6:17–19); she will be tested internally through her own prosperity in an Edenic-like land (chap. 8; cf. 6:10–16).[21] On the one hand, these verses continue and expand on concepts and themes already introduced. The famous Shema (6:4) and correlative command to love Yahweh completely (6:5) are the beginning of several chapters that, in the main, restate, interpret, and apply the First and Second Commandments.[22] On the other hand, this part of the book represents a marked rhetorical shift from chapters 1–5, both in its temporal focus and in its view of the role of Moab as the place of decision.[23] Though the

19. See the discussions of Israel's "heart" and the synergism between Yahweh's and Israel's actions in the next section, where some of the data from chaps. 6–8 will be incorporated.

20. Space constraints preclude discussion of the debate concerning the Shema in 6:4, particularly whether יהוה אחד should be translated as "Yahweh is one" or "Yahweh alone." The concern for exclusive devotion within the covenant relationship is the point of the passage, whatever translation one favors. See the discussions and references in Block, "How Many is God," 193–212; idem, *Gospel According to Moses*, 304–13; Tigay, "Excursus 10: The Shema (6:4)," in *Deuteronomy*, 438–41; and Weinfeld, *Deuteronomy 1–11*, 337–38.

21. The fact that chaps. 9–10 also focus on the theme of testing shows that demarcating 6:4—8:20 as a separate subunit is not absolute. Cf. Tigay (*Deuteronomy*, 83–84), who puts 7:1—10:22 together under the heading, "Avoiding Dangers to Faith and Obedience After the Conquest of the Promised Land." He sees the whole exhortation as stemming from the issue of the Canaanite presence in the land, and delineates the dangers as the following: the fear of a superior army and lure of idolatry (chap. 7); the sense of self-sufficiency (chap. 8); the notion that the conquest is proof of righteousness (chaps. 9–10). Nevertheless, Tigay finds a secondary division between chaps. 7–8 and 9–10.

22. After listing several allusions to the Decalogue in chap. 6, Tigay (*Deuteronomy*, 75–76) states, "In light of these allusions, the exhortations to love God, to remember Him, to teach children about His words and deeds, and all the other themes of chapter 6 can be regarded as a sermonic reflection on the first commandment, explaining what must be done to carry it out." The allusions in chap. 6 include the following: vv. 4, 14 restate the First Commandment; vv. 12, 21, 23 echo the preamble; v. 15 parallels the First and Second Commandments with the combination of prohibiting idolatry and warning of God's jealousy; vv. 5 and 17 echo the Second Commandment with the call to "love" and "keep"; v. 18 echoes the reward promised in the Fifth Commandment (6:2–3).

23. See especially the helpful discussion of chap. 6 in McConville and Millar, *Time*

address continues to refer to past experiences, there is a distinct emphasis now on Israel's future, as Moses' attention is clearly fixed on the coming occupation and settlement of the land.[24]

If the theme of exile were present in these verses, it would most naturally appear in the spelling out of consequences for disobedience. Since there is a strong emphasis on the conditionality of land entry and possession here, lists of blessings and curses abound. The blessings include well-being (6:18), life (6:24; 8:1; cf. 7:16), land entry and possession (6:18; 8:1), righteousness (6:25),[25] maintenance in covenant relationship with Yahweh (7:9, 12), multiplication and fruitfulness (7:13–14; 8:1), health (7:15), and victory over enemies (7:16).[26] While these blessings are always contingent upon heeding God's commandments generally, sometimes more specific elements are affixed: Israel must deal properly with enemy nations by thrusting (הרף) them out (6:19) and carrying out the policy of *ḥerem* against them (7:2–5); internal dispositions of fear (6:24; cf. 8:7) and love (7:9) are demanded; and Israel is called to remember Yahweh's past blessings as part of her obedience (8:2ff.). The curses are much more focused than the blessings. They employ the roots אבד and שמד almost exclusively: being "destroyed" by Yahweh (שמדה in 6:15;

---

*and Place*, 60–63. Concerning the role of Moab, Millar notes that in chaps. 1–5, Moab is "the place of recapitulation": as a new Horeb, it is a place of revelation; as a new Kadesh Barnea, it is a place of action. In. chaps. 6ff., Moab also becomes "the place of anticipation": the place of entry into the land; the place at which Israel must stay "spiritually" to occupy the land; and the place Israel must return after apostasy.

24. See 6:10, 20; 7:1, 2; 8:10, 12. Cf. McConville (*Deuteronomy*, 129), who emphasizes that the heart of the exhortation in chap. 6 (vv. 4–19) pictures life in the land as stretching into the distant future.

25. The meaning of צדקה, "righteousness," is notoriously difficult, and its exact meaning in 6:25 is debated. Whether forensic or ethical, or both, Israel's "righteousness" in 6:25 consists of an expression of her proper covenant relationship with Yahweh due to her obedience.

26. The statement in 7:16a—"And you shall consume all the peoples that Yahweh your God will give over to you"—could be taken as a command or blessing. Weinfeld (*Deuteronomy 1–11*, 374) notes that it "sounds indeed like a promise, though factually it has the meaning of an injunction." Others who take the statement as a command include Block, *Gospel According to Moses*, 293–94; Mayes, *Deuteronomy*, 187; and Merrill, *Deuteronomy*, 182–83. For the sense of a blessing see Craigie, *Book of Deuteronomy*, 180–81; McConville, *Deuteronomy*, 159–60; and Thompson, *Deuteronomy*, 132. Tigay (*Deuteronomy*, 89) thinks it can go either way, but favors a promise because the MT groups v. 16 with vv. 12–15. He also notes that the blessing was one promised to the patriarchs (see Gen 22:17).

7:4; הָאָבֵד in 7:10) and "perishing" (אבד in 8:19, 20[2x]).²⁷ Though these curses are generally the result of disobedience (e.g., 6:13; 7:11; 8:20), the sins that are emphasized are forgetting Yahweh (6:12; 8:11, 17), committing idolatry (6:14; 7:4; 8:19),²⁸ and lacking the internal dispositions of fear (6:13) and love (7:10). Twice, the curse specifies an intermediate step: idolatry first incurs Yahweh's anger, which then results in destruction (6:15; 7:4).

An allusion to exile is apparent when the language of the curses is compared with the antecedent threat of exile in chapter 4. As noted, the curses in chapters 6–8 use the same verbs of destruction—אבד (7:10; 8:19, 20[2x]) and שׁמד (6:15; 7:4)—that were used with respect to exile (4:26), and will be used again (28:63). Other terminological links include the following: "watch yourself lest you forget" (6:12; 8:11, 14; cf. 4:9, 23); the focus on idolatry (6:14; 7:4; 8:19; cf. 4:23, 25); Yahweh as "an impassioned God" (6:15; cf. 4:24); divine anger (6:15; 7:4; cf. 4:25); the qualification, "from off the face of the ground" (6:15; cf. 4:26);²⁹ the idea of the destruction happening "quickly" (7:4; cf. 4:26); the presence of a witness (Moses in 8:19; cf. creation in 4:26); and the construction of Qal infinitive absolute plus imperfect of אבד (8:19; cf. 4:26). Given these direct connections, if considered within the course of the book—within the sequence of Moses' speeches—it is difficult to hear the curses in the present text without thinking of the threat of exile in chapter 4.³⁰

Two further observations about the blessings and curses strengthen the plausibility that this text alludes to exile. First, the blessings and curses must be considered within the overall context of life in the land. This is clear with respect to the blessings; even the more general ones

---

27. I say "almost exclusively" because 7:10 speaks twice of God "repaying" (Pi. שׁלם) and once of him not being "slack" (Pi. אחר). These statements are parallel to God's destruction.

28. In 7:4, the curse of destruction immediately follows the sin of idolatry, but idolatry is viewed as the end result of not complying with the ḥerem policy in 7:2–3.

29. It must be admitted that this parallel is not exact. Deut 6:15 reads, "lest . . . he destroy (שׁמדה) you from off the face of the ground (אדמה)." Deut 4:26 reads, "you will soon utterly perish (אבד) from the land (ארץ) that you are going over the Jordan to possess." The NIV partially obscures the difference by translating אדמה as "land" (cf. LXX, which translates both אדמה and ארץ with γῆς). All other English translations have "earth" in 6:15, which would tend to argue against our thesis. I have chosen a more neutral rendering for אדמה in 6:15.

30. This is the proper reading of the book as it stands, no matter how one views the way the text was put together.

are closely linked to the land.[31] These blessings, therefore, constitute the establishment of complete *shalom* in the interweaving relationships of Yahweh, Israel, and the land. As such, when the land and the landed people are blessed, it is a sign that the covenant relationship between Yahweh and Israel is stable and operating. Conversely, a breach in the personal relationship causes disruption in the enjoyment and possession of the land. The dissolution of the People-Land relationship is, in fact, what constitutes exile.

This text exhibits great irony when it is viewed through the lens of the triangular relationship of God–People–Land. The very promise of blessing and harmony in the land represents the warning of chapter 8, whose center, verse 11,[32] equates forgetting Yahweh with disobedience.[33] This spiritual amnesia is a result of the feelings of self-sufficiency that might arise due to possessing such a rich land (8:7–10). Thus, it is Yahweh's fidelity that poses one of the greatest threats to Israel's survival in the land and in the covenant.[34]

The notion of Yahweh's fidelity leads to a second observation: the close connection between the lists of blessings and curses and Yahweh's promise to the patriarchs. The "fathers" are mentioned ten times in 6:4—

---

31. Thus, well-being and life are conjoined with land entry and possession (6:18; 8:1). Life (6:24), righteousness (6:25), and maintenance in covenant relationship (7:9, 12) follow specific commands about dealing with the enemies in the land (6:19; 7:2–5). The longest list of blessings (7:12–16) has direct parallels with the list of blessings in 28:1–14, which, of course, is land-focused.

32. Verse 11 is the point of transition from protasis to apodosis, and represents the shift in tone from positive to negative. There have been detailed studies and debates over the structure of chap. 8. Most recognize v. 11 as the center or at least part of it. So Block, *Gospel According to Moses*, 406–7; Lohfink, *Das Hauptgebot*, 195; McConville, *Deuteronomy*, 166–67; Tigay, *Deuteronomy*, 92; Weinfeld, *Deuteronomy 1–11*, 397; and Wright, *Deuteronomy*, 121. Some prefer to see vv. 7b–9 (the anticipated bounty in the land) as the center; cf. Fishbane, *Biblical Interpretation in Ancient Israel*, 328–29; and O'Connell, "Deuteronomy VIII 1–20," 437–52 (esp. pp. 439–40). For a helpful summary and critique of the main options, see Barker, *Triumph of Grace*, 57–65, who argues that v. 11 is the best option for the center.

33. The topic of chap. 8 is anticipated by the juxtaposition in 6:10–12 of Yahweh's gift of land, with all its blessings, and the warning about forgetting Yahweh. Cf. the statement by Block (*Gospel According to Moses*, 329) on 6:10–11: "When the triangle of relationships (Yahweh–people–land) is complete and operating as intended, when the ideal has become real, that is the time to watch oneself."

34. Cf. Block (*Gospel According to Moses*, 405): "By the end of the chapter, we learn that success may turn out to be a more discriminating test of one's spiritual condition than deprivation."

8:20.³⁵ The references with respect to the manna "that your fathers did not know" (8:3, 16) are nonspecific and irrelevant for our discussion.³⁶ There is no doubt that "fathers" should be identified as the patriarchs when the gift of land is the issue (six times: 6:10, 18, 23; 7:8, 13; 8:1).³⁷ The remaining two references appear in the phrase, "the covenant . . . that he swore to your fathers" (7:12; 8:18). The identity of the fathers here is significant, for this covenant is the basis of restoration in 4:31 ("He will not . . . forget the covenant with your fathers that he swore to them"). The standard interpretation understands the patriarchal covenant to be in view.³⁸ For 7:12, this position is supported by the language of 7:13, which clearly uses "fathers" for the patriarchs and speaks of God "multiplying" (from רבה; cf. 1:10) Israel. The reference in 8:18, then, would seem to follow suit, and is supported by ancient translations.³⁹ Block, however, sees the exodus/Horeb generation in view in 7:12 and 8:18 because the emphasis on material blessings in the immediate contexts (7:14–16; 8:7–9) is more easily associated with the covenant made at Horeb.⁴⁰ Even granting this point, at least for 7:13–16,⁴¹ it need not

---

35. Deut 6:10, 18, 23; 7:12, 13; 8:1, 3, 16, 18.

36. The phrase, "which you did not know, nor did your fathers know," in 8:3 (Deut 8:16 only has "that your fathers did not know") is a Deuteronomic expansion of Exod 16:15, "for they did not know what it was." According to Weinfeld (*Deuteronomy 1–11*, 389), this is typical Deuteronomic rhetoric "implying something never experienced before." Similar phrases appear in Deut 13:7[6]; 28:36, 64. Of course, if the "you" is the Moab generation, but now pictured in the wilderness, the "fathers" would have to antedate the exodus generation.

37. In 7:8, "land" is not explicitly mentioned, but שבעה, "oath," comes from the same root as the verb שבע, "to swear," which is consistently used in the other five references (cf. 1:8). See Weinfeld, *Deuteronomy 1–11*, 369.

38. Cf. McConville, *Deuteronomy*, 159, 172; Tigay, *Deuteronomy*, 88, 96; Weinfeld, *Deuteronomy 1–11*, 370; Wright, *Deuteronomy*, 117.

39. SP and LXX^(L.379) insert the names of Abraham, Isaac, and Jacob for "fathers" in 8:18.

40. Block, *Gospel According to Moses*, 387 (on 7:12), 437 (on 8:16). Block points to Exod 23:25–26 and Lev 26:1–13 as support. He anticipates the argument that "multiplying" in 7:13 implies the patriarchal covenant, and counters that the Horeb covenant also promises "multiplying" (Lev 26:9) (ibid., 388).

41. The "blessings" Block refers to in 8:7–9 actually constitute a description of the "good land" (8:7), which is the real blessing here. It is interesting, though, that the land is not referred to as a gift sworn to the fathers; instead, Moses states, "For Yahweh your God is bringing you into a good land" (v. 7), and "you shall bless Yahweh your God for the good land he has given you" (v. 10).

identify the covenant in 7:12 and 8:18 as the one made at Horeb. For Yahweh to "keep" (שמר in 7:12) or "confirm" (הקים in 8:18) his covenant with the patriarchs for a people that had already experienced Horeb, it would necessarily entail "Horeb-like" blessings that help specify how the promise of blessing to Abraham (cf. Gen 12:2) would be fulfilled for this people at this time.[42] It is best, therefore, to maintain consistency in identifying the "fathers" as the patriarchs throughout this section.

The reason it is important to establish this connection between the blessings and curses and the patriarchal promise is to highlight the conditional nature of the patriarchal covenant. Four of the references to the patriarchs belong to conditional blessings specified above (6:18; 7:12, 13; 8:18). In the other references (6:10, 23; 7:8; 8:18), where the sole actor is Yahweh, contingency and warning are nearby. The gift of a land that needs no Israelite cultivation—for it already has cities, houses, cisterns, and vineyards (6:10–11)—quickly turns into a warning about forgetting Yahweh (6:12). Yahweh's sovereign redemption of Israel in order to bring her to the land (6:22–23) is followed by the conditionality of life and righteousness (6:24–25). That this redemption was an outworking of divine choice, love, and fidelity (8:6–8) is placed between warnings of destruction for disobedience (8:4, 10). Yahweh alone enables Israel to get wealth (8:18), so forgetting him would spell certain doom (8:19–20). The significance of this discussion is threefold. First, the greatest threat facing Israel to covenant infidelity is not the loss of this-or-that blessing in the land, but the loss of the land—the blessing that allows all blessings—itself. This point suggests that the ultimate curse in the text may be none other than exile. If so, this would be consistent with the curse

---

42. Cf. Wright (*Deuteronomy*, 117): "Verses 13–15 add local color to the bare words [that Abraham's blessing promised posterity and land], describing what it would mean to have a growing population in a fertile land." This real issue is the relationship of the patriarchal covenant and Horeb (see chap. 5). Block himself would not disagree with my statement above, for he finds great continuity between the two covenants. See his discussions on 4:31 and 5:2–3 (in *Gospel According to Moses*, 190–93, 235–39). After arguing for "fathers" in 4:31 as the exodus generation, Block concludes, "Perhaps one does not need to choose between the Patriarchal covenant and the Israelite covenant [i.e., Horeb]. It seems to be a case of both/and" (ibid., 192). His reason is clear: "The covenant that Yahweh remembers is the one that he made with Abraham and confirmed with his descendants at Horeb" (ibid., 193). For the reference in 5:3 to the "fathers," whom Block considers to be the patriarchs—and so implying some type of contrast—he rejects the view that the contrast between the two covenants is in form and/or content (ibid., 237).

list in chapter 28, which climaxes in exile. Second, if there is an allusion to exile in the curses of the present passage, then exile can be interpreted along the lines of covenant reversal. This also would be consistent with our analysis of exile in chapter 28, but now the patriarchal covenant is in view. Third, focusing on the conditionality of the patriarchal covenant creates a tension when we compare it to the restoration texts in chapters 4 and 30. We have shown that the promise of restoration from exile is firmly rooted in the patriarchal covenant (cf. 4:31), emphasizing its gracious and "unconditional" nature. Though we cannot resolve this tension now, both of the last two points may help clarify the relationship between the various covenants (see chap. 5).

The line of thought thus far has focused on the lists of blessings and curses in 6:4—8:20. We have argued that an allusion to exile is established by the parallels with chapter 4 and supported by the focus on land and the conditionality of the patriarchal covenant. A potential objection might be raised with the *ḥerem* policy of chapter 7, which calls for the complete annihilation of the Canaanites and their gods.[43] How one understands this policy influences the meaning of אבד and שׁמד, whose remaining four references occur in 7:17–26 (אבד in vv. 20, 24; שׁמד in vv. 23, 24). Within the concentric pattern of chapter 7,[44] verses 17–26 correspond to verses 1–6, which outlines the ban.

These references to אבד and שׁמד relate to the conquest of the land and appear in a paragraph in which Moses is seeking to encourage Israel that she need not fear despite being outnumbered and seemingly outmatched (7:17–26):

> Yahweh your God will send hornets among them, until those who are left ... perish (אבד). (v. 20)
>
> Yahweh your God will give them over to you and throw them into great confusion, until they are destroyed (Ni. שׁמד). (v. 23).

---

43. Verse 2 reads, "When Yahweh your God gives them over to you, and you defeat them, you must utterly destroy them (החרם תחרים אתם). The noun is used twice in v. 26 to refer to the status of a pagan idol and what Israel would become if she would hoard such an idol. On the root חרם, see Stern, *Biblical Ḥerem*, 102; cf. Lohfink, "חֵרֶם," 99.

44. The correspondence is established by the root חרם in vv. 2 and 26. A concentric pattern for chap. 7 (and thus the unity of the chapter) is generally acknowledged. See the various schemes in Block, *Gospel According to Moses*, 355; Lohfink, *Das Hauptgebot*, 186–87; McConville, *Deuteronomy*, 151; Wright, *Deuteronomy*, 108. Against this pattern, Christensen (*Deuteronomy 1—21:9*, 162) considers 7:12–26 as a separate unit.

> He will give their kings into your hand, and you shall make their name perish (Hi. אבד) from under the heavens. (v. 24a)
>
> No one shall be able to stand against you until you have destroyed (Hi. שמד) them. (v. 24b)

The first, second, and fourth statements leave the nature of the enemies' demise somewhat unspecified; that is, the people theoretically could "perish" or "be destroyed" either by annihilation or removal. The same flexibility exists with parallel terms like ירש, "dispossess" (Hi.; v. 17), נשל, "clear away" (v. 22a), and כלה, "cease" (v. 22b). But the use of אבד in the idiom, "you shall make their name perish from under the heavens" (v. 24a) is not so flexible. Whatever its exact meaning,[45] this idiom speaks of certain death (cf. 9: 14; 29:19[20]). Though the fate is restricted to the kings of the nations, its use of אבד must color the rest of the text. After all, this is war rhetoric, and we should not seek to diminish the force of the text.

The issue, then, is how these proscriptions ought to be interpreted. On the face of it, the text commands unconditional annihilation, which is the clear meaning of the references to חרם elsewhere in Deuteronomy (2:34; 3:6[2x]; 13:16[15], 18[17]; 20:17).[46] Still, the question specifically is not the meaning of חרם,[47] but whether or not the command is to be

---

45. Tigay (*Deuteronomy*, 91) states, "To obliterate one's name is to leave no oral or written trace of his name on earth, that is, to leave him no survivor or monuments." Similarly, Block (*Gospel According to Moses*, 400) lists three possibilities: "[T]he people are lost to human history; the persons leave no surviving descendants to carry on their names; and they leave no memorials to their achievements."

46. The destruction of Sihon's kingdom in 2:34 makes clear the unconditional and complete nature of the action: "And we captured all his cities at that time and utterly destroyed (Hi. חרם) every city, men, women, and children. We left no survivors." The destruction of Og's kingdom in 3:6 is described similarly; though it lacks the final phrase, "we left no survivors," it states, "We utterly destroyed (Hi. חרם) them *as we did to Sihon the king of Heshbon.*" In 13:16–18[15–17], the ban involves killing people with a sword and burning objects as a whole burnt offering to Yahweh. The law of *ḥerem* spelled out in 20:15–18 qualifies the proscription of חרם (v. 17a) by the phrase, "you shall save alive nothing that breathes" (v. 16b). Based on a literal, straightforward reading, the standard critical position is that the authors of Deuteronomy—writing much later—inferred from common ANE practice that the disappearance of Canaanites was due to this policy. Thus, the policy was purely theoretical and did not exist when Israel entered the land. See Tigay, "The Proscription of the Canaanites (7:1–2, 7:16 and 20:15–18)," in *Deuteronomy*, 470–72.

47. Against Wright (*Deuteronomy*, 109), who rejects the common explanation of חרם as "devoting" things or people to Yahweh and prefers a sense of "renouncing": "it is an absolute and irrevocable *renouncing* of things or persons, a refusal to take any gain

taken literally. Several indications in the text suggest that a hyperbolic reading is preferable.[48] First, the *ḥerem* requirement in verse 2 is qualified or explained in verse 3 by the prohibition of making a covenant or intermarrying with the Canaanites. The latter would be illogical if the former were absolute.[49] Israel's co-existence with the Canaanites is also assumed in verse 22, which describes the conquest as a gradual process.[50] Second, verses 17–23 finds a parallel passage in Exodus 23, which prescribes expulsion rather than annihilation (Pi. גרש, "drive out," in Exod 23:28, 29, 30, 31).[51] Third, if the *ḥerem* ordinance concerning the Canaanites is taken literally, then so should the threat in Deuteronomy 7:26 of Israel becoming חרם, a thing devoted to destruction. A strictly literal reading, however, goes against the book's prediction of a remnant

---

or profit from them. Thus, in obedience to this command, things or persons could be renounced without necessarily being destroyed." This seems to take away the force of the rhetoric.

48. I use "hyperbolic" instead of "metaphorical" because the position in this study is not dependent upon following the traditional Jewish reading, which takes the policy in Deuteronomy metaphorically, thus not requiring unconditional proscription. See Tigay, *Deuteronomy*, 270. Several evangelicals have adopted this tradition; see Block, *Gospel According to Moses*, 350–62; Moberly, "Toward an Interpretation of the Shema," 124–44. We could add McConville (*Deuteronomy*, 151–64), who seems to take a more nuanced approach, often speaking about the balance or compromise between the ideal and real (see following footnote). My arguments for a hyperbolic reading are shared by those who take a metaphorical reading, though my conclusion is softer.

49. See Block, *Gospel According to Moses*, 359; cf. McConville (*Deuteronomy*, 153), who sees the juxtaposition as "an unexpected compromise between rigour and practicality." Concerning the ban in chap. 7, he states, "It is clear that Deuteronomy regards it as in some sense ideal, since it accepts an accommodation between the real and ideal" (ibid., 88).

50. McConville (*Deuteronomy*, 161) says this is consistent with the view that complete annihilation of the nations is always a kind of ideal, "symbolizing the need for radical loyalty to Yahweh on the part of Israel."

51. Noting Deut 7:20–23, cf. Exod 23:27–31: "I will send my terror before you and will throw into confusion all the people against whom you shall come, and I will make all your enemies turn their backs to you. And I will send hornets before you, which shall drive out the Hivites, the Canaanites, and the Hittites from before you. I will not drive them out from before you in one year, lest the land become desolate and the wild beasts multiply against you. Little by little I will drive them out from before you, until you have increased and possess the land. And I will set your border from the Red Sea to the Sea of the Philistines, and from the wilderness to the Euphrates, for I will give the inhabitants of the land into your hand, and you shall drive them out before you." See Weinfeld, "Ban on the Canaanites," 135–47.

that survives Yahweh's judgment (4:29–31; 30:1–10).⁵² This last point is especially relevant, for the "destruction" of Israel in verse 26 (signaled by חרם) corresponds to the "destruction" of Israel in verse 4 (signaled by שׁמד). A nuanced reading of חרם, thus, favors a nuanced reading of שׁמד, not only in 7:4, but throughout the passage.

We have sought to argue that allusions to exile occur in this text. The exile theme is "felt" when reading this text within the context of the book (i.e., following chap. 4) and by considering issues within the text itself. The *ḥerem* policy proves not to be an insurmountable obstacle, but can be read in a manner consistent with echoes of exile. We are not, however, trying to read exile into the text—as if אבד and שׁמד actually denote exile specifically and technically. These and other terms in the passage retain the rhetoric of death and destruction. But, given the genre and aim of the text, this does not eliminate the notion of exile completely. It is helpful to reconsider the influence in the opposite direction as well: the language of death becomes the language of exile explicitly in other texts (e.g., chaps. 4 and 28). This is an important insight as we develop the theology of exile.

## Deuteronomy 9:1—11:32

This section is bracketed by references to dispossessing "nations greater and mightier than yourselves" (9:1; 11:23), thus showing an affinity with the preceding chapters. It divides into two main parts (9:1—10:11; 10:12—11:32). 9:1—10:11 begins with an encouragement and warning with respect to the conquest (9:1-6), and then looks back in Israel's history and presents evidence for its thesis statement: "you are a stubborn people" (9:6).⁵³ The primary witness is the golden calf incident at Horeb

---

52. So Block, *Gospel According to Moses*, 360. Block also argues for a metaphorical reading based on the evidence of the biblical conquest narratives, which suggest that only in exceptional cases was the policy literally carried out (ibid., 360–62). The book of Joshua, for example, suggests that the literal application of the policy happened only three times; yet, Joshua is portrayed throughout as faithfully following Yahweh's commands.

53. Deut 9:1—10:11 is bounded by references to the journey theme: crossing the Jordan (9:1) and a command to continue the journey (10:11). See Block, *Gospel According to Moses*, 440; McConville, *Deuteronomy*, 191. Cf. Wright (*Deuteronomy*, 141): "The whole section ends, as it began in 9:1, with the onward movement of the people into the land of promise." Tigay (*Deuteronomy*, 96–97) puts all of chaps. 9–10 together based on recurrent motifs, but all his citations are in 9:1—10:11: (1) God's oath to the patriarchs (9:5; 10:11; cf. 9:27); (2) the danger of destroying Israel or Aaron (9:8, 14, 19, 20, 25, 26; 10:10); (3) the Tablets of the covenant (9:9–11, 15, 17; 10:1–5, 8);

(9:13–21), but also includes other times of rebellion in the wilderness (9:7, 22–24). Moses' intercession keeps Yahweh's wrath from consuming his people (9:18–19, 25–29; 10:10). Deuteronomy 10:12—11:32 represents a renewed call to covenant fidelity in the present and urges Israel to realize that its future depends on compliance with the command to love and obey Yahweh.[54] As Moses prepares to give the detailed laws of chapters 12–26, he rehearses many of his earlier themes and commands. We will focus our attention here primarily on allusions to exile and the overall assessment of Israel's spiritual condition.

The terms אבד and שמד are utilized with respect to four different stages in the life of Israel. First, the exodus proved fatal for the Egyptian army, whom Yahweh "destroyed" (Pi. אבד) in the Red Sea (11:4). The sense of complete destruction is confirmed by parallel phrases in the immediate context.[55] Second, at Horeb Israel's worship of the golden calf incurred Yahweh's wrath; repeatedly שמד (all Hi.) is employed to describe Yahweh's intent to destroy Israel (9:8, 14, 19, 20 [Aaron alone], 25). The sense of annihilation in this context is apparent, for Yahweh's full intent was to "blot out (מחה) their name from under heaven" and start over with Moses (9:14).[56] Third, the call to conquest comes with an assurance: "[Yahweh] will destroy (Hi. שמד) them and subdue (Hi. כנע) them before you. So you shall drive (Hi. ירש) them out and make them perish (Hi. אבד) quickly, as Yahweh has promised you" (9:3). Here, the parallel terms—הרף, "thrust out" (v. 4; cf. 6:19), and especially ירש, "possess, dispossess" (7x in vv. 1–6)[57]—qualify the terms of destruction

---

(4) Israel's rebellion, provocation, and stiff neck (9:6–8, 13, 22–23, 27; 10:16); and (5) Moses' forty-day fasts and prayers (9:9, 18, 25; 10:10; cf. 9:11).

54. The opening ועתה, "and now" (10:12), marks the transition from history to present exhortation based on it (cf. 4:1). Though several commentators divide this section further, Mayes (*Deuteronomy*, 207–8) makes a strong case for considering 10:12—11:32 as single section. He notes especially the common vocabulary, expressions, and structure between this section and 4:1–40. Mayes is followed by McConville, *Deuteronomy*, 198; Miller, *Deuteronomy*, 124–28; Thompson, *Deuteronomy*, 147ff.; Weinfeld, *Deuteronomy 1–11*, 429ff., 453–54. Cf. Craigie (*Book of Deuteronomy*, 201ff.), who puts 10:11—11:25 together.

55. Moses goes on to recount what Yahweh did to Dathan and Abiram in the wilderness, "how the earth opened its mouth and swallowed them up" (11:6).

56. Note also Yahweh's relenting, following Moses' intercession: "Yahweh was unwilling to destroy (Hi. שחת) you" (10:10). שחת seems to carry the sense of annihilation or obliteration (cf. 4:31).

57. Verses 1, 3, 4[2x], 5[2x], 6. On the meaning of ירש as conquest of another people

to convey the sense of removal. Fourth, in looking forward to Israel's life in the land, Moses warns her that if she proves unfaithful to Yahweh, she will incur divine anger and experience the covenant curses, with the result, "you will perish (אבד) quickly off the good land that Yahweh is giving you" (11:17). The qualifying phrase, "off the good land," most naturally depicts exile (cf. 4:26).[58] Thus, we see that אבד and שמד continue to carry various nuances. The distinguishing factor seems to be the land: when Israel is outside the land, these terms convey the full sense of annihilation; when the context is entering or possessing the land, the connotation of exile comes to the fore.[59]

The clear reference to exile in 11:17 comes in the middle of a large section that, similar to 8:7–9, develops a theology of land (11:8–25).[60] The land is considered to be both a promise (11:8–12, 22–25) and a test (11:13–21; cf. 6:10–15; 8:6–20). The presence of these two divergent claims explains why there is such an emphasis on choice in the broader context.[61] The entire unit (chaps. 5–11) ends, in fact, with a choice: "See, I am setting (נתן) before you today a blessing and a curse" (11:26).[62] The use of נתן, "give, set," is perhaps strategic. As McConville explains,

> To the question, 'What does Yahweh give?' the expected answer in deuteronomic terms is 'The land'; so here that presumed an-

---

(as here) see Norbert Lohfink, "371 ",יָרַשׁ.

58. Note also the double use of ירש in 11:23, referring to the conquest.

59. We could add an implied threat of exile behind some of the conditional blessings in chap. 11: "You shall keep the commandment ... that you may live long in the land that Yahweh swore to your fathers" (vv. 8–9); "You shall write them ... that your days and the days of your children may be multiplied in the land that Yahweh swore to your fathers" (vv. 20–21). These statements also support the conditional nature of the patriarchal covenant.

60. Block (*Gospel According to Moses*, 558–60) considers 11:8–25 to be the most comprehensive and systematic statement in the book on the theology of land. See chap. 5 of this study for a more thorough discussion of land in Deuteronomy.

61. Wright (*Deuteronomy*, 153) notes the importance of choice in chap. 11, but we could also consider chaps. 6–11 as a whole. The exhortation of 11:18–21 recalls 6:4–9: God's words shall be fixed on the heart; they shall be bound on the hand, face, and doorposts; and they shall be taught to future generations. In fact, choice is the essence of the Deuteronomic exhortation (cf. 30:19).

62. Deut 11:26–32 is actually a self-contained literary unit (note ראה, "see," in v. 26 as marking a beginning of a unit), and serves as a transitional paragraph. It forms an inclusion with 5:1b–5 to hold together chaps. 5–11 (cf. Block, *Gospel According to Moses*, 587), and, as we discussed in chap. 3, 11:26–32 has formal correspondence with Deut 12–28 (cf. Lohfink, *Das Hauptgebot*, 234; McConville, *Deuteronomy*, 205–6).

swer is anticipated with the correction, 'Yahweh gives the *possibility* of land.' The gift of land is in one sense an accomplished fact; in another, its possession is bound to be a matter of Israel's choice and agreement.... This covenantal rationale is at the root of the dialectic between divine gift and human responsibility everywhere in the book.[63]

The content of the blessing and curse are not spelled out here. Given the emphases in Moses preaching, however, we can assume that the blessing comprises "a long life of peace and prosperity in the land," and the curse entails "loss of the land, and consequently of life."[64] Of course, this is consistent with the list of blessings and curses in chapter 28.

The prominence of choice leads to the question of which choice Israel will make. Is the matter neutral at this point, or can one discern an overall assessment of Israel's spiritual condition? We know that a future generation will end up in exile (4:25–28), but does this have any bearing on the present generation? Though the initial portrayal of Israel's response at Horeb in chapter 5 is indeed positive (see 5:28), we noted the tension created by the addition of Yahweh's wish, "Oh that they had such a heart as this always, to fear me and to keep all my commandments" (5:29). From that point, there seems to be an increasingly negative tone in Moses' preaching,[65] culminating in the overt statements in chapter 9 concerning Israel's *present* state:

...you are a stiff-necked people (v. 6b)

---

63. McConville, *Deuteronomy*, 205.

64. Ibid., 206. Cf. Block (*Gospel According to Moses*, 576), commenting on 11:17 with a thought toward chap. 28: "The curse represents the complete opposite of the blessing: instead of divine favor, Israel incurs his wrath; instead of abundant rain in its season, drought; instead of fruit, infertility; instead of life abundant death—divorce from the land Israel had received as a gift."

65. A similar tension to 5:28–29 can be found in the structure of chap. 6, in which a section of warnings (vv. 10–19) is sandwiched between two very positive sections on Israel's response to Yahweh (vv. 4–9, 20–25). As mentioned, these warnings—of forgetting God because of affluence (vv. 10–13), of abandoning God because of surrounding idolatry (vv. 14–15), of doubting God because of hardship (v. 16)—are expanded in chaps. 7–8. This concentration on warning allows the hint of doubt in 5:29 to rise evermore to the surface. See Wright, *Deuteronomy*, 101–2. A similar structure is found in chap. 11, where the land as a test (vv. 8–21) comes between two sections on the land as promise (vv. 2–7, 22–25). The structure of chap. 8 is also telling. Block (*Gospel According to Moses*, 430) notes that the difference in amount of space given between the wrong response (vv. 11–17) and the right response (v. 18) reveals the level of Moses' concern.

> Yahweh said to me, "I have seen this people, and behold, it is a stiff-necked people." (v. 13)
>
> From the day you came out of the land of Egypt until you came to this place, you have been rebellious against Yahweh. (v. 7b)
>
> You have been rebellious against Yahweh from the day that I knew you. (v. 24)[66]

The supposition is that, based on her past record, Israel has a propensity to sin.[67] Whatever positive actions this generation has performed, therefore, must be considered temporary and "out of character."[68]

Israel's deep-seated problem is with her לבב, "heart" or "mind."[69] Moses emphasizes that true fidelity to the covenant is marked by the internalization of the law in the heart, not merely external obedience (6:5–6; 10:12; 11:18).[70] Having Yahweh's words on her heart engenders

---

66. Note also that Israel's history in the wilderness is marked by actions that "provoked Yahweh to wrath" (vv. 8, 22) and amount to unbelief (v. 23). In making and worshipping the golden calf, she "acted corruptly" (9:12) and did "what was evil in the sight of Yahweh" (9:18). The focus on the present generation falling under these indictments is important; this is no mere history lesson. Moses is not simply continuing the rhetorical use of anachronism as in 5:2–3—where he speaks as if the present generation, and none other, was at Horeb. Rather, he views Israel as a single entity in his declarations of her stubbornness and rebellion.

67. Barker (*Triumph of Grace*, 88) adds, Israel's "history is not of occasional blemishes amidst an otherwise good record. Israel's sin is persistent and deep-seated." Cf. Merrill, *Deuteronomy*, 191.

68. The positive assessments for this generation include their obedience in the conquest of the Transjordan territory (2:26—3:11)—in contrast to the unfaithful generation at Kadesh-barnea (1:19–46; cf. 2:16)—and their right response at Horeb (5:28). It is significant (and ironic), then, that two of the five examples in chap. 9 of Israel's rebellion are Kadesh-barnea and Horeb. The temporary nature of the positive response at Horeb, hinted at in 5:29 (as discussed above), is clear in 9:12: "They have turned aside quickly out of the way that I commanded them." From the perspective of Moses' preaching, the conquest of the kingdoms of Sihon and Og have just taken place; it remains to be seen whether Israel will continue to follow Yahweh's lead into the land. The evidence is decidedly against it. The distinction between the generations in chaps. 1–3 (note 2:16) is obliterated in 9:23, in which Israel (including the present generation) is charged with not believing or obeying Yahweh at Kadesh-barnea.

69. לבב occurs twelve times in chaps. 6–11: 6:5, 6; 7:17; 8:2, 5, 14, 17; 9:4; 10:12, 16; 11:16, 18.

70. As Tigay (*Deuteronomy*, 83) notes, "The proper attitude in observing the laws is as important as the laws themselves." The command to "love" Yahweh is repeated in these chapters in 10:12; 11:1, 13, 22; cf. 7:9. Elsewhere in Deuteronomy, see 13:4[3]; 19:9; 30:6, 16, 20.

the dispositions of love and reverential fear (e.g., 6:5; 10:12; cf. 5:29). Otherwise, the heart becomes the seat of the fear of man (7:17), pride (8:14, 17; 9:4), and deception (11:16). These dangers drive the repetitive exhortations to "remember" and "not forget,"[71] which have to do with regard or disregard for the covenant and not simply a retaining or loss of memory.[72] The negative statements in chapter 9 assert that the tendency of Israel's heart is indeed toward fear and idolatry (chap. 7), self-sufficiency (chap. 8), self-righteousness (chap. 9), and overall forgetfulness.[73] Clearly, Israel had failed the test of the wilderness through which Yahweh was "testing you to know what was in your heart, whether you would keep his commandments or not" (8:2).

The expectation is that Israel will continue to fail this test of the heart. Thus, Israel is still commanded, "Circumcise therefore the foreskin of your heart, and do not stiffen your neck anymore" (10:16). The allusion to 9:6 and 13 makes the idea of being stiff-necked a present-tense reality.[74] Only with a circumcised heart can she do what is required of her: "to fear Yahweh your God, to walk in all his ways, to love him, to serve Yahweh your God with all your heart and with all your soul, and to keep the commandments and statutes of Yahweh" (10:12–13; cf. 10:20; 11:1).[75] Forgiveness and covenant renewal—whether at Horeb (10:1–11)

---

71. זכר, "remember," in 7:18; 8:2, 18; 9:7; שכח, "forget," in 6:12; 8:11, 14, 19; 9:7; cf. 4:9, 23. The connection between heart and memory first arises in the book in 4:9: "Only take heed to yourself . . . lest you forget the things that your eyes have seen, and lest they depart from your heart." The same close connection is found especially in chap. 8 (vv. 2, 14, 17–19).

72. Block, *Gospel According to Moses*, 155.

73. Commenting on 7:17–26, Block (*Gospel According to Moses*, 397) remarks, "In his call to remember the past deeds of Yahweh, Moses acknowledges a fundamental problem in the human mind: the ability to keep fresh the memory of what one has experienced before."

74. The position here—that Israel still lacks a circumcised heart—is against that of Block, who thinks the present generation, by their clinging to Yahweh in the face of apostasy at Baal-peor (cf. 4:4), "have proved themselves to be circumcised of heart" (*Gospel According to Moses*, 534). But we have argued that, while the present generation has shown a positive disposition in the wilderness as of late, Moses thinks it is only temporary. Also, Block's attempt to explain away the force of the command in 10:16 is unconvincing: "If he [Moses] were trying to communicate the need for a fundamental change in disposition and orientation, Ezekiel's version of the metaphor is certainly more natural: 'Rid yourselves of all the offenses you have committed, and get a new heart and a new spirit' (Ezek. 18:31)" (ibid.).

75. On v. 16 as the central command of 10:12–22, see Lohfink, *Hauptgebot*, 220ff.

or now at Moab—offer fresh opportunity, but do not deal with the fundamental problem.[76] As Olson states, Horeb and Moab have "a shared pessimism about the ability of God's people to obey the commandments and laws of Horeb."[77]

If Israel has not undergone a change of heart, then why did Yahweh hear Moses' intercession and renew the covenant with Israel? Moses locates the basis of covenant renewal in Yahweh's fidelity to the patriarchs (10:15; cf. 9:27-29; 10:11, 22; 11:9, 21). We have emphasized the conditionality of the patriarchal covenant, but its conditionality is one-sided. On the one hand, Israel's enjoyment of the gift of land and long life is contingent upon her obedience (e.g., 11:8-9a); therefore, the promise is yet to be fulfilled. Israel's recalcitrance suggests that it may always be out of reach. On the other hand, Yahweh remains committed to fulfill his promise to the fathers in their offspring (e.g., 11:9b). In fact, Moses' statement that Israel is presently "as numerous as the stars of the heavens" (10:22; cf. 1:10; 26:5) shows that part of the promise is, in some sense, already fulfilled.[78] Its complete fulfillment will ultimately be realized, for Yahweh's covenant commitment to his people is eternal and, therefore, unconditional (see 11:21).[79] One could resolve the tension between conditionality and unconditionality by putting the onus on each generation to be faithful in order to receive the covenant blessings,[80] but this is only a temporary solution. As we have noted, Israel is most often viewed as

---

This subsection either ends at 10:22 or 11:1. The former is based on recognizing the framing of ועתה, "and now," in vv. 12 and 22; so Barker, *Triumph of Grace*, 103-6; McConville, *Deuteronomy*, 198; Tigay, *Deuteronomy*, 109-10. Ending at 11:1 recognizes the bracketing of the calls to love and obedience (10:12-13; 11:1); so Block, *Gospel According to Moses*, 525ff.; Mayes, *Deuteronomy*, 212; Weinfeld, *Deuteronomy 1-11*, 441. The latter seems preferable.

76. The reaffirmation of the Horeb covenant is symbolized by the cutting of the new tablets (10:1ff.) and the repetition of the basic covenant stipulations (10:12ff.). On the former, see Talstra, "Deuteronomy 9 and 10," 198-200. On the latter, see Barker, *Triumph of Grace*, 103.

77. Olson, *Deuteronomy and the Death of Moses*, 151. Cf. Barker (*Triumph of Grace*, 104), who argues that the context of the renewal of Horeb—which is needed because of past sin and not just because of a new situation, generation, or leader—is important for how we read the Moab covenant.

78. Cf. McConville, *Deuteronomy*, 201.

79. The phrase, "as long as the heavens are above the earth" (11:21) is a poetic way of saying "forever," alluding to the eternality of Yahweh's commitment (cf. Ps 89:30). See Block, *Gospel According to Moses*, 579.

80. Thus, Block, *Gospel According to Moses*, 580.

a single entity. If she (singular) is to see the promise fulfilled ultimately and finally, something will have to be done about her uncircumcised heart that prevents her from remaining faithful. The tension is only resolved, then, when God himself circumcises Israel's heart, transforming the command of love into a promise (30:6).

## Conclusion

Deuteronomy 5–11 alludes to exile through numerous links to chapter 4 (especially vv. 25–31): the focus on the First and Second Commandments; the stress on the conditionality of land entry and possession, often involving curses that employ אבד and שמד; the recognition of corporate solidarity; the question of Israel's ability to obey the commandments; the role of Moses as mediator; and the recalling of past experiences in facing future dangers. Concerning the patriarchal covenant, these chapters exhibit a tension: the stress in chapters 5–11 is on the conditionality of seeing the fulfillment of the promise to the fathers, though the unconditional side of the covenant (like in 4:31) is also present (cf. 9:27). It is clear, then, that exile as a theological concept exerts a profound influence on Moses' preaching.

### Deuteronomy 12:1—26:15

These chapters provide detailed laws for Israel's life in the land. Because the list of curses for violating these laws is reserved for chapter 28, references to exile in chapters 12–26 will be few.[81] Though we will look at a few texts within the corpus that have particular bearing on our theme, we will focus more on some overall observations and consider how they interact with the theme of exile.[82]

---

81. Of the vocabulary of exile considered in chap. 2, only two terms have an exilic connotation. שבה, "take captive," is used three times in 21:10–13 with reference to taking foreigners captive and dealing with the female captives appropriately. Deut 26:5 uses אבד as an adjective to describe Jacob as a "wandering (?) Aramean" (see discussion below). שוב, "turn, return," is not used of restoration, but of anti-exodus, as the king is prohibited from causing the people to "return" to Egypt (17:16). The other references from chapter 2 are non-exilic: נדח (13:6, 11, 14; 19:5; 20:19; 22:1); נתץ (12:3); רדף (16:20; 19:6 [but see discussion below]); רחק (12:21; 14:24); גלה in 23:1[22:30]; cf. 27:20; 29:28[29]); אבד (12:2, 3 [destroying foreign cultic sites]; 22:3 [lost animal]); שמד (12:30 [conquest]); שוב (13:18[17]; 23:15[14]).

82. Some of these observations come from Olson, *Deuteronomy and the Death of Moses*, 65–67.

The first observation is that the designation "lawcode" is somewhat inaccurate. The content is not comprehensive enough to function as such.[83] More importantly, this body of law is embedded within Moses' second speech, and exhibits much of the exhortative and motivational style of the former chapters.[84] Though debated in the details, there is also clearly a connection between the various laws here and the Decalogue in chapter 5,[85] including a heavy emphasis (as in chaps. 6–11) on the First and Second Commandments, which keep the specific laws under an anti-Canaanite cast.[86] In short, as applications of the revelation at Horeb, the laws in chapters 12–26 "serve the message of the book as a whole, and share the same outlook as the framework."[87] That "framework" includes chapters 4 and 28–30, as well as chapters 5–11. The laws, then, are embedded within a book overshadowed by the theme of exile (see discussion of macrostructure at the end of this chapter).

A second observation is the prominence of the exodus. Israel is constantly reminded of her origin of slavery in Egypt, from which Yahweh has rescued her.[88] We saw that the curse list in chapter 28 interprets exile as a reversal of the exodus—an anti-exodus. Therefore, any text that uses the exodus as motivation for obedience carries an implicit warning of

---

83. Fishbane (*Biblical Interpretation*, 91, 95) states that none of the biblical law collections (individually or collectively) "sufficiently cover the numerous areas required for an operative and positive lawcode.... [The collections] may best be considered as prototypical compendia of legal and ethical norms rather than comprehensive codes." Cf. Millar (*Now Choose Life*, 140), who speaks of "an increasing tendency in the laws to deal with the exception rather than the common case."

84. McConville, *Deuteronomy*, 212; Thompson, *Deuteronomy*, 160. Cf. Tigay (*Deuteronomy*, 117): "The most distinctive feature of Moses' presentation of the laws is the way he frequently devotes as much—or more—attention to exhorting the people to obey the laws as to presenting the laws themselves."

85. Cf. chap. 3, n. 128. For various analyses of the laws and their arrangement, see Carmichael, "Singular Method of Codification of Law," 19–24; Kaufman, "Structure of the Deuteronomic Law," 105–58; Merendino, *Das deuternomische Gesetz*; Rofé, "Arrangement of the Laws in Deuteronomy," 265–87; Braulik, *Die deuteronomischen Gesetze*; idem, "Sequence of the Laws in Deuteronomy 12–26," 313–35. Millar (*Now Choose Life*, 108), who has problems with the various proposals, still thinks the attempts (especially of Braulik and Kaufman) show that "a case can be made for reading chapters 12–26 as a literary work."

86. Deut 12:30–31; 13:3–8[2–7], 14[13]; 17:3; 18:20; 19:9; 20:18.

87. Millar, *Now Choose Life*, 145.

88. Deut 13:4[5]; 9[10]; 15:15; 16:1, 3, 6, 12; 17:16; 20:1; 23:4; 24:9, 18, 22; 25:17; 26:5–9.

exile for disobedience. This is most clear when comparing the return-to-Egypt motif in the king-law (17:16) and the curse of exile (28:68).[89] Moses envisions a time in the land when the people will desire a human king, and so offers several qualifications for the candidate. Positively, he must be a fellow Israelite chosen by Yahweh (17:15). Unlike the typical ANE king, Israel's king serves primarily as a model of devotion to Yahweh and his word (17:18–19).[90] Proscriptions of his service include multiplying "for himself" horses, women, and wealth (17:16–17).[91] The proscription of horses reads, "Only he must not multiply for himself horses or cause the people to return (Hi. שׁוּב) to Egypt in order to multiply horses, since Yahweh has said to you, 'You shall never return that way again'" (17:16). A return to Egypt signifies more than a desire to build a great army; it is a reversal of the journey Israel is now undertaking (cf. 2:1). Even so, it is this type of reversal that Yahweh himself will exact in exiling his people: "Yahweh will bring you back in ships to Egypt, a journey that I promised that you should never see again" (28:68). The king as a potential symbol of slavery (cf. 17:16)[92] explains, perhaps, why the king is singled out in the first reference to exile in the curses (28:36).

Israel's origins, of course, go further back than Egypt. The creedal statement in 26:5b–10a begins with the historical memory, "A wandering/perishing/fugitive (אֹבֵד) Aramean was my father. And he went down into Egypt and sojourned there, few in number, and there he became a nation, great, mighty, and populous" (v. 5).[93] The use of אבד in contexts of exile in Deuteronomy (e.g., 4:26; 28:63) suggests that exile is a reversal of this history. Not only will Israel "return to Egypt," but she will also return once again to the status of "landless," in which covenant promises are unfulfilled.[94]

---

89. See Reimer, "Concerning Return to Egypt," 217–29.

90. Cf. Miller, *Deuteronomy*, 147. One of the main roles of a typical ANE kings was prosecuting war; but this remains the prerogative of Yahweh in Israel. See Lind, *Yahweh Is a Warrior*, 155. Cf. Halbe, "Gemeinschaft, die Welt unterbricht," 55–75.

91. Olson (*Deuteronomy and the Death of Moses*, 82–83) maintains that 17:16-20 cover the same false "gods" as chaps. 7–12: militaristic power, materialism, and self-righteous moralism.

92. See Block, "Burden of Leadership," 264 n. 24: "This could account for later prophetic references to kings as symbols of slavery. See especially Samuel's speech in 1 Samuel 8:10–18 in response to the elders' demand for a king."

93. On the possible meanings of the adjective אֹבֵד see the discussion in chap. 2.

94. The patriarchal promise is at the forefront in the immediate context concerning

The concept of Israel as a "landed" nation brings up a third observation of the laws in chapters 12–26: the recurring triad of Yahweh, Israel, and the land.[95] The statutes and ordinances involve instructions on relating to God, to other human beings, and to the land. It is important to note, however, that these relationships are not equal. The goal of the horizontal relationships (to other humans, to the land) is always to maintain and express the right vertical relationship with Yahweh. This is most clearly evidenced, perhaps, with respect to Levites and others (e.g., slaves, sojourners, orphans, widows) who have no share in the land. In contexts of worship,[96] other Israelites are to make sure that these "landless" groups are included and cared for. This produces a spiral of blessings: Yahweh blesses the people with fruitfulness of the land; the people bless those dependent among them; together, all the people bless Yahweh in worship; and Yahweh continues to bless the people.[97] The point is that the land is a means to an end; it is "an arena of life" that allows Israel to enjoy fellowship with others and, ultimately, with God.[98] On the other hand, in Deuteronomic thought the land is a *necessary* means to an end. As McConville states, "The idea of life is never separated from that of

---

the offering of firstfruits (26:1–11). The major feature of these verses is the emphasis on the land as Yahweh's gift (vv. 1, 2, 3, 10, 11).

95. Olson (*Deuteronomy and the Death of Moses*, 66) finds all of these relationships in each of his ten sections the lawcode (corresponding to the Decalogue). Cf. Millar (*Now Choose Life*, 145): "The ethical demands of these chapters result from the application of the Deuteronomic theology of worship, of the land and of human relationships to Israel's new existence."

96. Cf. 12:12, 18–19; 14:27, 29; 16:11, 14; 18:1–8; 26:11, 12–13.

97. In this, we may recognize a certain "cost" to living obediently in the land. As McConville (*Law and Theology in Deuteronomy*, 15, 17) states, many laws "are in some way costly to the one who obeys.... The principle involved is in fact a paradox. Enjoyment of the land and its benefits depends upon a readiness to relinquish them. We have noticed that blessing was promised for the act of self-denial involved in slave release or the remittance of debts. But it is actually a regular principle that where blessing is promised it is in the context of self-restraint." Likewise, Olson (*Deuteronomy and the Death of Moses*, 66) speaks of obedient life as "faithful dying."

98. See Millar and McConville, *Time and Place*, 128. Millar (*Now Choose Life*, 146) states that "the land is pre-eminently the place where God is encountered. Yahweh brings Israel out of Egypt and gives her the land so that she may enjoy its bounty, but ultimately so that his people may enjoy his company." What Millar says about chap. 18 can be generalized: "Verses 1–2 remind Israel that while, for them, this land is the locus of their relationship with Yahweh, their goal is relationship with Yahweh himself" (*Now Choose Life*, 128).

the land in Deuteronomy."⁹⁹ Thus, a divorce between Israel and the land (i.e., exile) not only results from a broken covenant relationship, but also ensures that the relationship will remain broken. Because of this, future restoration must involve a return to the land (30:5).

A fourth relevant observation is the focus on death. The words "death" and "die" (from מות) occur 35 times in chapters 12–26.[100] The majority of these have to do with death penalties for various crimes,[101] often appearing with the stated purpose to "purge the evil from your midst/Israel."[102] The others have to do with natural death or situations of humans killing other humans (war, murder, and manslaughter).[103] Ironically, life in the land is dependent on dealing properly with the reality of death.[104] Moses concludes his third speech by setting the choice of "life or death, blessing or curse" before Israel (30:19; cf. v. 15). Since the ultimate curse for disobedience is exile (28:63ff.), exile must be considered the death of the nation. The death penalty for specific crimes committed by individuals is transferred to the nation as a whole. Thus, Yahweh will purge the evil by removing Israel from Israel!

This brings us back to a tension alluded to at various points in the paper—the tension between the corporate and the individual. Individual culpability is a major component of the laws.[105] Though some of the laws

---

99. Millar and McConville, *Time and Place*, 129.

100. Olson (*Deuteronomy and the Death of Moses*, 66) only counts 32 occurrences. Other than at four key points—the death of the wilderness generation (2:16); the death of Moses (4:22); the fear of dying at Horeb (5:25[2x]; cf. 18:16); and the death of Aaron (10:6)—chaps. 1–11 use terms of destruction (e.g., אבד, שמד) rather than מות. In chaps. 27–34, מות is used with reference to a dead body (28:26), the choice set before Israel (30:15, 19), the death of Moses (31:14, 27, 29; 32:50; 33:1), and the death of Reuben (33:6).

101. Deut 13:6[5], 10[9], 11[10]; 17:5[3x], 7, 12; 18:20; 19:6, 12; 21:21, 22[2x]; 22:21, 22, 24, 25, 26; 24:7, 16[3x].

102. Deut 13:6[5]; 17:7, 12; 22:21, 22, 24; 24:7.

103. Natural death (14:1; 24:3; 25:5[2x], 6; 26:14); dying in battle (20:5, 6, 7); murder (19:11); inadvertent manslaughter (19:5).

104. Cf. Olson (*Deuteronomy and the Death of Moses*, 65): "How one lives in the light of this reality of death in the past and in the future is the concern of the statutes and ordinances."

105. See Paul, *Studies in the Book of the Covenant*, 37–39. Paul lists individual culpability among ten distinctives of Israelite law: the classification of all crime as sin; the jurisdiction of the law over all of life; the divine prerogative in legislation and administration; the unmediated entrusting of the law to the nation as a whole; the open administration of justice; an essentially didactic purpose; the sacredness of human life;

require corporate obedience,[106] most of the commands directed toward the nation (or a governing group as representative of the nation) have to do with the proper administration of justice against individual lawbreakers. The lists of blessings and curses in chapter 28, however, are directed against the nation as a whole.[107] The question is, when do these national blessings and curses apply? Is it when the vast majority of individuals are either obedient or disobedient? Is it when the nation (or her official representatives) are properly or improperly administering justice? To state the question another way, what happens to the individual who is not behaving like the rest of the nation? It is clear that the individual lawbreaker amidst a faithful people can be dealt with according to statutes concerning a given crime, but there is no answer for the righteous person (or small remnant) living among an unfaithful people. It appears that such an individual must suffer the same fate as his brethren, including the curse of exile. How Yahweh deals with the righteous remnant in exile is only known after the fact; Deuteronomy is silent about the issue.

## Deuteronomy 31–34

The final chapters of Deuteronomy focus on the approaching death of Moses, and so continue the narrative of chapters 1–3.[108] Instead of looking at the past, however, this section looks toward the future, even the long-distant history of the nation. Though these chapters can be structured in various ways,[109] it is useful for our purposes to note several in-

---

class equality; individual culpability; and humane treatment of slaves.

106. E.g., destroying Canaanite cultic sites and worshiping at the "chosen" place (chap. 12), establishing the Sabbatical year (chap. 15), choosing a king (17:14-20), establishing cities of refuge (19:1-13), conducting warfare (chap. 20), making atonement for unsolved murders (21:1-9), and restricting access to the assembly of Yahweh (23:1-8)..

107. Contrast the anathemas against individuals in 27:15-26. True, some of the blessings and curses in chap. 28 may, in principle, affect individuals only (e.g., blessing or curse of a field, womb, or livestock; cf. vv. 3-6, 16-19, 38-44), but the overall thrust is national, especially the second halves of each list (vv. 7-14, 45-68).

108. Moses' death was anticipated in 1:37-38 and 3:23-29, but now becomes the central focus. The transfer of leadership from Moses to Joshua, which also frames chaps. 31-34, forms a frame around chaps. 4-30. See Christensen, *Deuteronomy 21:10—34:12*, 750. See chap. 1 for a discussion of the common view that Deut 1-3 and 31-34 introduce the "Deuteronomistic History" that extends through 2 Kings.

109. Christensen (*Deuteronomy 21:10—34:12*, 750-51) presents three different structures: an overall chiasm, whose center is the command to Moses to climb Mount

terwoven themes: Moses' death and the transfer of leadership to Joshua (31:1–8, 14–15, 23; 32:48–52; 34:1–12); the handling of the Torah, including writing a copy of it, placing it in the care of priests and elders, giving instructions for its public reading, and urging people to observe it (31:9–13, 24–26; 32:45–47); the teaching of a song or anthem (31:16–22, 28–30; 32:1–44); and a final blessing (chap. 33).[110] This outline shows that chapter 31 functions as an introduction to the rest of the chapters. To ensure continuity after Moses dies,[111] he is replaced by another human leader (31:3, 7–8, 14–15, 23), a normative text (31:9–13, 24–29), and a song (31:16–22).[112]

Though these chapters envision future judgment upon Israel for unfaithfulness (31:16–22, 26–27; 32:15–25), exile is not explicitly mentioned.[113] Instead, Yahweh expresses his judgment in other terms: "I will forsake them and hide my face from them, and they will be devoured. And many evils and troubles will come upon them . . ." (31:17; cf. 31:18, 21; 32:20, 22–24). Several considerations, however, suggest that there is at least an allusion to exile in these curses. First, the non-specificity is consistent with the overall tenor of the unit, in which there is hardly a specific reference to other major events in Israel's salvation history,

---

Nebo to "see" the land (32:48–52); a division into two concentric parts (31:1—32:47; 32:48—34:12), with centers of the Song of Moses (32:1–43) and Moses ascent of Mount Nebo (34:1–4); and a complex structure of four "wheels of the same likeness" (31:1–30; 31:30—32:45; 32:48—34:4; 34:5–12), which hinges on the summary command to observe all the words of the Torah (32:46–47). Most commentators follow variations of one of the first two options. Mayes (*Deuteronomy*, 371), however, finds three major sections (31:1–13; 31:14—32:44; 32:45—34:12).

110. Adapted from Tigay, *Deuteronomy*, 288.

111. Though many consider chaps. 31–34 as an "appendix" to the book, Craigie (*Book of D.euteronomy*, 367) helpfully considers these chapters under the rubric, "The Continuity of the Covenant From Moses to Joshua."

112. Olson, *Deuteronomy and the Death of Moses*, 133–38.

113. The closest we come is in a reference to Yahweh's judgment of Israel via her enemies: "How could one have chased (רדף) a thousand, and two have put to flight (Hi. נוס) ten thousand, unless their Rock had sold them, and Yahweh had given them up?" (32:30). A few of the other terms for exile (from chap. 2) are used, but do not connote exile specifically. 32:28 speaks of "a nation void (אבד) of counsel." שבה is used nominally to refer to foreign captives (32:42; cf. 28:41). שמד is used three times: Yahweh will "destroy" the nations in the conquest (31:3) just as he "destroyed" Sihon and Og (31:4), who suffered annihilation under the sentence of *ḥerem* (cf. 2:36; 3:6); the imperative in 33:27 for Israel to "destroy" her enemy whom Yahweh "thrust out" (Pi. גרש) is too general to interpret with precision. For restoration terminology, שוב is used, but refers to Yahweh "repaying" his enemies (32:41).

including the exodus and Horeb.[114] Second, in the context of the book, the prophetic picture of future judgment naturally recalls the prediction of exile in chapters 28-29. Also, the motif of having a "witness"—the Song itself in 31:19, 21; heaven and earth in 31:28—against Israel recalls the witness of heaven and earth in 4:26 concerning exile.[115] Third, Israel's judgment is followed by her vindication (32:26-43; cf. chap. 33), which fits with restoration beyond exile (cf. 30:1-10). Fourth, the overall thrust of moving toward the land of promise (e.g., 31:2-8, 13, 20; 32:47, 49, 52; 34:4) implies that future judgment will involve removal from the land.

We need to consider the grounds for both the pessimism and ultimate hope set forth in these chapters. That Israel will make the wrong choice between "life and death, blessing and curse" (30:19) is more pronounced here than anywhere in the book.[116] Yahweh predicts that the people will "whore after the foreign gods among them in the land that they are entering, and they will forsake me and break my covenant that I have made with them" (31:16; cf. 31:18, 20, 29; 32:5, 15-19).[117] The

---

114. There is only one quick reference to Horeb: Moses' blessing in chap. 33 begins with "Yahweh came from Sinai" (v. 2). With respect to chap. 32, Craigie (*Book of Deuteronomy*, 374) remarks, "However, the song does not refer to particular events; it is generally prophetic in expressing Moses' vision of the future, in both its gloomy and its brighter aspects, in a manner not unsimilar to the elaboration on the blessings and curses in chaps. 27-28." Concerning the lack of specific references in the Song, McConville (*Deuteronomy*, 461, 462) suggests that "deuteronomic themes have been deliberately eschatologized, with the playing down of Egypt, desert, exile and return, and the adoption of certain concepts familiar in prophetic visions of the future.... The lineaments of Israel's history have been partially obscured in order to highlight certain essential realities. In this context, Yahweh's relationship with the whole created order is in view."

115. The Song is a witness to the renewal of the covenant (in 31:9-13) in that Israel acknowledges her understanding of and agreement with the covenant's terms and implications (cf. Josh 24:22). See Kline, *Structure of Biblical Authority*, 141; cf. Craigie, *Book of Deuteronomy*, 373.

116. Cf. the introductory comment on chap. 31 by Tigay: "Sections 5 [31:16-22] and 7 [31:24-26], and the poem they introduce (chapter 32), interject an unexpected note of pessimism. Throughout his addresses, Moses has warned the people against disobedience with the aim of deterring it, and never insinuated that they are more likely to sin than to obey. In verses 12-13 he is hopeful, even optimistic, that regular reading of the Teaching will convince future generations to remain loyal and obedient. All of this is overridden by the announcement from God and Moses that the people are certain to sin, that they are even now planning rebellion (vv. 16,20,27,29)" (*Deuteronomy*, 289). While we reject Tigay's assessment of Israel's neutrality with respect to obedience in the rest of the book, his statement emphasizes the clarity of the present indictment.

117. The concentric structure of 31:9ff. has vv. 16-22 at its center (A/A' is handling the Torah [vv. 9-13, 24-29]; B/B' is the commissioning of Joshua [vv. 14-15, 23]). See

ultimate reason for Israel's inevitable infidelity is an issue of the heart (31:21b, 27).[118] A wooden translation of 31:21b reads, "For I know the intent that he is developing today before I have brought him into the land that I swore."[119] The word for "intent" (from יצר, "form, shape") is used in the flood account to speak of the tendency of the human heart to do evil (Gen 6:5; 8:21). The translation above, with singular pronouns, shows that Israel is viewed collectively as a single entity. Moses affirms Yahweh's evaluation, using the same terminology as in chapter 9: "For I know how rebellious and stiff-necked you are. Behold, even today while I am yet alive with you, you have been rebellious against Yahweh. How much more after my death!" (31:27; cf. 9:6, 13, 24) Thus, the pessimistic outlook is ultimately based on knowledge of Israel's depravity, which has already shown itself in continual rebellion at Horeb and in the wilderness. Her stubborn nature will prevail in the future.[120]

The positive end to the Song of Moses (32:26–43) comes as a surprise. The introduction of the Song in 31:16–20 only summarizes Israel's regression: God's faithfulness in giving the land (31:20; cf. 32:13–14) is countered by Israel's rejection of Yahweh, especially through idolatry (31:16, 20; cf. 32:16–18); so God in his anger will punish her (31:17–18; cf. 32:19–25).[121] The turning point from gloom to hope is found in 32:26–27:[122]

---

Tigay, *Deuteronomy*, 289; Wright, *Deuteronomy*, 296. Wright states, "If this concentricity is intentional, then even though the gloomy prediction of the people's future unfaithfulness haunts the center of the chapter, there is still a frame of words of promise that God will guarantee the gift of the land through Joshua." Even so, the presence of a chiasm more naturally puts the accent at the center; thus, even though God is giving the land, Israel's life in the land will be cut short. At the very least, we should note the tension between the themes.

118. Deut 32:15–18 includes a "secondary" reason: Israel has "grown fat" (v. 15; cf. 31:20) and "forgotten" God (v. 18). This seems to echo earlier warnings about Israel forgetting Yahweh because of the fruitfulness of the land (6:10–12 and 8:11–17). This is "secondary" in the sense that forgetfulness itself is a manifestation of a corrupt heart.

119. The phrase עשׂה הוא אשר יצרו את is translated variously: "their imagination which they frame" (ASV); "what they are inclined to do" (ESV); "their imagination how they do" (JPS); "their imagination which they go about" (AV); "their intent which they are developing" (NAS); "what they are disposed to do" (NIV); "the inclination of their behavior" (NKJ); "what they are inclined to do" (NRSV); "the purposes which they are already forming" (RSV).

120. Cholewinski, "Zur theologischen Deutung des Moabbundes," 107.

121. Cf. Olson, *Deuteronomy and the Death of Moses*, 137–38.

122. The pivotal nature of 32:26–27 is noted by Norbert Lohfink, "Der Bundesschluß im Land Moab," 53.

> I would have said, "I will cleave them to pieces;
> I will cause their remembrance to cease from humankind,"
> had I not feared provocation by the enemy,
> lest their adversaries misunderstand,
> lest they should say, "Our hand is triumphant,
> Yahweh has not wrought all this."

Similar to the golden calf incident, Yahweh relents from obliterating his people because of the wrong perception it would give to a foreign nation (cf. 9:28; 10:10).[123] There, the charge would be that Yahweh was weak (9:28); here, the enemy would take credit for the destruction of Israel, not realizing that it is merely an instrument of Yahweh (32:27–30).[124] In both cases, Yahweh is concerned about his own reputation. The basis of hope—of Israel's vindication (32:36)—is Yahweh's determination to vindicate himself against all competition:

> For their rock is not as our rock;
> our enemies are by themselves. (v. 31)

> Then he will say, "Where are their gods,
> The rock in which they took refuge?
> …
> Let them rise up and help you;
> Let them be your protection. (vv. 37, 38b)

> See now that I, even I, am he,
> And there is no god beside me. (v. 39a)

As we have shown, elsewhere in Deuteronomy restoration is always based on God's fidelity to his covenant with the patriarchs (4:31; 30:5–7; cf. 9:27). A closer look at the Song shows that the promise to the fathers is not absent, even though Yahweh's judgment has been put in a larger perspective.[125] Deuteronomy 32:7–9 develops Yahweh's election of Israel in the context of his purpose for all the nations of the world. Though each nation was established within its allotted boundaries (v. 8; cf. 4:19), Israel is given a special status as Yahweh's "portion" and "special posses-

---

123. Cf. also the similarity between 9:5 and 32:26–27 in the emphasis that Israel is not getting what she deserves.

124. In contrast to both chaps. 9 and 32, the foreign assessment in 29:25–28 of Israel's demise is completely accurate.

125. Following the discussion in McConville, *Deuteronomy*, 453–55, 459–60. See also Luyten, "Primeval and Eschatological Overtones," 341–47.

sion" (v. 9; cf. 4:20, 38; 9:26, 29).¹²⁶ This special relationship accounts for Yahweh's care of Israel in bringing her through the wilderness into the land (vv. 10-14), but it also explains the level of his passion and anger against her for turning to other gods (vv. 15-22).¹²⁷ Despite the universal scope in the latter part of the Song, Israel's sin and judgment resurface in the last phrase, which states that Yahweh will "atone for the land of/and his people" (32:43).¹²⁸ Thus, Israel's vindication and restoration to Yahweh will involve a re-establishment of the covenant triangle, Yahweh-Israel-Land. The function of the Song within the book is to point faithless Israel back to Yahweh, "to reverse the direction of her journey in a time of apostasy."¹²⁹ The destination of the journey is the land promised to the fathers.

The patriarchal promise is also the backdrop of chapter 33. Framed by praises focused on the uniqueness of Yahweh and of Israel (vv. 1-5, 26-29), Moses offers final blessings for each of the twelve tribes of Israel (vv. 6-25).¹³⁰ The tribal enumeration "is a vivid picture of the possession and filling of the land,"¹³¹ and so constitutes a fulfillment of the promise (cf. 1:7; 11:24). The blessings are similar to the subject matter of the laws in chapters 12-26—fruitful land, family, fertility, government, prosperity, security, teaching of Torah, and worship—and may elaborate on the blessings of 28:1-14.¹³² But the specific blessings in chapter 33 are not expressly predicated upon the condition of obedience.¹³³ It is better to

---

126. On translating נחלה as "special possession" rather than "inheritance," see Block, *Gods of the Nations*, 75-91; idem, *Gospel According to Moses*, 174-76. Block argues that a feudal social context is a better backdrop than inheritance.

127. Cf. Amos 3:2: "You only have I known of all the families of the earth; therefore I will punish you for all your iniquities."

128. The Hebrew reads וכפר אדמתו עמו, literally, "and he will atone for his land, his people." The difficulty of the last two words is overcome either by reading a bound phrase אדמת עמו, "land of his people" (so 4QDeutq, SP, LXX, Vg.), or by adding a waw-conjunctive before the last word: אדמתו ועמו, "his land and his people" (so Syr., Tg., Tg. Ps.-J.). See Christensen, *Deuteronomy 21:10—34:12*, 813 nn. 43.k and 43.l.

129. Millar, *Now Choose Life*, 96.

130. On the framework of chap. 33, see Christensen, "Two Stanzas of a Hymn in Deuteronomy 33," 382-89.

131. McConville, *Deuteronomy*, 473. McConville notes that the enumeration is organized .according to a south-to-north sweep of the land.

132. Merrill (*Deuteronomy*, 432) suggests that the list of tribal blessings in chap. 33 redresses the problem of the brevity of the blessing section in chap. 28.

133. Olson (*Deuteronomy and the Death of Moses*, 160) labels chap. 33 a "prayer,"

view them as concrete forms of the vindication of Israel in the Song of Moses (32:36, 43).[134] If so, the picture of Israel living safely in the land and in harmony with God is an "eschatological consummation,"[135] depicting a restored Israel, "a people saved by Yahweh" (33:29). This interpretation is consistent with the connection between the patriarchal promise and ultimate restoration.[136]

This glorious picture of Israel's future is bracketed by the darker reality of the present, symbolized in Moses' death (32:48–52; 34:1–12). Moses had earlier blamed Israel for Yahweh's anger against him (1:37; 3:26), but the reason given here for his death outside the land is his own sin against Yahweh in the wilderness (32:51; cf. Num 20:1–13; 27:12–14). His death serves as a warning to the nation, for he "dies at the point of decision, because of past failure."[137] As Olson states, "In his upcoming death, Moses becomes an embodiment of the song that he has just sung."[138] The emphases on both Moses' past sin and Israel's inevitable rebellion in the future demonstrate that Moses does not die as a substitute for the nation. "He does not die *instead* of the people but rather *ahead* of them."[139] For the nation, that death is none other than exile.

## THE MACROSTRUCTURE OF DEUTERONOMY

The first part of this chapter considered the theme of exile in Deuteronomy beyond the major texts analyzed in chapter 3. It was shown that exile and related themes cast their shadow over every part of the book. The pur-

---

and states, "The act of prayer is a confession of human limitations." This reinforces the unconditional nature of these blessings.

134. Mayes, *Deuteronomy*, 396; Olson, *Deuteronomy and the Death of Moses*, 161.

135. Millar, *Now Choose Life*, 96.

136. An eschatological perspective adds weight to McConville's proposal that a larger vision of God's purposes in the world is detected in the reference to "peoples" in 33:3 and 19 (*Deuteronomy*, 474). Though most take "peoples" as a reference to Israel (whether or not they follow the LXX reading of "his people" in v. 3; cf. the plural as referring to Israel in Gen 28:3; 48:4), it could refer to others beyond Israel. If so, then this text speaks of God's love for others (v. 3) and of a day when foreigners will come and worship Yahweh in the land (v. 19; cf. Isa 2:2–4). Cf. Tigay, *Deuteronomy*, 320–21. This would be a further outworking of the patriarchal promise, related specifically to the part, "in you all the families of the earth shall be blessed" (Gen 12:3b).

137. Millar, *Now Choose Life*, 97.

138. Olson, *Deuteronomy and the Death of Moses*, 150.

139. Ibid., 165.

pose of the following section is to see how the major texts on exile and restoration (4:25–31; 28:58–68; 30:1–10) fit within the macrostructure of the book. Rather than offering a new proposal, we will consider four of the leading structures that have been proposed: a treaty structure, a rhetorical-discourse structure, a rhetorical-superscription structure, and a concentric structure.[140] Though comments will be made about the strengths and weaknesses of each structure, we deem each one to be a viable way of grasping the organization of the book. All four of the structures reveal that exile and restoration are significant themes in the book.

## Treaty Structure

Before the discovery and intense study of many international treaties, von Rad had already made intriguing comments about the peculiar structure of Deuteronomy: history (chaps. 1–11); laws (12:1—26:15); mutual obligations (26:16–19); and blessings and curses (chaps. 27–28).[141] He suggested that the *Sitz im Leben* for the book was a feast of covenant renewal. The connection between Deuteronomy's literary structure and covenant was confirmed as scholars became aware there had been a fairly consistent form in ANE treaties for centuries.[142] Deuteronomy, thus, can be organized according to a treaty structure. In simplest form,[143] the outline is as follows:

---

140. Wright (*Deuteronomy*, 1–5) also summarizes four "valid and helpful" approaches. His "expanded Decalogue" is not a structure of the whole book, however, for it only deals with the ordering of the legal material in chaps. 12–26. This is expanded under the structure labeled "Rhetorical-Superscription" here.

141. Von Rad, *Problem of the Hexateuch* (New York: McGraw-Hill, 1966), 1–78. See chap. 1 for a discussion of the history of research.

142. As discussed in chap. 1, there are formal differences between second-millennium Hittite treaties and first-millennium neo-Assyrian treaties. The main discussions are by Mendenhall, "Ancient Oriental and Biblical Law," 26–46; idem, "Covenant Forms in Israelite Tradition," 50–76; Baltzer, *Covenant Formulary*; Kline, *Treaty of the Great King*; idem, *Structure of Biblical Authority*; Hillers, *Treaty-Curses and the Old Testament Prophets*; Frankena, "Vassal-Treaties of Esarhaddon," 122–54; Weinfeld, "Traces of Assyrian Treaty Formulae," 417–27; idem, *Deuteronomy and the Deuteronomic School* (Oxford: Clarendon, 1972), 116–29; McCarthy, *Treaty and Covenant*, 172–82; Kitchen, *Ancient Orient and Old Testament*, 90–102; idem, "AncientOrient," 1–24; idem, *On the Reliability of the Old Testament*, 283–307; Wenham, "Structure and Date of Deuteronomy," 206–12. Cf. Craigie, *Book of Deuteronomy*, 24–29; Nicholson, "Covenant in a Century of Study since Wellhausen," 78–93; Steymans, *Deuteronomium 28*.

143. See Craigie, *Book of Deuteronomy*, 23; Merrill, *Deuteronomy*, 30–31; Wright, *Deuteronomy*, 3.

I. Preamble (1:1–5)
II. Historical Prologue (1:6—4:49)
III. General Stipulations (chaps. 5–11)
IV. Specific Stipulations (chaps. 12–26)
V. Blessings and Curses (chaps. 27–28)
VI. Witnesses (see 30:19; 31:19; 32:1–43)

Other components that are often put within the structure include document clause (chap. 27), oath imprecation (29:9–28), deposit of document (10:1–5; 31:24–26), periodic reading (31:9–13), and duplicates and copies (17:18–19; 31:25–26).

The main strength of viewing Deuteronomy through the lens of contemporary treaties is that it highlights the covenantal elements and themes of the book. Deuteronomy is wholly concerned with the relationship between Yahweh and Israel, which is expressed through various covenants (e.g., patriarchal, Horeb, Moab). The book, which is itself a type of covenant renewal document, establishes procedures for future covenant renewal (e.g., chaps. 27; 29; 31:9–13). Deuteronomy's resemblance to ancient treaty forms also allows the transfer of leadership from Moses to Joshua to have an important place within the book.

The main problem with this type of structure is that Deuteronomy is *not* a treaty document *per se*, nor is the correspondence with ANE treaties exact. The simple outline above masks the difficulties and lack of consensus scholars have had in incorporating other elements into more detailed structures.[144] Certain elements appear at various places in the book.[145] Some units exhibit the treaty structure within themselves (e.g., chaps. 4 and 29–30).[146] More seriously, as the outline above shows, parts of the book are left out (much of chaps. 29–34).[147] The covenant character

---

144. Sees Kitchen, *Ancient Orient*, 96–98; Kline, *Treaty of the Great King*, 7–8; Weinfeld, *Deuteronomy and the Deteronomic School*, 116–29.

145. E.g., invocation of witnesses (4:26; 30:19; 31:19, 28); blessings and curses (11:26–29; 27; 28; 30:15–20; cf. chaps. 6–9); deposit of document (10:1–5; 31:24–26); making duplicates and copies (17:18–19; 31:25–26).

146. See especially the attempts to discern the covenant formulary within segments of Deuteronomy in Balzer, *Covenant Formulary*; and McCarthy, *Treaty and Covenant*.

147. Thompson (*Deuteronomy*, 18–20) discusses this discrepancy. Drawing on the work of Wenham ("Structure and Date of Deuteronomy"), he notes that the Old Testament covenant form ends with a section titled "Recapitulation" that is not found in ANE treaties. For Deuteronomy the "Recapitulation" is in chaps. 29–30, thus ex-

of Deuteronomy, then, is better viewed as a *substructure* of the book.[148] While it is clear that Deuteronomy draws on the ANE treaty tradition for its form, vocabulary, and themes, we should be more concerned with discerning how and why Deuteronomy exploits treaty forms and concepts. An example we have mentioned several times is the polemical nature of Deuteronomy; by drawing on similarities, the uniqueness of Yahweh, Israel, and the relationship between them can be emphasized.

The difficulties summarized above affect the way we view the texts on exile and restoration within the treaty structure. While the curse of exile in 28:58–68 naturally concludes "Blessings and Curses," the placements of 4:25–31 and 30:1–10 in this outline are tenuous. Chapter 4 has been particularly difficult to fit within the form. Some have it within the "Historical Prologue" (like the example above), but others put chapter 4 within the "General Stipulations."[149] The problem is that chapter 4 is a formal subunit in itself and embraces most of the elements of the covenant scheme.[150] Even verses 25–31 contains the elements of stipulation (v. 25), divine witnesses (v. 26a), curses (vv. 26b–28), and blessings (vv. 29–31). Chapters 29–30 are sometimes linked with chapters 27–28 under a general heading of "covenant sanctions" or the like, but more naturally fall outside of the ANE treaty structure.[151] Even if chapter 29 is considered as an "oath imprecation," nothing similar can be said of 30:1–10. As we argued in chapter 3, the Deuteronomic vision of restoration is rather unique; no ANE treaty would offer a scheme of blessing–curse–blessing.

Noting the problems, however, actually points to the importance of our texts within the book. Chapter 4 (especially vv. 25–31) is a pivotal

---

pressly outside of the treaty form. He also notes that chaps. 31–34 do not belong to the covenant form as such, but sees a connection in that they are in the context of covenant renewal (p. 20). Kline (*Treaty of the Great King*, 7–8) has a different outline than the one above and seeks to incorporate the entire book. The first four elements are essentially the same, but the last two are "The covenant sanctions: covenant ratification, blessings and curses, covenant oath" (chaps. 27–30) and "Dynastic disposition: covenant continuity" (chaps. 31–34). This may be an appropriate way to outline Deuteronomy, but it still seems to be a departure from the ANE treaty form.

148. See the helpful distinctions between literary structure, covenantal substructure, and theological structure in Miller, *Deuteronomy*, 10–14.

149. E.g., Kitchen, *Ancient Orient*, 97; Thompson, *Deuteronomy*, 19.

150. McCarthy, *Treaty and Covenant*, 131ff. Cf. Thompson, *Deuteronomy*, 18, who also sees the same issue with chaps. 29–30 (which includes another major text).

151. See chap. 3, n. 269.

text. It bridges the gap between the "historical prologue" in chapters 1–3 and the "general stipulations" in chapters 5–11, as well as introduces blessings and curses that are expanded in chapter 28. Deuteronomy 30:1–10 falls outside the treaty structure due to its unique vision, and is thus emphasized in comparison to ancient documents. Deuteronomy 28:58–68 is allowed greater significance here than in the other structures, perhaps, because the present structure is the only one that gives an independent heading to the blessings and curses in chapters 27–28.

### Rhetorical-Discourse Structure

The next two structures to be analyzed are "rhetorical" in that they divide the text based on formal clues in the text itself. The present one is labeled "rhetorical-discourse" because it is organized around the three (or four) discourses of Moses.[152] Mayes' outline is a good representative of this approach:

I. First Address of Moses to Israel (1:1—4:43)
   A. Introduction (1:1–5)
   B. Historical review (1:6—3:11)
   C. Conclusion. Possession of the land under Joshua's leadership (3:12–29)
   D. General command to obey the law (4:1–40)
   E. Cities of refuge in East Jordan (4:41–43)
II. Second Address of Moses to Israel (4:44—28:68)
   A. Introduction (4:44–49)
   B. Exhortation to covenant faith (5:1—11:32)
   C. The law of the covenant (12:1—26:15)
   D. The sealing of the covenant (26:16—27:26)
   E. Declaration of the blessings and the curses (28:1–68)
III. Third Address of Moses to Israel (29:1—30:20)
   A. Exhortation to obedience to the covenant law (29:1–9)

---

152. We discussed the issue of the number of main speeches in chap. 3. Though most recognize three, some argue on the basis of the superscriptions (see on "Rhetorical-Superscription" structure below) that a fourth main speech is given in Deut 33. So, e.g., Miller (*Deuteronomy*, 10–14), who, like Mayes (and Tigay), organizes his commentary around Moses' speeches (though Miller has the third "speech" ending at the end of chap. 32).

      B. Present and future generations enter into covenant relationship (29:10–15)
      C. Warning against idolatrous worship (29:16–21)
      D. Punishment for disobedience (29:22–28)
      E. Repentance and restoration (29:29—30:14)
      F. Choice between life and death (30:15–20)
  IV. Appendix (31:1—34:12)
      A. Moses' provision for the future (31:1–13)
      B. Yahweh's provision for the future, and the Song of Moses (31:14—32:44)
      C. Conclusion (32:45—34:12)[153]

A progression of the speeches of Moses is the most natural reading of Deuteronomy. Each is introduced with similar phrases: "These are the words" (1:1); "This is the law" (4:44); and "These are the words" (28:69[29:1]). The final chapters, then, are considered as a kind of appendix or epilogue. On this reading, the book is seen as a "last will and testament" of a dying leader.[154] A focus on Moses' speaking consists well with the repeated emphases, as we have seen, on the parenetic style of the whole book (including the "lawcode") and the role of Moses.[155] This structure also has the advantage of subsuming the laws in chapters 12–26 into a larger context.

The simplicity of this structure also accounts for some of its weaknesses. By focusing on the three major discourses, one is still left with a lot of material to be organized and divided. Intuitively and otherwise, readers discern other natural breaks (e.g., 6:4; 12:1; 27:1; 28:1; 33:1). Thus, as in the example above, one must flesh out the details of the text by other means if the structure is to be of any use. Also, this approach downplays the fact that Moses actually gives more than three speeches (see 31:7-8, 10-13, 25-29; 31:30—32:44, 45-46; 33:2-29).[156] Conversely,

---

153. Adapted from the more detailed outline (with third- and fourth-level subdivisions) in Mayes, *Deuteronomy*, 108-10.

154. See especially Weinfeld, *Deuteronomy 1–11*, 4.

155. See also Miller, *Deuteronomy*, 11.

156. Deut 27:1–10 contains two short speeches issued conjointly by Moses and the elders (vv. 1–8) and Moses and the Levitical priests (vv. 9–10). Deut 27:12–26 is a dictation of the curses to be recited in a covenant renewal ceremony. Deut 32:46b-47 is an exhortation in the narrative conclusion to the Song of Moses. The voice of Moses is also found in two poems at the end: The Song of Moses (32:1–43) and The Blessing of Moses (33:2–29). See Block, "Recovering the Voice of Moses," 391.

the second major speech is "interrupted" by chapter 27.[157] Lastly, the final chapters, being considered an appendix, are often treated as secondary, which makes it more difficult to put Deuteronomy within the larger narrative of Genesis–Kings (see chap. 1).

The quibbles over this approach do not deter from the significant placement of the major texts on exile and restoration. Each of the major texts appears at a final or penultimate position within the speeches. This is a powerful argument for maintaining the implicit presence of our theme throughout the book.

### Rhetorical-Superscription Structure

Another approach to the rhetorical structure of Deuteronomy is based on its five editorial superscriptions (1:1; 4:44; 6:1; 28:69[29:1]; 33:1).[158] Since three of these five superscriptions are the headings of Moses' three main speeches, the present approach is an expansion or advancement of the previous structure. Olson's monograph is the most rigorous example.[159] His outline of the book is as follows:

I. "These Are the Words": A Story of Faithfulness and Rebellion (1–4)
   A. Moses, Death, and the Old Generation (1)
   B. Israel among the Nations and Foretastes of the Conquest (2–3)
   C. Interpreting the Past for the Sake of the Future (4:1–40)
   D. The Cities of Refuge (4:41–43)
II. "This Is the Torah": Blueprint of Deuteronomy's Structure and Themes (5)
   A. The Central Concern of Deuteronomy (5:1–5)
   B. A Past Story Captured in a Snapshot (5:6)

---

157. Ibid., 391 nn. 35 and 36; 396–97.

158. The significance of the superscriptions has been recognized for some time, but has been particularly developed by McBride and Lohfink. See McBride, "Polity of the Covenant People," 62–77; Lohfink, "Bundesschluß im Land Moab," 35–56. Cf. Polzin, *Moses and the Deuteronomist*, 30; Seitz, *Redaktionsgeschichtliche Studien zum Deuteronomium* . For an analysis of Lohfink's interpretive strategy, see Robinson, *Roman Catholic Exegesis*, 105–48.

159. Olson, *Deuteronomy and the Death of Moses*. His first chapter (ibid., 6–22) presents his overall methodology. He takes the form of Deuteronomy as *torah*, which he defines as a program of "catechesis" (ibid., 7–14). The structure is based on the five superscriptions (ibid., 14–17). The recurring theme is the death of Moses (ibid., 17–22).

C. The Law for the Present—The Ten Commandments (5:7–21)
   D. The Covenant for the Future—Moses' Commission as Mediator and Teacher (5:22–31)
   E. The Blessing—"That It May Go Well with You" (5:32–33)
III. "This Is the Commandment": The Great Commandment for the Present (6–11)
   A. The Great Commandment—Love the One Lord Alone (6:1–9)
   B. The Giftedness of Israel's Existence (6:10–25)
   C. The Gods of Death—Militarism, Materialism, and Moralism (7–10)
   D. Life and Death, Blessing and Curse (11)
IV. "These Are the Statutes and the Ordinances": Expansions of the Ten Commandments (12–28)
   A. No Other Gods (First Commandment)—God's Presence and Word (12:1—13:18)
   B. God's Name (Second Commandment)—Purity, Boundaries, and Power (14:1–21)
   C. The Sabbath (Third Commandment)—Letting Go and Setting Free (14:22—16:17)
   D. Parents and Authority (Fourth Commandment)—The Limits of Human Power (16:18—18:22)
   E. Killing (Fifth Commandment)—Life and Death (19:1—22:8)
   F. Adultery (Sixth Commandment)—God, Sex, and Foreigners (22:9—23:18)
   G. Stealing (Seventh Commandment)—Money, Freedom, and Life (23:19—24:7)
   H. Bearing False Witness (Eight Commandment)—God and the Ox (24:8—25:4)
   I. Coveting a Neighbor's Wife (Ninth Commandment)—Rules and Exceptions (25:5-12)
   J. Desiring (Tenth Commandment)—Power, Business, and Bullies (25:13—26:15)
   K. Sealing the Relationship "Today" (26:16–19)
   L. A Publishing Party and a Curse on Secret Sins (27)
   M. The Law—Short on Blessing, Long on Curse (28)

V. "These Are the Words of the Covenant": The New Covenant for the Future (29–32)
   A. Three Versions of the New Covenant of Moab (29:1—32:47)
      1. The Liturgical Form (29–30)
      2. The Human and Textual Form (31)
      3. The Poetic Form (32:1–47)
   B. Moses—A Sin Remembered, Death Foretold (32:48–52)
VI. "This Is the Blessing": God's Blessing, Moses' Death (33–34)
   A. Moses' Prayer for God's Blessing (33)
   B. The Death of Moses outside the Land (34)

Like the previous approaches to structure, this approach has the advantage of identifying the divisions based on explicit markings in the text. It improves upon the former by noting further breaks at significant transition points (6:1; 12:1; 33:1) and by giving the final chapters equal standing with the rest of the book. Though not apparent in the outline, Olson's full program gives chapter 5 a central position within the book, allowing the arguments for an "expanded Decalogue" in chapters 12–26 to be incorporated into a coherent understanding of the whole book.[160]

This structure, especially as developed by Olson, is appealing in many respects, but it has its drawbacks. First, Olson is inconsistent in his stated methodology by considering 6:1 and 12:1 as verses with superscriptions. Neither, however, is an *editorial* superscription; both fall within Moses' second speech. Further, 6:4 ("Hear, O Israel!") is a more natural dividing point than 6:1. Second, considering chapters 29–32 as a single unit is problematic; Moses' third speech (chaps. 29–30) is a discreet unit that is clearly marked off from chapters 31–32. This is an example where the previous structure is to be preferred. Third, it is unnatural to unite chapters 33 and 34. Even Olson's heading for this section does not evidence a consistent theme. Chapter 34 has clearer links to chapters 1–3, chapter 31, and the end of chapter 32. Fourth, while

---

160. Ibid., 14–17, 40–48. Olson considers chap. 5 to be a key structural chapter because it is a miniature version of the structure of the whole book, "the *torah* of Deuteronomy *en nuce*" (p. 15). That is, the rest of the book is linked to statements in chap. 5: Past Story (chaps. 1–4; 5:6); Law for the Present (chaps. 6–28; 5:7–21); New Covenant for the Future (chaps. 29–32; 5:22–31); and Blessings for Future: Through Death to Life (chaps. 33–34; 5:32–33) (see diagram on p. 16). The outline above is adapted from his Table of Contents on pp. vii–x.

welcome for theological reasons, the emphasis on the Decalogue suffers the same criticisms leveled against those positions that seek a one-to-one correspondence between the Ten Commandments and the laws in chapters 12–26.[161] Finally, a minor criticism is that this approach must assume that 28:69[29:1] is a superscription rather than a subscription. Our discussion of the text showed, though, that it is one of several that are pivot points in the text; therefore, 28:69 functions both as a subscription and superscription.

This structure appears to downplay the themes of exile and restoration somewhat, but not entirely. This is especially true for 30:1–10, which is reduced in the outline to a part of one form of "The New Covenant at Moab." As just argued, however, this is a weakness in the system. While 4:25–31 and 28:58–68 retain their positions at the end of the first and fourth units, respectively, the addition of two units in-between (chaps. 5 and 6–11) makes our major texts less prominent. Seen from a different angle, however, these additional units elucidate the importance of our themes. We have observed a strong link with Horeb and the Decalogue in chapter 4, so the centrality given to the Decalogue (witnessed by the relative independence of chap. 5 in the outline) reinforces the link; if and when Horeb and the Decalogue are referred or alluded to in other parts of the book, the connections with exile and restoration must be kept in mind. Also, we saw that the curse at the end of chapter 11 (see subheading in outline above) has exile in mind. By making chapters 6–11 a separate unit, then, we have an additional section of the book that ends with the theme of exile.

### Concentric Structure

The final structure stems from Christensen's analysis on the poetic features of the composition of the text of Deuteronomy. Having observed carefully balanced structures "at virtually all levels of analysis within the

---

161. Olson's attempt to link other parts of chap. 5 with the rest of Deuteronomy also seems forced (see previous footnote). Connecting chaps. 1–4 with the preamble to the Decalogue (5:6) based on a shared concern with the past is an overstep; it is not even the same historical period in view in the two texts (and the exodus is referred to throughout the book). Finding a link between 5:22–31 and chaps. 29–32 is troubling, since the former text does not speak of Moses as a future covenant mediator, as Olson maintains (also the parallel between Horeb and Moab is a consistent theme throughout the book). Similar criticisms can be made about the connection between 5:32–33 and chaps. 33–34 around the theme of blessing.

book" and numerous textual links and echoes, Christensen created the following five-part concentric design:

   A  Outer Frame: A Look Backward (chaps. 1–3)
      B  Inner Frame: The Great Peroration (chaps. 4–11)
         C  Central Core: Covenant Stipulations (chaps. 12–26)
      B'  Inner Frame: The Covenant Ceremony (chaps. 27–30)
   A'  Outer Frame: A Look Forward (chaps. 31–34)[162]

The corresponding parts can be read continuously: the Outer Frame (chaps. 1–3, 31–34) is held together by the figure of Joshua (only found in chaps. 3, 31, and 34), who will lead Israel into the land; the Inner Frame (chaps. 4–11, 27–30) is unified by references in the join to blessings and curses connected with the ceremony on Mount Gerizim and Mount Ebal (11:26–32; 27:1–14). Concentric patterns are also found in each of the five major parts of this broad structure.

This structure takes seriously the nature of the book itself, exploiting the literary skill and artistry that is now readily observed by scholars.[163] Our study of several texts has confirmed the common use of chiasms, and has found that later texts often allude to—while still advancing—earlier themes. The notion of "framework" has appeared frequently in our discussion, especially with respect to the links between what is here referred to as the Inner Frame. Further, the division between chapters 26 and 27 represents a natural break in the text that is obscured by the rhetorical structures above. Finally, this structure overcomes the difficulties concerning chapters 31–34 in the previous structures: it gives a prominent place to chapters 31–34 (like the rhetorical-superscription structure) while recognizing the natural division after chapter 30 (like the rhetorical-discourse structure).

    162. Christensen, *Deuteronomy 1–11*, xli. Though others have followed Christensen's lead (e.g., McConville and Millar, *Time and Place*; Wright, *Deuteronomy*, 3–4), Christensen himself moved away from this structure in the revised addition of his commentary. While he still considers the concentric pattern a legitimate outline, he considers a "more instructive" literary structure to be one based on "the sequence of eleven 'weekly portions' in the lectionary cycle of traditional Jewish usage" (*Deuteronomy 1—21:9*, lviii). An examination of his revised commentary shows that Christensen still finds concentric patterns throughout Deuteronomy.

    163. Incidentally, the underpinnings of this structure raise questions regarding the common critical view of Deuteronomy's formation—a basic lawcode that has undergone a lengthy process of additions and redactions. See chap. 1.

The weaknesses of this approach to Deuteronomy would be most evident if it were to be used exclusive of another structure. A major concern is that, in practice, an undue focus on concentricity can drive one to force such a pattern on any given text, even if not apparent.[164] Also, connections between texts by way of echo or allusion go beyond the corresponding parts of the outline above. We have witnessed many themes that permeate the book. Finally, since the center of a chiasm usually indicates the most important point, the placing of the covenant stipulations as the Central Core might suggest that these laws take front-and-center stage in the book. These laws, however, should be seen as embedded within, and taking a back seat to, the larger concerns of the book.

The major texts on exile and restoration are given a different sort of emphasis in this structure. Significantly, they all appear in the Inner Core, and do so at its beginning and ending. Connecting chapter 4 with chapters 5–11 suggests that chapter 4 introduces the sustained parenesis of those chapters. As we found, allusions to exile abound in chapters 5–11. Another positive feature of this structure is that the later texts on exile (28:58–68) and restoration (30:1–10) are united within the same unit. This reinforces our contention that the latter texts are expounding upon the brief paragraph in 4:25–31. Finally, the last section, "A Look Forward" (chaps. 31–34), lets the concerns of Israel's immediate future (entry into the land) and distant future (exile and restoration) stand side by side.

## CONCLUSION

Deuteronomy 4:25–31 introduced the theme of exile at a significant point. Deuteronomy 4 ends Moses' first speech and functions as an overture to the rest of the book. It is not surprising, then, that the theme is developed further in Moses' other speeches. In chapter 3 of this study, we noted this development in two main texts (28:58–68; 30:1–10). The present chapter has shown that exile and its related themes are interwoven throughout the book, both in its parts (specific texts) and in its whole (macrostructure). What remains is the need for a theological synthesis of the data and conclusions drawn. This is the concern of chapter 5.

---

164. Christensen often comes up with unique structures and divisions, even when there is a virtual consensus on a given text's structure. Also, Christensen sometimes presents a structure that is far too sophisticated and complicated to be intentional. See, e.g., his structure of chap. 28 (*Deuteronomy 21:10—34:12*, 665–66). For a critique of Christensen's analysis, especially his designation of Deuteronomy as "didactic poetry," see DeRouchie, "Call to Covenant Love," 40–46.

# 5

# The Theology of Exile

UNDERSTANDING THE THEME OF exile in Deuteronomy *theologically* has been the aim of this entire study. This chapter seeks to summarize and synthesize the conclusions of the previous chapters. Though exile is explicit in a few texts, it casts a shadow over the whole book.[1] The importance of this theme for the entire book has not been fully appreciated. We contend that discussions of major theological topics in the study of Deuteronomy are inadequate if the theme of exile is not given due consideration. Thus, following a summary of the theological dimensions of the theme of exile itself, we will discuss the relationship of exile to broader topics in the theology of Deuteronomy.

## EXILE AS A THEOLOGICAL CONCEPT

Simply defined, exile involves removal of a population from its homeland. On the brink of Israel entering the land promised to her, Moses repeatedly raises the topic of exile in the midst of exhorting her to fidelity in her unique covenant relationship with Yahweh. Our examination of Deuteronomy shows, however, that exile is more than an historical event; it is a theological concept that signifies Israel's death. A study of the vocabulary of exile in Deuteronomy alerted us to the utilization of destruction language for the topic (see chap. 2). The roots אבד and שמד, in particular, are prominent. Though exile certainly involves destruc-

---

1. McConville makes this point for both Deuteronomy and the Deuteronomistic History in "Restoration in Deuteronomy," 12–15. In Joshua–Kings, exile is raised explicitly in only a few texts (1 Kgs 8:15–53; end of 2 Kings; cf. echoes of loss of land in general way in Josh 23:13; 1 Sam 12:25; 1 Kgs 9:6–9; 14:15–16; 2 Kgs 14:26–27), but clearly the whole narrative must be read with an exile perspective. For restoration in Deuteronomy, McConville adds, "Restoration, indeed, may be said to be in the warp and woof the book (*sic*)" (ibid., 39).

tion of land and property and death of individuals, the presence of these terms in the contexts of exile cannot be explained simply as colorful commentary on the processes of invasion and deportation. The people will continue to exist physically in exile; yet, as a single entity, Israel is said to "perish" and "be destroyed." So, it is not Israel as an historical or socio-religious people, but Israel as Yahweh's elect son and servant (1:31; 7:6; 14:1), that is put to death.

Considering the interplay of this construct (exile = death) with some basic conclusions on the theme of exile in Deuteronomy will elucidate the theological contours of exile and restoration. However, speaking of exile as Israel's death might draw unwarranted inferences. Therefore, a note of clarification is in order lest the reader misunderstand the present thesis. It is crucial to realize that the equation of exile with death is theological rhetoric and hyperbole. We are *not* suggesting that exile constitutes complete dissolution of the covenant between Yahweh and Israel as an *historical actuality*. Such a literal reading would contradict the patriarchal promises, which ground the promise of restoration beyond exile. Rather, the *rhetoric* of death allows for a proper theological understanding of the *reality* of exile and, especially, of restoration.

One basic observation is that exile is threatened as a consequence of infidelity (e.g., 4:25-28; 28:58-68). The threat is based on the conditional nature of the covenant Yahweh made with Israel at Horeb, which is continued in the covenant at Moab.[2] If Israel proves unfaithful, she will incur the curses of the covenant. The fact that exile is the final or ultimate curse (chap. 28) suggests that it is a consequence of prolonged and wholesale disobedience. In Deuteronomy, sin can be judged and dealt with in ways that fall short of exile. Specific laws prescribe the administration of justice for crimes performed by individuals or groups. Even the nation as a whole may go wayward at times, but it can be restored through repentance and a return to following the covenant. Therefore, exile assumes that Israel would have continually rejected many opportunities to repent and continue her relationship with Yahweh. Thus, exile is the result, not of a violation here or there, but of complete abandonment of the covenant itself (29:24) and total rejection of Yahweh's commands

---

2. The place of the patriarchal covenant in this discussion will be addressed shortly. As we shall see in the discussion below, the word "conditional" is problematic when used with respect to the covenant. Here we mean that Israel's blessing and fulfillment of the mission is conditional upon her fidelity to the covenant.

(e.g., 28:15, 58). Specifically, exile is the result of idolatry (4:25), a violation of the First and Second Commandments, because idolatry is the symbol of wholesale rejection of Yahweh (28:20).

Exile thus constitutes a rupture of the covenant triangle involving Yahweh, Israel, and the land. A rift in the Yahweh-Israel connection (via idolatry) results in a breach of the Israel-Land connection (via exile).[3] Certain aspects of the portrayal of exile in Deuteronomy might *suggest* (note the rhetoric) that this brokenness is permanent. Israel will "surely perish" and be "utterly destroyed" (4:26; cf. 28:63). Her exile entails the reversal of covenant history—an anti-exodus return to Egypt (28:68). In exile, Israel will be forced to perpetuate her crime of worshiping other gods (4:28; 28:64). Thus, the catalyst becomes the consequence; what got them there will keep them there.

The punishment of exile consists with the Deuteronomic emphasis on retributive justice, modeled in the so-called *lex talionis*: "life for life, eye for eye, tooth for tooth, hand for hand, foot for foot" (Deut 19:21; cf. Exod 21:23–25; Lev 24:17–20). Not only is the measure-for-measure principle witnessed—Israel abandons Yahweh, so Yahweh abandons Israel, but the punishment fits the crime (which is at the heart of *lex talionis*): as capital punishment is the just penalty for the individual idolater (e.g., Deut 4:3; 13:2–6, 7–11, 13–16; 17:2–7; cf. 22:13–14 [concerning adulterous acts]), so corporate "death" is the appropriate punishment for national idolatry.

Without understanding this rhetoric of the finality of Israel's broken relationship with Yahweh—that Israel is dead to Yahweh—we will not fully grasp the force and meaning of restoration from exile. If restoration is to come, it must involve more than a healing of wounds and settling of grievances; it must involve some kind of "new" covenant relationship. Also, the restoration can in no way be something that is due Israel.

A second basic conclusion concerning exile in Deuteronomy is that exile is predicted as an eventual fact in Israel's future. The major texts on exile strongly suggest this inevitability, such as with the כי-clause in 4:25 and the overall tone of 28:45–68. By the end of the book, however,

---

3. Cf. the statement by Talmon, "'Exile' and 'Restoration,'" 111: "Exilation not only disrupts the unity of family and community, and tears apart the bond of the deported with their land, it also dissolves the solidarity of YHWH and his people." It must be emphasized, however, that the dissolution is the cause of the exile rather than a mere result of it.

the inevitability of exile is beyond doubt. It is impossible to read the assumption of Israel's demise in a purely conditional sense in the promise of restoration (30:1–10) and the Song of Moses (chap. 32). How do we account for the juxtaposition of the "conditionality" (*if*) and "unconditionality" (*when*) of exile? A simple answer would be that the threat of exile serves as a negative motivation for obedience for each generation still in the land, but that some future generation will indeed fail and go into exile. Given the sense of corporate solidarity, however, this bifurcation is not completely satisfactory. The failure of a future generation indicates the failure of "all Israel." We will return to this tension in the next section.

For the present discussion, the more pressing question is why the certainty of exile? The primary basis of this certainty is knowledge of Israel's corrupt nature and heart (e.g., 9:6; 12:8; 29:3; 31:18–21; cf. 5:29). Israel *will* not because she *can*not (i.e. be faithful). Therefore, exile—Israel's death—is the exposure and inevitable result of a deadness that already exists internally. Israel is untrustworthy (5:29), stubborn (9:6, 13; 31:27), rebellious (9:7, 24; 31:27), corrupt (9:12; 31:29), untamed (12:8), prone to idolatry (31:16–21), and her heart is uncircumcised (10:16) and without understanding (29:3). These descriptions make clear that Israel's restoration, if it is to come, must begin with a new disposition and ability to heed Yahweh.

A third basic conclusion about exile in Deuteronomy is that Yahweh himself will send Israel into exile. This is a logical consequence of the covenant-focused reasons for exile given above. Given the treaty parallels, Yahweh as the suzerain exacts punishment on the rebel vassal.[4] Yahweh's direct role is also explicit in the text. Repeatedly, his personal involvement is heightened by descriptions of his anger being provoked prior to the actual punishment of exile (e.g., 4:25; 29:22–26[23–27]; cf. 28:63). The description of exile in 4:26–27 does not even mention mediate agents; the only explicit agent is Yahweh himself. Even in chapter 28, which mentions the destruction brought on by foreign peoples (vv. 25, 33, 48–53), these are expressly brought to Israel by Yahweh (vv. 48, 49). In the main paragraph on exile (28:58–68), Yahweh again is the sole agent of Israel's affliction (vv. 59–61), destruction (vv. 62–63a), removal from

---

4. In the ANE treaties, the suzerain often appealed to the gods to exact this punishment. But, of course, there is no higher authority to which can be appealed in the case of Yahweh.

the land to other places (vv. 63b–64), psychological trauma (vv. 65–67), and return to Egypt (v. 68). Far from the expected implication that Israel fell because of the impotence of her god (cf. 9:28), the foreigner will interpret the actions of Yahweh rightly (29:21–27). Exile displays Israel's death, but Yahweh is very much alive.

The combination of the last two observations—the inevitability of exile and Yahweh's sovereign superintendence—implies that exile is part of a larger divine plan (cf. 29:28).[5] This is not the place to venture into the theological and philosophical conundrum of reconciling divine sovereignty with human freedom, but in Deuteronomy, what Yahweh wants of Israel is something only Yahweh can give, even as he chooses not to—at least not (on a national scale) before exile. In light of this, Yahweh's longing for Israel to have a heart of fear and obedience (5:29) is set against the reality that Yahweh has not given her "a heart to understand or eyes to see or ears to hear" (29:3). Also, while the circumcision of Israel's heart is commanded (10:16), it will only happen by a work of (post-exilic) grace (30:6). The latter point can be extended to all the commandments, summed up in the call to love Yahweh with complete heart and soul (6:5; cf. 30:6). Developing this larger divine plan would necessitate placing Deuteronomy within the larger story (for the Christian, this would include the New Testament), but the Deuteronomic vision of exile and restoration helps set the stage. It begins with the declaration,

> See now that I, I am he,
> And there is no god besides me;
> I kill and I make alive. (32:39)

As we have argued, a major rationale for Deuteronomy's focus on exile as death is to provide the theological framework in which to interpret restoration from exile. The observations above have already advanced the discussion on the topic of restoration, but it is worth summarizing the Deuteronomic vision in a more straightforward manner. In Deuteronomy, restoration from exile is both possible and predicted (4:29–31; 30:1–10). This restoration will involve both a return to Yahweh and a return to the land. The order of events in the process is sharply debated (see chap. 3 on 30:1–10), but is extremely important theologically. It appears to us, at least, that the process involves the following order of events, which reflect various uses of שׁוּב‎ : 1) a preliminary "turn" of

---

5. Cf. McConville, "Restoration in Deuteronomy," 14.

the heart in exile (i.e., conviction) (4:30; 30:1a); (2) a spiritual "return" to Yahweh with a desire to obey his voice (i.e., repentance) (4:29–30; 30:1b–2); (3) a return to the land by the power of Yahweh (30:3–5); and (4) a "return" to obeying all the commandments, enabled by the divine circumcision of the heart (4:30; 30:6, 8).

The identification of conviction as the initial step in the process of restoration is most telling for our understanding. We take the temporal phrases in 4:30 ("[when] all these things find you") and 30:1 ("When all these words come upon you") to indicate an initial work of divine grace upon Israel's heart that allows her to recognize her desperate condition and desire to seek Yahweh and be obedient. When this occurs, Yahweh will bring Israel back to the land and circumcise her heart, allowing for unending covenant faithfulness. In this reading, Israel's repentance is prompted by divine revelation and activity; the first action is not something that Israel does, but one that is done to her.[6]

This ordering of events allows a more satisfactory explanation than either of the two competing options that are more popular on "the relationship between Yahweh's decision to restore Israel and Israel's willingness to repent and be redeemed."[7] The first option takes repentance as the initial step in restoration; thus, Yahweh's return to Israel in relationship and Israel's circumcision of heart and return to the land are predicated upon her return to Yahweh.[8] While we agree that Israel's repentance precedes the circumcision of her heart, the view that Israel's repentance is the initial step in restoration runs counter to at least three other conclusions: the condition of Israel's heart prior to any divine work of grace; the inevitability of restoration; and the fact that restoration is explicitly based on Yahweh's promise to the patriarchs (4:31). The second alternative considers the divine circumcision of the heart to precede Israel's repentance and return to the land.[9] While this view is correct in that it maintains divine priority, it forces an improbable interpretation of the structure of 30:1–10.[10]

---

6. In 30:1, Israel's first action is not an "action" at all, but a "taking to heart" the things that have been revealed.

7. McConville, *Deuteronomy*, 423–24.

8. For references, see chap. 3. This view of Deut 30 is assumed in Schmid and Steck, "Restoration Expectations," 76–77.

9. For references, see chap. 3.

10. We argued in chap. 3 that the center of 30:1–10 is most likely v. 8 rather than v.

When considering Moses' preaching solely from the angle of motivation for obedience, in which exile is a threat for persistent disobedience, the announcement of future restoration appears illogical and unwarranted.[11] But the other conclusions of exile above must be kept in mind. The inevitability of exile is predicated upon a problem with Israel's heart. This is why the centerpiece of restoration is the circumcision of the heart (30:6). Thus, in being restored, Israel is also changed, ensuring that her future life in the land will be one of continual obedience and fidelity to Yahweh and the covenant. The sovereign work of Yahweh in restoring Israel answers to his direct and ultimate agency in Israel's exile. Since the restoration is based on Yahweh's promise to the patriarchs (e.g., 4:31), in the end, Israel's entire history is viewed as under the complete control of Yahweh.

If exile is death, then restoration is resurrection—a return to life from death. This new life is altogether *new*. In other words, the hope is not simply for a *restitutio in integrum*—a return to how things were.[12] Were this the case, Israel would be doomed to fail again. Rather, the resurrected life involves an anthropological transformation (i.e., heart circumcision) that will guarantee obedience for every generation henceforth (note "and the heart of your offspring" in 30:6). Therefore, the newness of the "new covenant" relationship is not so much in the demands of the covenant (see discussion on covenant below) as much as the ability and willingness of Israel to keep them.

---

6 because of the chain of *waw*-consecutives in vv. 3–7.

11. Thus, the common assumption that the predictions of restoration (4:29–31; 30:1–10) are later interpolations; e.g., Tigay, "Excursus 5: The Promises of Reinstatement (4:29–31 and 30:1–10)," in *Deuteronomy*, 432. For a similar view with respect to the promise of restoration in Amos see Carroll, "Deportation and Diasporic Discourses," 69: "Thus the ending of the book of Amos (9:13–15) effectively reverses the force of most of the contents of the scroll . . ."

12. McConville ("Restoration in Deuteronomy," 39–40) calls this restoration "eschatological" because "it refuses to be bound to any one realization of its vision, and lives with an unresolved tension between the real and ideal." Carroll ("Deportation and Diasporic Discourses," 68) assumes that the idiom שוב שבות, "restore the fortunes," is a conventional phrase in the prophetic scrolls that "tends to indicate a notion of the restoration of things to how they were in the past." While this may be the case elsewhere, the conventional sense does not fit the use of the idiom in Deut 30:3. This misunderstanding of the Deuteronomic vision is apparent, e.g., in Pate et al., *Story of Israel*, 96: "The prophets, however, do not proclaim a restoration after the destructive exile that simply returns to the old Deuteronomic status quo." Surely, Deut 30 envisions something greater than the "status quo"!

## EXILE AND THE THEOLOGY OF DEUTERONOMY

Since exile is such a pervasive theme in Deuteronomy, it naturally interacts with other themes in the book. As McConville notes, "Deuteronomy's exilic vision is in line with its primary theology."[13] As we have discussed these themes and their relationship to exile, we have seen that they usually involve complexities and dialectics well known in Deuteronomic (and OT) studies. This is why the subheadings below are labeled "problems": The "Problem" of History; The "Problem" of Covenant; The "Problem" of Land; The "Problem" of Israel's Ability; and The "Problem" of the Individual. The purpose of this section is to highlight the tensions and see how the theme of exile interacts with them. In some instances, appreciation of exile may aid in resolving certain debates. In other instances, an understanding of exile will intensify the perceived tension.

### *The "Problem" of History*

Despite the future orientation of Moses' speeches in Deuteronomy, he draws heavily on the past experiences of the nation. The issues of history interrelates with the other theological concerns in this section, but the primary tension that concerns us here involves the continuities and discontinuities between various Israelite generations. As such, it is an issue of the identity of "Israel." Though generations are sharply distinguished at times,[14] Deuteronomy usually considers Israel to be a singular identity that transcends the generations. She is on a journey that began with the patriarchs and, following a long stint in Egypt, has continued through several rough and windy roads in the desert. On the brink of the land, Moses calls Israel to continue her journey into the land.[15] In two senses, however, entry into the land does not mark the final stopping point. First, in a metaphorical sense, true rest in the land involves an ongoing

---

13. McConville, "Restoration in Deuteronomy," 31. McConville's statement comes in the midst of an argument against the view that the exile theme in Deuteronomy is "merely a reflex based on the defeat of its first hopes" (ibid.).

14. E.g., 2:16; 11:2; cf. 5:3, though the rhetoric of the text actually emphasizes solidarity rather than distinction (see below).

15. The journey motif is expounded most fully in McConville and Millar, *Time and Place*. Concerning corporate solidarity and the promise of land, Miller ("Gift of God," 454) states, "The land is given 'to them' or 'to you' or 'to us.' Deuteronomy can say that Yahweh swore to give it to our fathers or Yahweh swore to our fathers to give it to *us*. There is no real distinction. The promise to the fathers was a promise to us. The gift to the fathers was a gift to us. The recipients coalesce."

"journey" of faith in and dependence upon Yahweh. A faithful Israel is a nation that is always "on the move." Second, in a more literal sense, Moses predicts that Israel's initial possession of the land is not the final stage in her journey. In the future, Israel will be exiled into a foreign land—an anti-exodus trek that constitutes a reversal of Israel's history. In the end, however, Israel will return to the land and remain there forever.

The conflation of generations is most notable in Moses' use of anachronistic address. He identifies the present generation at Moab with the people who experienced events in the past, including election (7:7; cf. 32:6), suffering in Egypt (6:21; 26:6-7; 29:16; cf. 10:19), the exodus,[16] Horeb,[17] and various stages in the wilderness.[18] The rhetoric is most pronounced in Moses' claim that it was "with us" and "not with our fathers" that Yahweh made a covenant at Horeb (5:2-3). Also, Moses description of events in Israel's distant future takes the same form. The "you" that Moses addresses is the "you" that will go into exile (4:25-28; 28:58-68; cf. 31:16-21, 29) as well as be restored (4:29-31; 30:1-10).[19]

Several reasons may account for this stance. Positively, the oneness of Israel allows Yahweh to be faithful to his promise to the patriarchs, in which he swore to give them the land.[20] The "fathers" did not see the fulfillment in their own day, but they would receive it, in effect, when their descendants finally possessed the land. Conversely, each succeeding generation can find hope in Yahweh's past pledge (cf. 6:20-23). Ideally, Israel would see her possession of the land as an unmerited gift based on an ancient promise (cf. 9:4-5). However, the possibility exists that a given generation would claim an unwarranted, absolute entitlement to the land based on its solidarity with the patriarchs. This danger is offset

---

16. Throughout Deuteronomy, the present generation is assumed to be part of the group Yahweh brought out of Egypt. See 4:20; 6:22-23; 7:8, 19; 8:14; 9:7; 11:3-4; 13:4[5], 9[10]; 15:15; 16:1, 3, 6, 12; 17:16; 20:1; 23:4; 24:9, 18, 22; 25:17; 26:8; 29:1[2]. Cf. 34:12.

17. Cf. 1:6, 9-18; 4:10-14, 23, 34-36; 5:2-33; 9:8-19; 10:10; 33:2.

18. The wilderness period that "you" or "we" experienced (anachronistically) includes more general overviews (2:15; 8:2-4, 15-16; 9:7; 29:4-5[5-6]) as well as specific incidents: the initial refusal to enter the land at Kadesh-barnea (1:19-46); idolatry at Beth-peor (4:3); and testing Yahweh at Massah, Taberah, and Kibroth-hattaavah (6:16; 9:22).

19. Moses does speak of descendants in 4:25 and 30:6, but the present generation is included in both the exile and the restoration. Cf. 6:20-25.

20. For variations of the land-grant formula with respect to the patriarchs, see, e.g., 1:8; 6:10, 18, 23; 7:8; 8:18; 9:5; 11:9; 30:20.

by the emphasis on the conditionality of the patriarchal covenant (see below on the "problem" of covenant).

Another positive purpose of stressing continuity is to show that the covenant renewal at Moab is a sign of Yahweh's continued allegiance to Israel (on the relationship of the covenants see below on the "problem" of covenant). Yahweh has effectively forgiven the sins of the wilderness generation, therefore the present (and each succeeding) generation's relationship with Yahweh is on the same basis as the past. This provides hope for continual renewals in the land.[21] This is the point of the never-ending "today" of faithful response to the covenant.

Negatively, corporate solidarity explains the pessimism of Yahweh and Moses about Israel's ability to obey the commandments. A major function of the accounts of Israel's stubbornness and faithlessness at Horeb (chap. 9) and in the desert (chaps. 1–2; 9:7, 22–24) is to demonstrate the corrupt nature of Israel's heart and will. Moses' thesis statement in 9:6b states it succinctly: "You are a stiff-necked people." Thus, the lesson of these past experiences for the present generation is not simply an imperative, "Don't be like your predecessors," but an indicative, "You are like your predecessors!" This raises the question of the function of the laws and commands in the book which we will discuss later (see below on the "problem" of Israel's ability).

It appears, then, that the accent concerns historical continuity and corporate solidarity. Therefore, the theme of exile complicates the matter. Exile does manifest aspects of continuity. Since all the curses are directed toward Israel as a whole (to "you"), exile, as the ultimate curse, is also threatened to the present generation (note "you/your" throughout 4:25–28; 28:58–68). Moreover, the corrupt nature of Israel's heart explains why exile is presented as ultimately inevitable. The continuities, however, are overshadowed by the discontinuities ushered in by the exile. The death of the nation means the end (and failure) of the journey and the covenant relationship. Along this horizon, exile is unlike the wilderness period in which God halted Israel's anti-exodus journey (cf. 2:2f.) after waiting for one generation to die (cf. 2:14), therefore renewing the covenant (cf. 5:2–3). Instead, exile is the culmination of a thorough anti-exodus (cf. 28:68) with no termination point (cf. 29:27) and *apparently*

---

21. Cf. McConville, "Restoration in Deuteronomy," 39: "The fusing of the generations is of the essence of the deuteronomic paranesis. And its effect is to generate the possibility of constant renewals."

signifies a completely broken covenant (29:24; 31:16, 20).[22] Also, unlike the positive functions of the wilderness as a time of divine providential care and instruction (2:7; 8:2–5), the exile is consistently portrayed as the display of divine retribution and abandonment (28:65–68).

Israel's restoration must be understood first from the sense of discontinuity due to exile. The finality of exile makes restoration something much more than another stage in an ongoing journey. In essence, it is the start of a new journey[23] that will involve a new covenant that seems to go beyond the covenant renewals of the past (see below). Israel herself will be new; she will have a new heart that will enable an obedience she quite knew before, and she will have the prospect of a future life with God that will never end.

The "newness" of Israel's restoration has its limits. What is not new is Israel's covenant partner. The exile had not changed Yahweh. He needed no correction, growth, or transformation of heart. The constancy of Yahweh is the basis for the elements of continuity that are found in restoration. The basic demand to heed his voice and love him wholeheartedly (30:2, 6) is unaffected in the new order of things. The basis of restoration—the promise to the patriarchs—also remains the same. Continuity of the divine plan, in the end, is the fundamental issue in solving the "problem" of Israel's history.

### The "Problem" of Covenant

ברית, "covenant," refers to three[24] different covenants in Deuteronomy: the patriarchal covenant (4:31; 7:12; 8:18), the covenant at Horeb,[25] and

---

22. Note the emphasis on the word, "apparently." I am not saying that exile actually shattered the covenant relationship; otherwise, there would be a contradiction with the fact that restoration is based on the patriarchal covenant. Rather, the imagery of death is part of the theological rhetoric so that the full force of the newness of restoration can be emphasized.

23. Cf. Yahweh's intent, following Israel's idolatry of the golden calf, to "start over" and transfer the promise to the descendants of Moses: "Let me alone, that I may destroy (Hi. שׁמד) them and blot out their name from under heaven. And I will make of you a nation mightier and greater than they" (9:14). The use of שׁמד, which is connected to exile in Deuteronomy, implies a radical disjunction.

24. A fourth use of ברית is used in the prohibition of making a "covenant" with the nations of the land (7:2).

25. Deut 4:13, 23; 5:2, 3; 7:9; 9:9, 11, 15; 10:8; 28:69.

the Moab covenant.[26] The main issue at hand is the relationship among these covenants. It is strategic to begin with the relationship between Horeb and Moab. We have demonstrated that Moab is not a replacement of Horeb. To express the continuity between the two covenants, we have used terms like "repetition," "augmentation," "extension," "identification," "recapitulation," and "renewal." Support for this understanding of the relationship is found, especially, in the identification of the Moab generation with those at Horeb (4:9–24; 5:2–31), and in the juxtaposition of Moab and Horeb (28:69; cf. 29:24; 31:9, 16, 20, 25, 26).

The connection between Horeb and Moab allows us to make a couple of significant observations. First, as covenant renewal, Moab signals Yahweh's forgiveness of Israel's sins in the wilderness and his readiness to continue his covenant relationship (from Horeb) with her. The notion of renewal is intrinsic to the nature of Moab. Within the narrative of chapters 1–3, Moab functions as a second Kadesh Barnea.[27] Kadesh was supposed to be the point of entry into the land (1:2), but instead it became the place of rebellion (1:26–46). Israel turned eleven days into forty years, much of which was spent at Kadesh (1:46). Thus, Kadesh became the launching point of a reversal of Israel's journey to the land— an anti-exodus back toward Egypt (2:1). Moab, then, is a symbol of Yahweh's reversal of the reversal. Therefore, Moab is more than a place of entry into the land—it is a symbol of divine grace and commitment to the people. This fundamental stance of grace must be kept in mind.

Second, the Moab covenant is an application of the Horeb covenant to life in the land. By this, we mean much more than the fact that the laws in Deuteronomy are geared specifically for landed existence.[28] The recounting of Horeb in chapter 5 contains three aspects that are paral-

---

26. Deut 17:2; 28:69; 29:8, 11, 13, 18, 20, 24; 31:9?; 16, 20, 25?, 26?; 33:9. It is not clear which covenant is in view in the phrase, "the ark of the covenant of Yahweh" (31:9, 25, 26). In 10:8, Horeb is clearly in view. But 31:9 states that Moses wrote down "this law," which refers to the Torah in Deuteronomy (and so is connected more directly to Moab). Because Moab is an extension of Horeb, however, the exact identification in 31:9 is insignificant.

27. On Moab as a second Kadesh Barnea, see McConville and Millar, *Time and Place*, 41, 61.

28. Cf. the contention by Lohfink ("Die '*huqqîm umišpāṭîm*'," 1–27) that the final redaction of the lawcode of Deuteronomy was valid only for the time when Israel occupied the land. He argues that "in the land" and "all the days that you live upon the earth" (12:1) should be taken in a restrictive sense, in contrast to the view in 5:29 and 31 that considers the law valid for all time.

leled in Moab: Yahweh's giving of commandments (5:6-21); Israel's right response of fear and intent to obey (5:23-29); and Yahweh's declaration that a heart of reverence and submission yields long life (5:29). The accent on grace—not only in the declaration of redemption that prefaces the "law" (5:6), but also in God's unconditional forgiveness of Israel's infidelity in the wilderness, should prevent a legalistic reading of the passages that speak of fidelity to the words given at Moab as resulting in possession and continued occupation of the land (e.g., 4:1; 5:32-33; 6:1-3, 18, 24; 11:8-9). The call to decision at Moab is first and foremost a call to remember what Yahweh has done—in the exodus (e.g., 4:20), at Horeb (e.g., 4:9-10), and in the wilderness (e.g., 8:2-5). Israel's posture of dependence upon Yahweh at Moab, which had just been demonstrated in Israel's following Yahweh's lead in the defeat of Sihon and Og (2:26—3:11), is the key to a successful future. As Millar states, "Life for Israel is to be life at Moab, even when firmly rooted in Canaan."[29] As we shall see, however, Israel's positive posture at Moab was temporary and fleeting, just as it was at Horeb (cf. 5:29; 9:6ff.).

The emphasis on continuity between Horeb and Moab raises the question whether or not Moab offers anything "new." The additional laws of Moab can hardly be said to be "new," since these laws tend to be extensions and applications of similar laws in the Book of the Covenant (cf. Exod 21-24).[30] In anticipation of the following comparison between the patriarchal and Horeb covenants, it is significant that Moab embeds the Horeb covenant within Israel's story, which runs from the patriarchs to future restoration from exile. This juxtaposition itself is not new, for Leviticus 26 ends its list of blessings and curses (cf. Deut 28) with a paragraph about the possibility of restoration beyond exile that appears to exhibit a sensitive juxtaposition of the two covenants:

> If they confess their iniquity and the iniquity of their fathers . . .
> —if then their uncircumcised heart is humbled and they make

---

29. Ibid., 61. Cf. Brueggemann, *Land*, 44-45: "That moment [at Moab] stands as a paradigm for what is under way at the boundary of the new land, fraught with problems and loaded with promise." On the importance of remembering see McConville and Millar, *Time and Place.*, 61 n. 87: "Forgetting Yahweh is tantamount to forgetting the decisions faced and made at Moab, and turning from the life of decision (which by definition must be a life of uncertainty and dependence) to a life of complacency, betraying an underlying pride of achievement."

30. The connections between the laws in Deut 12-26 and the Decalogue strengthen this point (see chap. 4).

amends for their iniquity, then I will remember my covenant with Jacob, and ... my covenant with Isaac and my covenant with Abraham, and I will remember the land. ... and they shall make amends for their iniquity, because they spurned my rules and their soul abhorred my statutes. Yet for all that, when they are in the land of their enemies, I will not spurn them, neither will I abhor them so as to make an end of them utterly and break my covenant with them, for I am Yahweh their God. But I will for their sake remember the covenant with their forefathers, whom I brought out of the land of Egypt in the sight of the nations, that I might be their God: I am Yahweh. (Lev 26:40a, 41b–42, 43b–45)[31]

Though a full comparison between Leviticus 26:40–45 and the restoration texts in Deuteronomy (4:29–31; 30:1–10) is beyond the scope of the present study, some initial observations hint at a distinguishing feature of Moab. First, Leviticus, being strictly conditional, lacks Deuteronomy's strong sense of the inevitability of future (exile and) restoration. Second, Leviticus appears more optimistic than Deuteronomy concerning Israel's ability to change her ways. Leviticus 26:40 makes human repentance the clear first step. Also, the need for the uncircumcised heart to be merely "humbled" (Lev 26:41) is much weaker than the divine circumcision in Deuteronomy 30:6. Third, the vision of restoration in Leviticus seems no more than a return to how things were before exile. Thus, if the text in Leviticus 26 can serve at all as representative of the outlook of Horeb, then Moab might be unique in its recognition of its own limitations—that ultimately it is unable to deliver.[32] Conversely, Moab's vision of restoration includes a "return" to a different reality than the present—in which the command becomes the promise—and an entrance into better circumstances than ever existed for pre-exilic Israel.

The inevitability of the storyline of Moab means that, in a sense, Israel cannot break the Moab covenant, for it incorporates the unfolding plan of a sovereign God. When Moses speaks of Israel abandoning or breaking the covenant (Deut 29:24; 31:16, 20), he only means that Israel will renege on her commitment to keep the terms of the covenant

---

31. For a helpful discussion of the difficulties and debates of Lev 26:40–45, see Milgrom, *Leviticus 23–27*, 2329–42.

32. See Cholewinski, "Zur theologischen Deutung des Moabbundes," 106; Millar, *Now Choose Life*, 106.

presented to her and will be unfaithful to Yahweh.[33] But Israel cannot keep Yahweh from doing what he has purposed to do.[34] Therefore, the Moab covenant is both conditional and unconditional, depending on the perspective from which it is approached.

Whether or not this tentative difference between Horeb and Moab is correct, Moab's juxtaposition of the patriarchal and Horeb covenants within a unified storyline calls for care in considering the relationship between the latter two covenants. A common view is to see a complete contrast between an unconditional covenant (patriarchal) and a conditional covenant (Horeb).[35] The fundamental problem is that both covenants are "conditional" and "unconditional" (albeit in different senses), especially in light of Moab.

First, the Horeb covenant is "conditional" in that different conditions of the covenant (fidelity or infidelity) will yield different outcomes for the people (blessing or curse). Since both possibilities are written into the covenant, however, the covenant itself will be fulfilled one way or the other. The certainty of fulfillment makes Horeb "unconditional." The new aspect of the covenant of Moab of Israel's certain failure and exile, followed by restoration and blessing, increases the confusion.

Second, the patriarchal covenant is clearly "conditional" in Deuteronomy.[36] Two of the three explicit references to the patriarchal

---

33. This is clear by the parallel phrases of "forsaking me" (31:16) and "despising me" (31:20). The emphasis on idolatry as the foundational sin generally makes the same point.

34. We suggested in chap. 3 that the wisdom maxim in 29:28 may actually have to do with this distinction. Thus, while the facts of exile and return are now being revealed to Israel, how and when they occur are still a mystery known only to Yahweh. Israel's occupation in the present is to obey and teach those things of which they have full knowledge and possession.

35. This view is witnessed, e.g., in Pate et al., *Story of Israel*, 96: "Based on the conditional Mosaic covenant of Deuteronomy, the prophets proclaim judgment for sin committed. However, the prophets also reach back to the unconditional Abrahamic and Davidic covenants as the basis for their hope of a future restoration." Cf. Merrill, *Deuteronomy*, 129, on 4:31: "Once more the conditional nature of the Sinai covenant is oriented to the unconditional nature of the so-called Abrahamic."

36. Some view the conditionality of the land in Deuteronomy as a late imposition on an earlier unconditional promise. Von Rad (*Problem of the Hexateuch*, 85) sees a tension in Deuteronomy between an "historical" conception of land (i.e., unconditional, based on the patriarchal promises) and a later "cultic conception"(i.e., conditional, based on Yahweh's ownership). Noth (*Deuteronomistic History*, 135) and Perlitt (*Bundestheologie im Alten Testament*, 46) think the conditional element arose as early (unconditional)

covenant occur in conditional blessings (7:12; 8:18; cf. 6:18; 7:13). The "unconditional" character of this covenant is retained in the focus on land as something Yahweh "swore" to the fathers,[37] or more generally as the land that Yahweh is "giving" to Israel based on the promise to the fathers.[38] Still, some of these references also emphasize that Israel must go and take possession of the land[39] or that obedience is a condition to possessing the land.[40]

It seems, then, that the language of "conditional" and "unconditional" proves unhelpful in understanding the relationship between the covenants. We have yet to establish the nature of the connection. Since both the patriarchal and Horeb covenants exhibit "conditional" and "unconditional" elements, one could argue for continuity between the two. Indeed, we noted the debate in identifying the "fathers" as either the patriarchs or the Horeb generation in several texts (4:31; 5:3; 7:12; 8:18). The juxtaposition of election and the blessings of obedience in 7:6–16, especially, blurs the distinction between the covenants. Though we argued that "the covenant ... that he swore to your fathers" (7:12) refers the patriarchal covenant, the material blessings of 7:13–16 are more easily associated with the covenant at Horeb. From this perspective, the Horeb covenant (now reapplied in the Moab covenant) is a particular, national expression and application of the patriarchal covenant. The conditions of the Horeb covenant are conditions of the patriarchal covenant appropriately specified for and applied to the nation. Exile and restoration show this continuity most clearly: exile results from the breaking of the Horeb/Moab covenant and results in the loss of the land sworn to the

---

Deuteronomic material was reinterpreted by the Deuteronomistic circle. Against these positions is Plöger (*Literarkritische, formgeschichtliche und stilkritische*), who sees the gift of the land as unconditional, while seeing Israel's occupation of the land as conditional. Plöger's position is more consistent with those who see both conditionality and unconditionality as fundamental to the rhetoric of the book. See the discussion and references in Millar, *Now Choose Life*, 56–60.

37. Deut 1:8, 35; 4:31; 6:10, 18, 23; 7:8, 13; 8:1; 10:11; 11:9, 21; 26:3, 15; 28:11; 30:20; 31:20, 21, 23; 34:4. Other verses speak of aspects of the patriarchal covenant other than the land that Yahweh "swore" to the fathers: covenant (7:12; 8:18); word (9:5); multiplication (13:18[17]); and covenant relationship (29:12[13]).

38. Deut 1:20, 25; 2:29; 4:1, 21, 40; 5:16, 31; 9:6; 11:17, 31; 12:9, 10; 15:4, 7; 16:20; 17:14; 18:9; 19:1, 2, 10, 14; 21:1, 23; 24:4; 25:15, 19; 26:1; 27:2, 3; 28:8; 32:49, 52.

39. Deut 1:8; 6:18; 8:1; 10:11; 11:9, 31; 30:20.

40. Deut 4:1, 40; 5:16, 31; 16:20.

fathers; restoration results from Yahweh's commitment to the patriarchs and results in Israel receiving the blessings of the Moab covenant.

On the other hand, Deuteronomy maintains a distinction between the patriarchal and Horeb covenants that argues another perspective. More generally, there is a difference in some of the terminology used with respect to each covenant. Horeb/Moab has no parallel to the promissory language (i.e., "sworn," "oath," "giving") of the patriarchal covenant. Instead, Moab speaks of "blessing" for obedience (11:26-27; 27:12; 28:1-14). Though we do not want to revert to the common view contested above, the different emphases between gift and reward must not be overlooked. While the elements of the patriarchal promise may or may not come with conditions, depending on the context, the blessings of Horeb/Moab are always contingent.

More specifically, the greatest note of discontinuity between the patriarchal covenant and the Horeb covenant arises in the context of restoration beyond exile. This is clearest in chapter 4, where the basis of restoration is distinctly Yahweh's remembrance of "the covenant of your fathers which he swore to them" (4:31). A contrast with Horeb seems intentional, for "covenant" refers to Horeb in 4:13 and 23, and exile is specifically the result of violating the Horeb covenant (4:23-28). A distinction also occurs in 30:1-10, but in a different fashion. The sequence of blessing-curse (30:1), symbolizing the Moab covenant, takes place before the restoration (based on the patriarchal covenant[41]) occurs. Though the object of obedience in the land will be the same commands of Moab (cf. 30:2, 6, 8, 10), there is no apparent threat of curse since it will be unnecessary.

This last point raises a question: what type of covenant relationship will exist in the future? We know that Moab is not the final place for having a covenant ceremony because chapter 27 commands certain rituals that must take place after Israel enters the land (e.g., at Shechem). Clearly, however, the ceremonies depicted in chapter 27 constitute covenant renewal. As Moab is the continuation or reaffirmation of Horeb, so these future "covenants" are a continuation of Moab. Even so, can the same be said for the covenant relationship in the time of restoration? Though Deuteronomy does not give an answer directly, inferences can be drawn

---

41. There is no explicit reference to the patriarchal covenant in 30:1-10, but we argued in Chapter 3 that numerous allusions to the covenant imply that it serves as the basis of restoration.

from what we have discerned already. The discontinuities of restoration suggest against a simple return to the covenant of Horeb/Moab/Shechem. Since restored Israel is still constituted as a nation and committed to obeying the commands of Moab, the covenant relationship cannot simply be a return to the situation of the patriarchs. It must be some kind of "new covenant." As we stated in the opening section of this chapter, what is new in this relationship is the ability and certainty of Israel to reciprocate fidelity to the covenant. In this setting, all the tensions between the previous covenants disappear, for the command becomes the promise (cf. 10:16; 30:6) and the conditions become realized.[42]

## The "Problem" of Land

As one of the three major components of the covenant triangle, and as the centerpiece of the patriarchal promise, land is directly connected with the above discussion of covenant. The focus on land in Deuteronomy, however, justifies a separate section on the theme. The position of Israel just outside the land causes Moses to be preoccupied with it.[43] The promise to the patriarchs involves several other components that are alluded to in Deuteronomy: special relationship with Yahweh,[44] exalted status in the world,[45] multiplication,[46] and curse upon enemies.[47] Still, the number of these references pale in comparison to the focus on the gift of land. Also, the Moab covenant is an extension of the Horeb covenant with stipulations suited specifically for a landed people. Since the loss of this land hangs over the people as a constant threat, it is important to see how the theme of exile relates to the larger theology of land in Deuteronomy.

---

42. Likewise, Mayes (*Deuteronomy*, 78–79) states that the possibility of repentance and forgiveness in the final chapters of Deuteronomy helps resolve "the tension between the idea that Israel's status as the people of Yahweh precedes and is independent of the covenant, and the idea that disobedience to the covenant demands bring punishment and destruction."

43. Israel's story in the Pentateuch begins (Gen 12) and ends (Deuteronomy) with Yahweh's promise of land. The function of Deuteronomy in the Pentateuch, then, is to bring this theme to a climax. See McConville, "Restoration in Deuteronomy," 11.

44. E.g., 4:6–8, 19–20, 32–38; 7:6–11; 8:5; 9:29; 10:15; 26:16–19; 28:9–10; 29:12; 30:9; 32:6–14; 33:29.

45. Deut 4:6–8; 7:14; 26:19; 28:1,10, 13.

46. Deut 1:10–11; 7:13; 8:1; 10:22; 11:21; 13:18; 26:5; 30:5.

47. Deut 7:15–16; 28:11; 30:7; 32:43; 33:27; cf. 2:26—3:11; 7:1ff.; 9:1ff.; 11:23, 25; 31:3–5.

The tension concerning land in Deuteronomy is that its status as gift and its elevated importance are challenged by other themes in the book. A Deuteronomic theology of land begins with the land as a divine gift.[48] It is described as a "good land" (1:25; 8:7), already nourished by Edenic resources (8:7–10; 11:9–12) and endowed with the props for civilization (6:10–11) that Israel would need to be satisfied as a landed people. Indeed, it is a land given *sola gratia*, "in which you will lack nothing" (8:9) from the outset.

But the land is also recognized as a place of testing and a catalyst for temptation.[49] The existence of Canaanites in the land poses a dual temptation: fear and unbelief for those seeking to enter the land (1:26–33; 7:17–23; 20:1–4; cf. 1:38; 3:2, 28; 31:6–8, 23); and the seduction of idolatry for Israel once in the land (7:1–5).[50] The blessings of the land also become a test. It is significant that descriptions of the land are followed by warnings of forgetting Yahweh and the graciousness of his gift (6:12; 8:11–17; 11:16). The loss of memory spoken of in these warnings is again manifested by the potential seduction of idolatry (6:14; 8:19; 11:16). These temptations are the reason why the notion of gifted land is balanced by the conditionality of land possession.[51] Obedience to the lawgiver—both to the commands to enter the land and to the detailed laws controlling life in the land—is the demonstration of faith in, and the path to remembering, the land-giver.[52] This dialectic of promise and command is at the heart of the tension concerning the nature of the patriarchal covenant discussed above.

Land, then, is important because it is a symbol of life with Yahweh. It is an arena in which Israel can have fellowship with her God and experience his blessings and care. The heightening of this symbolic value,

---

48. See discussion and references in previous section of the "problem" of covenant. For a helpful analysis of "gift" language in Deuteronomy see Plöger, *Literarkritische, formgeschichtliche und stilkritische*, 121–29.

49. Brueggemann, *Land*, 50–65.

50. Our position that the *herem* policy in chaps. 7 and 20 is hyperbolic makes this threat a constant one for Israel.

51. See Brueggemann, *Land*, 49; Diepold, *Israels Land*, 100.

52. Cf. Brueggemann (*Land*, 56, 57): "Israel's Torah is markedly uninterested in a religion of obedience as such. It is rather interested in care for land, so that it is never forgotten from whence came the land and to whom it is entrusted and by whom. . . . Torah exists so that Israel will not forget whose land it is and how it was given to us."

however, tends to mitigate the significance of land as turf and of the blessings of the land as primarily material. Millar states,

> The land is also the locus of Israel's relationship with Yahweh. . . . While physical abundance in the land does not lie outside his concerns, the primary matter is Israel's relationship with God as signified by the land. In the wilderness, the survival or physical comfort of the nation was not the ultimate purpose of Yahweh's intervention (see e.g. 8:3). In Yahweh's land, material blessing should sharpen the focus on the potential intimacy occupation of this land provides. The ultimate indicative is not the land which Yahweh gives, but the relationship which that land affords.[53]

It must be remembered that the setting of Deuteronomy is outside the land even as Yahweh is already in covenant relationship with Israel.[54] This is consistent with the whitewashed assessments of Israel's experience in the wilderness:

> For Yahweh your God has blessed you in all the work of your hands. He knows your going though this great wilderness. These forty years Yahweh your God has been with you. You have lacked nothing. (2:7)

> And you shall remember the whole way that Yahweh your God has led you these forty years in the wilderness, that he might humble you, testing you to know what was in your heart, whether you would keep his commandments or not. And he humbled you and let you hunger and fed you with manna, which you did not know, nor did your fathers know, that he might make you know that man does not live by bread alone, but man lives by every word that comes from the mouth of Yahweh. Your clothing did not wear out on you and your foot did not swell these forty years. (8:2–4)

The statement that Israel "lacked nothing" (2:7) in the wilderness is stark, for it is the same reality promised for existence in the land (8:9).

---

53. Millar, *Now Choose Life*, 56.

54. McConville ("Restoration in Deuteronomy," 33–34) uses the setting of Deuteronomy outside the land in support of his understanding of the altar-law or place-formula (e.g., 12:5) to refer to any place where Israel might meet God. He states, "The covenant of Yahweh with Israel will not be confined to one time or place, or even one possible history, but is ready for 'land' in the broadest sense, and adaptable to many new beginnings" (ibid., 34). For a full discussion of his position see McConville and Millar, *Time and Place*, 89–139.

Though the blessings of the land make "no lack" a believable prospect from the start (not just retrospectively, like the wilderness), the point is that Israel had a vital relationship with Yahweh outside the land—despite Israel's consistent unfaithfulness. The land affords the opportunity for Yahweh to fulfill his promises and to work out his plan for Israel in the sight of the world (e.g., 26:19; 28:10), but it is not an indispensable component to establishing or maintaining a covenant relationship with his people. Unlike the other gods, Yahweh is not limited to a local territory, for the whole earth is his.[55]

The themes of exile and restoration relate to these tensions of the land directly. Exile shatters the covenant triangle by dismantling the connection between two of its components, Israel and the land. Still, our examination of chapter 28 showed that the Israelite perspective understands the fundamental covenant relationship to be between Yahweh and Israel in direct contrast to the usual ANE perspective that considered deity-land as primary.[56] Therefore, exile is the result, rather than the cause, of the rupture between Yahweh and Israel. In fact, Deuteronomy is virtually silent about a "relationship" between Yahweh and the land, except that he owns it along with the rest of the earth. The closest we get is in the *foreign* response to Yahweh's judgment in 29:21-27. The foreigners are preoccupied with the land—its devastation (29:21-22); Yahweh's judgment upon it (29:23, 26); and the people's removal from it to another land (29:27). Even if "land" is a metonym for "the people of the land" in some of the references, the perspective is unique in Deuteronomy. This text is "the exception that proves the rule"—the rule that land is secondary to the covenant.

On the other hand, this passage in chapter 29 is an indication that land, while secondary, is not irrelevant. It might be a stretch to say that Deuteronomy is missiological,[57] but the book offers glimpses of God's larger concern for the world (cf. 2:4-23). The acknowledgment that the world is watching (4:6-8; 26:19), and that Yahweh is concerned about foreign evaluation (9:28; 28:9-10, 25, 37; 29:21-23), at least suggests that the covenant relationship between Yahweh and Israel serves as a

---

55. On Yahweh's control over the whole earth, see 4:26, 32, 39; 10:14; 14:2; 28:49, 64; 30:19; 31:28; 32:1.

56. See Block, *Gods of the Nations*, especially 21-33.

57. On the missiological significance of Deuteronomy, see Wright, *Deuteronomy*, 8-17. Cf. Block, "Privilege of Calling," 387-405; Millar, *Now Choose Life*, 147-60.

type of witness to others about the character and power of Yahweh. Because land is central in the minds of others, Yahweh's covenant with Israel must take place with reference to a specific land in order for this witness to have an effect.

The theme of restoration both lessens and emphasizes the significance of the land. The restoration envisioned in 4:29–31 downplays the land. Though the reference to the patriarchal covenant (4:31) implies that return to land is involved, the text only explicitly states that Israel returns to Yahweh in repentance and obedience (4:29–30). The emphasis is consistent with the points made above concerning the unique Israelite perspective and the ability of Israel to have a relationship with Yahweh outside the land. The restoration envisioned in 30:1–10, however, highlights the importance of land in at least three ways. First, restoration involves return to the land (30:5). Second, the circumcision of the heart, the needed surgery to repair Israel's root problem of rebellion, is held off in the restoration process until Israel is in the land (30:6). In our reading, this order of events is necessary because the outcome of the circumcision of the heart is a constant, perpetually operating covenant relationship. Given the notion of witness, the land is the proper context for Israel's display of complete obedience to Yahweh and for Yahweh's display of commitment to his people. Third, only in the land can there be resolution to the tensions of the patriarchal covenant itself, and to the uncertain relationship between the patriarchal and Horeb covenants.

Therefore, we must be careful how we speak of the importance of land in the Deuteronomic vision of Israel's future. Israel's possession of the land is significant in its function as the ideal context in which the covenant relationship can be enjoyed by Israel and witnessed by the world, but it is not indispensable to the existence of the covenant relationship itself. This latter point is hinted at by the fact that the covenant is renewed in *Moab*, a place outside the land. The land becomes an indispensable piece, however, in the ultimate (eschatological) fulfillment of Yahweh's plan, as pictured in Israel's restoration.[58]

## The "Problem" of Israel's Ability

Deuteronomy is focused on the concept of decision. One of the most striking features of the book is its preoccupation with exhortation.[59] At Moab, Israel is reminded of her past experiences in order to make the right choice in the present—to be faithful to Yahweh by obeying his commands to enter the land and keep the laws of the covenant while in the land. Will Israel obey in the long run? More importantly, will Israel be able to obey? Scholars debate whether Deuteronomy is optimistic or pessimistic on the matter.[60] The optimistic view is based on two lines of thought. First, the giving of commands and exhortations implies ability to keep them. Otherwise, why offer a choice (e.g., 30:20) in the first place?[61] Second, Deuteronomy recounts several positive examples

---

58. Cf. the statement in McConville ("Restoration in Deuteronomy," 38): "Possession of the ancient land remains the deuteronomic ideal, but the significant qualification entered by the story of the end of Judah is that the life of the covenant people could continue without it." I agree that there is this qualification, but it already exists in Deuteronomy before it is demonstrated in Israel's history. I do not agree, however, with an earlier statement: "The framing of the story [from Deuteronomy to Kings] in non-landedness is, paradoxically, a ground of hope. It is not necessary to suppose that the origin of the story in the promise to the patriarchs entails that the land is an indispensable part of the restored life of the people" (ibid., 37–38). While the covenant relationship can be maintained apart from land, the Deuteronomic vision of restoration cannot be fulfilled without it.

59. Amsler, "La motivation de l'éthique," 11–22. Millar (*Now Choose Life*, 49–51) outlines at least fifteen ways the language of Deuteronomy refers to the action to be taken in response to the divine command. Millar concludes, "The unmatched concentration of paranetic vocabulary confirms that the prevailing atmosphere of the book is the ethical decision facing Israel" (ibid., 51).

60. For a discussion and summary of positions, see Millar, *Now Choose Life*, 161–80. Millar thinks a good case can be made for both sides, but his presentation seems to favor the pessimistic view. The "optimists" include McBride, "Polity of the Covenant People," 62–77; Mayes, "On Describing the Purpose of Deuteronomy," 13–33; Lenchak, '*Choose Life*'; Tigay, *Deuteronomy*. The "pessimists" include Barker, *Triumph of Grace*; Olson, *Deuteronomy and the Death of Moses*; Stulman, "Encroachment in Deuteronomy," 613–32; idem, "Sex and Familial Crimes," 47–63.

61. On philosophical grounds, one could also argue that it would be unjust for God to punish a lawbreaker if he is ultimately unable to comply. This is beyond the scope of our study, but points to the need to be aware of presuppositions that we all bring to

of Israel's past fidelity, which implies that Israel can do likewise in the future. Individuals who proved faithful include the patriarchs (9:27), Caleb (1:36), Joshua (1:38), and Moses himself (34:10–12). The nation as a whole was faithful at Horeb (5:24–28) and in the conquest of Sihon and Og (2:26—3:11). At Moab, Israel appears to be in good position to follow Yahweh into the land (cf. 4:4; 31:1–13). Since our study has supported the pessimistic view, we need to explain how such a position deals with the positive elements in the text.

We begin by rehearsing the negative portrait of Israel's nature and heart in Deuteronomy. The positive portrayal of Israel's response at Horeb (5:24-28) is tempered by a hint of doubt by Yahweh concerning Israel's chances of sustaining a posture of fear and obedience (5:29). Israel's right response indeed proved fleeting, as she quickly turned to idolatrous worship of the golden calf (9:8–21). This experience proved paradigmatic for Israel's continual rebellion in the wilderness (9:7, 22–24; cf. 1:26–43), with the added indictment that Israel, at her core, is stiff-necked (9:6, 13; cf. 9:24; 12:8). This inner corruption is never overcome; the positive scenes in the wilderness (e.g., 2:26—3:11; 6:22; 10:22; 11:2–7; cf. conquest in 7:18–23) are overshadowed by the reality that Israel's heart is still uncircumcised at Moab (10:16). Yahweh tells Moses that the people will be unfaithful in the land (31:16, 20; cf. 32:15ff.) because he knows "what they are inclined to do" (31:21). The larger theological reality is that Yahweh has not given Israel the heart she needs to be faithful (29:3). Therefore she will fail, with the inevitable result of suffering the ultimate curse of exile (4:25–28; 28:58–68).

The positive elements need to be understood within this larger negative perspective. First, the sustained exhortation to obey does not engender optimism in the end. As Millar states,

> These repeated appeals seem to imply that Israel has the ability to comply. On the surface, this is the case. There may be a sub-text, however. The forceful repetition of the demand of obedience may in fact reveal a certain amount of desperation, presupposing the waywardness of Israel. Within the rhetoric of Deuteronomy, even calls to obedience become ambiguous.[62]

the table.

62. Millar, *Now Choose Life*, 166.

One of the most prominent exhortations is the call to "remember" (or not "forget") Yahweh and his acts. The memory motif is a subtle indictment of Israel's tendency to forget, and so serves as support of the pessimistic view.[63] Second, accounts of the nation's past fidelity are always followed by negative elements. The description of the defeat of Sihon and Og (2:26—3:11) is followed by Moses' exclusion from the land (3:25-26). The submission at Horeb (5:24-28) is followed by Yahweh's doubt (5:29), not to mention the sin that followed (9:8ff.). The hope in the leadership of Joshua (31:1-13) is followed by knowledge of future failure (31:14-29). Thus, the text never lets Israel's display of fidelity go unchallenged.[64] Third, when things did go well in the wilderness, the emphasis was always on Yahweh's initiative and grace rather than Israel's obedience (e.g., 2:26—3:11; 6:22; 10:22; 11:2-7).

Fourth, the examples of faithful individuals seem to be the exceptions that prove the rule. These references to individual fidelity are overshadowed by the prominent theme of the death of Moses in the book (1:37; 3:25-26; 4:21-22; 31:1, 14, 16, 29; 32:48-52; 34:1-12).[65] What chance will Israel have in the land if her great leader was excluded? As a caveat, however, the individual Israelite who seeks to be faithful to Yahweh amidst a sinful generation can be assured that he or she is not forgotten by Yahweh (see the fuller discussion below on the "problem" of the individual).

The theme of exile and the question of Israel's ability are intimately related. The inevitability of exile is grounded in the pessimistic portrayal of Israel's heart and nature. It is only in restoration that Israel's heart will be circumcised, enabling her to be fully and continually obedient (30:6). From this ultimate horizon, then, the pessimism is reversed into a resounding optimism. Millar concludes,

> Chapter 30 ensures that Deuteronomy is ultimately an optimistic book. Its doctrine of the sinfulness of human nature may mean that Israel is bound to fail, but the promise of God's radical intervention, setting up a new covenant which does change the hearts of his people, means that the book is transformed by a theology

---

63. Brueggemann, *Land*, 50–55.

64. Pate et al. (*Story of Israel*, 44) further note that chaps. 1–11 begin and end with negative events (failure at Kadesh and the golden calf incident).

65. On the prominence of this theme, see Olson, *Deuteronomy and the Death of Moses*. Note also the death of Aaron in 10:6.

of hope. That is why Moses can preach on (30:15–20), calling Israel to persevere in obedience, walking with Yahweh, facing a lifetime of decisions. God's people may be bound to fail today, but they are not trapped in failure for ever, for God's solution is coming.[66]

Millar's comment helps us understand the function of the laws and exhortations in Deuteronomy. We noted in chapter 3 that exile in Deuteronomy 4 and 28, in line with the dual nature of the Moab covenant (see discussion above), serves both as a potential threat (conditional *if*) and an inevitable future reality (unconditional *when*). The function of the commands must be viewed from both angles. The choice before Israel is a real choice that each generation must make. Israel should be encouraged by Yahweh's proven faithfulness to lead Israel in her journey of faith and to reward those who put their confidence in him.[67] The hope of Yahweh's continued faithfulness beyond exile should motivate Israel in the present ("today") to turn to him whenever she sins. However, from the perspective of the storyline that finds Israel (pen)ultimately in exile, the law also functions as a catalyst and conduit for the manifestation of Israel's stubbornness and unbelief. The law is holy, but Israel is not. Her ultimate refusal to be obedient to what Yahweh commands reveals her deep-seated rejection of Yahweh himself.

The future restoration of Israel causes the law to transcend both these functions. Israel's obedience will still serve as a mirror to her heart, but since the heart will have been transformed, the reflection will be one of trust and confidence in Yahweh. Also, Israel will still be responsible to choose the right path, but she will no longer need the promise of blessing or the threat of curse to motivate her to obedience. Paradoxically, her choice will be inevitable.

### The "Problem" of the Individual

The "problem" of the individual is comparable to the "problems" of history and Israel's ability discussed above. The notion of corporate solidarity conflates the generations so as to speak of one "Israel." Israel's inability to be faithful in the past is evidence that "all Israel" will be unfaithful and ultimately receive the death penalty of exile because her heart remains

---

66. Millar, *Now Choose Life*, 180.

67. Ibid., 204, states that the primary function of the laws is to keep Israel on the move, avoiding stagnation.

uncircumcised throughout her history. What does all this have to do with the individual Israelite? Also, what is the position of the individual with respect to the themes of exile and restoration, both of which are national concerns?

Before looking at Deuteronomy, it is worth noting that this issue is part of the debate taking place in NT studies that we mentioned at the end of chapter 1. Many NT scholars now believe that the normative belief of first-century Jews was that they were still in exile, awaiting the full restoration Yahweh had promised.[68] N. T. Wright, the leading proponent of this view, summarizes the position:

> Most Jews of this period, it seems, would have answered the question 'where are we?' in language which, reduced to its simplest form, meant: we are still in exile. They believed that, in all the senses which mattered, Israel's exile was still in progress. Although she had come back from Babylon, the glorious message of the prophets remained unfulfilled. Israel still remained in thrall to foreigners; worse, Israel's god had not returned to Zion.[69]

It is significant that a systematic approach, such as Wright's, that focuses on exile also tends to de-emphasize the individual. Wright states, for instance,

> Exile will be undone when sin is forgiven.... If [Israel's] sin has caused her exile, her forgiveness will mean her national re-establishment. This needs to be emphasized in the strongest possible terms: the most natural meaning of the phrase 'the forgiveness of sins' to a first-century Jew is not in the first instance the remission of *individual* sins, but the putting away of the whole nation's sins. And, since the exile was the punishment for those sins, the only sure sign that the sins had been forgiven would be the clear and certain liberation from exile. This is the major, national,

---

68. E.g., Wright, *New Testament and the People of God*, 152-66, 268-72, 299-301; idem, *Jesus and the Victory of God*, xvii-xviii, 126-27, 203-6, 268; Evans, "Aspects of Exile and Restoration," 299-328; Hafemann, "Paul and the Exile of Israel," 329-71; Meier, "Jesus, the Twelve, and the Restoration of Israel," 365-404; Bauckham, "Restoration of Israel in Luke–Acts," 435-87; Pate et al., *Story of Israel*, 20-22, 105-18. For the prominence in recent studies of the historical Jesus and Luke–Acts see the references in Bauckham, "Restoration of Israel in Luke-Acts," 437 nn. 7 and 8. See also the references concerning responses to Wright in chap. 1.

69. Wright, New Testament and the People of God, 268-69.

context within which all individual dealing-with-sin must be understood.[70]

While it is beyond the scope of this study to evaluate the merits of these positions,[71] Wright's construct illustrates the "problem" of the individual with which we are concerned.

For all of its national focus, however, Deuteronomy does recognize the existence and significance of the individual.[72] We have discussed the frequent change between singular and plural "you" as Moses addresses the people (i.e., the *Numeruswechsel*). While the focus is usually on the nation as a whole, the presence of this stylistic feature assumes that the

---

70. Ibid., 273 (emphasis original). Cf. Wright, *New Testament and the People of God*, 334: "Individual Jews would find their own 'salvation' through their membership within Israel, that is, within the covenant." See also Wright, *Jesus and the Victory of God*, 271: "From the point of view of a first-century Jew, 'forgiveness of sins' could never simply be a private blessing, though to be sure it was that as well, as Qumran amply testifies. Overarching the situation of the individual was the state of the nation as a whole . . . ." Cf. Schmid and Steck ("Restoration Expectations in the Prophetic Tradition," 59), who argue that within the framework of prophetic salvific statements "[t]he fate of the individual . . . is scarcely included."

71. Wright's de-emphasis of the individual in the NT understanding of repentance and forgiveness has been sharply criticized by, e.g., Stein, "N. T. Wright's *Jesus and the Victory of God*: A Review Article," 211–14. Stein objects to many of Wright's interpretations of texts in which Wright reads a national sense to advice, warnings, and parables of Jesus that appear, on the surface, to speak of individuals. Concerning Wright's use of repentance texts, Stein remarks, "Wright so emphasizes the corporate nature of many of these texts that he neglects (or at least minimizes) their individualistic dimension" (ibid., 212). Also, Stein objects to seeing forgiveness of sins as another way of saying "return from exile": "Clearly, however, this is at best an overstatement. There is much in the Gospels concerning the great joy in heaven over one sinner who repents and receives forgiveness (Luke 15:7, 10). It is difficult to see in Jesus' forgiving the paralytic's sins (Mark 2:1–12), in his forgiving of the sinful woman (Luke 7:36–50), in the story of Zacchaeus (Luke 19:1–10), and in all the accounts of the forgiving of sinners the theme of the return of the nation from exile as being more central than the forgiveness of these individuals. Furthermore, what do we do with such references as Pss 25:18; 32:1, 5; 38:18; 51:2–3; 103:3, 10; 130:4, that speak of individual forgiveness, and the individual sacrifices for forgiveness described in Lev 4:26, 31, 35; 5:10, 13, 16, 18; 6:7; 19:22 and Num 15:27–28" (ibid., 212–13).

72. Critical scholars tend to find an emphasis on the individual arising in the deuteronomic movement in the time of Hezekiah or later with the pre-exilic prophets, Jeremiah and Ezekiel. See, e.g., Halpern, "Jerusalem and the Lineages," 1–107; Sanders, "Exile and Canon Formation," 55–56. Because these scholars also date Deuteronomy relatively late, speaking of some sort of "individualism" in Deuteronomy is not a problem typically. Conservative scholars, however, would argue for a much earlier recognition of the individual, not only from Deuteronomy but also from the Davidic psalms.

nation is made up of individuals, each responsible to heed Moses' words and pass them on to his or her children (e.g., 4:9; 6:20-25). Individuals are also singled out amidst a generation for behaving in contrast to the bent of the nation. Caleb and Joshua alone are faithful at Kadesh-barnea (1:36, 38). Yahweh differentiates between those who followed the Baal of Peor and those who clung to Yahweh (4:3-4). Moses seems to escape the indictment of the nation at Horeb and in the wilderness (9:6—10:11). Finally, the individual who breaks the covenant by committing idolatry is sifted out from the community by Yahweh, who himself exacts judgment on the person (29:17-20).

These examples raise a series of tensions and questions about the role of the individual. The first issue concerns the relationship between individual and national disobedience. Individual lawbreakers, of course, can be dealt with in a way that prevents the community from suffering. This is done through punishment of the individual either by humans (e.g., much of the legislation in chaps. 12-26) or by Yahweh himself (27:15-26; 29:19-20).[73] The curses in chapter 28, however, concentrate on national disobedience and judgment. The inference is that the corporate judgment, climaxing in exile, will come when a majority, if not all, of the people prove unfaithful. But how does this square with the sense of inevitability we have established for the curses in chapter 28? The answer must be that the indictment against the nation of being stubborn (קשה [ערף], "stiff [of neck]"; 9:6, 13; 31:27; cf. verb form in 10:16) and rebellious (מרה; 9:7, 24; 31:27[2x]) applies to each individual within the nation. Similar terminology is used in 29:18, where the individual thinks to himself, "I shall be safe, though I walk in the stubbornness of my heart."[74] In the latter case, the individual transgressor is a picture of the nation, evidenced by Moses' abrupt shift in 29:21 to the consequences of covenant breach for the nation (29:21-27). Millar seems to have it

---

73. Deut 29:20-21 explicitly states Yahweh will single the individual out. The list of curses against individuals in 27:15-26 ("Cursed be anyone who . . .") do not specify concrete (human-enacted) punishment for offence since the sins in view are those which are committed in secret. The assumption is that Yahweh, who alone knows the sin, exacts the punishment. See Bellefontaine, "Curses of Deuteronomy 27," 58; Weinfeld, *Deuteronomy and the Deuteronomic School*, 276-78. The formal connection between chaps. 27-28 (see chap. 3) suggests that the curses in view in chap. 27 are somehow related to the curses in chap. 28, which involve punishments meted out by Yahweh himself.

74. The word for "stubbornness" here is שרר, a synonym of קשה. Note also the "stubborn" (סרר) and "rebellious" (מרה) son in 21:18, 20.

right: "National catastrophe results from national breach of covenant. The likelihood of each individual falling into apostasy translates into the nation as a whole spurning the grace of Yahweh."[75]

This leads into a second issue: how does the position of universal corruption account for the presence of righteous individuals? In the case of Israel displaying corporate fidelity, the answer was that such displays were temporary and/or external.[76] This same logic might explain many individual acts of righteousness as well (e.g., 4:4), but cannot explain every instance. The assessment of Caleb is especially noteworthy: "he has wholly followed Yahweh" (1:36). Caleb's obedience seems to be an outworking of an internal disposition of fidelity.[77] Did Caleb (and Joshua) somehow escape the Israelite (and human) plight of heart rebellion? It is difficult to answer this question within the bounds of Deuteronomy, but we will attempt a conjecture. Certain individuals like Caleb (I would include, at least, Joshua and Moses) appear already to possess what the nation as a whole lacks: a circumcised heart. We know that, within the divine plan, the nation will only receive this after the exile (30:6), but since Yahweh is the one who must give such a heart (cf. 29:3), perhaps he chooses to dispense it to certain individuals beforehand. These positive examples of faithfulness, then, would serve both to condemn the nation for its lack and to offer hope by pointing to the reality that awaits all Israel in the future. All this reasoning (and, admittedly, theological bias), however, takes us too far afield from the text. The tension must be allowed to stand.

The presence of righteous individuals in the nation brings us to the third issue: what about the individual and the exile? It is possible that when Israel is exiled there are no righteous individuals among the people. In this case there would be no problem, for every person would

---

75. Millar, *Now Choose Life*, 174. Cf. Driver, *Critical and Exegetical Commentary on Deuteronomy*, 326.

76. The difference between external and internal participation in the covenant was noted in the discussion of chap. 29. The renewal of the covenant in vv. 9–14, which shows the nation's outward willingness to abide by the covenant, comes between the darker realities of the absence of the right heart (v. 3) and future judgment (vv. 21–27).

77. Cf. the description of Caleb in Num 14:24 as a man who "has a different spirit and has followed me fully . . . ." Though Joshua is not described the same way explicitly, his constant connection with Caleb as faithful spies and as exceptions to Yahweh's judgment on the people implies that Joshua also should be viewed in the same way as Caleb.

receive his or her just deserts. If we assume that there are righteous individuals, what will become of them? It appears that they will be exiled along with the others, receiving the indictment and judgment that befalls the nation as a whole. This is prefigured already in the person of Moses. Though Moses was not perfect (cf. 32:51), he would certainly be classified as one of the righteous. His death—his loss of the land—is due, in large part, to the sins of the people (1:37; 3:26; 4:21). Like all other Israelites—righteous and unrighteous—Moses' "restoration" rests in the future restoration of the nation.

Deuteronomy does not add much to a development of the "remnant" motif.[78] The few who remain through the experience of exile are "left . . . among the nations" (4:27)—not to be spared because of their righteousness, but to suffer the concomitant curses of forced idolatry (4:28; 28:64), psychological trauma (28:65–67), and slavery (28:68). Recalling the sinful individual within the community in 29:17–20, there is no contrasting parallel that pictures Yahweh singling out a righteous individual to avoid judgment. Otherwise, exile would be amputation, not death. Moreover, 30:1–10 envisions the restoration of *all* Israel. It entails resurrection from the dead, not mere survival through devastation.

Deuteronomy has plenty to say about the individual, but only enough to frustrate the reader asking the sort of questions we have posed here. The theme of exile does subsume the concerns of the individual into a larger, corporate sphere. Thus, righteous individuals, in the day of judgment, would not escape exile (cf. Daniel and his friends). Nevertheless, the individual is not lost altogether. The restoration of Israel includes the restoration of each individual within the nation. Thus, what may be prefigured in individuals like Joshua and Caleb is the hope for all of God's people. Therefore, those who draw on Deuteronomy for its themes of exile and restoration—such as Wright and other NT scholars[79]—would do well to pay attention to what it offers concerning the individual.

---

78. This is supported by the near absence of references to Deuteronomy in the classic work on the development of remnant theology: Hasel, *Remnant*.

79. See chap. 1 for Wright's references to Deuteronomy. Cf. Bauckham ("Restoration of Israel in Luke–Acts," 435), who locates the primary sources of hope in Deut 30–33 and Isa 40–66. See also Harrington, "Interpreting Israel's History," 59–68. Hafemann ("Paul and the Exile of Israel," 344) argues that "curse of the Law" in Gal 3:10 is taken from Deut 27–32 "read as a conceptual whole." Evans ("Aspects of Exile and Restoration," 327), however, thinks Jesus drew on the traditions of Daniel, Zechariah, and Second Isaiah, but Evans makes no mention of Deuteronomy.

# Bibliography

Ackroyd, Peter R. *Exile and Restoration: A Study of Hebrew Thought of the Sixth Century B. C.* OTL. Philadelphia: Westminster, 1968.
Aejmelaeus, A. "Function and Interpretation of *kî* in Biblical Hebrew." *JBL* 105 (1986): 193-209.
Albright, William F. *From the Stone Age to Christianity: Monotheism and the Historical Process.* Garden City, NY: Doubleday, 1957.
Alt, Albrecht. *Essays on Old Testament History and Religion.* Sheffield: JSOT Press, 1989.
Alter, Robert. *The Art of Biblical Narrative.* New York: Basic Books, 1981.
Amsler, S. "La motivation de l'éthique dans la par én èse due Deut éronome." In *Beiträge zur alttestamentlichen Theologie: Festschrift für Walther Zimmerilie*, ed. H. Donner, R. Hanhart, and R. Smend, 11-22. Göttingen: Vandenhoeck & Ruprecht, 1977.
Anbar, M. "The Story of the Building of an Altar on Mount Ebal." In *Das Deuteronomium: Entstehung, Gestalt und Botschaft*, ed. Norbert Lohfink, 304-10. BETL, no. 68. Leuven: Leuven University Press, 1985.
Andersen, Francis I. "The Theology of Deuteronomy 27." *TynBul* 49 (1998): 277-303.
Arnold, Bill T. "בוא." In *NIDOTTE* 1:615-18.
Austel, Hermann J. "שָׁמַד." In *TWOT* 2:935.
Baker, David W. "נהג." In *NIDOTTE* 3:42-43.
Baltzer, Klaus. *The Covenant Formulary in Old Testament, Jewish, and Early Christian Writings.* Philadelphia: Fortress, 1971.
Barker, Paul A. *The Triumph of Grace in Deuteronomy: Faithless Israel, Faithful Yahweh in Deuteronomy.* Paternoster Biblical Monographs. Philadelphia: Paternoster, 2004.
———. "The Theology of Deuteronomy 27." *TynBul* 49 (1998): 277-303.
Barr, James. *The Concept of Biblical Theology: An Old Testament Perspective.* Minneapolis: Fortress, 1999.
———. *The Semantics of Biblical Language.* Oxford: Oxford University Press, 1961.
———. "Common Sense and Biblical Language." *Bib* 49 (1968): 377-87.
Barstad, Hans. *The Myth of the Empty Land: A Study in the History and Archaeology of Judah During the "Exilic" Period.* SO, no. 28. Oslo: Scandinavian University Press, 1996.
Barton, John, and David J. Reimer, eds. *After the Exile: Essays in Honor of Rex Mason.* Macon, GA: Mercer University Press, 1996.
Barth, C. "נָתַץ *nātaṣ*." In *TDOT* 10:108-14.
Bauckham, Richard. "The Restoration of Israel in Luke-Acts." In *Restoration: Old Testament, Jewish, and Christian Conceptions*, ed. James M. Scott, 435-87. JSJSup, no. 72. Leiden: Brill, 2001.
Baumann, Eberhard. "שוב שבות. Eine exegetische Untersuchung." *ZAW* 47 (1929): 17-44.

Begg, Christopher. "'Bread, Wine, and Strong Drink' in Deut 29:5a." *Bijdragen* 41 (1980): 266–75.

———. "The Literary Criticism of Deut 4,1–40: Contributions to a Continuing Discussion," *ETL* 56 (1980): 10–55.

Bellefontaine, Elizabeth. "The Curses of Deuteronomy 27: Their Relationship to the Prohibitives." In *A Song of Power and the Power of Song: Essays on the Book of Deuteronomy*, ed. Duane L. Christensen, 256–68. SBTS, vol. 3. Winona Lake, IN: Eisenbrauns, 1993.

Blenkinsopp, Joseph. *The Pentateuch: An Introduction to the First Five Books of the Bible*. New York: Doubleday, 1992.

Block, Daniel I. *The Gods of the Nations*. 2nd ed. ETS Studies: Studies in Ancient Near Eastern National Theology. Grand Rapids: Baker, 2000.

———. *The Gospel According to Moses: A Commentary on Deuteronomy*. Draft, Spring 2005.

———. "The Burden of Leadership: The Mosaic Paradigm of Kingship (Deut. 17:14–20)." *BSac* 162 (2005): 259–78.

———. "How Many is God? An Investigation into the Meaning of Deuteronomy." *JETS* 47 (2004): 193–212.

———. "The Privilege of Calling: The Mosaic Paradigm for Missions (Deut. 26:16–19)." *BSac* 162 (2005): 387–405.

———. "Recovering the Voice of Moses: The Genesis of Deuteronomy." *JETS* 44 (2001): 385–408.

Blomberg, Craig. "The Wright Stuff: A Critical Overview of *Jesus and the Victory of God*." In *Jesus and the Restoration of Israel: A Critical Assessment of N. T. Wright's Jesus and the Victory of God*, ed. Carey C. Newman, 19–39. Downers Grove, IL: InterVarsity, 1999.

Boorer, Suzanne. *The Promise of the Land as Oath: A Key to the Formation of the Pentateuch*. BZAW, no. 205. Berlin: de Gruyter, 1992.

Botterweck, G. Johannes, et al., eds. *TDOT*. Translated by John T. Willis et al. 14 vols to date. Grand Rapids: Eerdmans, 1974–.

Braulik, Georg. *Deuteronomium*. 2 vols. Die Neue Echter Bibel. Würzburg: Echter Verlag, 1986, 1992.

———. *Die Mittel deuteronomischer Rhetorik*. AnBib, no. 68. Rome: Biblical Institute Press, 1978.

———. "Die Ausdrücke für Gestz im Buch Deuteronomium." *Bib* 51 (1970): 39–66.

———. "Review of Mittmann, *Deuteronomium 1:1—6:3 Literarkritisch und traditionsgeschichtlich untersucht*." *Bib* 59 (1978): 351–78.

———. "The Sequence of the Laws in Deuteronomy 12–26." Translated by L. M. Maloney. In *A Song of Power and the Power of Song: Essays on the Book of Deuteronomy*, ed. Duane L. Christensen, 313–35. SBTS, vol. 3. Winona Lake, IN: Eisenbrauns, 1993.

Bright, John. *History of Israel*. 3rd ed. Philadelphia: Westminster, 1981.

Brown, Colin, ed. *NIDNTT*. Translated by C. Brown with additions and revisions. 3 vols. Grand Rapids: Zondervan, 1975, 1976, 1978.

Brown, Francis, et al. *The Brown-Driver-Briggs Hebrew and English Lexicon*. Peabody, MA: Hendrickson, 1996.

Brueggemann, Walter. *Cadences of Home: Preaching Among Exiles*. Louisville: Westminster John Knox, 1997.

———. *Deuteronomy*. Nashville: Abingdon, 2001.

———. *The Land: Place as Gift, Promise and Challenge in Biblical Faith.* 2nd ed. OBT. Minneapolis: Fortress, 2002.

———. *Theology of the Old Testament: Testimony, Dispute, Advocacy.* Minneapolis: Fortress, 1997.

———. *To Build, To Plant: A Commentary on Jeremiah 26–52.* Grand Rapids: Eerdmans, 1991.

———. "Imagination as a Mode of Fidelity." In *Understanding the Word: Essays in Honour of B. W. Anderson*, ed. J. T. Butler, et al., 1–27. JSOTSup, no. 37. Sheffield: JSOT Press, 1985.

———. "A Shattered Transcendence? Exile and Restoration." In *Biblical Theology: Problems and Perspectives: In Honor of J. Christiaan Beker*, ed. Stephen J. Kraftchick, et al., 169–72. Nashville: Abingdon, 1995.

———. "Weariness, Exile and Chaos (A Motif in Royal Theology)." *CBQ* 34 (1972): 19–38.

Brueggemann, Walter, and Hans W. Wolff. *The Vitality of Old Testament Traditions.* Atlanta: John Knox, 1975.

Bryan, Steven M. "Jesus and Israel's Traditions of Judgment and Restoration." PhD diss., University of Cambridge, 1999.

Buis, Pierre. "Deutéronome xxvii 15–26: Malédictions on exigences de l'alliance." *VT* 17 (1967): 478–79.

Buis, Pierre, and Jacques Leclerq. *Le Deutéronome.* Sources bibliques. Paris: Gabalda, 1963.

Cairns, Ian. *Deuteronomy: Word and Presence.* International Theological Commentary. Grand Rapids: Eerdmans, 1992.

Carmichael, Calcum M. *Law and Narrative in the Bible.* Ithaca, NY: Cornell University Press, 1985.

———. *The Laws of Deuteronomy.* Ithaca, NY: Cornell University Press, 1974.

———. "A Singular Method of Codification of Law in the Mishpatim," *ZAW* 84 (1972): 19–24.

Carroll R., M. Daniel. "נדח." In *NIDOTTE* 3:34–35.

———. "פוץ." In *NIDOTTE* 3:585–89.

Carroll, Robert P. "Deportation and Diasporic Discourses in the Prophetic Literature." In *Exile: Old Testament, Jewish, and Christian Conceptions*, ed. James M. Scott, 63–85. JSJSup, no.56. Leiden: Brill, 1997.

———. "Exile! What Exile? Deportation and the Discourse of Diaspora." In *Leading Captivity Captive: 'The Exile' as History and Ideology.*, ed. Leslie L. Grabbe, 62–79. JSOTSup, no. 278. Sheffield: Sheffield Academic, 1998.

Carson, D. A. *Exegetical Fallacies.* 2nd ed. Grand Rapids: Baker, 1996.

Carson, D. A., et al., eds. *Justification and Variegated Nomism.* Vol. 1 of *The Complexities of Second Temple Judaism.* Grand Rapids: Baker, 2001.

———. *The Paradoxes of Paul.* Vol. 2 of *The Complexities of Second Temple Judaism.* Grand Rapids: Baker, forthcoming.

Casey, Maurice. "Where Wright Is Wrong: A Critical Review of N. T. Wright's *Jesus and the Victory of God.*" *JSNT* 69 (1998): 95–103.

Cazelles, H. "Passages in the Singular within Discourse in the Plural of Dt 1–4." *CBQ* 29 (1967): 213–14.

Childs, Brevard S. *Introduction to the Old Testament as Scripture.* Philadelphia: Fortress, 1979.

———. *Old Testament Theology in a Canonical Context.* Philadelphia: Fortress, 1985.

———. "Retrospective Reading of the Old Testament Prophets." *ZAW* 108 (1996): 362–77.

Cholewinski, Alfred "Zur theologischen Deutung des Moabbundes." *Bib* 66 (1985): 96–111.

Christensen, Duane L. *Deuteronomy 1–11.* WBC, vol. 6A. Dallas: Word, 1991.

———. *Deuteronomy 1—21:9.* Rev. ed. WBC, vol. 6A. Nashville: Thomas Nelson, 2001.

———. *Deuteronomy 21:10—34:12.* WBC, vol. 6B. Nashville: Thomas Nelson, 2002.

———. "The *Numeruswechsel* in Deuteronomy 12." In *A Song of Power and the Power of Song,* ed. D. L. Christensen, 394–402. SBTS, vol. 3. Winona Lake, IN: Eisenbrauns, 1993.

———. "Two Stanzas of a Hymn in Deuteronomy 33." *Bib* 65 (1984): 382–89.

———, ed. *A Song of Power and the Power of Song: Essays on the Book of Deuteronomy.* Sources for Biblical and Theological Study, vol. 3. Winona Lake, IN: Eisenbrauns, 1993.

Clements, Ronald E. *Deuteronomy.* OTG. Sheffield: JSOT Press, 1989.

Clines, David J. A. *The Theme of the Pentateuch.* JSOTSup, no. 10. 2nd ed. Sheffield: Sheffield Academic, 1989.

Coggins, Richard J. "The Exile: History and Ideology." *ExpTim* 110 (1999): 389–93.

Cohen, Gary G. "שָׁבָה." In *TWOT* 2:895–96.

Coppes, Leonard J. "נָהַג." In *TWOT* 2:558–59.

———. "נָדַח." In *TWOT* 2:556–57.

———. "קָבַץ." In *TWOT* 2:783–84.

Craigie, Peter C. *The Book of Deuteronomy.* NICOT. Grand Rapids: Eerdmans, 1976.

———. "Deuteronomy and Ugaritic Studies." In *A Song of Power and the Power of Song: Essays on the Book of Deuteronomy,* ed. Duane L. Christensen, 109–122. SBTS, vol. 3. Winona Lake, IN: Eisenbrauns, 1993.

Cross, Frank M., Jr. *Canaanite Myth and Hebrew Epic.* Cambridge, MA: Harvard University Press, 1973.

———. "The Themes of the Book of Kings and the Structure of the Deuteronomistic History." In *Reconsidering Israel and Judah: Recent Studies on the Deuteronomistic History,* ed. J. G. McConville and G. N. Knoppers, 79–94. SBTS, vol. 8. Winona Lake, IN: Eisenbrauns, 2000.

Crüsemann, Frank. *The Torah: Theology and Social History of Old Testament Law.* Minneapolis: Fortress, 1996.

Davies, Philip R. *In Search of 'Ancient Israel'.* JSOTSup, no. 148. Sheffield: JSOT Press, 1992.

De Tillesse, G. Minette. "Sections 'Tu' et section 'Vous' dans le Deutéronome." *VT* 12 (1962): 29–87.

DeRouchie, Jason S. "A Call to Covenant Love: Text Grammar and Literary Structure in Deuteronomy 5–11." PhD diss., The Southern Baptist Theological Seminary, Louisville, 2005.

Dever, William G. *What Did the Biblical Writers Know and When Did They Know It?* Grand Rapids: Eerdmans, 2001.

Diepold, Peter. *Israels Land.* Beiträge zur Wissenschaft vom Alten und Neuen Testament, no. 15. Stuttgart: Kohlhammer, 1972.

Dietrich, Ernst Ludwig. "שׁוּב שְׁבוּת. Die Endzeitliche Wiederherstellung bei den Propheten." Beiheft zur *ZAW,* no. 40. Giessen: Alfred Töpelmann, 1925.

Dietrich, Walter. *Prophetie und Geschichte*. FRLANT, no. 108. Göttingen: Vandenhoeck & Ruprecht, 1972.
Donner, Herbert. *An Israelite and Judean History*. Edited by J. M. Miller and J. H. Hayes. Old Testament Library. Philadelphia: Westminster, 1977.
———. "The Separate States of Israel and Judah." In *Israelite and Judean History*, ed. J. Maxwell Miller and John H. Hayes, 381–434. OTL. Philadelphia: Westminster, 1977.
Driver, G. R. "Hebrew Roots and Words." *WO* 1 (1950): 406–15.
Driver, Samuel. R. *A Critical and Exegetical Commentary on Deuteronomy*. 2$^{nd}$ ed. ICC. Edinburgh: T. & T. Clark, 1902.
Dumbrell, William J. "רדף." In *NIDOTTE* 3:1057–62.
Elliger, Karl, and Wilhelm Rudolph, eds. *BHS*. Stuttgart: Deutsch Bibelgesellschaft, 1977.
Els, J. J. S. "לקח." In *NIDOTTE* 2:812–17.
Evans, Craig A. "Aspects of Exile and Restoration in the Proclamation of Jesus and the Gospels." In *Exile: Old Testament, Jewish, and Christian Conceptions*, ed. James M. Scott, 299–328. JSJSup, no. 56. Leiden: Brill, 1997.
———. "Jesus and the Continuing Exile of Israel." In *Jesus and the Restoration of Israel: A Critical Assessment of N. T. Wright's* Jesus and the Victory of God, ed. Carey C. Newman, 77–100. Downers Grove, IL: InterVarsity, 1999.
Even-Shoshan, Abraham, ed. *A New Concordance of the Bible*. Jerusalem: Kiryat Sefer, 1990.
Fensham, F. Charles. "Malediction and Benediction in Ancient Near Eastern Vassal-Treaties and the Old Testament." In *A Song of Power and the Power of Song: Essays on the Book of Deuteronomy*, ed. Duane L. Christensen, 247–55. SBTS, vol. 3. Winona Lake, IN: Eisenbrauns, 1993.
Fishbane, Michael. *Biblical Interpretation in Ancient Israel*. Oxford: Clarendon, 1985.
Fisher, Milton C. "נָתַץ." In *TWOT* 2:609–10.
Foster, Raymond S. *The Restoration of Israel: The Return from the Exile*. London: Darton, Longman and Todd, 1970.
Frankena, R. "The Vassal Treaties of Esarhaddon and the Dating of Deuteronomy." *OTS* 14 (1965): 122–54.
Freedman, David Noel. "Divine Commitment and Human Obligation: The Covenant Theme." *Int* 18 (1964): 419–31.
Friedman, Richard Elliott. "From Egypt to Egypt: Dtr$^1$ and Dtr$^2$." In *Traditions in Transformation*, ed. Baruch Halpern and Jon D. Levenson, 167–92. Winona Lake, IN: Eisebrauns, 1981.
García Martínez, et al., eds. *Studies in Deuteronomy in Honour of C. J. Labuschagne on the Occasion of his 65$^{th}$ Birthday*. VTSup, no. 53. Leiden: Brill, 1994.
———. "Analyse littéraire de Deutéronome, V–XI." *RB* 84 (1977): 481–522.
———. "Analyse littéraire de Deutéronome, V–XI." *RB* 85 (1978): 5–49.
Ginsberg, H. L. *The Israelian Heritage in Judaism*. New York: Jewish Theological Seminary, 1982.
Goldingay, John E. *Theological Diversity and the Authority of the Old Testament*. Grand Rapids: Eerdmans, 1987.
Gowan, Donald E. *Theology of the Prophetic Books: The Death and Resurrection of Israel*. Louisville: Westminster John Knox, 1998.
———. "The Beginnings of Exile-Theology and the Root *glh*." *ZAW* 87 (1975): 204–7.

———. "The Exile in Jewish Apocalyptic." In *Scripture in History and Theology: Essays in Honor of J. Coert Rylaarsdam*, ed. A. L. Merill and T. W. Overholt, 205-23. PTMS, no. 17. Pittsburgh: Pickwick, 1977.

Grabbe, Lester L., ed. *Can a "History of Israel" Be Written?* JSOTSup, no. 245. Sheffield: JSOT Press, 1997.

———. *Leading Captivity Captive: 'The Exile' as History and Ideology*. JSOTSup, no. 278. European Seminar in Historical Methodology, no. 2. Sheffield: Sheffield Academic, 1998.

Gross, W. "נהג." In *TDOT* 9:255-59.

Gruber, M. I. "Hebrew *da 'ăbôn nepeš* 'Dryness of Throat': From Symptom to Literary Convention." *VT* 37 (1987): 365-69.

Gunn, David M. "New Directions in the Study of Biblical Hebrew Narrative." In *Reconsidering Israel and Judah: Recent Studies on the Deuteronomistic History*, ed. J. G. McConville and G. N. Knoppers, 566-77. SBTS, vol. 8. Winona Lake, IN: Eisenbrauns, 2000.

Habel, Norman C. *The Land is Mine: Six Biblical Land Ideologies*. OBT. Minneapolis: Fortress, 1995.

Hafemann, Scott J. "Paul and the Exile of Israel in Galatians 3-4." In *Exile: Old Testament, Jewish, and Christian Conceptions*, ed. James M. Scott, 329-71. JSJSup, no. 56. Leiden: Brill, 1997.

Hall, Gary H. "שמד." In *NIDOTTE* 4:151-52.

Halpern, Baruch. *The First Historians: The Hebrew Bible and History*. San Francisco: Harper & Row, 1988.

———. "Jerusalem and the Lineages in the seventh century BCE: Kinship and the Rise of Individual Moral Liability." In *Law and Ideology in Monarchic Israel*, ed. Baruch Halpern and D. W. Hobson, 1-107. JSOTSup, no. 124. Sheffield: Sheffield Academic, 1991.

Hamilton, Victor P. "פוץ." In *TWOT* 2:719-20.

———. "שוב." In *TWOT* 2:909-10.

Haran, Menahem. "Behind the Scenes of History: Determining the Date of the Priestly Source." *JBL* 100 (1981): 321-33.

Harrington, D. J. "Interpreting Israel's History: The *Testament of Moses* as a Rewriting of Deut. 31-34." In *Studies on the Testament of Moses*, ed. G. W. E. Nickelsburg, 59-68. SBLSCS, no. 4. Missoula, MT: Scholars Press, 1973.

Harris, R. L., et al., eds. *TWOT*. 2 vols. Chicago: Moody, 1980.

———. "אָבַד." In *TWOT* 1:3-4.

Hasel, Gerhard F. *The Remnant: The History and Theology of the Remnant Idea from Genesis to Isaiah*. Berrien Springs, MI: Andrews University Press, 1972.

Hatch, Edwin, and Henry A. Redpath. *A Concordance to the Septuagint and Other Greek Versions of the Old Testmaent (Including the Apocryphal Books)*. 2nd ed. Grand Rapids: Baker, 1998.

Hatina, Thomas R. "Exile." In *Dictionary of New Testament Background*, ed. C. A. Evans and S. E. Porter, 348-51. Downers Grove, IL: InterVarsity, 2000.

Head, Peter M. "The Curse of Covenant Reversal: Deuteronomy 28:58-68 and Israel's Exile." *Churchman* 111 (1997): 218-26.

Hermann, Siegfried. "Die konstruktive Restauration: Das Deuteronomium als Mitte biblischer Theologie." In *Probleme biblischer Theologie: Gerhard von Rad zum 70. Geburtsag*, ed. Hans W. Wolff, 155-70. Munich: Kaiser, 1971.

Hillers, Delbert R. *Treaty-Curses and the Old Testament Prophets*. Biblica et orientalia, no. 16. Rome: Pontifical Biblical Institute, 1964.

Hoffman, Yair. "The Deuteronomist and the Exile." In *Pomegranates and Golden Bells: Studies in Biblical, Jewish, and Near Eastern Ritual, Law, and Literature in Honor of Jacob Milgrom*, ed. D. P. Wright, et al., 659–76. Winona Lake, IN: Eisenbrauns, 1995.

Holladay, William L. *The Root šûbh in the Old Testament with Particular Reference to its Usages in Covenantal Contexts*. Leiden: Brill, 1958.

Holter, Knut. "Literary Critical Studies of Deut 4: Some Criteriological Remarks." *BN* 81 (1996): 91–103.

Howard, David M., Jr. "גלה." In *NIDOTTE* 1:861–64.

———. "דבר." In *NIDOTTE* 1:912.

———. "שבה." In *NIDOTTE* 4:18–19.

Hurvitz, Avi. "The Evidence of Language in Dating the Priestly Code." *RB* 81 (1974): 24–56.

Jenni, Ernst. "אבד *'bd* to punish." In *TLOT* 1:13–15.

———. "בוא *bô'* to come." In *TLOT* 1:201–4.

———. "Faktitiv und Kausativ von אבד, zugrunde gehen." VTSup 16 (1967): 143–57.

Jenni, Ernst, and Claus Westermann, eds. *TLOT*. Translated by Mark E. Biddle. 3 vols. Peabody, MA: Hendrickson, 1997.

Johnson, Luke Timothy. "An Historiographical Response to Wright's Jesus." In *Jesus and the Restoration of Israel: A Critical Assessment of N. T. Wright's* Jesus and the Victory of God, ed. Carey C. Newman, 210–16. Downers Grove, IL: InterVarsity, 1999.

Joüon, Paul. *A Grammer of Biblical Hebrew*. 2 vols. Translated and revised by T. Muraoka. Subsidia Biblica, no. 14. Rome: Editrice Pontificio Istituto Biblico, 1996.

Kaiser, Walter C. "לָקַח." In *TWOT* 1:481–82.

Kaukfman, Stephen A. "The Structure of the Deuteronomic Law." *Maarav* 1–2 (1978–79): 105–58.

Kaufmann, Yehezkel. *From the Babylonian Captivity to the End of Prophecy*. Vol. 4 of *The History of the Religion of Israel*. Translated by C. W. Effroymson. New York: Ktav, 1977.

Kitchen, Kenneth A. *Ancient Orient and the Old Testament*. Chicago: Inter-Varsity, 1966.

———. *The Bible in its World: The Bible and Archaeology Today*. Downers Grove, IL: InterVarsity, 1979.

———. *On the Reliability of the Old Testament*. Grand Rapids: Eerdmans, 2003.

———. "Ancient Orient, 'Deuteronomism,' and the Old Testament." In *New Perspectives on the Old Testament*, ed. J. B. Payne, 1–23. Waco: Word, 1970.

———. "The Fall and Rise of Covenant, Law and Treaty." *TynBul* 40 (1989): 118–35.

Kittel, G., and G. Friedrich, eds. *TDNT*. 10 vols. Translated and edited by Geoffrey W. Bromiley. Grand Rapids: Eerdmas, 1964–76.

Klein, Ralph W. *Israel in Exile: A Theological Interpretation*. Philadelphia: Fortress, 1979.

Kleinert, P. *Untersuchungen zur alttestamentlichen Rechts- und Literaturgeschichte I: Das Deuteronomium und der Deuteronomiker*. Leipzig: Velhagen & Klassing, 1872.

Kline, Meredith G. *By Oath Assigned: A Reinterpretation of the Covenant Signs of Circumcision and Baptism*. Grand Rapids: Eerdmans, 1968.

———. *The Structure of Biblical Authority*. Grand Rapids: Eerdmans, 1972.

———. *The Treaty of the Great King: The Covenant Structure of Deuteronomy.* Grand Rapids: Eerdmans, 1963.
Klingbeil, M. G. "Exile." In *Dictionary of the Old Testament: Pentateuch*, ed. T. Desmond Alexander and David W. Baker, 246–49. Downers Grove, IL: InterVarsity, 2003.
Knapp, Dietrich. *Deuteronomium 4: Literarische Analyse und theologische Interpretation.* Göttingen: Vandenhoeck & Ruprecht, 1987.
Knibb, Michael A. *The Qumran Community.* Cambridge: Cambridge University Press, 1987.
———. "The Exile in the Literature of the Intertestamental Period." *Heythrop Journal* 17 (1976): 253–72.
Knoppers, Gary N. *Two Nations Under God: The Deuteronomistic History of Solomon and the Dual Monarchies.* 2 vols. HSM, nos. 52–53. Atlanta: Scholars, 1993, 1994.
Kraabel, A. T. "Unity and Diversity among Diasporia Synagogues." In *The Synagogue in Late Antiquity*, ed. Lee I. Levine, 49–60. Philadelphia: American Schools of Oriental Research, 1987.
Kühlewein, S. "רחק *rḥq* to be distant." In *TLOT* 3:1230–32.
Labuschagne, C. J. *Deuteronomium.* Vol. 1A. De Prediking van het Oude Testament. Nijkerk: Uitgeverij Callenbach, 1987.
Lemaire, André. "Concerning the Redactional History of the Books of Kings." In *Reconsidering Israel and Judah: Recent Studies on the Deuteronomistic History*, ed. J. G. McConville and G. N. Knoppers, 446–61. SBTS, vol. 8. Winona Lake, IN: Eisenbrauns, 2000.
Lemche, Niels P. *Ancient Israel: A New History of Israelite Society.* Biblical Seminar. Sheffield: JSOT Press, 1988.
———. *Early Israel.* VTSup, no. 37. Leiden: Brill, 1985.
Lenchak, Timothy A. *"Choose Life": A Rhetorical-Critical Investigation of Deut 28, 69—30, 20.* AnBib, no. 129. Rome: Pontifical Biblical Institute, 1993.
Levenson, Jon D. *The Death and Resurrection of a Beloved Son.* New Haven: Yale University Press, 1993.
Lewy, I. "The Puzzle of Dueteronomy 27: Blessings Announced, but Curses Noted." *VT* 12 (1962): 207–11.
Liddell, H. G., and R. Scott. *Greek-English Lexicon.* Revised and supplemented. Oxford: Clarendon, 1996.
Lohfink, Norbert. *Das Hauptgebot: Eine Untersuchung literarischer Einleitungsfragen zu Dtn 5–11.* AnBib, no. 20. Rome: Pontifical Biblical Institute, 1963.
———. *Die Väter Israels im Deuteronomium: Mit einer Stellungnahme von Thomas Römer.* OBO, no. 111. Göttingen: Vandenhoeck & Ruprecht, 1991.
———. *'Höre Israel!' Auslegung von Texten aus dem Buch Deuteronomium.* Die Welt der Bibel, no. 18. Düsseldorf: Patmos, 1965.
———. "Auslegung deuteronomischer Texte: IV. Verkündigung des Hauptgebots in der jüngsten Schicht des Deuteronomiums (Dt 4,1–40)." *BK* 19 (1964): 247–56.
———. "The Cult Reform of Josiah of Judah: II Kings 22–23 as a Source for the History of Israelite Religion." In *Ancient Israelite Religion: Essays in Honor of Frank Moore Cross*, ed. P. D. Hanson, 459–75. Philadelphia: Fortress, 1987.
———. "Darstellungskunst und Theologie in Dtn 1,6—3,29." *Bib* 41 (1960): 105–134.
———. "Der Bundesschluß im Land Moab: Redaktionsgeschichtliches zu Dt 28,69—32,47." *BZ* 6 (1962): 32–56.

――. "Deutéronome et *Pentateuque*: État de la recherche." In *Le Pentateuque: Débats et recherches*. Lectio Divina, no. 151. Paris: du Cerf, 1992.

――. "Die '*huqqîm umispatim*' im Buch Deuteronomium und ihre Neubegrenzung durch Dtn 12,1." *Bib* 70 (1989): 1–27.

――. "חָרַם *ḥāram*." In *TDOT* 5:180–99.

――. "יָרַשׁ *yrš*." In *TDOT* 6:368–96.

――. "Recent Discussion on 2 Kings 22–23: The State of the Question." In *A Song of Power and the Power of Song: Essays on the Book of Deuteronomy*, ed. Duane L. Christensen, 36–61. SBTS, vol. 3. Winona Lake, IN: Eisenbrauns, 1993.

――. ed. *Das Deuteronomium: Entstehung, Gestalt und Botschaft*. BETL, no. 68. Leuven: Leuven University Press, 1985.

Long, V. Philips, ed. *Israel's Past in Present Research: Essays on Ancient Israelite Historiography*. SBTS, vol. 7. Winona Lake, IN: Eisenbrauns, 1999.

Longman, Tremper, III, and Daniel G. Reid. *God Is a Warrior*. Studies in Old Testament Biblical Theology. Grand Rapids: Zondervan, 1995.

Luyten, J. "Primeval and Eschatological Overtones in the Song of Moses (Dt 32,1–43)." In *Das Deuteronomium: Entstehung, Gestalt und Botschaft*, ed. Norbert Lohfink, 341–47. BETL, vol. 68. Leuven: Leuven University Press, 1985.

Marsh, Clive. "Theological History? N. T. Wright's *Jesus and the Victory of God*." *JSNT* 69 (1998): 77–94.

Martens, Elmer A. "בּוֹא." In *TWOT* 1:93–95.

Mason, Rex. "Restoration." In *The NIDOTTE* 4:137–40.

Mayes, A. D. H. *Deuteronomy*. NCB. Grand Rapids: Eerdmans, 1981.

――. "Deuteronomy 4 and the Literary Criticism of Deuteronomy," *JBL* 100 (1981): 23–51. Reprinted in *A Song of Power and the Power of Song: Essays on the Book of Deuteronomy*, ed. Duane L. Christensen, 195–224. SBTS, vol. 3. Winona Lake, IN: Eisenbrauns, 1993.

――. "Exposition of Deuteronomy 4:25–31." *IBS* 2 (1980): 67–83.

――. "The Nature of Sin and its Origin in the Old Testament." *Irish Theological Quarterly* 40 (1973): 250–63.

――. "On Describing the Purpose of Deuteronomy." *JSOT* 58 (1993): 13–33.

McBride, S. Dean. "Polity of the Covenant People: The Book of Deuteronomy." In *A Song of Power and the Power of Song: Essays on the Book of Deuteronomy*, ed. Duane L. Christensen, 62–77. SBTS, vol. 3. Winona Lake, IN: Eisenbrauns, 1993.

McCarthy, Dennis J. *Treaty and Covenant*. Rev. ed. AnBib, no. 21a. Rome: Pontifical Biblical Institute, 1981.

――. "Notes on the Love of God in Deuteronomy and the Father-Son Relationship Between Yahweh and Israel." *CBQ* 27 (1965): 144–47.

McConville, J. Gordon. *Deuteronomy*. AOTC, vol. 5. Downers Grove, IL: InterVaristy, 2002.

――. *Grace in the End: A Study in Deuteronomic Theology*. Studies in Old Testament Biblical Theology. Grand Rapids: Zondervan, 1993.

――. *Law and Theology in Deuteronomy*. JSOTSup, no. 33. Sheffield: JSOT Press, 1984.

――. "Deuteronomic/-istic Theology." In *NIDOTTE* 4:528–37.

――. "Exodus." In *NIDOTTE* 4:601–5.

———. "Faces of Exile in Old Testament Historiography." In *Israel's Past in Present Research: Essays on Ancient Israelite Historiography*, ed. V. Philips Long, 519-34. SBTS, vol. 7. Winona Lake, IN: Eisenbrauns, 1999.

———. "The Old Testament Historical Books in Modern Scholarship." *Themelios* 22 (1997): 3-13.

———. "Restoration in Deuteronomy and the Deuteronomic Literature." In *Restoration: Old Testament, Jewish, and Christian Conceptions*, ed. James M. Scott, 11-40. JSJSup, no.72. Leiden: Brill, 2001.

———. "Singular Address in the Deuteronomic Law and the Politics of Legal Administration." *JSOT* 97 (2002): 19-36.

McConville, J. Gordon, and Gary N. Knoppers, eds. *Reconsidering Israel and Judah: Recent Studies on the Deuteronomistic History*. SBTS, vol. 8. Winona Lake, IN: Eisenbrauns, 2000.

McConville, J. G., and J. G. Millar. *Time and Place in Deuteronomy*. JSOTSup, no. 179. Sheffield: Sheffield Academic, 1994.

Meier, John P. "Jesus, the Twelve, and the Restoration of Israel." In *Restoration: Old Testament, Jewish, and Christian Conceptions*, ed. James M. Scott, 365-404. JSJSup, no.72. Leiden: Brill, 2001.

Mendenhall, George. *Law and Covenant in Israel and the Ancient Near East*. Pittsburgh: Biblical Colloquium, 1955.

———. "Covenant Forms in Israelite Tradition." *BA* 17 (1954): 50-76.

———. "Samuel's 'Broken *Rîb*': Deuteronomy 32." In *A Song of Power and the Power of Song: Essays on the Book of Deuteronomy*, ed. Duane L. Christensen, 169-80. SBTS, vol. 3. Winona Lake, IN: Eisenbrauns, 1993.

Merendino, Rosario P. *Das Deuteronomische Gesetz: Eine Literarkritische, Gattungs-und Überlieferungsgeschichtliche Untersuchung zu Dt 12-26*. Bonn: P. Hanstein, 1969.

Merrill, Eugene H. *Deuteronomy*. NAC, vol. 4. Nashville: Broadman & Holman, 1994.

Milgrom, Jacob. *Leviticus 23-27*. AB, vol. 3B. New York: Doubleday, 2000.

Millar, J. Gary. *Now Choose Life: Theology and Ethics in Deuteronomy*. Grand Rapids: Eerdmans, 1998.

Millard, A. R. "A Wandering Aramean (Deut 26:5)." *JNES* 39 (1980): 153-55.

Miller, Patrick D. *Deuteronomy*. IBC. Louisville: John Knox, 1990.

———. "The Gift of God: The Deuteronomic Theology of the Land." *Int* 23 (1969): 451-65.

Mittmann, Siegfried. *Deuteronomium 1:1—6:3 literarkritisch und traditionsgeschichtlich untersucht*. Berlin: Töpelmann, 1975.

Moberly, R. W. L. *The Old Testament of the Old Testament: Patriarchal Narratives and Mosaic Yahwism*. OBT. Minneapolis: Fortress, 1992.

Moberly, R. W. L. "Toward an Interpretation of the Shema." In *Theological Exegesis: Essays in Honor of Brevard S. Childs*, ed. Christopher Seitz and K. Greene-McCreight, 124-44. Grand Rapids: Eerdmans, 1999.

Moran, William. L. "The Ancient Near Eastern Background of the Love of God in Deuteronomy." *CBQ* 25 (1963): 77-87.

———. "The End of the Unholy War and the Anti-Exodus." In *A Song of Power and the Power of Song: Essays on the Book of Deuteronomy*, ed. Duane L. Christensen, 147-55. SBTS, vol. 3. Winona Lake, IN: Eisenbrauns, 1993.

Naudé, Jackie A., "חרם." In *NIDOTTE* 2:276-77.

Nelson, Richard D. *The Double Redaction of the Deuteronomistic History*. JSOTSup, no. 18. Sheffield: JSOT Press, 1981.

Neusner, Jacob. *Self-fulfilling Prophecy: Exile and Return in the History of Judaism*. Boston: Beacon, 1987.

Newman, Carey C., ed. *Jesus and the Restoration of Israel: A Critical Assessment of N. T. Wright's Jesus and the Victory of God*. Downers Grove, IL: InterVarsity, 1999.

Newsome, James D., Jr. *By the Waters of Babylon: An Introduction to the History and Theology of the Exile*. Atlanta: John Knox, 1979.

Nicholson, Ernest W. *Deuteronomy and Tradition: Literary and Historical Problems in the Book of Deuteronomy*. Philadelphia: Fortress, 1967.

———. "Covenant in a Century of Study Since Wellhausen." In *A Song of Power and the Power of Song: Essays on the Book of Deuteronomy*, ed. D. L. Christensen, 78–93. SBTS, vol. 3. Winona Lake, IN: Eisenbrauns, 1993.

Niehaus, Jeffrey J. "Deuteronomy: Theology of." In *NIDOTTE* 4:537–44.

Nielsen, E. *Deuteronomium*. Handbuch zum Alten Testament, vol. 1. Tübingen: Mohr Siebeck, 1995.

Noth, Martin. *The Deuteronomistic History*. 2nd ed. JSOTSup, no. 15. Sheffield: JSOT Press, 1981.

———. *A History of the Pentateuchal Traditions*. Translated by Bernard Anderson. Englewood-Cliffs, NJ: Prentice-Hall, 1972.

O'Connell, Robert H. "Deuteronomy VIII 1-20: Asymmetrical Concentricity and the Rhetoric of Providence." *VT* 40 (1990): 437–52.

———. "רחק." In *NIDOTTE* 3:1099–1103.

Oded, Bustenay. *Mass Deportations and Deportees in the Neo-Assyrian Empire*. Wiesbaden: Reichert Verlag, 1979.

———. "Observations on the Israelite/Judean Exiles in Mesopotamia During the Eighth-Sixth Centuries BCE." In *Immigration and Emigration within the Ancient Near East, Festschrift E. Lipinski*, ed. K. van Lerberghe and Antoon Schoors, 205–12. OLA, no. 65. Leuven: Peeters, 1995.

Olson, Dennis T. *The Death of the Old and the Birth of the New*. Chico, CA: Scholars, 1985.

———. *Deuteronomy and the Death of Moses: A Theological Reading*. OBT. Minneapolis: Augsburg, 1994.

Otto, Eckart. *Das Deuteronomium im Pentateuch und Hexateuch*. Forschungen zum Alten Testamentum, no. 30. Tübingen: Mohr Siebeck, 2000.

Otzen, Benedikt. "אָבַד 'ābad." In *TDOT* 1:19–23.

Park, Sang Hoon Park. "שאר." In *NIDOTTE* 4:11–17.

Pate, C. Marvin, et al. *The Story of Israel: A Biblical Theology*. Downers Grove, IL: InterVarsity, 2004.

Paul, Shalom M. *Studies in the Book of the Covenant in the Light of Cuneiform and Biblical Law*. VTSup, no. 18. Leiden: Brill, 1970.

Payne, David F. *Deuteronomy*. DSB. Philadelphia: Westminster, 1985.

Peckham, Brian. "The Composition of Deuteronomy 5–11." In *The Word of the Lord Shall Go Forth: Essays in Honor of David Noel Freedman in Celebration of His Sixtieth Birthday*, ed. Carol L. Meyers and Michael O'Connor, 217–40. American Schools of Oriental Research, no. 1. Winona Lake, IN: Eisenbrauns, 1983.

Perlitt, Lothar. *Bundestheologie im Alten Testament*. Neukirchen: Neukirchener Verlag, 1969.

———. *Deuteronomium*. Biblischer Kommentar: Altes Testament, vol. 5. Neukirchen-Vluyn: Neukirchener Verlag, 1990.

Plöger, J. G. *Literarkritische, forgeschichtliche und stilkritische Untersuchungen zum Deuteronomium*. BBB, no. 26. Bonn: Peter Hanstein, 1967.

Polzin, Robert. *David and the Deuteronomist. Part Three, A Literary Study of the Deuteronomic History*. Bloomington: Indiana University Press, 1993.

———. *Moses and the Deuteronomist. Part One, A Literary Study of the Deuteronomic History*. New York: Seabury, 1980.

———. *Samuel and the Deuteronomist. Part Two, A Literary Study of the Deuteronomic History*. San Francisco: Harper & Row, 1989.

———. "Reporting Speech in the Book of Deuteronomy: Toward a Compositional Analysis of the Deuteronomic History." In *A Song of Power and the Power of Song: Essays on the Book of Deuteronomy*, ed. Duane L. Christensen, 355–74. SBTS, vol. 3. Winona Lake, IN: Eisenbrauns, 1993.

Preuschen, Erwin. "Die Bedeutung שבות שוב im Alten Testament." *ZAW* 15 (1895): 1–74.

Preuss, Horst Dietrich. *Deuteronomium*. Erträge der Forschung, no. 164. Darmstadt: Wissenschaftliche Buchgesellschaft, 1982.

———. "בוא *bô'*." In *TDOT* 2:20–49.

———. "Zum deuteronomistischen Geschichtswerk." *TRu* 58 (1993): 229–64, 341–95.

Price, Robert E. "A Lexico-graphical Study of *glh*, *šbh*, and *šwb* in Reference to Exile in the Tanach." PhD diss., Duke University, 1977.

Pritchard, James B., ed. *ANET*. Princeton: Princeton University Press, 1969.

Rad, Gerhard von. *Deuteronomy: A Commentary*. Translated by Dorothea Barton. OTL. Philadelphia: Westminster, 1966.

———. *Holy War in Ancient Israel*. Translated and edited by Marva J. Dawn. Grand Rapids: Eerdmans, 1991.

———. *The Problem of the Hexateuch and Other Essays*. Translated by E. W. Trueman Dicken. New York: McGraw-Hill, 1966. ET of *Das formgeschichtliche Problem des Hexateuchs*. BWANT, no. 78. Stuttgart: Kohlhammer, 1938.

———. *Studies in Deuteronomy*. SBT. 1st series, no. 9. Chicago: Regnery, 1953.

———. "The Form-Critical Problem of the Hexateuch." In *The Problem of the Hexateuch and Other Essays*, 1–78. Translated by E. W. Trueman Dicken. Philadelphia: Fortress, 1984.

Rahlfs, Alfred, ed. *Septuaginta: Id est Vetus Testamentum graece iuxta LXX interpretes*. Stuttgart: Deutsche Bibelgesellschaft, 1935, 1979.

Raitt, Thomas M. *The Problem of the Process of Transmission in the Pentateuch*. JSOTSup, no. 89. Sheffield: JSOT Press, 1990.

———. *A Theology of Exile: Judgment/Deliverance in Jeremiah and Ezekiel*. Philadelphia: Fortress, 1977.

Reimer, Dennis J. "Concerning Return to Egypt: Deut xvii 16 and xxviii 68 Reconsidered." In *Studies in the Pentateuch*, ed. J. A. Emerton, 217–29. VTSup, no. 41. Leiden: Brill, 1990.

Ridderbos, Jan. *Deuteronomy*. Grand Rapids: Zondervan, 1984.

Ringgren, Helmer. "פוץ *pûṣ*." In *TDOT* 11:509–12.

Robinson, Robert B. *Roman Catholic Exegesis Since Divino Afflante Spiritu: Hermeneutical Implications*. Atlanta: Scholars Press, 1988.

Rofé, Alexander. "The Arrangement of the Laws in Deuteronomy." *ETL* 64 (1988): 265-87.

———. "The Covenant in the Land of Moab (Deuteronomy 28:69—30:20): Historico-Literary, Comparative, and Formcritical Considerations." In *A Song of Power and the Power of Song: Essays on the Book of Deuteronomy*, ed. Duane L. Christensen, 269-80. SBTS, vol. 3. Winona Lake, IN: Eisenbrauns, 1993.

Rogers, Cleon L., Jr., and I. Cornelius, "קבץ." In *NIDOTTE* 3:862-65.

Rogerson, John W. "The Hebrew Conception of Corporate Personality: A Re-Examination." *JTS* 21 (1970): 1-16.

Römer, Thomas. "Deuteronomy in Search of Origins." In *Reconsidering Israel and Judah: Recent Studies on the Deuteronomistic History*, ed. J. G. McConville and G. N. Knoppers, 112-38. SBTS, vol. 8. Winona Lake, IN: Eisenbrauns, 2000.

Römer, Thomas, and Albert de Pury. "L'historiographie deutéronomiste (HD): Histoire de la recherche et enjeux du débat." In *Israël construit son histoire: L'historiographie deutéronomiste à la lumière des recherches récentes*, ed. Albert de Pury, Thomas Römer, and Jean-Daniel Macchi, 9-120. Le Monde de la Bible, no. 34. Geneva: Labor et Fides, 1996.

Ross, Allen P. "Exile." In *NIDOTTE* 4:595-601.

Sanders, E. P. *Judaism: Practice and Belief 63 BCE-66 CE*. Philadelphia: Trinity Press International, 1992.

Sanders, James A. *Torah and Canon*. 2nd ed. Philadelphia: Fortress, 1974.

Sawyer, J. F. A. "קבץ *qbṣ* to assemble." In *TLOT* 3:1099-1102.

Schenker, Adrian Schenker. "Umwiderrufliche Umkehr und neuer Bund: Vergleich zwischen Dt 4:25-31, 30:1-14; Jer 31:31-34." *Freiburg Zeitschrift für Philosophie und Theologies* 27 (1980): 99.

Schley, Donald G., Jr. "'Yahweh Will Cause You to Return to Egypt in Ships' (Deuteronomy XXVIII 68)." *VT* 35 (1985): 369-71.

Schmid, H. H. "לקח *lqḥ* to take." In *TLOT* 2:648-51.

Schmid, Konrad, and Odil Hannes Steck. "Restoration Expectations in the Prophetic Tradition of the Old Testament." In *Restoration: Old Testament, Jewish, and Christian Conceptions*, ed. James M. Scott, 41-81. JSJSup, no.72. Leiden: Brill, 2001.

Schökel, L. Alonso. "Narrative Art in Joshua-Judges-Samuel-Kings." Translated by Daniel Legters. In *Reconsidering Israel and Judah: Recent Studies on the Deuteronomistic History*, ed. J. G. McConville and G. N. Knoppers, 255-78. SBTS, vol. 8. Winona Lake, IN: Eisenbrauns, 2000.

Schoors, Antoon. "שבי and גלות in Is 40-55: Historical Background." *Proceedings of the World Congress of Jewish Studies* 5 (1969): 90-101.

———. "The Particle כי." *OTS* 21 (1981): 240-76.

Schrieber, Paul L. "'Choose Life and Not Death': Life-and-Death Issues in Light of Deuteronomy 30:15-20." *Concordia Journal* 24 (1998): 346-56.

Scott, James C. *Domination and the Arts of Resistance: Hidden Transcripts*. New Haven: Yale University Press, 1990.

Scott, James M. "Exile and the Self-Understanding of Diaspora Jews in the Greco-Roman Period." In *Exile: Old Testament, Jewish, and Christian Conceptions*, ed. James M. Scott, 173-218. JSJSup, no.56. Leiden: Brill, 1997.

———. "Paul's Use of the Deuteronomic Tradition." *JBL* 112 (1993): 645-65.

———, ed. *Exile: Old Testament, Jewish and Christian Conceptions*. JSJSup, no. 56. Leiden: Brill, 1997.

———, ed. *Restoration: Old Testament, Jewish and Christian Conceptions*. JSJSup, no. 72. Leiden: Brill, 2001.
Seifrid, Mark A. *Christ Our Righteousness: Paul's Theology of Justification*. NSBT, no. 9. Downers Grove, IL: InterVarsity, 2000.
———. "Blind Alleys in the Controversy Over the Paul of History." *TynBul* 45 (1994): 73–95.
———. "The 'New Perspective' on Paul and Its Problems." *Themelios* 25 (2000): 4–18.
———. "Paul's Approach to the Old Testament." *TJ* 6 (1985): 3–37.
Seitz, Christopher R. *Theology in Conflict: Reactions to the Exile in the Book of Jeremiah*. New York: de Gruyter, 1989.
Seitz, Gottfried. *Redaktionsgeschichtliche Studien zum Deuteronomium*. Stuttgart: Kohlhammer, 1971.
Ska, Jean Louis. *"Our Fathers Have Told Us": Introduction to the Analysis of Hebrew Narratives*. Subsidia Biblica, no. 13. Rome: Pontifical Biblical Institute, 1990.
Sklba, Richard J. "The Call to New Beginnings: A Biblical Theology of Conversion." *BTB* 11 (1981): 67–73.
Smend, Rudolf. "The Law and the Nations: A Contribution to Deuteronomistic Tradition History." Translated by P. T. Daniels. In *Reconsidering Israel and Judah: Recent Studies on the Deuteronomistic History*, ed. J. G. McConville and G. N. Knoppers, 95–110. SBTS, vol. 8. Winona Lake, IN: Eisenbrauns, 2000.
Smith, Daniel L. *The Religion of the Landless: The Social Context of the Babylonian Exile*. Bloomington, IN: Meyer-Stone Books, 1989.
Smith, George Adam. *The Book of Deuteronomy*. Cambridge: Cambridge University Press, 1918.
Smith-Christopher, Daniel L. *A Biblical Theology of Exile*. OBT. Minneapolis: Fortress, 2002.
———. "Reassessing the Historical and Sociological Impact of the Babylonian Exile (597/587–539 BCE)." In *Exile: Old Testament, Jewish, and Christian Conceptions*, ed. James M. Scott, 7–36. JSJSup, no. 56. Leiden: Brill, 1997.
Soggin, J. A. "שׁוב *šûb* to return." In *TLOT* 3:1312–17.
Sonnet, J.-P. *The Book within the Book: Writing in Deuteronomy*. Biblical Interpretation Series, no. 14. Leiden: Brill, 1997.
Speckermann, Hermann. *Juda unter Assur in der Sargonidenzeit*. FRLANT, no. 129. Göttingen: Vandenhoeck & Ruprecht, 1982.
Stager, Lawrence. "The Fury of Babylon: Ashkelon and the Archaeology of Destruction." *Biblical Archaeologist Reader* 22 (1996): 56–69, 76–77.
Stein, Robert H. "N. T. Wright's *Jesus and the Victory of God*: A Review Article." *JETS* 44 (2001): 207–18.
Stern, Philip D. *The Biblical Ḥerem: A Window on Israel's Religious Experience*. Atlanta: Scholars, 1991.
Steuernagel, C. *Der Rahmen des Deuteronomiums*. Halle: J. Krause, 1894.
———. *Deuteronomium und Josua*. Göttingen: Vandenhoeck & Ruprecht, 1900.
Steymans, Hans Ulrich. *Deuteronomium 28 und die adê zur Thronfolgeregelung Asarhaddons: Segen und Fluch im Alten Orient und in Israel*. Orbis biblicus et orientalis, no. 145. Göttingen: Vandenhoeck & Ruprecht, 1995.
———. "Eine assyrische Vorlage für Deuteronomium 28, 20–44." In *Bundesdokument und Gesetz: Studien zum Deuteronomium*, ed. Georg Braulik, 118–41. Freiburg: Herder, 1995.

Stulman, L. "Encroachment in Deuteronomy. An Analysis of the Social World of the Deuteronomic Code." *JBL* 109 (1990): 613-32.

———. "Sex and Familial Crimes in the D Code." *JSOT* 53 (1992): 47-63.

Talmon, Shemaryahu. "'Exile' and 'Restoration' in the Conceptual World of Ancient Judaism." In *Restoration: Old Testament, Jewish, and Christian Conceptions*, ed. James M. Scott, 107-46. JSJSup, no. 72. Leiden: Brill, 2001.

Talstra, Eep. "Deuteronomy 9 and 10: Synchronic and Diachronic Observations." In *Synchronic or Diachronic? A Debate on Method in Old Testament Exegesis*, ed. Johannes C. de Moor, 187-210. OTS, no. 34. Leiden: Brill, 1995.

Thielman, Frank. *From Plight to Solution: A Jewish Framework for Understanding Paul's View of the Law in Galatians and Romans*. Leiden: Brill, 1989.

———. *Paul and the Law: A Contextual Approach*. Downers Grove, IL: InterVarsity, 1994.

Thompson, J. A. *Deuteronomy*. TOTC. Downers Grove, IL: InterVarsity, 1975.

Thompson, J. A., and Elmer A. Martens. "שוב." In *NIDOTTE* 4:55-59.

Thompson, Thomas L. *The Historicity of the Patriarchal Narratives: The Quest for the Historical Abraham*. BZAW, no. 133. Berlin: de Gruyter, 1974.

———. *The Mythic Past: Biblical Archaeology and the Myth of Israel*. London: Basic, 1999.

Tigay, Jeffrey H. *Deuteronomy*. JPSTC, vol. 5. Philadelphia: The Jewish Publication Society, 1996.

Torrance, Thomas Forsythe. "The Israel of God." *Int* 10 (1956): 305-322.

Torrey, Charles C. *Ezra Studies*. New York: Ktav, 1970.

Van Dam, Cornelis. "אבד." In *NIDOTTE* 1:223-25.

———. "נתץ." In *NIDOTTE* 3:212-13.

Van Rooy, H. F. "Deuteronomy 28,69—Superscript or Subscript?" *JNSL* 14 (1988): 215-22.

Van Seters, John. *In Search of History: Historiography in the Ancient World and the Origins of Biblical History*. New Haven: Yale University Press, 1983.

VanGemeren, Willem A., ed. *NIDOTTE*. 5 vols. Grand Rapids: Zondervan, 1997.

Vanoni, G. "Der Geist und der Buchstabe: Überlegungen zum Verhältnis der Testamente und Beobachtungen zu Dtn 30,1-10." *BN* 14 (1981): 65-98.

Veijola, Timo. "Principal Observations of the Basic Story in Deuteronomy 1-3." In *A Song of Power and the Power of Song: Essays on the Book of Deuteronomy*, ed. Duane L. Christensen, 137-46. SBTS, vol. 3. Winona Lake, IN: Eisenbrauns, 1993.

Vermeylen, Jacques. "Les sections narratives de Deut 5-11 et leur relation à Ex 19-34." *Das Deut* (1985): 174-207.

Verseput, Donald J. "The Davidic Messiah and Matthew's Jewish Christianity." SBLASP, no. 35 (1995): 102-116.

Vetter, D. "שמד *šmd* to destroy." In *TLOT* 3:1367-69.

Waltke, Bruce K. "גָּלָה." In *TWOT* 1:160-61.

Waltke, Bruce, and Michael O'Connor. *An Introduction to Biblical Hebrew Syntax*. Winona Lake, IN: Eisenbrauns, 1990.

Watts, James W., ed. *Persia and Torah: The Theory of Imperial Authorization of the Pentateuch*. SBL Symposium Series, no. 17. Atlanta: SBL, 2001.

Watts, John D. W. *Deuteronomy*. In vol. 2 of BBC. Edited by Clifton J. Allen, 175-296. Nashville: Broadman Press, 1970.

———. "The Deuteronomic Theology." *RevExp* 74 (1977): 321-26.

Weinfeld, Moshe. *Deuteronomy and the Deuteronomic School*. Oxford: Clarendon, 1972.

———. *Deuteronomy 1–11*. AB, vol. 5. New York: Doubleday, 1991.

———. "The Ban on the Canaanites and Its Development in Israelite Law." *Zion* 53 (1988): 135–47.

———. "*Berit*—Covenant vs. Obligation." *Bib* 56 (1975): 120–28.

———. "The Covenant of Grant in the Old Testament and in the ANE." *JAOS* 90 (1970) 184–203; *JAOS* 92 (1972) 468–69.

———. "Deuteronomy: The Present State of Inquiry." In *A Song of Power and the Power of Song: Essays on the Book of Deuteronomy*, ed. Duane L. Christensen, 21–35. SBTS, vol. 3. Winona Lake, IN: Eisenbrauns, 1993.

———. "The Emergence of the Deuteronomic Movement: The Historical Antecedents." In *Das Deuteronomium: Entstehung, Gestalt und Botschaft*, ed. Norbert Lohfink, 79–83. BETL, no. 68. Leuven: Leuven University Press, 1985.

———. "Jeremiah and the Spiritual Metamorphosis of Israel." *ZAW* 88 (1976): 17–56.

———. "The Loyalty Oath in the ANE." *Ugarit-Forschungen* 8 (1976): 379–414.

———. "Traces of Assyrian Treaty Formulae in Deuteronomy." *Bib* 46 (1965): 417–27.

Weippert, Helga. "Das deuteronomistische Geschichtswerk: Sein Ziel und Ende in der neueren Forschung." *TRu* (1985): 213–49.

———. "'Histories' and 'History': Promise and Fulfillment in the Deuteronomistic Historical Work." In *Reconsidering Israel and Judah: Recent Studies on the Deuteronomistic History*, ed. J. G. McConville, J. G. and G. N. Knoppers, 47–61. SBTS, vol. 8. Winona Lake, IN: Eisenbrauns, 2000.

Welch, Adam R. *The Code of Deuteronomy*. London: Oxford University Press, 1924.

———. *Deuteronomy: The Framework to the Code*. London: Oxford University Press, 1932.

Wellhausen, Julius. *Die Komposition des Hexateuchs und der historischen Bücher des Alten testaments*. Berlin: Georg Reimer, 1889.

———. *Prolegomena to the History of Ancient Israel*. Edinburgh: A. and C. Black, 1885. Reprint: Magnolia, MA: Peter Smith, 1977.

Wenham, Gordon J. *Genesis 1–15*. WBC, vol. 1. Waco: Word, 1987.

———. "Deuteronomy and the Central Sanctuary." In *A Song of Power and the Power of Song: Essays on the Book of Deuteronomy*, ed. Duane L. Christensen, 94–108. SBTS, vol. 3. Winona Lake, IN: Eisenbrauns, 1993.

———. "The Structure and Date of Deuteronomy." PhD diss., London University, 1971.

Westermann, Claus. *Die Geschichtsbücher des Alten Testaments: Gab es ein deuteronomisticisches Geschichtwerk?* TBu, no. 87. Munich: Chr. Kaiser, 1994.

Westermann, Claus, and R. Albertz. "גלה *glh* to uncover." In *TLOT* 1:314–20.

White, William. "רָדַף." In *TWOT* 2:834.

———. "רָהַק." In *TWOT* 2:843–44.

Whitelam, Keith W. *The Invention of Ancient Israel: The Silencing of Palestinian History*. London: Routledge, 1996.

Whybray, R. Norman. *Introduction to the Pentateuch*. Grand Rapids: Eerdmans, 1995.

———. *The Making of the Pentateuch: A Methodological Study*. JSOTSup, no. 53. Sheffield: JSOT Press, 1987.

Widengren, Geo. "Yahweh's Gathering of the Dispersed." In *In the Shelter of Elyon: Essays on Ancient Palestinian Life and Literature in Honor of G. W. Ahlström*, ed.

W. Boyd Barrick and John P. Spencer, 227-45. JSOTSup, no. 31. Sheffield: JSOT Press, 1984.

Wilkie, John M. "Nabonidus and the Later Jewish Exiles." *JTS* 2 (1951): 36-44.

Wilson, Ian. *Out of the Midst of the Fire: Divine Presence in Deuteronomy*. SBLDS, no. 151. Atlanta: Scholars, 1995.

Wiseman, D. J. "Vassal-Treaties of Esarhaddon." *Iraq* 20 (1958): 1-100.

Wolff, Hans W. "The Kerygma of the Deuteronomic Historical Work." In *The Vitality of Old Testament Traditions*, by Walter Brueggemann and Hans W. Wolff, 83-100. Atlanta: John Knox, 1975.

Wright, Christopher J. H. *Deuteronomy*. NIBC. Peabody, MA: Hendrickson, 1996.

———. *God's People in God's Land*. Grand Rapids: Eerdmans, 1990.

Wright, G. Ernest, Henry H. Shires, and Pierson Parker. "Deuteronomy." In *The Interpreter's Bible*. Edited by George Arthur Buttrick, 309-537. New York: Abingdon, 1953.

Wright, N. T. *The Climax of the Covenant: Christ and the Law in Pauline Theology*. Minneapolis: Fortress, 1991.

———. *Jesus and the Victory of God*. Vol. 2 of *Christian Origins and the Question of God*. Minneapolis: Fortress, 1996.

———. *The New Testament and the People of God*. Vol. 1 of *Christian Origins and the Question of God*. Minneapolis: Fortress, 1992.

———. *What Saint Paul Really Said: Was Paul of Tarsus the Real Founder of Christianity?* Grand Rapids: Eerdmans, 1997.

Yamauchi, Edwin. "Slaves of God." *Bulletin of the Evangelical Theological Society* 9 (1966): 31-49.

Zimmerli, Walther. "Das Zweite Gebot." In *Gottes Offenbarung: Gesamelte Aufsätze zum Alten Testament*, 234-48. Tbu, no. 19. München: Chr. Kaiser, 1963.

Zobel, Hans-Jürgen. "גָּלָה *gālāh*." In *TDOT* 2:476-88.

www.ingramcontent.com/pod-product-compliance
Lightning Source LLC
Chambersburg PA
CBHW071241230426
43668CB00011B/1542